PURITY OF HEART IN EARLY ASCETIC AND MONASTIC LITERATURE

Essays in Honor of Juana Raasch, O.S.B.

Harriet A. Luckman
Linda Kulzer, O.S.B.

Editors

A Liturgical Press Book

THE LITURGICAL PRESS
Collegeville, Minnesota

Cover design by Greg Becker

© 1999 by The Order of St. Benedict, Inc., Collegeville, Minnesota. All rights reserved. No part of this book may be reproduced in any form or by any means, electronic or mechanical, including photocopying, recording, taping, or by any retrieval system, without the written permission of The Liturgical Press, Collegeville, Minnesota 56321. Printed in the United States of America.

1   2   3   4   5   6   7

Library of Congress Cataloging-in-Publication Data

Purity of heart in early ascetic and monastic literature : essays in honor of Juana Raasch, O.S.B. / Harriet Luckman, Linda Kulzer, editors.
    p.   cm.
   Includes bibliographical references and index.
   ISBN 0-8146-2485-5 (alk. paper)
   1. Asceticism—History—Early church, ca. 30–600. 2. Monastic and religious life—History—Early church, ca. 30–600. 3. Heart—Religious aspects—Christianity—History of doctrines—Early church, ca. 30–600. I. Raasch, Juana, 1927–1974. II. Luckman, Harriet, 1956– .
III. Kulzer, Linda.
BV5023.P87   1999
248.4'7—dc21   98-37386
                                                                                  CIP

Contents

Preface v
    Linda Kulzer and Harriet A. Luckman

Acknowledgments viii

Abbreviations ix

Introduction 1
    Columba Stewart, O.S.B.

The Concept of Purity of Heart in the Old Testament 17
    Irene Nowell, O.S.B.

The Phrase "Purity of Heart" in Early Syriac Writings 31
    Deirdre Ann Dempsey

The Place of the Heart: Geography and Spirituality in the *Life of Antony* 45
    Douglas Burton-Christie

Christ as Virtue in Didymus the Blind 67
    Placid Solari, O.S.B.

Basil of Caesarea and Purity of Heart 89
    Harriet A. Luckman

Temple and Throne of the Divine Glory: "Pseudo-Macarius" and Purity of Heart, Together with Some Remarks on the Limitations and Usefulness of Scholarship 107
    Hieromonk Alexander Golitzin

A Reflection on the Use of "Heart" in Select Prayer Texts in Early Christianity 131
    Mary Anthony Wagner, O.S.B.

Apatheia and Purity of Heart in Evagrius Ponticus 141
    Jeremy Driscoll, O.S.B.

Purity of Heart in the Life and Words of Amma Syncletica   161
    Mary Forman, O.S.B.

Purity of Heart in St. Augustine   175
    Gertrude Gillette, O.S.B.

The Beginning and End of Purity of Heart: From Cassian to the Master and Benedict   197
    Benedict M. Guevin, O.S.B.

"The Deepest Conviction of the Heart": A Probe into an Expression of St. Benedict (*RB* 7.51)   215
    Terrence G. Kardong, O.S.B.

Epilogue: The Life of Sister Juana Raasch, O.S.B., 1927–1974   223
    Linda Kulzer, O.S.B.

Contributors   237

Greek Terms   241

Hebrew Terms   242

Latin Terms   243

Syriac Terms   244

General Index   245

Preface

Part One by
LINDA KULZER, O.S.B.

The essays in this volume honor Sr. Juana Raasch, O.S.B. (1927–74), for her outstanding research on the topic of purity of heart in early Christian texts. Over the years since her death we, her sisters in community, have become more and more aware of the significance of her work. We continue to receive letters attesting to the high regard in which her work is held. Requests come for information about her work and about the possibility of reprinting all or parts of her research. Recently we received volume 5 of the series *La Tradición Benedictina: Ensayo histórico* by Rev. García M. Colombás, O.S.B., of Montserrat. He sent us a copy because he had dedicated this volume to Sister Juana, with the dedication page reading: "Dedicated to the memory of Sister Juana Raasch, O.S.B. Benedictine Institute of Sacred Theology, Saint Joseph, Minnesota."

Upon receiving this volume from Father García we decided the time had come for our own community to plan a publication that would honor Sr. Juana Raasch's memory. I felt honored to be asked to consider such a project. I asked Harriet Luckman to co-edit this volume with me. Ms. Luckman is a doctoral candidate in historical theology at Marquette University, Wisconsin. I knew she had the background to understand the special significance of Sister Juana's work. Together we decided on a format of essays that would expand the pioneering research Sister Juana had begun. The essayists were chosen on the basis of their previous work in the area of monastic studies and patristic literature.

Part Two by
HARRIET A. LUCKMAN

As early as 1966, Sister Juana began to isolate the major terms, define concepts, mention major texts, and draw the primary lines of argument concerning the issue of purity of heart as understood by the early Church witnesses. Sixteen contemporary monastic and patristic scholars have joined together in this volume to honor her work. They have built on the foundations she began and added new insights into the various texts and authors of the period as scholarship in the area has advanced since the time of Juana's writings.

While this book does not presume to be an exhaustive study of purity of heart, we have attempted to look at some major writers who discussed purity of heart in their works and the influences surrounding the writing of those works. Our book deals exclusively with the subject of what the early ascetic and later monastic writers understood by the term purity of heart and how that understanding would work its way out in various scriptural, theological, philosophical, and spiritual writings and practice. The time period covered by these sixteen essays includes a chapter on the Old Testament notion of a "pure and upright heart" through to the writings of Augustine and finally to Benedict of Nursia.

This book begins with an introduction outlining for the reader the basic concepts behind the notion of purity of heart. It examines generally what those concepts meant for the ascetic community and in many ways for the young Christian Church as a whole via the ascetic influences. It also discusses briefly the writings of John Cassian within that tradition. The essays then move to the concept of "heart" in the Hebrew and later Syrian traditions, into the writings of the major schools of the first centuries of the Common Era. The importance of geography for the early desert tradition following Anthony of Egypt is examined, as well as the role "heart" played in that early large scale ascetical movement. The essays next move the reader into the place and understanding the various virtues held in witnessing to purity of heart. They discuss Didymus the Blind's notion of Christ as virtue, Basil of Caesarea's communal concept of purity of heart, Pseudo-Macarius' notion of the Temple and the throne of glory, a short reflection on the term "heart" in certain early prayer texts, Evagrius Ponticus' Christian adaptation of the stoic concept of *apatheia*, followed by Amma Syncletica's interpretation and teachings. The book then moves into Augustine of Hippo's writings on purity of heart, perhaps the only early Christian writer who may not have been composing "ascetical" literature strictly speaking, but whose writings have had an inestimable impact on Western Christianity. The final articles examine the notion of purity of heart in the monastic legislator known only as "the Master," and move finally to Benedict of Nursia and his widely influential Rule.

The contributors to this volume are to be commended for their work on the subject and for bringing to light once again the centrality of the notion of purity of heart for the early Christian community—a concept which included everything from right and proper belief to right and proper behavior and prayer. The exegesis of Matt 5:8, "Blessed are the pure of heart for they shall see God," and the varying forms the notion of "purity" and "heart" would take within the early Christian tradition is both a fascinating and intriguing study. It is also a study which surprisingly has seen little attention aside from the original five articles written by Juana Raasch in *Studia Monastica* between 1966 and 1970 and the articles in this volume. As these essays convincingly show, there was no separation in the early Church between a right believing Christian and the witness of Christianity, no separation between the "mind" and the "heart." It is perhaps one of the most important lessons to be learned—among many—from this early Christian period.

In conclusion, I add it has been both an honor and a great privilege for me to have been asked to co-edit this volume on purity of heart. It has also been a very rewarding collaboration with scholars who often went out of their way to make working with them a real pleasure. Working with my co-editor Linda Kulzer, O.S.B., has been nothing but a joy, and once again a great debt of gratitude goes out to all those mentioned in this collection who have helped make this volume a reality. There is also, of course, the firm desire that this work will do justice to the memory of Sr. Juana Raasch, O.S.B., and the project she so earnestly began in the mid 1960s.

Acknowledgments

It is impossible to thank all those individuals who help make a book come into being. The support they offer both as the idea of a book takes shape as well as once the actual writing and compiling has begun is invaluable. As co-editors we are particularly indebted to those scholars and monastics who willingly and generously shared both their time and talents to help make this volume a reality, particularly those individuals whose essays make up the body of this work. Their efforts and contributions, as well as their enthusiasm for this project, are gratefully acknowledged.

We would like to thank Michael Naughton, O.S.B., and the editors of The Liturgical Press for their interest and willingness to undertake the publication of this collection of essays, as well as the many sisters of St. Benedict's Monastery, St. Joseph, Minnesota, who encouraged us in this project and shared their memories of Sister Juana. In particular we would like to thank Sr. Ruth Boedigheimer, O.S.B., whose help with archival materials went far beyond the call of duty, and Sr. Johanna Becker, O.S.B., whose persistent hopes for this volume helped make it a reality. Peg Emmet Corcoran, a long-time friend of Sister Juana, deserves special thanks for donating original materials about Sister Juana. We also give special recognition and gratitude to Avis Raasch Worthington, Sister Juana's only sibling, whose writings about Sister Juana have so enriched our account of her life.

Special acknowledgment must be made to Fr. García Colombás, O.S.B., of Montserrat, whose initial encouragement led Juana into the study of purity of heart in early Christian texts.

> Harriet A. Luckman and Linda Kulzer, O.S.B., Editors
> St. Benedict's Monastery
> March 31, 1998

Abbreviations

BRev	*Biblical Review*
CCL	Corpus christianorum, series latina
CSCO	Corpus scriptorum christianorum orientalium
CSEL	Corpus scriptorum ecclesiasticorum latinorum
CSQ	*Cistercian Studies Quarterly*
CSS	Cistercian Studies Series
DSp	*Dictionnaire de spiritualité*
HTR	Harvard Theological Review
JAC	*Jahrbuch für Antike und Christentum*
JECS	*Journal of Early Christian Studies*
JJS	*Journal of Jewish Studies*
JR	*Journal of Religion*
LSJ	H. G. Liddell, R. Scott, and H. Stuart Jones, *A Greek-English Lexicon*
NT	*New Testament Studies*
OCP	*Orientalia christiana periodica*
PG	Patrologia Graeca, ed. J. P. Migne.
PL	Patrologia Latina, ed. J. P. Migne.
PS	Patrologia Syriaca
PO	Patrologia Orientalis
RB	Rule of St. Benedict
RM	Rule of the Master
SC	Sources chrétiennes
SA	Studia Anselmiana
SM	*Studia Monastica*
SP	*Studia Patristica*
TDOT	*Theological Dictionary of the Old Testament*
TDNT	*Theological Dictionary of the New Testament*
VigChr	*Vigiliae Christianae*
ZPT	*Zetischrift für Philosophie und Theologie*

Introduction

COLUMBA STEWART, O.S.B.

PRELIMINARIES

A Conversation Begun

I never knew Juana Raasch. Although her monastery and mine are neighbors, she died some years before I came to Saint John's. I met her, as so many have, through her extraordinary articles on purity of heart. Having learned more about her as this memorial volume developed, I now wish even more that I had known her. I suspect we would have had many things to talk over, and not only about early monastic writings. One of them would have been that the scholar's work is often lonely and little understood, even in monasteries. Evidently that was the case for her. These essays are meant to signify the conversation partners Sister Juana may have longed for as she crafted her fine, insightful contribution to our understanding of this fundamental Christian theme. Now she no longer needs us, for she has the reward promised the pure of heart. I hope, however, that she is delighting in the work we offer in her memory and is remembering us to the God whom she now sees face to face.

The landscape of early Christian studies has changed remarkably in the thirty years since her work. Some of the essays contained here revisit ancient authors studied by Sister Juana, while others supplement her survey. Good editions are now more abundant and the tools for studying them are impressive, even if they do not always live up to their promises. Sister Juana did her work by searching the texts with her own eyes, sensing the spirit as well as locating the letter. Even so, neither her work nor anyone else's can be the last word. The thematic studies we offer complement and develop her fundamental investigation.

In this introduction I will offer some general observations about how we approach an ancient Christian theme like purity of heart, situate the notion of purity in its cultural and religious context, introduce the two early monastic theologians most responsible for the classic monastic doctrine of *puritas cordis*, and finally consider some aspects of purity of heart, particularly as they are found in the writings of John Cassian.

Language and Understanding

"Purity of heart" is a theological prism refracting an extraordinary spectrum of biblical, philosophical, and ascetical themes. The monastic use of the phrase that so intrigued Juana Raasch integrated biblical perspectives with themes grounded in Hellenistic philosophical schools. Theology and asceticism converged as "purity of heart" acquired its technical meaning of perfection attained through a disciplined life. The ideas and practices essential to monastic purity of heart were not new. However, the phrase which came to house them in monastic tradition developed its integrative meaning slowly, co-existing with or replacing other ways of describing the same goal. The essays in this book trace the biblical and early Christian development of the language and concepts that informed the monastic understanding of purity of heart. The evolution of ideas and of the language that conveys them is always exceedingly complex. This case is no exception, with its interplay of biblical, philosophical, and theological terminology. We should reflect for a moment on the significance and implications of that interplay.

The Judeo-Christian world has always been culturally eclectic. Moses was raised in a Pharaonic household and even his name is Egyptian. Paul of Tarsus was born a Greek-speaker of the Diaspora in Asia Minor. John Cassian, the key figure in the Latin tradition of purity of heart, was bilingual and well-traveled.[1] This eclecticism strikes us most vividly when we read early Christian theological and spiritual writings and find, alongside familiar biblical imagery, terminology obviously related to Hellenistic philosophical traditions. One reader will find such language disturbing and regard it as a contamination or aberration of Christian thought. Another will fix upon it and overlook the theological context in which it appears. Both may be imperfectly sensitive to the way that language becomes modified in both conversational and literary usage.

In the world of early Christianity, the flux of intellectual and linguistic cultures was so great that it is usually impossible for us to know how and when an author acquired a particular idea or term.

---

[1] For Cassian's life, see ch. 1 of my *Cassian the Monk* (New York: Oxford University Press, 1998).

Simply because we can find it in a specific source we must not too readily assume our predecessor did the same. Some ideas were imbedded in the languages adopted by the Christians who had to use the language and intellectual tools available to them, just as we do. We all write from where we live, and the language which makes communication possible also betrays our temporal and cultural location. The methodological pitfall for modern readers of ancient Christian texts is to approach the Christian use of philosophical terminology via concordance. We find a certain word in a Christian text, recognize it as "Platonic," and check Plato and Plotinus. Locating a "source" and sketching a line toward the early Christian text at hand, we presume that illumination will occur when the connection is complete. We forget the thousand pathways that language and concepts can travel. Having only texts, we forget that the authors had more, and we project a purer sense of Platonism or Stoicism onto Christian texts than their authors' own understandings would bear. Or, we impose our own imperfectly reasoned sense of a word on someone else's use of it. The hermeneutical care we exercise in actual conversation can be oddly inactive just when one would think it most likely to be in the very forefront of consciousness, when reading a text from a very different time, place, and set of circumstances from our own.

As an analogy, consider the saturation of modern discourse with language inspired by psychology. The various schools of psychology and their pop versions have poured word upon word into our daily vocabulary. People in general, and religious and academic types in particular, glibly use words like neurosis, complex, hang-up, phobia, shadow, ego, addiction, psychotherapy, schizophrenia, paranoia, "issues," self-image. But how many have read the actual writings of Freud, Jung, or their hosts of successors and critics? We have picked up language with a vestigial mark of its original or technical signification and made it our own. And, of course, my appropriation of a word will differ from someone else's. Beneath the tip of my use of, for example, "phobia" is an iceberg of meaning, much (perhaps most) of it intuitively and emotionally, rather than rationally, delineated. It may be that I have actually read some Freud or someone influenced by him. But the terminology has become mine, interpreted within the matrix of my own experience and then offered to others out of that matrix. A sensitive interlocutor will catch my nuance and engage my sense of the term with her own, though probably in a largely unconscious manner.

As we encounter philosophical vocabulary in early Christian writings we also have to keep in mind that there is by no means unanimity among scholars about its meaning either in its original or its

Christian context. There may not in fact be a single Ur-meaning. A classic instance is the Platonic notion that the objects of knowledge are eternal, immutable "forms." Efforts to establish exactly what Plato (or Socrates) meant have been frustrated by the various understandings of the concept within the Platonic corpus itself. This reminds us that every occurrence of a term or concept is both a new creation and an epiphany. It stands with new meaning even while revealing something of its history of meanings.

Finally, we need to remember that the fundamental task of all philosophies and religions is to make sense of human existence in a universe marked by the inevitable death of all living things. The promise of release from that inevitability has tantalized thinkers across cultures, whether they have seen the path as running through death to a life beyond it, or above death by an intellectual or religious transcendence of mortality. When we are disturbed by what seem to be dualist or escapist traits in ancient texts we need to acknowledge the stark presence of decay and death in those societies where living to forty was an unusual achievement. In the political security of North America or western Europe today, we must also remember the collapse of social stability that marked the late antique period in which foundational Christian texts were written. Mortality, both personal and imperial, provided powerful incentives for facing death squarely and for seeking ways beyond it. It should be little surprise that our ancestors used every available means—biblical, theological, and philosophical—in that fundamental endeavor.

PURITY IN THE MEDITERRANEAN WORLD

The contents of this volume prove the theme of purity of heart to be woven from several strands. "Heart" is a comfortable term for the modern reader even though the biblical and early Christian use of the term is surprisingly complex. The religious understanding of "purity" is surely less accessible, for we tend to use the word with reference either to sanitation or hygiene. When it is used morally, the context tends to be almost exclusively sexual and the signification to be naïveté. In the ancient Mediterranean world that shaped Christianity, purity had a far greater range of meanings and signified not lack of experience but coming to grips with it. For the purpose of overview, we can distinguish three kinds of purity: ritual and bodily purity, moral purity, and metaphysical purity. All three contributed to the classic monastic doctrine of purity of heart.

Ritual Purity

Concern for ritual purity is a near-universal element of human religious systems, evident in purificatory washings or baths, restraint from sexual activity before performing religious duties, etc. Ritual purity is most familiar to Jewish and Christian readers from their reading of the Hebrew Scriptures. The details of the Levitical holiness code distinguishing clean from unclean seem arcane to modern Westerners, but are rooted in human instincts that are universal. The basic point was delineating the realm of the holy, which was both place (as an altar or Temple) and state (being purified for the sake of ritual performance). The holiness codes of the people of Israel staked out God's arena and the qualifications for entry into it.

Christian baptism has ties to the purifying rituals of proselyte and penitential baptism in the Judaism of Jesus' day, and the reminder of baptism in the ritual use of holy water upon entering a church or beginning a liturgy links Christian practice to that broad world of concern for ritual purity. It is also true that in Christian practice the Jewish holiness code has been applied selectively and often in a misogynistic manner. As in the Levitical code, menstruating women and those who had recently given birth were regarded as "impure" (see Leviticus 12). Latin rituals for "churching" women after childbirth contained elements both of purification (sprinkling with holy water) and thanksgiving (the prayer texts). In both East and West the marital intercourse of priests was seen as dissonant to service at the altar; abstention from intercourse on the eve of eucharistic celebration became extended for the Western church into an argument for clerical celibacy.[2] This sexual aspect of purity will be considered later as it pertains to purity of heart and chastity.

Moral Purity

The prophets and sages of Israel reminded their people that ritual purity is really about intention and disposition, and thus inseparable from moral purity. The opening lines of Isaiah put the argument starkly, pushing even to the point (rhetorical as it may be) of rejecting any ritual practice offered without moral integrity. The emphasis on inner disposition so evident in the Psalms and Wisdom literature (perhaps especially in Sirach) is where the moral genius of Israel meets that of the Stoics and kindred Hellenistic schools of "philosophical"

---

[2] For an overview of this trend, see Roger Gryson, *Les origines du célibat ecclésiastique du premier au septième siècle*, Recherches et Synthèses de Sciences Religieuses (Gembloux: Duculot, 1970) 45–201.

behavior. The pure or single heart characterizes the moral integrity fundamental to right worship.

The early Christian authors whom Juana Raasch studied inherited both the biblical emphasis on purity of intention/singleness of heart and the Greek emphasis on clarity of purpose exemplified by the commonplace maxim, *gnothi seauton* (γνῶθι σεαυτόν), "know thyself."[3] The practices of self-awareness and discernment developed by the philosophical schools of antiquity influenced Christian *askesis* (ἄσκησις) and were further developed by Christian authors.[4] Athanasius notes that Antony would write down his thoughts.[5] This Pythagorean and Stoic practice had been transposed to the desert, and can be seen in Evagrius' recommendation of tracking the thoughts to detect recurring patterns, Poemen's humility in returning to his spiritual father to offer a previously forgotten thought for discernment, John Climacus' mention of the monk who kept a wax tablet tied to his belt so that he could record his thoughts as they arose.[6] A host of other examples could be added to these particularly arresting ones.[7]

The difference between philosophical and Christian self-knowledge lay not in technique but in purpose. For Christians, cultivation of virtue and clarity of thought were more than means of harmonizing one's own life with the *logos* (λόγος) which governed the universe. Even when Christians adopted *logos* language to understand the relationship between God the Father, God the Son, and the created universe, the transcendent monotheism and specifically christological orientation established a further horizon which shifted perspective to a vaster scale. Nowhere is this more apparent than in the biblical text which so inspired Cassian, "Blessed are the pure in heart, for they shall see God" (Matt 5:8).

---

[3] The standard work on this perennial theme is Pierre Courcelle's *Connais-toi toi-même. De Socrate à saint Bernard*, 3 vols. (Paris: Études augustiniennes, 1974–75).

[4] This development has been traced by Pierre Hadot; see, for example, the essays in *Philosophy as a Way of Life: Spiritual Exercises from Socrates to Foucault*, ed. Arnold I. Davidson; trans. Michael Chase (Oxford: Blackwell, 1995). Hadot's famous article "Exercices spirituels" is translated in that collection.

[5] See *Vita Antonii* 55.9 (*SC* 400, p. 284): τὰς πράξεις καὶ τὰ κινήματα τῆς ψυχῆς, ὡς μέλλοντες ἀλλήλοις ἀπαγγέλλειν, σημειώμεθα καὶ γράφωμεν.

[6] Evagrius: *Praktikos* 43 (*SC* 171, pp. 598–600); Poemen: the first saying attributed to him in the Alphabetical Collection (*PG* 65, col. 317A); Climacus: *Ladder of Divine Ascent*, Step 4 (*PG* 88, col. 701CD).

[7] For an overview of the practice of manifestation of thoughts to a spiritual elder, see my "The Desert Fathers on Radical Honesty About the Self," *Sobornost* 12 (1990) 25–39, 131–56; reprinted in *Vox Benedictina* 8 (1991) 7–53.

Metaphysical/Cosmological Purity

A third strand is metaphysical or cosmological purity. Traceable to both Platonic and Stoic schools and culminating in the syntheses of the philosopher Plotinus and his Christian contemporary Origen, this conception of purity was grounded in two fundamental and related assumptions. The first was a pronounced body-soul dualism based on the notion that the soul as immaterial and eternal is superior to the body. Some Platonic texts go so far as to identify the human person exclusively with the soul and to denigrate the body as, in the famous words of the *Phaedo*, a "prison" for the soul.[8] A tendency in this direction is discernible in some Christian writers. However, quick judgments about the anti-body attitudes of writers like Origen and Augustine must be nuanced not only by their convictions about the role of the body in Christian life (Origen and his followers are rather more optimistic than Augustine on this point)[9] but also by their teaching on bodily resurrection. Their emphasis on this fundamental doctrine was far greater than is the case for most modern Christians.

The second assumption was that simplicity and unity are marks of the divine, while complexity and multiplicity are characteristics of the created order. When understood cosmologically, this perspective underlies models of creation. For both Origen and Plotinus, outward movement from the primordial unity of God generated multiple orders of creation. The corollary is that the diverse creation will eventually return to the primordial unity.[10] Origen understood the return in christological terms and in a way that preserved the individuality of each created being, though this highly speculative aspect of his thought has remained controversial, as has the version taught by his follower Evagrius.[11] Whatever its ramifications, the movement from

---

[8] The text is *Phaedo* 62b3; for various interpretations of it, see John Dillon, "Rejecting the Body, Refining the Body: Some Remarks on the Development of Platonist Asceticism," *Asceticism*, ed. Vincent Wimbush and Richard Valantasis (New York: Oxford University Press, 1995) 80–7.

[9] See Peter Brown's *The Body and Society: Men, Women, and Sexual Renunciation in Early Christianity* (New York: Columbia University Press, 1988) 160–77 (Origen), 420–3 (Augustine and Cassian); also ch. 4 of my *Cassian the Monk*.

[10] For Origen, see the cogent overview by Rowan Greer in the introduction to his translation of some of Origen's major treatises, *Origen: An Exhortation to Martyrdom, Prayer, etc.*, Classics of Western Spirituality (New York: Paulist Press, 1979) 7–17. On Plotinus, see Pierre Hadot, "Plotinus and Porphyry," *Classical Mediterranean Spirituality*, trans. Jane Curran; ed. A. H. Armstrong (New York: Crossroads, 1986) 230–49; and Pierre Hadot, *Plotinus, or the Simplicity of Vision*, trans. Michael Chase (Chicago: University of Chicago Press, 1993).

[11] On Evagrius, see particularly Gabriel Bunge, "*Mysterium unitatis*. Der Gedanke der Einheit von Schöpfer und Geschöpf in der evagrianischen Mystik," *Freiburger Zeitschrift für Philosophie und Theologie* 36 (1989) 449–69.

One to many and then back to One operated as a fundamental principle in early Christian texts.

MONASTIC SYNTHESIS: JOHN CASSIAN AND HIS TEACHER, EVAGRIUS PONTICUS

As Juana Raasch noted, the monastic theologian identified most obviously with the theme of purity of heart is John Cassian.[12] Sister Juana's work can be understood as a textual archaeology of the traditions underlying Cassian's choice of purity of heart as his premier definition of Christian and monastic perfection. Cassian borrows much of his teaching on this theme from his master, Evagrius Ponticus. Evagrius, however, had synthesized the theological, philosophical, and ascetical traditions under the Stoic label *apatheia* (ἀπάθεια), rather than the biblical "purity of heart." Cassian's shift of terminology from *apatheia* to *puritas cordis* shows both a keen appreciation of biblically-based pedagogy and a recentering of Evagrius' understanding of Christian perfection. By using the phrase familiar from the Matthean beatitude, "Blessed are the pure in heart, for they shall see God" (Matt 5:8), Cassian highlighted the interplay of moral worthiness, physical integrity, and psychological balance in the process of attaining Christian maturity.[13]

Evagrius' *apatheia* was equally inclusive, but his use of the nonbiblical, Stoic term opened the door to misunderstandings of various kinds.[14] Critics like Jerome chose to interpret the term literally and narrowly as suggesting sinlessness, which of course is a quality attributable to God alone.[15] Even those without Jerome's political agenda have found the Stoic overtones of *apatheia* to be problematic, wishing for a more explicitly Christian frame of reference. If properly understood, Evagrius' concept is theologically viable. He never claims that human beings are sinless or passionless, as the term *apatheia* might seem to suggest. Instead, he is describing the integration of attractions and repulsions in a tranquil personality shaped by grace. The name he gave to this state, however, got in the way. His terse, dense writing style did

---

[12] Juana Raasch, "The Monastic Concept of Purity of Heart and Its Sources," *Studia Monastica* 1 (1969) 8.

[13] For Cassian's teaching on purity of heart, see my *Cassian the Monk*, 41–61. I have not yet seen the article by Mark Sheridan, "The Controversy over ἀπάθεια: Cassian's Sources and His Use of Them," cited in Jeremy Driscoll's essay in this volume.

[14] For an overview, see Antoine and Claire Guillaumont's introduction to Evagrius' *Praktikos* (SC 170, pp. 98–112), and Jeremy Driscoll's contribution to this collection.

[15] See Jerome's *Letter 133 to Ctesiphon*, esp. sec. 3.5-6 (*CSEL* 56) 246.

not contribute to understanding, nor did it adequately defend him from his enemies.

Cassian's renaming of *apatheia* as "purity of heart," though seemingly a departure from his master's teaching, may actually have been inspired by Evagrius himself. Evagrius was partial to beatitudinal formulae and quite frequently cited Matt 5:8 specifically in his writings.[16] The contemplative emphasis on "seeing God" suited Evagrian spiritual theology with its heavily Platonic and contemplative coloring. The concept of "purity," *katharotes* (καθαρότης), is an equally prominent theme throughout his work. One aspect of it, a Platonic approach mediated particularly through Origen, is a metaphysical purity characterizing encounter with God without material or conceptual mediation. Closely allied to this understanding of prayer is purity from the devastating effects of anger and other passions.[17] Evagrius typically prefers "intellect/mind" (νοῦς) to "heart" (καρδία), though when commenting on biblical texts he follows their use of heart. As he notes, "it is customary in Scripture to have καρδία [heart] instead of νοῦς [mind]."[18] Evagrius' intellectual emphasis was characteristic of the Alexandrian school which formed him. Although the language and approach may seem more philosophical than Christian to some modern readers, Evagrius was being quite traditional within the lineage of the Jewish theologian Philo and the Christians Clement and Origen. Cassian frequently used the Latin term *mens*, the equivalent for νοῦς,[19] in a way akin to Evagrius, but his decision also to highlight the more biblical "heart" language was a prudent public relations move. Writing about heart allowed him a more explicit emphasis on love. In a sort of pastoral condensation of Evagrius' schema of the monastic life Cassian defines purity of heart as the "perfection of apostolic love" (*Inst.* 4.43, *Conf.* 1.6). Love is the bridge between life now and life eternal (*Conf.* 1.10), so that purity of heart is the Christian staging ground for life in heaven. It is anticipation of eternity, for what is begun now

---

[16] See my *Cassian the Monk*, 56.

[17] Thus Evagrius' teaching on "pure" prayer as in, for example, *On Prayer* 66/67–73/74 and 114–7 (*PG* 79.1181A–84A and 1192D–94A). For the teaching of both Evagrius and Cassian on imageless prayer, see my *Cassian the Monk*, 86–90 and 95–9.

[18] *Schol. in Ps.* 15:9 (*PG* 12.1216A).

[19] He notes their equivalence in *Inst.* 8.10 and *Conf.* 7.4.2. Cassian's *Institutes* and *Conferences* were edited by Michael Petschenig in *CSEL* 18 and 13, respectively. The English translation of the *Institutes* by E.C.S. Gibson in the Library of Nicene and Post-Nicene Fathers, Second Series, 11, omits *Inst.* 6 on lust; it has been translated by Terrence Kardong in *Cassian on Chastity* (Richardton, N.D.: Assumption Abbey Press, 1993) 21–30. Boniface Ramsey's new and complete translation of the *Conferences*, Ancient Christian Writers 57 (New York: Paulist Press, 1997) replaces Gibson's, which omitted *Conf.* 12 and 22.

through the gift of love will abide forever: love never passes away (1 Cor 13:8).

ASPECTS OF PURITY OF HEART

Purity of Heart as Process

The American writer Flannery O'Connor wrote to a friend, "The phrase 'naive purity' is a contradiction in terms. I don't think purity is mere innocence; I don't think babies and idiots possess it. I take it to be something that comes with experience or with Grace so that it can never be naive."[20] Cassian would heartily endorse her conviction. In modern discourse, purity is conceived in pristine terms, as a primordial condition which can only degenerate with the passage of time and the accumulation of experience. "Pure as the driven snow" suggests that, like snow, the one so characterized will inevitably become dirty. Similarly, Ivory soap is reckoned as "pure" because nothing pollutes it.

The understanding of purity operative among ancient philosophers and theologians, however, was opposite to our static assumptions. It is helpful to remember that the Greek word meaning pure, *katharos* (καθαρός), actually means purified, for it derives from the verb *kathairo* (καθαίρω), meaning "take away" and thus, "cleanse." The starting point, then, was messiness and confusion. A Platonist might have blamed this on embodiment and immersion in the material world. Christian thinkers with their generally more appreciative view of material creation speak in terms of fallen human nature as the starting point of a slow educative process for the human race in general (salvation history) and each person in particular (repentance and conversion). The advantage does not necessarily go to those who have not known travail or how painfully tangled life can be. A certain amount of experience, in fact, is usually needed to understand just what the stakes are. Such awareness is perhaps the best incentive for undertaking the ascetical process which cultivates purity of heart.

Cassian, for example, notes that eunuchs are at a distinct *dis*advantage when it comes to chastity. Because eunuchs experience less *physical* struggle with sexuality than others do, they can fail to realize how important integrity of thought and action really is.[21] The heroes of the monastic movement were people like Moses, the repentant bandit and murderer, or Mary of Egypt, the prostitute who became an icon of ascetical tenderness. Because they had known in their own experience

---

[20] *The Habit of Being*, ed. Sally Fitzgerald (New York: Farrar, Straus, Giroux, 1979) 126.
[21] *Conf.* 12.5.1 and 12.10.3.

how vicious the human lot can be, they longed for the transforming work that only God can effect in human hearts and bodies.

Purity of heart is the goal of what Benedict called *conversatio morum* and his Greek predecessors called *askesis* (ἄσκησις) or the *praktike* (πρακτική).[22] Cassian begins his *Conferences* by mapping the monastic life as a journey toward both a near goal and an ultimate one (*Conf.* 1.1–5). The ultimate goal, of course, is heaven. But within sight and imagination is the nearer goal of purity of heart. The nearer goal provides a mark to aim for and to steer by. Even more, it determines the kind of travel. A mountain peak requires ascent as well as progress. Purity of heart demands a program of spiritual discipline as well as simply the passage of time.

Purity of Heart and Prayer

An axiom of early monastic theology often overlooked or underplayed by modern scholars is that ascetical effort alone can attain nothing of abiding spiritual significance. Furthermore, sheer grit cannot sustain ascetical discipline. Only God's assistance can begin and complete the quest for purity of heart. But grace is not a sort of spiritual vitamin grabbed on the run. It is more like the manna of the Israelites, given fresh each morning but needing collection. The Israelites found that greed provided no advantage and that ingratitude imperilled access to such providential nourishment. It is the same with fruitful asceticism, which requires acknowledgment of need (I must be fed), self-limitation (I cannot feed myself), and dependence on God (only God can feed me). The monastic writers often write of this dynamic in terms of compunction, that acute awareness of limitation and brokenness joined to deep thanksgiving for the abundant mercies of God.[23]

The repentance and trust fundamental to Christian asceticism are experienced most directly in prayer. Whether the goal be labeled *apatheia* or purity of heart, prayer is central. Here Evagrius' emphasis on "pure prayer" and Cassian's on "purity of heart" intersect, for both emphasize focused intention. The synergy between divine and human

---

[22] On these Greek terms, see my overview in *Cassian the Monk*, 50–1, and Pierre Hadot, "Les divisions des parties de la philosophie dans l'Antiquité," *Museum Helveticum* 36 (1979) 201–23.

[23] On this theme, see Irénée Hausherr, *Penthos: The Doctrine of Compunction in the Christian East*, trans. Anselm Hufstader, Cistercian Studies Series 53 (Kalamazoo, Mich.: Cistercian Publications, 1982). For Evagrius, see Jeremy Driscoll, "Penthos and Tears in Evagrius Ponticus," *Studia Monastica* 36 (1994) 147–64; on Cassian, see my *Cassian the Monk*, 122–9.

in prayer, which is at least part of what we call grace, grounds the possibility of everything else. The deeper the grounding—the more one has been opened to God in compunction—the clearer will be the eyes of the heart which "see God." Prayer is the heart of any Christian asceticism. Isolating particular disciplines, even practices of prayer, from the immediacy of the divine presence in prayer will inevitably miss the whole point of Christian asceticism.

Monastic writers have often been reticent when describing their actual experience of prayer, preferring to describe attitude, setting, and problems. Their reticence is appropriate before such a mystery and also recognizes that the experience of prayer varies widely from individual to individual. We must be careful not to exclude another's experience of prayer through our own ill-crafted definitions. Whatever one's own experience of prayer, whether it be an apophatic "presence in absence" or a richly kataphatic encounter, fidelity to prayer defines the pure of heart.

Purity of Heart and Contemplation

In his dialogue with the Zen master Daisetz T. Suzuki, Thomas Merton compared the monastic teaching on purity of heart with the Zen notion of "suchness."[24] One who is pure of heart has an immediate apprehension of the way things really are. In Evagrius' teaching, the concept of "purity" is linked most closely with his teaching on pure prayer and contemplation. For Cassian, too, contemplative focus is the essence of Christian perfection. All human energies, supported and strengthened by grace, are gathered into the project of seeing. The beatitudinal assertion that the pure of heart "see God" is attractive but very vague. What does the contemplative contemplate?

There is nothing esoteric or intellectualized about the early monastic understanding of contemplation. The media are the Bible and all of creation. The dynamic is one of deepening insight as the heart clarifies through prayer and discipline. One sees to understand and understands through seeing. The visual metaphor, used both by the philosophers and the Christians, reminds us not to confuse their tendency toward spiritualization with a denial of human experience. Thus the seeming paradox of Evagrius' insistence on both imageless prayer and on *theoria* (θεωρία), contemplation. Contemplative media are essential as long as they are truly media, means, leading toward an ultimate ob-

---

[24] Thomas Merton, *Zen and the Birds of Appetite* (New York: New Directions, 1968) 100.

ject. To idolize the means, whether it be a pious image of God or even the biblical text, is to miss the object.[25]

Cassian follows his monastic predecessors in describing the interplay of ascetical maturity and deepening insight.[26] He notes that the very face of Scripture changes as we change, for we see with sharper spiritual vision (*Conf.* 14.11.1). This is why for the believer the Bible is different from *War and Peace* or any other great work of literature. Tolstoy's great novel rewards, and even requires, rereading. But the Bible is read and meditated day in and day out for a lifetime, and is always revelatory. It is not the Bible that changes, but the reader. At the same time, the Christian disciplines that foster growth in purity of heart remain a part of daily life. Cassian posits Mary of Bethany as the icon of perfect contemplation, but then adds that such perfection awaits us in heaven (*Conf.* 1.8–10). Meanwhile we have many things to do, both in our own lives and for others. Yet as we do them, we grow in the love which is purity of heart, and as we become purer of heart we can see more and more.

Purity of Heart and Anger

One of the experiential markers of purity of heart is tranquility. Not a zombie-like state, this kind of tranquility means that one responds appropriately and completely to each person and every situation one encounters. Athanasius described Antony the Great as fully present to everyone he met because he was not prey to extreme emotional reactions.[27] Evagrius and Cassian, like so many other early Christian writers, worked out of a basic Platonic anthropology that identified two major energy sources in the human personality.[28] One of these was a source of desire and attraction. The other was a source of resistance and repulsion. The pathology of the first was lust, of the second anger. The health of the first was love for God and for other people, and attraction to virtue. The health of the second was resistance to sin and fierce struggle against temptation. Purity of heart, then, is another way of speaking about the healthy soul. Later I will say more about purity of heart and chastity. Here I want to focus on the other part of the soul and its malaise of anger.

---

[25] This is Cassian's point in the opening chapters of *Conf.* 10. See my *Cassian the Monk*, 51–4 and 95–9.

[26] See Cassian's *Conf.* 14, with its echoes of Evagrius' *Gnostikos;* for an overview, see my *Cassian the Monk*, 90–9.

[27] *Vita Antonii* 14.4–6 (*SC* 400, pp. 172–4).

[28] For Evagrius, see especially *Praktikos* 89 and the commentary by Antoine and Claire Guillaumont (*SC* 171, pp. 680–9); for Cassian, see *Conf.* 24.15–17 and my remarks in *Cassian the Monk*, 64–6.

Readers are often struck both by the frequency and insightfulness of remarks about anger in early monastic writings. The theoretical background of the parts of the soul explains some of that emphasis on anger, but of course the model itself was based on observation of human behavior. Anger is endemic to human experience and often interwoven with other traits. One zealous for virtue, for example, can become enraged when others interrupt the day's routine. Evagrius and Cassian wrote of the fraudulent anchorites who went away to the desert to get away from other people.[29] Because their *fuga mundi* really was a flight from the world rather than a choice for God, the very foundation of their monastic lives was rotten. Cassian recommended the common life of the cenobium as the way to identify and address problems of anger (*Conf.* 19.13). However, he was not romantic about community life. His treatise on friendship, *Conference* 16, is largely about the corrosive effects of anger on human relationships. Like Benedict, Cassian urged his readers to run the path of the commandments so that their hearts could be expanded through the exercise of charity, leaving no room for anger to hide (*Conf.* 16.27.5).

Purity of Heart and Chastity

Cassian's emphasis on the heart suggests an incarnational understanding of purity. One could argue that his most distinctive contribution to early monastic theology was to link the spiritualized understanding of purity characteristic of both non-Christian and Christian Platonism more evidently to the human experience of embodiment.[30] The body is not left behind or ignored in the pursuit of purity of heart but becomes an essential and even sacramental element in God's transformation of the whole person. Cassian's teaching on chastity parallels his teaching on purity of heart, anchoring the same basic point about moving toward God in another aspect of human experience.[31]

Cassian suggests that purity of heart develops gradually. Clarification of intention and insight is a trajectory rather than an immediate achievement.[32] When he writes about the maturing of sexuality in chastity, he is more explicit about the developmental stages. He acknowledges that the process itself is invisible, like physical growth,

---

[29] For Evagrius, see, for example, *Praktikos* 22 (*SC* 171, p. 552). For Cassian, see *Inst.* 8.16-19, *Conf.* 1.6, 19.10–14.

[30] See ch. 4 of my *Cassian the Monk*.

[31] For Cassian's teaching on chastity, see especially *Inst.* 6, *Conf.* 12 and 22.

[32] One can compare Evagrius' more explicit outline in the *Praktikos* of stages of *apatheia* (*Prak.* 57–70 as in *SC* 171, pp. 634–57). See the introduction by Antoine and Claire Guillaumont in *SC* 170, pp. 108–11.

though the results are measurable and progress can be marked. The six stages he describes, geared to his originally male monastic readership, depict a process of internalization which moves from a purely physical baseline into thoughts, memory, and even dreams (*Conf.* 12.7). The progress is really a return, a return to the natural condition of the human person so terribly disrupted by the Fall. In the tranquil chastity of the pure in heart, body and soul work together in transparency to God and humankind.[33] The chaste person, pure in heart and in body, is totally available to God and to the needs of other human beings. Desire has been clarified and now serves the will of the God who implanted it in our hearts in the first place.

VALEDICTION

The advantage of serving the hors d'oeuvre of this collection is that I am spared the task of conclusion. From the overview provided here the reader can now proceed to detailed investigations of the sources and elements of the rich and complex theme of purity of heart. What I can do, however, is thank Sister Juana for providing the occasion for us to continue her work: may we be worthy successors.

---

[33] See *Conf.* 12.8.5 for Cassian's description of transparent chastity.

The Concept of Purity of Heart in the Old Testament

IRENE NOWELL, O.S.B.

INTRODUCTION

The most thorough study of "purity of heart" in the Old Testament to date is that done by Sr. Juana Raasch, O.S.B., in 1966.[1] She begins with the Greek *katharos* (καθαρός, "clean"), which in the Septuagint translates several Hebrew terms. Of the Hebrew terms, she notes particularly *ṭāhôr* (טהור, clean). However, the texts she uses include also the Hebrew terms *bār* (בר, Ps 24:4, pure), *yāšār* (ישר, straight, Ps 11:7; see 11:2 for the reference to "heart"), *kibbēs* (כבס, cleanse, Jer 4:14). She analyzes the concept of purity, which includes moral purity but "most often denotes mere ritual cleanness."[2] She describes the heart as "the source of the interior life," "thinking, planning, remembering."[3] She defines purity of heart as "a metaphor which stands for the removal of inner defilement, that is, sin, in its very principle: the interior disposition."[4] It is purity of heart which is necessary for and leads to the vision of God (Ps 24:3-4; Matt 5:8). The source of impurity is the evil inclination (*yāṣer hārā'*, יצר הרע) of the heart (see Gen 6:5). Only God

---

[1] Juana Raasch, "The Monastic Concept of Purity of Heart and Its Sources," *Studia Monastica* 8 (1966) 11–21. Other scholars before and since relegate "purity of heart" to a paragraph at most. See A. R. Johnson, *The Vitality of the Individual in the Thought of Ancient Israel*, 2d. ed (Cardiff: University of Wales, 1964) 83–4; H. W. Wolff, *Anthropology of the Old Testament*, trans. Margaret Kohl (Philadelphia: Fortress Press, 1974) 52–3; H.-J. Fabry, "*lēb, lēbāb*," *TDOT* 7.430; F. Baumgärtel, "*kardia*," *TDNT* 3.607. Jan G. Bovenmars (*A Biblical Spirituality of the Heart* [New York: Alba House, 1991] 9–12) has the longest consideration, using Pss 7:10; 9:2; 24:3-4; 51:10; 73:1, 12, 13; 86:11; 97:11; 101:2; 112:7, 8; 119:34; Prov 20:9; 22:11; Wis 1:1.

[2] Raasch, "The Monastic Concept of Purity of Heart," 12.
[3] Ibid., 13.
[4] Ibid.

can cleanse the human heart and create a new heart (see Ezek 36:25-27; Ps 51:12).

The following study is dedicated to Sister Juana, who isolated the major terms, defined the concepts, mentioned some of the major texts, and drew the lines of the argument. I intend to expand her work by first considering the meaning of the Hebrew concept "heart" and the nuances in the various words for purity. Then I will discuss each of the passages in the Old Testament where the concept "purity of heart" occurs in order to describe the characteristics of a pure heart, the way to obtain and maintain a pure heart, and the consequences of being pure of heart. Finally, I will draw a few conclusions.

TERMINOLOGY AND CONCEPTS

Heart

The term heart (*lēb*, *lēbāb*; לב, לבב) in the Old Testament appears 853 times in Hebrew and 8 times in Aramaic. It does not refer to the specific physical organ which pumps blood through the human body. There is no evidence that the people of Ancient Israel knew the function of the beating heart. The location of the heart is, however, understood to be in the chest area and seems to include most of the organs in the central torso.[5]

The primary biblical use of the term heart is not physical at all. The heart refers to: (1) the source of thought and reason,[6] (2) the source of volition and decision,[7] (3) the center of emotions, (4) the seat of human wisdom. It thus comes to connote the interior disposition as contrasted with exterior actions, symbolized often by "hands" (see Ps 24:3-4).[8] The heart may also signify the whole person.

---

[5] See Johnson, *Vitality*, 75–6; Wolff, *Anthropology*, 40–3; Fabry, *TDOT* 7.411–2; cf. Baumgärtel, *TDNT* 3.606; R. North, "Brain and Nerve in the Biblical Outlook," *Bib* 74 (1993) 594. R. North ("Did Ancient Israelites Have a Heart?" *BRev* 11:3 [1995] 33) shows a second-century B.C.E. Etruscan statue which has a "window" in the torso showing "the internal organs of cognition."

[6] North, "Brain and Nerve," gives the most thorough defense for the understanding of *lēb*/*lēbāb* as the organ of both knowledge and volition. Wolff, *Anthropology*, entitles his chapter on the heart "Reasonable Man."

[7] B. Gemser ("The Object of Moral Judgment in the Old Testament," *Adhuc Loquitur: Collected Essays of Dr. B. Gemser* [Leiden: Brill, 1968] 86–7) points out the primacy of the "heart" in biblical descriptions of "sinning in thought."

[8] See T. McCreesh, "Heart," *Collegeville Pastoral Dictionary of Biblical Theology*, ed. Carroll Stuhlmueller (Collegeville: The Liturgical Press, 1995) 422.

Purity

There is a cluster of terms that signify purity in the phrase "purity of heart."[9] They have various nuances of meaning.

(1) The noun *tōm* (תם) signifies completeness, and thus perfection or integrity. "One dies in his full [*tummô*, תֻּמּוֹ] vigor" (Job 21:23).[10] God "is the shield of those who walk honestly" (*tōm*, תֹם, Prov 2:7). The adjective *tām* has the same range of meaning.

(2) The adjective *bār* (בר, from the root *brr*, ברר) means pure in the sense of free, clear, empty, open. "The command of the LORD is clear [*bārâ*, בָּרָה], / enlightening the eye" (Ps 19:9). "Where there are no oxen, the crib remains empty" (*bār*, בָּר, Prov 14:4).

(3) The verb *yāšar* (ישר) means to go/make straight. "The cows went straight [*yiššarnâ*, יִשַּׁרְנָה] for the route to Beth-shemesh" (1 Sam 6:12). "Make straight [*yaššĕrû*, יַשְּׁרוּ] in the wasteland a highway for our God!" (Isa 40:3). The adjective *yāšār* thus comes to connote upright, honest. The noun *yōšer* has the same range of meaning and is often translated as integrity.

(4) The adjective *zāk* (זָךְ) signifies purity of oil or frankincense. Applied to people, both adjective and verb (*zākâ*, זכה) signify moral purity. "You shall order the Israelites to bring you clear [*zāk*, זָךְ] oil of crushed olives, to be used for the light" (Exod 27:20). "I am clean [*zak*, זַךְ] and without transgression; I am innocent; there is no guilt in me" (Job 33:9).

(5) The adjective *ṭahôr* (טהור, clean) and the verb *ṭhr* (טהר, to be clean) usually refer to cultic cleanness. To be clean in a cultic sense (as opposed to unclean) means that a person or thing is fit for worship. For example, "all who are clean" may partake of the sacrifices (Lev 7:19). Pure (*ṭahôr*, טָהוֹר) gold may be used for the ark, the lampstand, the table, the cups and plates for the sanctuary (Exod 25:11, 24, 29, 31). By contrast, anything that has a scaly condition, whether human skin or a moldy garment, is unclean (Lev 14:54-57). Less often this root refers to moral purity (see Hab 1:3; Ps 12:7). "Too pure [*ṭĕhôr*, טְהוֹר] are your eyes to look upon evil" (Hab 1:13). "The fear of the LORD is pure" (*ṭĕhôrâ*, טְהוֹרָה, Ps 19:10).

In the deutero-canonical books, the primary term is *katharos* / *katharizō* (καθαρός, καθαρίζω, "clean") with *kardia* (καρδία).

---

[9] Johnson (*Vitality*, 83) lists the roots *brr*, *tmm*, *yšr*; Fabry (*TDOT* 7.430) lists *tōm*, *yōšer*, *kibbēs*, *zākâ*, *bar*, and *ṭāhôr*; Baumgärtel (*TDNT* 3.606–7) lists *bar*, *ṭāhôr*, *yāšār*, *tōm*.

[10] All translations are from the *New American Bible* unless otherwise noted

PURITY OF HEART

Characteristics of a Pure Heart

Whole

The pure heart is whole (*tōm*, תם). In Psalm 101 the king promises to "walk with integrity of heart" (*tom-lĕbābî*, תָם־לְבָבִי) within the royal court (Ps 101:2). Psalm 101 is a royal psalm, a pledge of the king to rule according to God's law. Wholeness (or integrity) is a key word throughout the psalm. The king promises to be wise regarding the way of wholeness or integrity (*derek tāmîm*, דֶּרֶךְ תָּמִים, 101:2). Then he announces that only those who "walk in the way of integrity" (*derek tāmiîm*, דֶּרֶךְ תָּמִים, 101:6), those who are "the faithful of the land," will be allowed into his service. Such people are also God's delight (Prov 11:20; see also Pss 18:31, 33; 119:1; Prov 11:5). Thus the king's purity of heart will be given flesh both in his own actions and in the actions of those who serve him.

The pledge of the king is set under the opening statement: I will sing of love [*ḥesed*, חסד] and justice [*mišpāṭ*, משפט] / to you, LORD, I sing praise" (Ps 101:1). The psalm ends with the promise to "rid the LORD's city of all evildoers" (101:8). The king acts in purity of heart (and surrounds himself with others who are pure of heart) in order to establish God's rule of love and justice. He acts for the sake of the community.

The idea of wholeness of heart is particularly related to kings. Twice David is identified as "whole of heart." Psalm 78, a historical psalm, ends with a reference to David, chosen by God to shepherd God's people.

> [God] chose David his servant,
>   took him from the sheepfold,
> From tending sheep God brought him,
>   to shepherd Jacob, his people,
>   Israel, his heritage.
> He shepherded them with a pure heart [*tom lĕbābô*, תָם לְבָבוֹ];
>   with skilled hands he guided them (Ps 78:70–72).

In this psalm we see the parallel between heart and hand. David's inner self (heart) is whole and his actions (hands) are insightful. Psalm 78 has many wisdom elements, so it is not surprising that the psalm ends on a wisdom note. David has integrity (heart) and wisdom (hands). Purity of heart is linked with wisdom.

When Solomon finishes building palace and temple, he has a second encounter with God, paralleling the encounter at Gibeon when he asks for a "listening heart" (1 Kgs 3:9). In this second encounter, God promises that the divine eyes and heart will remain in the Temple for all time (1 Kgs 9:3). Solomon, however, must emulate his father David:

> As for you, if you will walk before me, as David your father walked, with wholeness of heart [*tom-lēbāb*, תָם־לֵבָב] and uprightness, doing according to all that I have commanded you, and keeping my statutes and my ordinances, then I will establish your royal throne over Israel forever, as I promised your father David (1 Kgs 9:4).

Otherwise the Temple will become a "heap of ruins" and the people will be driven from the land (1 Kgs 9:6-9).

Walking in wholeness of heart is paralleled with uprightness (*yōšer*, see below) and defined as obedience to all God's commands. Psalm 119 makes a similar statement: "May I be wholehearted [*libbî tāmîm*, לִבִּי תָמִים] toward your laws, / that I may not be put to shame" (Ps 119:80). Its opposite is defined as turning away from God and following other gods, failing to obey God's commandments but instead worshiping and serving other gods (1 Kgs 9:6). Wholeness of heart is measured by obedience and fidelity.

There is a third story of a king with a pure heart. Abraham tells Abimelech, king of Gerar, that Sarah is his sister and Abimelech takes her into his house. (This is the second of the three wife-sister stories in which a patriarch, in order to save himself, says that his wife is his sister; see Gen 12:10-20; 26:1-11.) But God reveals to Abimelech that Sarah is really Abraham's wife. A horrified Abimelech pleads with God for his life because he did not know the true relationship between Abraham and Sarah:

> "Did he not himself say to me, 'She is my sister'? And she herself said, 'He is my brother.' I did this in the integrity of my heart [*tom-lēbābî*, תָם־לְבָבִי] and the innocence of my hands." Then God said to him in the dream, "Yes I know that you did this in the integrity of your heart [*tom-lēbābkā*, תָם־לְבָבְךָ]; furthermore it was I who kept you from sinning against me. Therefore I did not let you touch her" (Gen 20:5-6).

Abimelech claims innocence because he acted in wholeness of heart and cleanness of hands. He links his inner disposition (heart) and outward actions (hands). But God claims responsibility for Abimelech's integrity, preventing him from touching Sarah and thus preventing his sin, however inadvertent it may be.

A new theme is added here to the cluster of ideas surrounding purity of heart: fear of the Lord. When asked why he did not tell Abimelech that Sarah was his wife, Abraham replies, "I was afraid because I thought there would surely be no fear of God in this place" (Gen 20:11). The implication is that Abimelech, who acted in wholeness of heart and cleanness of hands, does indeed fear God. Proverbs tells us that fear of the Lord is the beginning of wisdom (Prov 9:10; see also Prov 1:7). Abimelech is a wise man.

Wholeness of heart can also be described in other ways. We pray for singleness of heart:

> Teach me, LORD, your way
> that I may walk in your truth,
> single-hearted [*yaḥēd lĕbābî*, יַחֵד לְבָבִי] and revering your name (Ps 86:11).

In Ezekiel God promises: "I will give them one heart [*lēb ʾeḥād*, לֵב אֶחָד], and put a new spirit within them" (Ezek 11:19 NRSV; see also Jer 32:39). This oneness of heart signifies the people's relationship to the king and obedience to his laws: "The rest of Israel was likewise of one mind [*lēb ʾeḥād*, לֵב אֶחָד] to make David king" (1 Chr 12:39). "In Judah, however, the power of God brought it about that the people were of one mind [*lēb ʾeḥād*, לֵב אֶחָד] to carry out the command of the king and the princes in accordance with the word of the LORD" (2 Chr 30:12). In the Wisdom of Solomon rulers are exhorted to seek God in simplicity of heart (ἐν ἁπλότητι καρδίας, Wis 1:1).

In contrast to wholeness of heart Psalm 101 presents "the crooked heart" (*lēbāb ʿiqqēš*, לֵבָב עִקֵּשׁ, Ps 101:4, see below) and "the arrogant heart" (lit. broad of heart, *rĕḥab lēbāb*, רְחַב לֵבָב, Ps 101:5; see also Prov 21:4). The king declares, "I shun the devious of heart [*lēbāb ʿiqqēš*, לֵבָב עִקֵּשׁ]; the wicked I do not tolerate" (Ps 101:4). These wicked are false in word (Ps 101:3, 5, 7) and in deed (Ps 101:3, 7). Proverbs adds that the "crooked of mind [*ʿiqqeš-lēb*, עִקֶּשׁ־לֵב] do not prosper" (Prov 17:20 NRSV); "crooked minds [*ʿiqqeš-lēb*, עִקְּשֵׁי־לֵב] are an abomination to the LORD" (Prov 11:20 NRSV).[11]

In Psalm 12 the enemies "speak with deceiving lips and a double heart" (*lēb wālēb*, לֵב וָלֵב, Ps 12:3). The members of David's army, however, do not have such a double heart (1 Chr 12:34). Ben Sira warns us not to approach fear of the Lord with a divided heart (ἐν καρδίᾳ δισσῇ, Sir 1:28).[12] Those of shallow heart (κοῦφος καρδίᾳ) go after temporary pleasures and sin against their own life (Sir 19:4)

Worst of all are those who are without a heart (*ʾên lēb*, אֵין לֵב) or lacking heart (*ḥăsar-lēb*, חֲסַר־לֵב). They "have eyes and see not, . . . ears and hear not," and they fail to fear the Lord (Jer 5:21-22). They turn away from God and go after idols (Jer 5:19) and foreign alliances (Hos

---

[11] For a thorough study of the word pair *tm*/*qš*, see W. Brueggemann, "A Neglected Sapiential Word Pair," *ZAW* 89 (1977) 234–58.

[12] See P. W. Skehan and A. A. Di Lella, *The Wisdom of Ben Sira* (New York: Doubleday, 1987) 146.

7:11). They commit adultery (Prov 6:32; see also 7:7) and belittle others (Prov 11:12). They follow worthless pursuits (Prov 12:11; see also 17:18), delight in folly (Prov 15:21), and neglect their own vineyard (Prov 24:30). They sin and think God does not see (ἐλαττούμενος καρδία, Sir 16:23).[13] Wisdom calls to them (Prov 9:4, 16). Those who do not listen to her destroy themselves (Prov 6:32; 10:13, 21; see also Sir 6:20).[14]

Empty and Open

> Who may go up the mountain of the LORD?
> Who can stand in his holy place?
> The clean of hand and pure of heart [*bar-lēbāb*, בַר־לֵבָב],
> who are not devoted to idols,
> who have not sworn falsely (Ps 24:3-4).

The pure heart is open and free (*bār*, בר), empty of evil. In Psalm 24, an entrance liturgy, the pure heart is parallel to clean hands (*nĕqî kappayim*, נְקִי כַפַּיִם), i.e., hands that are also free of evil. This person is innocent of wrongdoing both within (heart) and without (hands), both in thought and deed. The remainder of the verse expands on this innocence. The soul (*nepeš*, נֶפֶשׁ) has not been lifted up toward what is worthless, i.e., idols; nor has a deceptive oath been sworn. This is the person who may enter God's presence.

The description is stated in negative terms. This is a person who has been swept clean of wrong doing and deceit and is pure of heart. The emptiness makes it possible for the heart and hands to be filled with the Lord's blessings and to enjoy the gift of right relationship (*ṣĕdāqâ*, צְדָקָה) with God (24:5). The stanza ends with the declaration that these are the characteristics of those who seek God intensely, who seek the face of the God of Jacob (24:6). The consequence of purity of heart in Psalm 24 is blessing and righteousness. The goal of purity of heart is to see the face of God.

Psalm 73 is the psalm of the heart. "Heart" (לֵבָב) occurs six times in this psalm of twenty-eight verses (73:1, 7, 13, 21, and twice in 26). Psalm 73 is a wisdom psalm, a meditation on the seeming unfairness of life. Why do the wicked prosper and the righteous suffer? The first verse is a declaration of faith and the thesis statement of the psalm. In spite of appearances, God is indeed good to the just. "How good God

---

[13] The Cairo manuscripts indicate that the Hebrew is *ḥăsar-lēb*; see Skehan and Di Lella, *The Wisdom of Ben Sira*, 275.

[14] Greek ἀκάρδιος represents Hebrew *ḥăsar-leb* in the Cairo manuscripts; see Skehan and Di Lella, *The Wisdom of Ben Sira*, 193.

is to the upright, / the Lord to those who are clean of heart!" (*bārê lēbāb*, בָּרֵי לֵבָב, Ps 73:1).

Psalm 73 begins not with the conditions, but with the consequence of purity of heart. The result of emptying the heart of evil is the experience of God's amazing goodness. The only good is the nearness of God. In the sanctuary the psalmist realizes that nothing else matters.

> I am always with you;
>   you hold my right hand.
> You will guide me with your counsel,
>   and afterward you will receive me with glory.
> Whom have I in heaven but you?
>   Nothing else delights me on earth.
> Though my flesh and my heart fail,
>   God is the rock of my heart, my portion forever (Ps 73:23-26).

The psalmist concludes by returning to the opening statement: God is good to the pure of heart. Now the psalmist knows in what that goodness consists; it is the nearness of God: "As for me, to be near God is my good" (Ps 73:28).

In contrast to the emptiness of the pure of heart, the wicked are full—full of health and wealth, pride and malice. "Evil thoughts flood their hearts" (Ps 73:7). They are similar to the enemies who come to visit the sick person in Psalm 41: "Their hearts store up malice" (Ps 41:7). They are self-satisfied and self-sufficient. But as the psalmist prays, it becomes evident that the wicked are on a slippery road to ruin (Ps 73:18-20). They will end far from God (Ps 73:27).

Upright and Honest

The pure heart is upright, honest, sincere (*yāšār*, יָשָׁר). God warns the Israelites not to assume that it is because of their own righteousness or uprightness of heart (*yōšer lĕbābkā*, יֹשֶׁר לְבָבְךָ) that they are taking possession of the land, but rather because of God's fidelity to the promise made to the ancestors and because of the wickedness of the nations whom they are dispossessing (Deut 9:5). David claims that his offerings to the Temple were brought with "a sincere heart" (*yōšer lĕbābî*, יֹשֶׁר לְבָבִי). He knows that God tests hearts (*bōḥēn lēbāb*, בֹּחֵן לֵבָב, see below) and takes pleasure in uprightness (1 Chr 29:17). When Solomon asks for a listening heart at Gibeon, he acknowledges that God was good to David because he walked before God in faithfulness, justice, and with "an upright heart" (*yišrat lēbāb*, יִשְׁרַת לֵבָב, 1 Kgs 3:6). The Levites in the time of Hezekiah are praised for being more upright of heart (*yišre lēbāb*, יִשְׁרֵי לֵבָב) than the priests in sanctifying themselves (2 Chr 29:34). In the book of Job, the young Elihu claims to have reason to speak because he is upright of heart (*yōšer libbî*, יֹשֶׁר־לִבִּי) and speaks sincerely (Job 33:3).

The upright of heart are found frequently in the Psalms. The wicked threaten them so they take refuge in God:

> In the LORD I take refuge; how can you say to me,
> "See how the wicked string their bows,
>   fit their arrows to the string
>   to shoot from the shadows at the upright of heart" (*yišrē lēb*, יִשְׁרֵי־לֵב, Ps 11:1-2).

Their trust is well placed, for God saves them and defends them:

> A shield before me is God
>   who saves the honest heart (*yišrê-lēb*, יִשְׁרֵי־לֵב, Ps 7:10).
> Continue your kindness toward your friends,
>   your just defense of the honest heart (*yišrê-lēb*, יִשְׁרֵי־לֵב, Ps 36:11).
> Do good, LORD, to the good,
>   to those who are upright of heart (*lîšārîm bĕlibbôtām*, לִישָׁרִים בְּלִבּוֹתָם, Ps 125:4).

Therefore the upright of heart are happy and give glory to the God who saves them:

> Be glad in the LORD and rejoice, you just;
> exult all you upright of heart (*yišrê-lēb*, יִשְׁרֵי־לֵב, Ps 32:11).
> Light dawns for the just;
>   gladness, for the honest of heart (*yišrê-lēb*, יִשְׁרֵי־לֵב, Ps 97:11).
> The just will rejoice and take refuge in the LORD;
>   all the upright [*yišrê-lēb*, יִשְׁרֵי־לֵב] will glory in their God (Ps 64:11).

They renew their commitment to live by God's law:

> I will praise you with sincere heart [*yōšer lēbāb*, יֹשֶׁר לֵבָב]
>   as I study your just edicts (Ps 119:7).
> Judgment shall again be just,
>   and all the upright of heart [*yišrê-lēb*, יִשְׁרֵי־לֵב] will follow it (Ps 94:15).

In these psalms the upright of heart are often described as righteous (*ṣedeq/ṣaddîq*, צדק/צדיק, Pss 7:9-10; 11:3; 32:11; 64:11; 97:11, 12; 125:3; see also 94:15) and good (*ṭôb*, טוב, Ps 125:4). They are God's friends, those who know God (*yōdĕʾîm*, ידעים, Ps 36:11). God's love (*ḥesed*, חסד) surrounds them (Ps 32:10; see also 36:8, 11).

Morally Pure

The heart that is whole, clean, upright is morally pure (*zāk/zākâ*, זך / זכה), cleansed of sin. However, no human being has the power to create a pure heart; no human being has the power to cleanse the

heart. "Who can say, 'I have made my heart pure [*zikkîtî libbî*, זִכִּיתִי לִבִּי],
I am cleansed of my sin?'" (Prov 20:9). Even keeping one's heart pure
is difficult, especially in face of life's seeming unfairness. "Is it in vain
that I have kept my heart clean [*zikkîtî lĕbābî*, זִכִּיתִי לְבָבִי], washed my
hands in innocence?" (Ps 73:13).

The psalmist is afflicted daily, yet the wicked continue to prosper
(Ps 73:3-5, 14). The struggle leads to the temptation to speak as the
wicked do, to ask if God really knows anything (Ps 73:15, 11). But to
succumb would be a betrayal of God's people. Purity of heart implies
not only individual morality, but also community responsibilities and
communal consequences. The psalmist must choose between association with the wicked and fidelity to God's people. Choosing the wicked
is equivalent to abandoning purity of heart. The effects of this betrayal
are felt not by oneself alone but by the whole believing community.

The temptations of the heart are temptations of thought: to think
like the wicked (Ps 73:15) or to claim the wisdom of God (Ps 73:16). Purity of heart lies in recognizing the impossibility of understanding the
thoughts of God. "Though I tried to understand all this / it was too
difficult for me" (Ps 73:16). The resolution of the psalmist's struggle is
found not in penetrating the thoughts of God but rather in experiencing God's nearness (Ps 73:17). In the sanctuary, God's holy place, the
psalmist knows two things: the wicked are far from God (Ps 73:27) and
the pure of heart enjoy God's presence (Ps 73:28). The nearness of God
answers the psalmist's anguished question: It is not in vain that you
keep your heart pure and your hands clean (see Ps 73:13). God is indeed good to the pure of heart (see Ps 73:1).

Cultically Clean

The pure heart—whole, free, honest, good—is thus fit for worship
(*ṭāhôr*, טָהוֹר), fit to be brought into God's presence (see Ps 24:4). Ben Sira
advises one who is sick to prepare to offer sacrifice: "Flee wickedness;
let your hands be just, cleanse your heart of every sin" (καθάρισον καρδίαν, Sir 38:10).[15] But only God can cleanse the heart. "A clean heart [*lēb
ṭāhôr*, לֵב טָהוֹר] create for me, God; / a steadfast spirit renew within me"
(Ps 51:12).

Psalm 51 takes the thought of Prov 20:9 one step further. If one cannot cleanse one's own heart from sin, then one must beg God to do it.
With the psalmist we acknowledge that the sinfulness which has
plagued us from the first moment of our existence (Ps 51:7) continues

---

[15] The Cairo manuscripts indicate that the Hebrew is *ṭahēr lēb*. See Skehan and Di
Lella, *Wisdom of Ben Sira*, 440.

to stare us in the face (Ps 51:5). Only God can free us. Therefore we beg God not only to cleanse our hearts but to begin again. We ask to be created anew. The verb *bara'* (ברא), to create, is predicated only of God in the Hebrew Bible. No one else can accomplish this new creation. God's new creation of our inner selves will be a clean heart, fit for worship.

The psalm gives other descriptions of this inner being to be created by God. God's desire for us is truth within us, even in our entrails, so we ask for wisdom in our secret, hidden being (Ps 51:8). The clean heart is paralleled by the steadfast spirit (Ps 51:12), the spirit that is established and stable. We ask also for a generous, willing spirit (Ps 51:14).

God's creation of the new, however, will require a shattering of the old. But what is shattered is not lost; the old is in the new. The clean heart, fit to worship, offers itself in sacrifice as a broken, humbled heart, a broken spirit (Ps 51:19). This is a sacrifice acceptable to God (Ps 51:18).

The relationship between God and the clean heart is even clearer in Prov 22:11: "The LORD loves the pure of heart" (*těhôr lēb*, מהור־לב, Prov 22:11). In Psalm 24 the pure of heart may approach God's sanctuary. In Psalm 73 the nearness of God in the sanctuary is their good. Proverbs 20:9 cautions that no human is able to cleanse the heart. Psalm 51 answers by asking God to create a new, clean heart and to accept a broken heart in sacrifice. Proverbs 22:11 reveals that God loves the clean of heart. God's love is drawn by what is inside a person, the heart.

Obtaining and Maintaining a Pure Heart

God's Action

It is clear that only God can create a pure heart (Ps 51:12; Prov 20:9). It is God also who watches to maintain the pure heart. Jeremiah gathers the concepts: "You, O LORD, know [*ydᵉ*, ידע] me; you see [*rᵉh*, ראה] me, and test [*bḥn*, בחן] me—my heart is with you" (Jer 12:3 NRSV). The vocabulary of testing includes *bāḥan* (בחן) and *ṣārap* (צרף), which are often used for the smelting and purifying of precious metals, and *ḥāqar* (חקר), which has to do with investigation or spying.

God "knows the secrets of the heart" (Ps 44:22). God sees the heart (Jer 20:12). God declares, "I the LORD test the mind [*ḥōqēr lēb*, חקר לב] and search the heart,[16] to give to all according to their ways, according to the fruit of their doings" (Jer 17:10 NRSV). Thus we trust God to purify us and to punish the wicked:

---

[16] In Jer 17:10 the Hebrew word *lēb* is translated "mind" and *kĕlāyôt*, which means "kidneys," (and thus the innermost and most secret part of a person), is translated "heart." So also Jer 11:20; 20:12; Pss 7:10; 26:2.

> Bring the malice of the wicked to an end;
>   uphold the innocent,
> O God of justice,
>   who tries hearts [*bōḥēn libbôt*, בֹחֵן לִבּוֹת] and minds (Ps 7:10; see also Ps 17:3; 26:2 [*ṣĕrôpâ . . . libbî*, לִבִּי . . . צְרוֹפָה]; Prov 17:3; 1 Chr 29:17).

So in our prayer we beg:

> Probe me [*ḥāqrēnî*, חָקְרֵנִי], God, know my heart [*da' lĕbābî*, דַּע לְבָבִי];
>   try me [*bĕḥānēnî*, בְּחָנֵנִי], know my concerns.
> See if my way is crooked,
>   then lead me in the ancient paths (Ps 139:23-24).

Only God knows, sees, tests the human heart. Only God can create a pure heart. Only God can re-create it.

Human Action

There are, however, actions expected of human beings in order to maintain purity of heart. The psalmist of Psalm 73 reveals that it will be a struggle (Ps 73:13-14). The heart may be shattered in the process (Ps 51:19).

The person who is pure of heart is expected to fear the Lord (Gen 20:5-6, 11; Ps 86:11). Fear of the Lord will lead to trust in God's protection (Pss 11:1; 32:10; 64:11) and obedience to God's law (1 Kgs 3:6; 9:4; see also Ps 94:15; 119:80). God's law, God's covenant, requires that a person be faithful to the community (see 1 Kgs 9:4-9; Pss 73:13, 15; 101:2, 6-8). Such purity of heart is the responsibility especially of the king or ruler (Gen 20:5-6; 1 Kgs 9:4; Pss 78:72; 101:2; Wis 1:1) This inward purity of heart is demonstrated by exterior actions (clean hands; Gen 20:5; Ps 24:4; see also 2 Chr 29:34) and sincerity of speech (Job 33:3). These are the people God loves (Prov 22:11).

Consequences of Being Pure of Heart

The consequence of being pure of heart is the nearness of God (Ps 73:1, 28). God saves and defends the pure of heart (Ps 7:11; 36:11), does good to them (Ps 97:11), and fills them with blessings (Ps 24:5). God delights in them (1 Chr 29:17). Purity of heart leads to the ultimate goal: to see the face of God (Ps 24:6). There is no greater joy. "Blessed are the clean of heart, for they will see God" (Matt 5:8).

CONCLUSION

A study of the texts reveals that purity of heart is a sign of wisdom. The concept is found primarily in the psalms where it describes the wise person, characterized by wholeness, openness to God, honesty, moral integrity, and fitness for worship. The contrast to the pure heart—the crooked heart, the empty heart, the absent heart—occurs primarily in the wisdom books, Proverbs and Sirach, where it describes the fool and the wicked person. In the historical books the pure heart is a necessity for a wise king. It is also a characteristic of a wise people, obedient and prepared to worship God. The goal of wisdom is life, the good life. Purity of heart is thus a necessity for all who "yearn for life and desire to see good days" (Ps 34:13; *RB* Prol. 15).

I am grateful to the members of the Old Testament Colloquium and to the summer faculty of St John's University for their suggestions concerning earlier versions of this essay.

The Phrase "Purity of Heart" in Early Syriac Writings

DEIRDRE ANN DEMPSEY

A copious Christian religious literature was produced during the first millennium after Christ by Syriac-speaking theologians who lived in regions that would now fall within the borders of Iran, Turkey, Lebanon, Iraq, Syria, and the Gulf states. These theologians wrote in the Syriac language, a Semitic language related to Arabic and Hebrew.[1] Sr. Juana Raasch, O.S.B., in her series of *Studia Monastica* articles on "The Monastic Concept of Purity of Heart and Its Sources," dealt in some detail with the writings of some of the early Syriac fathers.[2] In this article, I should like to expand on that aspect of Sister Juana's investigation of the concept "purity of heart." My intention is to consider how some of the early Syriac theologians used the phrase "purity of heart." I shall begin by looking at the phrase and its variations in Syriac: What are the biblical (Old Testament and New Testament) antecedents of the phrase? What does the Syriac word translated

---

[1] Syriac was a Semitic language widely used by Christians in the Near East during the first millennium after Christ. Syriac is a dialect of Aramaic; it belongs to the eastern subdivision of Late Aramaic (See Joseph Fitzmyer, "The Phases of the Aramaic Language," *A Wandering Aramean: Collected Aramaic Essays* [Missoula, Mont.: Scholars Press, 1979] 57–84, esp. 62, for more on the classification of Syriac). Syriac survives in an extensive Christian religious literature composed between the end of the second century and the beginning of the fourteenth century; it remains the liturgical language for a range of churches from Lebanon to the Malabar Coast of India, most of whose members speak Arabic or (in India) Malayalam. For readers interested in more information on Syriac Christianity, David Bundy's contribution to *The Anchor Bible Dictionary* (New York: Doubleday, 1992), with its extensive bibliography, might prove useful ("Christianity in Syria," a subsection of the article on "Christianity," *The Anchor Bible Dictionary,* vol. I, 970–9).

[2] For example, Sister Juana deals with Aphrahat in an article entitled, "The Monastic Concept of Purity of Heart and Its Sources (IV)," *Studia Monastica* 11 (1969) 269–314; the section on Aphrahat is on 272–82.

most often as "purity" connote? The Syriac word for "heart"? Then I shall turn to some of the Syriac works that contain references to the concept "purity of heart." These will include writings from Aphrahat (also known as Aphraates), *Liber Graduum*, *The Letter to Cyriacus*, as well as works by Isaac of Nineveh, Martyrius (also known as Sahdona), and Dadisho.

In biblical Hebrew, a language closely related to Syriac, as can be seen by a comparison of vocabulary,[3] several words can be translated into English as "pure." This semantic range is seen also in the Peshitta, the Syriac Bible.[4] In the Hebrew text of Ps 51:12, the psalmist asks God for a *lēb tāhôr*, a Hebrew phrase translated as either "a pure heart" (*Revised English Bible* [REB]) or "a clean heart" (*New Revised Standard Version* [NRSV], *New American Bible* [NAB], and *New Jerusalem Bible* [NJB]). This phrase is rendered in the Peshitta as *lebbâ dakyâ*, the noun *lebbâ*, "heart," followed by the participle of the root *dky*, "to be or to be made pure or clean." Throughout the Peshitta Old Testament some form of this root *dky* is used, whenever the Hebrew has a form of the root *ṭhr*. Perhaps the clearest example of this preference for some form of the Syriac root *dky* is Prov 20:9, which reads in Hebrew *mî yōʾmar zikkîtî libbî ṭāhartî mēḥattāʾtî*: "Who can say, 'I have made my heart clean, I am purified of my sin'?" (NRSV); "Who can say, 'I have made my heart clean, I am cleansed of my sin'?" (NAB). In this verse, the two Hebrew verbs differ; a form of the verb *zky* ("I have made . . . clean") is used in the first colon, a form of the verb *ṭhr* ("am purified," "I am cleansed") in the second colon. In the Peshitta, two forms of the same verb, *dky*,[5] are used in both cola. In Prov 22:11 ("The one who loves a pure heart and who is gracious in speech will have the king as a friend"), the Hebrew reads *ṭehor-lēb*, "a pure heart" (NRSV), while the Peshitta reads *dkê blebbeh* (the first word of this phrase is again a passive participle of the root *dky*). The Hebrew of Job 14:4 ("But will

---

[3] Syriac, a dialect of Aramaic, is usually classified as a Northwest Semitic language, as is Hebrew. In some of what is to follow, vocabulary similarities are striking. For example, the Hebrew word for "heart" is *lēb*—the Syriac word in the absolute state is the same; in this article the Syriac word for "heart" will usually appear in its emphatic, or definite, state, *lebbâ*. There are some slight differences: in some words, a *z* in a Hebrew word will turn up as a *d* in Syriac—so, for example, the root of Hebrew word for "to clean" is *zky*, while the Syriac root is *dky*.

[4] The Syriac word *peshitta* is usually translated as "simple" or "clear"; this is similar to the use of the term "vulgate" for the Latin translation. The Peshitta Old Testament is basically a translation from the Hebrew, although there seems to be some influences from the Septuagint in those books that were most used in the liturgy.

[5] As I mention in note 3, a *z* in a Hebrew word will often turn up as a *d* in Syriac—so, for example, the root of Hebrew word for "to clean" is *zky*, while the Syriac root is *dky*. The Hebrew *zky* and the Syriac *dky* come from the same common root.

anyone produce the pure from what is impure?" [NJB]; "Who can bring a clean thing out of an unclean?" [NRSV]) reads *ṭāhôr*, while the Peshitta reads *dakyâ*. In the Hebrew text of Ps 73:13, the psalmist asks *ʾak-rîq zikkîtî lebābî*:[6] "Is it in vain that I have kept my heart clean?" (NAB). In the Peshitta this question is rendered with a form of the verb *dky*, the Syriac equivalent of the Hebrew verb *zikkîtî*. In the Hebrew text of Job 16:17, Job states *tepillātî zakkâ*,[7] "my prayer is pure" (NRSV and NJB; the REB and the NAB translate "my prayer is sincere"). The Syriac version is a form of the root *dky*. Other Hebrew and Syriac words can be translated into English as "pure" or "clean." In the Hebrew Bible, Psalm 73 begins by announcing how good God is to Israel, to the *bārê lēbāb*, the "pure of heart" ("Indeed God is good to Israel, the Lord to those who are pure of heart" [NJB]; "How good God is to the upright,[8] the Lord, to those who are clean of heart" [NAB]). In the Peshitta, this is rendered with *brîray lebbâ*. In the Hebrew text of Ps 24:4, the one who will stand in the Lord's holy place is one whose hands are clean *(nāqî)* and who is *bar-lēbāb*, "pure of heart." In the Peshitta, the Hebrew *bar-lēbāb*, "pure of heart," is translated into Syriac with *gbê blebbeh*, a passive participle from the root *gby*, "chosen, eminent, pure."

In the Hebrew Bible, then, there are a few different words that can be translated as "pure" or "clean"; these are built off of the roots *thr* (Ps 51:10), *zky* (Ps 73:13), *zkk* (Job 16:17), and *brr* (Pss 24:4; 73:1). The preference in the Peshitta is for some form of the root *dky* (Pss 51:10; 73:13; Job 16:17); occasionally forms of the roots *brr* (Ps 73:1) and *gby* (Ps 24:4) are used. In the Peshitta, and then in the writings of the Syriac theologians, the word used to connote "pure" or "purity" is usually a form of *dky*. The Syriac theologians, of course, are influenced by Matt 5:8. In Greek, this verse reads *makarioi hoi katharoi tē kardia,* "blessed are the pure in heart" (NRSV, NJB); "blessed are the clean of heart" (NAB). In the Syriac rendering of this verse, *hoi katharoi tē kardia* becomes *dkên blebbehôn*, the masculine plural absolute passive participle of the Syriac verb *dky*, "to be or to be made clean or pure," with the preposition *b*, "in," attached to the Syriac word for "heart," *lebbâ*, with a third person masculine plural possessive suffix, "*their* heart." Noun forms built off of this root become the norm, in the writings of the Syriac fathers, when the concept "purity of heart" is considered. So, for example, when the writer Aphrahat begins his treatise on

---

[6] *Lēbāb* is another Hebrew word for "heart," related to the word *lēb*.
[7] This adjective, *zakkâ*, is related to the root *zky*.
[8] Several of the translations, including the NRSV, NAB, and the REB, emend the Hebrew text ("to Israel") and read "to the upright." The Peshitta reads "to Israel."

prayer, he starts with the statement: "Purity of heart [*dakyût lebbâ*] is prayer greater than all the prayers prayed aloud."⁹ The word *dakyût* here is built off of the root *dky*.

What then is the basic meaning of the word translated here as "purity," *dakyûtâ*?¹⁰ As noted above, the root of this noun, *dky*, has the base meaning of "to be or to be made clean or pure." The root *dky* in Syriac has both a literal and a metaphorical sense: "pure" and "clean" literally, or "pure," "clean," or "innocent" metaphorically. The noun *dakyûtâ*, built off of this root, can also be used literally and metaphorically. So, for example, the noun can be used to describe a quality of the sky, in terms of clarity or transparency, or to describe the quality of metals, in terms of their purity. The noun is often used metaphorically, to describe a state of mind or, more often, a state of heart.

In Syriac, the word for heart, *lebbâ*, has the same wide range the word *lēb* has in biblical Hebrew. The heart, in both Syriac and Hebrew, is the vital center—in the heart is concentrated the physical nature of the individual; it is the affective center—the heart is the seat of human emotions; and it is the voluntative center—the heart functions as the driving force behind the voluntative endeavors of the individual, it engages in conceiving and planning.¹¹ So, for example, the Peshitta identifies, as does the Hebrew text, the heart as the source of life, in Prov 4:23; it is the heart, in Deut 15:10, that is displeased, "bad," in both the Hebrew text and in the Peshitta; and in Ps 19:15, in both the Hebrew text and the Peshitta, the psalmist dedicates to the Lord the words of his mouth and the meditations of his heart, all his intentions and plans.¹²

---

⁹ The Syriac text of *Demonstration* IV is available in the edition by J. Parisot, *Patrologia Syriaca* 1 (Paris: Firman-Didot, 1894) cols. 137–82. An English translation is available in Sebastian Brock's *The Syriac Fathers on Prayer and the Spiritual Life* (Kalamazoo, Mich.: Cistercian Publications, 1987) 2–28.

¹⁰ The form of the noun in the phrase taken from the treatise by Aphrahat, *dakyût*, is the construct state, "purity of . . . ." This form *dakyûtâ* is the emphatic, or definite, form of the noun, "purity."

¹¹ A good overview of the range of *lēb* in Hebrew can be found in the article on *lēb* in the *Theological Dictionary of the Old Testament*, vol. 7 (Grand Rapids, Mich.: Eerdmans, 1995).

¹² It is interesting that the Greek translation of the Hebrew Bible, the Septuagint, although generally translating the Hebrew *lēb* or *lēbāb* with *kardia*, sometimes substitutes other words. The most common substitute is *dianoia*, "understanding." For example, the Hebrew text of Job 9:4 reads *hăkam-lēbāb*, "wise in heart"; the Greek substitutes the word *dianoia*, "understanding," for "heart" (the Peshitta keeps "heart"). Again, at Num 15:39, where the Hebrew text reads *lĕbabkem*, "your heart" ("and not follow the dictates of your own heart" [NJB]), the Greek text uses the plural of *dianoia*. Again, the Peshitta follows the Hebrew and reads "your hearts."

The writings of St. Ephrem the Syrian, a fourth-century Syriac writer whose works are of immense importance for Syriac-speaking Christianity, reflect this broad understanding of the word "heart."[13] Ephrem was born about 306, in or around Nisibis (a city in what would now be the southeastern corner of Turkey). He was ordained a deacon in this city, and served there as a catechetical teacher. After the city of Nisibis, which had been part of the Roman empire, was handed over to the Persian empire in 363, Ephrem left with the rest of the Christian population and eventually made his way to Edessa, one hundred miles west of Nisibis and still, during Ephrem's lifetime, part of the Roman empire. He spent the last ten years of his life in Edessa, writing, teaching choirs of women to sing his hymns (some of Ephrem's hymns have remained central in both the East and West Syrian liturgical traditions), and working in the local church. He died on June 9, 373.

Ephrem was a prolific author; he left behind some five hundred hymns, collected into cycles: *On the Nativity, On Virginity, On the Church, On Nisibis, Against Heresies, On Unleavened Bread, On Paradise, On the Fast, Against Julian,* and fifty-one hymns preserved only in Armenian. The image of the heart is used often in these hymns. The heart, for Ephrem, is the place where faith is planted and grows. He speaks of "root of faith" planted in the heart;[14] this image meshes well with an image from a different set of hymns, the image of Christ as the farmer who works "the soil of the heart."[15] This faith planted and taking root in the heart can be destroyed; in Ephrem's *Hymns on Faith* Zacharias declares that he lost "the faith of his heart" *(haymānûtâ dlebbeh)* through "the questioning of his mouth."[16] The heart can become unclean through deceit *(ṭma' lebban bneklê)*, or even become drunk enough to forget loved ones.[17] The heart can go astray. In his *Hymns on Faith*, Ephrem writes that "the feet never divide themselves along two paths—the heart *[lebbâ]* is divided, hurrying along two roads at the same time, along the two paths of darkness and light."

---

[13] For more on Ephrem see Sebastian Brock, trans., *The Harp of the Spirit: Twelve Poems of St. Ephrem* (London: Fellowship of St. Alban and St. Serguis, 1975); Kathleen McVey, *Ephrem the Syrian: Hymns* (New York: Paulist Press, 1989), particularly the introduction, 3–48; and Sidney Griffith, "Faith Adoring the Mystery": Reading the Bible with St. Ephraem the Syrian (Milwaukee: Marquette University Press, 1997).

[14] Edmund Beck, *Des heiligen Ephraem des Syrers Hymnen de Ecclesia*, Corpus scriptorum Christianorum Orientalium, vols. 198 and 199 (Louvain: Peeters, 1960) XXV:15.

[15] Edmund Beck, *Des heiligen Ephraem des Syrers Hymnen de Nativitate (Epiphania)*, Corpus scriptorum Christianorum Orientalium, vols. 186 and 187 (Louvain: Peeters, 1959) VIII:7.

[16] Edmund Beck, *Des heiligen Ephraem des Syrers Hymnen de Fide*, Corpus scriptorum Christianorum Orientalium, vols. 154 and 155 (Louvain: Peeters, 1955) IX:10.

[17] Beck, *Hymnen de Ecclesia*, XIV:8, XVI:6.

The cause of this division is the heart's *ḥîrûtâ*, "freedom."[18] The heart is also the seat of desire, counsel, and discernment. So, for example, in one of his *Hymns on the Church* Ephrem remarks, in a section surrounded by strophes dealing with the Fall, that "when a heart is filled with desire [*reḥmĕtâ*] of something, then there is no longer room for counsel [*melkâ*] and discernment [*bûyānâ*]."[19] For Ephrem, then, counsel, discernment, and love all *could* be located in the heart. Finally, the heart is also the place where anger can be located; in the *Hymns on the Church*, Ephrem speaks of "the wrath of our heart" *(rgûzyâ dlebban)*.[20] These are only a few examples of Ephrem's use of "heart"; they give a sense, though, of the range the word had, not only for Ephrem, but for all theologians writing in Syriac.

One of these theologians is Aphrahat, "the Persian Sage." Sister Juana dealt at some length with this Syriac writer in her "The Monastic Concept of Purity of Heart and Its Sources."[21] Very little is known about Aphrahat. He lived in the first half of the fourth century, in what is now Iraq, in the Persian empire. Aphrahat is the author of 23 *Demonstrations*, or homilies, which contain teachings on a variety of topics. *Demonstration* 1, for example, is on faith; *Demonstration* 2 is on love. In *Demonstration* 6, Aphrahat provides the earliest references to an institution of early Syriac Christianity, "the Sons and Daughters of the Covenant."[22] Aphrahat's *Demonstration* 4 is devoted to prayer. As Sebastian Brock remarks, this *Demonstration* "has the distinction of being the earliest extant Christian treatise on prayer which is not primarily concerned with the Lord's Prayer, as is the case with the well-known works on prayer by Tertullian, Origen, and Cyprian."[23] Aphrahat, in *Demonstration* 4, emphasizes the need for purity of heart if prayer is to be acceptable to God; the *Demonstration* begins with the statement that

---

[18] Beck, *Hymnen de Fide*, XX:14.
[19] Ibid., XLVI:4.
[20] Beck, *Hymnen de Ecclesia*, XIV:7.
[21] Raasch, "The Monastic Concept of Purity of Heart and Its Sources," 272—82.
[22] The exact nature of these "Sons and Daughters of the Covenant" is disputed among scholars. Some have wanted to see the "Sons and Daughters of the Covenant" as precursors to monasticism, pointing out the emphasis on solitary living, abstinence from sexual relations, and ascetic food practices. Others have argued that they functioned as deacons or ascetics within society. According to Sebastian Brock, some of the members will have lived in their parent's house, while others would live a communal life in groups of two or three. Men and women sometimes lived together, but this practice was already frowned upon by Aphrahat in the first part of the fourth century, and was later condemned (see Sebastian Brock, *Spirituality in the Syriac Tradition*, Mōrān ʿEthō Series 2 [Kerala, India: SEERI, 1989] 52). On p. 54 of this work, Brock writes that it is likely that both Aphrahat and Ephrem belonged to the "Sons of the Covenant."
[23] Brock, *The Syriac Fathers on Prayer*, 2.

dakyût lebbâ, "purity of heart," "is prayer greater than all the prayers prayed aloud." Aphrahat goes on to allude to Mal 1:11 ("and in every place incense is offered to my name, and a pure offering") when he writes: "see how our righteous forefathers excelled in their prayer before God, and how it served them as a *pure offering [qûrbānê dakyê]*."[24] Throughout this *Demonstration*, Aphrahat presents prayer as a kind of interior offering or sacrifice. Aphrahat goes on to list the biblical examples of the efficacy of prayer:

> It was through prayer that offerings were accepted, and it was prayer again that averted the Flood from Noah; prayer has healed barrenness, prayer has overthrown armies, prayer has revealed mysteries, prayer has divided the sea, prayer made a passage through the Jordan, it held back the sun, it made the moon stand still, it destroyed the unclean, it caused fire to descend. Prayer closed up the heaven, prayer raised up from the pit, rescued from the fire, and saved from the sea.[25]

Offerings were accepted through prayer, and purity of heart *is* prayer: "It was through Abel's purity of heart *[bdakyût lebbeh dhābêl]* that his offering was accepted by God. . . . But Abel's purity of heart was his prayer."[26]

For Aphrahat, the concept of pure prayer, and hence purity of heart, is bound up with the necessity of forgiveness and reconciliation. Aphrahat writes in *Demonstration* 4:

> You who pray should remember that you are making an offering before God: let not Gabriel who presents the prayers be ashamed by an offering that has a blemish. When you pray to be forgiven, and acknowledge that you yourself forgive, consider first in your mind whether you really do forgive, and only then acknowledge "I forgive." You must not act deceitfully with God and say "I forgive" when you do not really forgive; for God is not like you, a mortal, whom you can deceive.[27]

Aphrahat goes on to say that if forgiveness is lacking, Gabriel will refuse to bring the "unclean offering" before God. Prayer is also giving rest to the weary, visiting the sick, and making provision for the poor. As Sister Juana notes, Aphrahat's "purity of heart"

> is envisioned from God's point of view and means readiness to please him, especially by acts of mercy and kindness toward men, with whom God identifies, and by having a heart free from anger and ready to forgive. . . . Thus the heart's purity, its attitude of love and faith expressed

[24] Translation from ibid., 5.
[25] Translation from ibid.
[26] Translation from ibid., 6.
[27] Translation from ibid., 17–8.

in life and actions, is more important than any specific ascetical or religious practice and is itself the goal of all such practices and of the Christian ascetical life.[28]

Aphrahat ends his *Demonstration* with two concrete examples of how *not* to act, one of which follows:

> Judge in yourself what I am going to tell you: suppose you happen to go on a long journey and, parched with thirst in the heat, you chance upon one of the brethren; you say to him, "refresh me in my exhaustion from thirst," and he replies, "It is the time for prayer; I will pray, and then I will come to your aid"; and while he is praying, before coming to you, you die of thirst. What seems to you the better, that he should go and pray, or alleviate your exhaustion?[29]

The second Syriac theologian dealt with in this article who uses the phrase "purity of heart" is anonymous. He was the author of *The Book of Steps*, also know by its Latin title, *Liber Graduum*.[30] *The Book of Steps* is a collection of thirty discourses, or homilies, on the spiritual life. A reference to the Zab, a river flowing into the Tigris, suggests that the author of these thirty homilies lived in the Persian empire. The date of composition of *The Book of Steps* is usually set in the late fourth or early fifth century. One theme consistently emphasized in *The Book of Steps* is the distinction between two stages of the spiritual life. The first stage is that of "the upright," who follow the "small commandments" of the Gospel; these "small commandments" concern the life of active charity, and are summed up by the Golden Rule, "one should not do to anyone what is hateful to oneself; and what one wishes others to do to oneself, one should do to those one meets" (*Discourse* I.4).[31] It is the "full grown" who go on to the second stage of the spiritual life, who, at this stage, keep the "great commandments," renouncing family and possessions. In *Discourse* XII ("On the Ministry of the Hidden and the Manifest Church") mention is made of "the pure of heart," *dkên blebbehôn*, in the context of a discussion of the concept of the three different churches: the heavenly church, the visible church on earth, and the interior church of the heart. As Sebastian Brock remarks:

> Christian growth is seen as a growth in awareness, and the discovery, made possible by the functioning of the visible Church, of the hidden

---

[28] Raasch, "The Monastic Concept of Purity of Heart and Its Sources," 273–4.
[29] Translation from Brock, *The Syriac Fathers on Prayer*, 20.
[30] The Syriac text of the *Liber Graduum (The Book of Steps)* was edited by Michael Kmosko, *Patrologia Syriaca* 3; I have used an English translation of *Discourse* XII and *Discourse* XVIII, from Brock, *The Syriac Fathers on Prayer*, 42–61.
[31] See Brock, *The Syriac Fathers on Prayer*, 43.

church of the heart. This discovery then leads to an awareness of the heavenly Church upon which the visible Church had been modelled by Christ and his apostles. Awareness of the existence and functioning of the heavenly Church in turn results in a deepened perception of the significance and reality of the sacraments of the visible Church which had been the starting point in this process of growth.[32]

How, then, does the concept "purity of heart" occur in *Discourse* XII of *The Book of Steps*? The saints of the "church on high," the heavenly Church, were called "pure in heart," *dkên blbbehôn;* this purity of heart, then, is worthy of emulation, if the visible Church is to reflect the heavenly Church ("those who are diligent in this visible Church become like that heavenly Church as they follow after it").[33] According to *Discourse* XII:

> If however, we should have doubts and despise this visible church, with its visible altar and visible priesthood, and this baptism that brings forgiveness, then our body will not become a temple, neither will our heart become an altar or a well-spring of praise. Nor shall we have revealed to us that church on high with its altar, its light and its priesthood, where are gathered all the saints who are pure in heart, who dwell in its glory.[34]

The author of *Discourse* XII goes on to specify what it means to be "pure in heart":

> For even though our Lord is in every place, he is only to be seen openly in that church which is in heaven, and only by those who have abased themselves and become at rest, gentle toward everyone, people who have struggled and done battle on their own with evil spirits, who have purified their hearts of evil thoughts. . . . Those who have fought with Satan and vanquished him become worthy of this church which is above all, in which our Lord shines out openly, and they receive the glorious light of his countenance. For our Lord said, *"Blessed are those who are pure in heart [dkên blebbehôn], for they shall see God."*[35]

This emphasis on the "pure of heart" as a lack of hidden sin and evil thoughts is evident also in *Discourse* XVIII, "On the Tears of Prayer." In this homily the author writes:

> Thus it is appropriate for men who are in Christ to *raise up their hands everywhere and in every place, without anger and without any evil thoughts* [1 Tim 2:8]; they should shed tears in their love and yearning for our Lord, waiting for when they shall come and see him face to face, as it is written:

[32] See ibid., 43–4.
[33] Translation from ibid., 48.
[34] Translation from ibid., 47.
[35] Translation from ibid., 53.

> *Blessed are the pure in heart [dkên blebbehôn], for they shall see God* [Matt 5:8] in this world, as Paul said, *as though in a mirror, in the eyes of our hearts we behold our Lord; but in that world, face to face* [1 Cor 13:12]. The heart does not become pure, then, unless hidden sin has disappeared from it, and any evil thoughts that had been hidden away in it through the strength of the sin that dwells there have come to a complete end. Neither will this sin be eradicated from our heart, nor will the evil thoughts and the sin's other fruits disappear unless we pray just as our Lord and all who preached him prayed.[36]

The concept "purity of heart" is also taken up in the *Letter to Cyriacus*.[37] According to the title provided in the Syrian Orthodox manuscripts which contain the work, this *Letter to Cyriacus* was written by "Babai whom the wicked Barsauma killed." This would make the author of the *Letter* Baboway, the patriarch of Seleucia-Ctesiphon, who was put to death by the Persian king Peroz in 484. Scholars have doubts about this identification;[38] all that can be said with any certainty about the *Letter* is that it comes out of Persian Christianity, and that a composition date in the first half of the sixth century seems likely. The *Letter* concerns the solitary life and offers practical advice to Cyriacus. The *Letter* begins with a description of the worship performed by the angels:

> It demands the following: purity of heart, true love of God, wariness over thoughts, reflection on Christ, prayer without ceasing, assiduous fasting consisting of an eager struggle against unclean thoughts, continuous conflict with the body, abstinence from luxurious foods, rest of soul, true joy . . . refusal of everything attractive, cessation of all cares, escape from all evils, abstinence from the sight of people's faces, an uninterrupted course night and day, a wakeful mind unmingled with worldly cares, a scanty diet, the arena of the diligent, the tree of self-effacement.[39]

Later in the *Letter* "purity of heart" is mentioned again:

> See, O brother who loves God . . . strive after the following: wariness over all thoughts, meditation on God, unceasing prayer, purity of heart, a clear conscience, an understanding of what the battle against Satan means, discernment, wariness against shameful passions, recollection and a strict guard against transgressions, the raising up of the soul above the world, and besides all this, continuous fasting, reading of the holy Scriptures, recitation of the psalms, meditation on glorious things.[40]

---

[36] Translation from ibid., 57.
[37] I use here the section on Babai in ibid., 136–65.
[38] See ibid., 136
[39] Translation from ibid., 138–9.
[40] Translation from ibid., 146.

As was the case for the author of *The Book of Steps*, the impediment to "purity of heart," according to the author of the *Letter,* is "unclean thoughts":

> Let it be your care to cultivate the soil of your soul with continual prayer and recitation of the psalms. Do not neglect your soul, but persevere in stilling unclean thoughts in its depths, for these habitually hinder the heart from progressing in purity and holiness by making it impure. For it is these in particular which are bearers of destruction for humanity. They are like rust to iron for people with a pure mind; they are like blindfolds over the eyes of the soul, so that it cannot see clearly what it is doing.[41]

St. Isaac of Nineveh (who is also called St. Isaac the Syrian) speaks of "purity of heart," *dakyût lebbâ*, in his discourse on pure prayer. Isaac was born in Qatar, in the Persian Gulf; he was appointed bishop of Nineveh, in what is now north Iraq, in the last quarter of the seventh century. Isaac resigned after only five months and retired to the mountains of Khuzistan, to live the life of a hermit, attached to the monastery of Rabban Shabur. Isaac's writings on spirituality seem to date from his old age; his works were translated into Arabic and Greek and became very influential. Isaac gives his definition of "purity of heart" in a treatise on pure prayer:

> Purity of prayer, O disciple of truth, and the recollection of mind that exists in it, consist in the exact reflection on virtue in which we carefully engage at the time of prayer. Just as purity of heart *[dakyût lebbâ]*, concerning which the Fathers diligently exhort, is not a matter of someone being totally without thought or reflection or stirring, but rather it consists in the heart being purified of all evil, and in gazing favourably on everything, and considering it from God's point of view, so it is the same with pure and undistracted prayer. This does not mean that the mind is entirely devoid of any thought or wandering of any kind, but that it does not wander about on empty subjects during the time of prayer.[42]

The phrase "purity of heart" is used frequently by two other seventh-century Syriac writers, Martyrius (also known as Sahdona) and Dadisho. Martyrius was born around Kirkuk, in what would now be Iraq. He became a monk at a monastery in north Iraq and eventually became a bishop sometime in the late 630s. Martyrius became embroiled

---

[41] Translation from ibid., 145.

[42] Translation from Sebastian Brock, *Isaac of Nineveh (Isaac the Syrian): "The Second Part," Chapters IV–XLI,* Corpus scriptorum Christianorum Orientalium, vol. 555 (Louvain: Peeters, 1995) 84. Brock remarks, in footnote 2 on this same page, that the allusion Isaac makes to "the Fathers" is too vague to identify; Brock suggests that Isaac might have had in mind Aphrahat and his *Demonstration* 4.

in the christological controversies of the time, and was twice forced into exile; he spent the last years of his life living a solitary life, probably attached to a monastery, somewhere around Edessa. The most important of the works of Martyrius which have survived is *The Book of Perfection*. This long work is "one of the masterpieces of Syriac monastic literature."[43] Five letters to fellow monks also survive, along with a set of maxims. The phrase "purity of heart," *dakyût dlebbâ*, occurs several times in *The Book of Perfection*; allusions to Matt 5:8 and references to "pure heart," *lebbâ dadkê*, abound in that work, as well as in other writings of Martyrius. So, for example, in the chapter devoted to faith in *The Book of Perfection*, paragraph 13 ends with the phrase: "It is not able to put into words what God is; he is ineffable for language and inconceivable for the mind. Only to the 'pure of heart' is he credible, because the 'pure of heart' sees God by faith."[44]

In *The Book of Perfection* a connection is made between purity of heart and love *(hûbâ)*. Chapter 4 of *The Book of Perfection* has love as its theme; Brock translates a section of this chapter:

> Happy is that person of love who has caused God, who is love, to dwell in his heart. Happy are you, O heart, so small and confined, yet you have caused him whom heaven and earth cannot contain to dwell spiritually in your womb, as in a restful abode. Happy that luminous eye of the heart which, in its purity, clearly beholds him before whose sight the seraphs veil their face. . . . *Blessed indeed are the pure in heart, for they shall see God.* . . . Blessed are you, O heart that is luminous, the abode of the Divinity; Blessed are you, heart that is pure, which beholds the hidden Being.[45]

Dadisho was born, like Isaac of Nineveh, in Qatar, in the Persian Gulf; also like Isaac, Dadisho went north, to the region now known as Iraq. Very little is known about Dadisho, but most scholars will place him in the second half of the seventh century. Dadisho wrote a work on pure prayer, a treatise on solitude and prayer, and a commentary on the writings of Abba Isaiah. This Abba Isaiah was the author of a collection of ascetic writings, written for the edification of anchorites, *îḥîdāyê*. Abba Isaiah has usually been identified as Isaiah of Gaza, who wrote in the late fifth century. As Brock remarks, this identification is

---

[43] Brock, *The Syriac Fathers on Prayer*, 198. The Syriac text of the parts of *The Book of Perfection* used in this article, as well as a French translation, are available in André de Halleux, *Martyrius (Sahdona): Oeuvres spirituelles, II*, Corpus scriptorum Christianorum Orientalium, vols. 214 and 215 (Louvain: Peeters, 1961).

[44] De Halleux, *Martyrius (Sahdona)*, ch. 2, para. 13.

[45] Translation from Brock, *The Syriac Fathers on Prayer*, 200.

"entirely certain."[46] Dadisho himself seems to have placed Abba Isaiah in the late fourth century, identifying him with the Egyptian monastic movement.[47] Dadisho, when he is quoting or explaining Abba Isaiah, uses the phrase "purity of heart," *dakyût lebbâ,* and makes frequent use of Matt 5:8, either in direct quotation or allusion.

In his commentary on the writings of Abba Isaiah, Dadisho writes, expanding on Abba Isaiah's comment about people who say: "I do not commit adultery, I do not fornicate, nor do I love money, therefore I am a just person," that sin is not just of the body (passions involving the stomach, sleep, fornication, money, and the like). There are also "subtle and hidden passions." One can be freed from these "subtle and hidden passions" through the help of the Lord, and be favored by "purity of heart," *dakyût lebbâ.* These "subtle and hidden passions," which keep the heart impure, are listed. Dadisho follows each of Abba Isaiah's examples with his own explanation: "lack of fear" (Dadisho quotes from Luke 18:2, "he neither feared God nor respected people"); "haughtiness" (Dadisho comments: "This is arrogance, boasting, and pride"); "lack of faith" (Dadisho explains that this is "when someone doubts the promises of our Lord"); "envy" (according to Dadisho, "hate, enmity, jealousy, and anger are born" from this); "deceit" (which comes from malice and lack of love, in Dadisho's explanation); "hypocrisy" and obsequiousness, which are born of love for transient glory. These, according to Dadisho's quote of Abba Isaiah, are what one must combat in one's thoughts.[48] It is through this combat with evil thoughts that one arrives at "purity of heart," *dakyût lebbâ,* by the "grace of our Lord," *ṭaybûteh dmāran.*[49]

Dadisho goes on in his "explication of the seventh discourse of Abba Isaiah" to state that, according to Abba Isaiah, it is impossible for the anchorites *(îḥîdāyê)* to be saved from the passions of sin and to purify their hearts of evil thoughts unless they first remove themselves from the world, from its cares and distractions.[50] Twenty "virtues" *(myattĕrātâ)* are listed, practices which will lead to "purity of heart" *(dakyût lebbâ)* for the anchorite. These include: not eating much, wakefulness, sleeping on the ground, the office of the Psalms, reading Scripture, manual labor, prayer, mourning, tears, and weeping. Through the practice of these virtues, the anchorite will then see God and find

---

[46] Brock, *Spirituality in the Syriac Tradition,* 31.
[47] René Draguet, *Commentaire du livre d'Abba Isaïe (logoi I–XV) par Dadiso Qatraya (VIIe s.),* Corpus scriptorum Christianorum Orientalium, vols. 326 and 327 (Louvain: Peeters, 1972) vol. 327, 15–6.
[48] Ibid., III:11.
[49] Ibid., III:8.
[50] Ibid., VII:1.

the fruits of the Spirit. The twenty fruits of the Spirit then listed include love, joy, peace, goodness, kindness, and patience; first and foremost of these fruits, however, is the vision of the Lord in a manifestation of light.[51]

This article does not pretend be an exhaustive survey of the use of the phrase "purity of heart" in early Syriac writings; such a survey would require a volume of its own. It does attempt to give the reader some idea (1) of the variety of writers who used the phrase *dakyût lebbâ* (or some variation of this phrase) and (2) of the variety of ways the phrase was used. I hope that it helps to advance Sister Juana's solid and interesting work on the Syriac Fathers' concept of "purity of heart."

---

[51] Ibid., XIV:17.

The Place of the Heart: Geography and Spirituality in the *Life of Antony*

DOUGLAS BURTON-CHRISTIE

"[For the one who] wishes to live in solitude in the desert . . . there is only one conflict . . . and that is with the heart."
—*Antony of Egypt*[1]

INTRODUCTION

Thirty-five years of ascetic struggle at the edge of the Egyptian wilderness brought the early Christian monk Antony to a crucial turning point. Having withdrawn from his village and lived alone for many years within a deserted fortress not far from the Nile river, he was now surrounded almost constantly by crowds of people seeking his help and advice. He responded generously to these demands. But he also realized that if he hoped to remain faithful to the vision that had brought him to the desert in the first place, he would have to move from this place. At first he thought to go to the upper Thebaid, where no one knew him. But as he sat by the banks of the river waiting for a boat to take him there, he heard a voice telling him that if he truly wished to be alone, he should go instead to the inner desert—a wild, solitary place in the Arabian desert. Some Saracens who were traveling in that direction offered to show Antony the way; they embarked together, traveling for three days and three nights, eventually

---

[1] *Verba Seniorum* II.2. *PL* 73:858A; also Antony 11 (*Alphabetical Collection*) *PG* 65.77C. The quotation represents a slight conflation of two versions of this saying. The Latin version does not mention the word desert, while the Greek version does. But the Latin version views solitary life in the desert as a struggle of the heart while the Greek version sees it as a struggle against lust or fornication.

arriving at place where there was a high hill, a spring, and a few date palms. Antony, we are told, "fell in love with the place."[2]

This moment marks a striking turn in Athanasius' *Life of Antony*. Having moved from one place to another during the preceding years, Antony from this moment forward gives himself completely to this place, leaving it only on rare occasions. It becomes "his own home,"[3] the place where Antony learns to keep his heart awake.[4] It becomes a place of recognizable power, transformed by the ascetic's long practice and deep desire for God.

This confluence of topography and spiritual longing recurs throughout the literature of early Christian monasticism. Nor is place merely a backdrop to the spiritual questions arising among the monks; rather it is integral to those questions, giving them shape and substance. As, for example, it does in the saying of Antony cited above, where the desert is identified as the place of the heart. To give oneself fully to the solitude of the desert, Antony suggests, means facing up to the long and difficult struggle with the heart. To probe the heart, honestly and deeply, means, at least to some degree, giving oneself over to the harsh reality of solitary struggle in the desert. Place, in other words, is not incidental to the spiritual quest but informs it profoundly.

How, precisely, did the geography of the early monastic world affect its thought? How was its thought and spirituality shaped by its relationship to landscape out of which it arose? These are the questions I want to explore in this essay. Too often landscape is seen either as setting for the early monastic experiment (and therefore largely invisible) or as a suggestive metaphor; seldom is it taken seriously as a place in its own right. I want to ask what it would mean to locate the monastic quest for purity of heart more carefully within the physical and symbolic landscape of the desert. How, for example, did the physical features of the desert, such as space, light, distance, aridity, affect the monastic quest both individually and communally? How and why did monks and early monastic writers engage in their characteristic symbolic constructions of the desert—creating of the desert landscape a deeply mythologized place capable of carrying their deepest fears and

---

[2] VA 50.1; Gregg, 68. References to the *Life of Antony (VA)* are from Bartelink's critical edition (chapter and paragraph number); translations, unless otherwise indicated, are from Robert Gregg's English translation (Gregg). Athanase d'Alexandrie, *Vie d'Antoine*, introduction, critical text, translation, notes and index by G.J.M. Bartelink (Paris: Cerf, 1994); Athanasius of Alexandria, *The Life of Antony and the Letter to Marcelinus*, trans. and intro. Robert C. Gregg (New York: Paulist Press, 1980). Occasionally I have made my own translations or have emended Gregg's translations (indicated by: [m]).

[3] VA 50.2; Gregg, 68.

[4] VA 59.6; Gregg, 75.

desires? What kind of relationship existed *between* the two landscapes, one exterior and the other interior, within which the monks lived? To inquire into these questions is to begin exploring the geography of the heart, that mysterious region at once physical and spiritual, in which the early monks sought and sometimes discovered the presence of God.

In this essay I want to explore that geography, particularly in relation to Athanasius' *Life of Antony*, asking how the notion of place is construed within the unfolding narrative of Antony's quest for God.[5] There are good reasons for examining the sense of place in this classic text from early Christian monasticism. Athanasius' depiction of Antony's ascetic quest is framed in largely geographical terms: as the ascetic moves from village to nearby desert to ever more remote parts of the desert, he comes to a clearer self-knowledge and awareness of God.[6] But there is more to it than this. The idea of place figures as a prominent theme in the work (the word *topos* is used at least twenty times, often at significant junctures). Particular places (the village, the church, the house, the cell) also shape the narrative in important ways. Entire landscapes or features of the landscape (the desert, the mountain) and the means for reaching or traversing them (the path) also recur throughout the work. There is careful attention to the movement away from, into, and around certain places. And certain places are framed in relationship to one another—earth and heaven, village and desert, inside and outside—as a way of signaling key tensions and issues in the hero's ascetic struggle (and in Athanasius' own theological and ecclesial struggles). In all of this there is a fluidity to the language

---

[5] For another view of this question, see Judith Sutera, "Place and Stability in the *Life of Antony*," *Cistercian Studies Quarterly* 27:2 (1992) 101–14. The question of authorship of the *Life of Antony* has been a matter of serious debate. However, David Brakke's recent work on the subject has, to my mind, shifted the balance in favor of Athanasian authorship. See his "The Authenticity of the Ascetic Athanasiana," *Orientalia* 63 (1994) 17–56. See also chapter four of his *Athanasius and the Politics of Asceticism* (Oxford: Clarendon Press, 1995) 201–65, which demonstrates the coherence of the *Life*'s contents with that of other Athanasian works.

[6] Whether or not it happened in anything like this way is far from clear; what we encounter in the *Life of Antony* is of course a literary-theological creation, aimed at promoting a certain vision of the monastic life. As such it creates a more schematic, symbolized rendering of the monastic sense of the desert than a broad reading of the evidence would support. And, it is only *one* view of the question. Still, the vision of monastic life and of the relationship of that life to the place in which it evolved that emerges from the *Life of Antony* is both intriguing and instructive. Given the enormous influence of this text, both among early monastics and among later generations of monastic seekers, it is worth asking how it envisioned "the place of the heart." On the issue of the literary-theological construction of the desert, see James Goehring, "The Encroaching Desert: Literary Production and Ascetic Space in Early Christian Egypt," *Journal of Early Christian Studies* 1 (fall 1993) 281–96.

of this work that allows for a recognition of both the concrete particularity of places and their symbolic resonance. Spirituality in the *Life of Antony* is indisputably mediated by, grounded in, the sense of place.

BEGINNINGS: FROM DOMESTIC SPACE TO WILD SPACE

Home, church, and village loom large in the early part of Athanasius' narrative. When we meet Antony as a young man, we hear that he is cognizant of little else besides his parents and "his home," that he desires nothing more than to live, simply, "in his home."[7] He is a model of domestic piety. But it is not only his parents' house that occupies his attention; he is also a regular visitor, with his parents, to the "Lord's house."[8] Following his parents' death, though, the relationship between these two houses becomes more complex for Antony. At probably no more than twenty years of age he becomes responsible "for both the home and his sister."[9] We are not told how heavily these new domestic responsibilities weighed upon him; but the implication is that the domestic space had become more problematic, more burdensome for Antony.

One hint of this is found in the description of Antony's state of mind some six months later. Apparently, his thoughts are focused on the possibility of relieving himself of these burdens. Going by himself to the Lord's house, his mind is filled with the example of Jesus' followers who forsook everything to follow him (Matt 4:20) and of the early Christian community that shared all things in common (Acts 4:35). Athanasius tells us that Antony "went into the church pondering these things," and that when he heard the Gospel text telling of Jesus' challenge to the rich man to sell his possessions and give them to the poor (Matt 19:21), Antony "went out from the Lord's house" and gave the townspeople his possessions and his land (keeping a little for his sister) "so that they would not disturb him or his sister in the least."[10] But returning and "entering the Lord's house once more," he hears the text in which Jesus exhorts his followers not to be anxious about tomorrow (Matt 6:34). "He could not remain any longer," says Athanasius, "but going out," he gave his remaining possessions to those in need.

---

[7] *VA* 1.3; Gregg, 30.
[8] Ibid.
[9] *VA* 2.1; Gregg, 31.
[10] *VA* 2.2–4; Gregg, 31.

It is striking to note the extent to which space mediates the crucial action in this opening sequence. The most significant instance of this is the movement from the domestic space of the home to the sacred space of the church (the Lord's house) to the ascetic space that lies beyond both of these. The narrative hints that Antony's relationship to home and family is already becoming ambiguous; he is wondering about new possibilities of detachment and more radical self-giving. But it is only when he *enters into* the Lord's house (and listens to the texts read there) that his sense of attachment to and responsibility toward the domestic sphere begins to loosen. Still, if the church is a charged space that helps loosen Antony's hold on the domestic (or its hold on him), he does not stay there but moves through it into a new, as yet unexplored space. The narrative registers this clearly in terms of a dynamic movement through space. Antony "enters into" and "goes out from" the Lord's house twice, each time deepening his sense of what he is being called to do and where he is being called to go. The second time, his sense of restless urgency is palpable: "He could not remain any longer" (in the Lord's house) but "going out" gave the rest of his possessions to those in need.

It is at this point that he makes his first significant break with his old life, devoting himself from then on, Athanasius says, "to the discipline rather than the household."[11] This is a telling remark. In juxtaposing "household" and "discipline" in this way, Athanasius signals, in spatial terms, Antony's shift of allegiance. In fact, Antony has not yet left the village. But in Athanasius' terms, the discipline *(askesis)* is itself a kind of space, akin to but different from and preferred to the domestic space of the household. To occupy this new space is to reorient oneself, psychologically, around a different center. It is to dwell in a different "world" driven by its own particular concerns and questions. Before Antony takes a single step outside the village, he has already traveled a great distance.

This interior shift does eventually lead Antony to move, physically, from the space of the household (the village) to the space of the discipline (a place of isolation outside the village). Here too, spatial language reveals and mediates the interior movement in Antony's life. Dwelling at first "in places proximate to his village," he "goes forth" from there in search of other ascetics from whom he can learn. Athanasius notes that Antony "did not go back to his own place," unless he had seen the person he was looking for. Then, "as though receiving from him certain supplies for traveling the road to virtue, he returned." Antony spent the beginning stages of his discipline "in that

[11] *VA* 3.1; Gregg, 32.

place" and "would not look back on things of his parents, nor call his relatives to memory."[12] The word *topos* occurs three times in this brief section. Significant too are verbs suggestive of movement ("going forth," "returning," etc.). Together this language helps both to locate Antony physically and to suggest something of the character and struggle of his discipline—especially the tension between place and movement within his ascetic practice.

Antony's location at the edge of the village places him within the ascetic culture which already existed at that time in and around Egyptian villages. Athanasius, however, provides a hint of the provisional and tentative nature of Antony's presence within this culture of "village asceticism," noting that "there were not yet many monasteries in Egypt and no monk knew at all the great desert"[13] (the clear implication being that this will soon change as Antony takes up his abode there). But even if transitional, this is a significant moment in Antony's development. It is here that he learns to *dwell* in a single place. "He began," Athanasius says, "by *remaining*" in places close to his village. The earlier stages of his awakening to the ascetic life had been marked by the opposite impulse; having heard the call to the ascetic life, Antony was unable to "remain" in the Lord's house, but went forth to embark on his new life. Now, having entered into the practice of the discipline, he remains in place.

But the call to abide in a single place carries within it a further call—to go forth in search of wisdom. The discipline, at least as Antony understands it at this stage, seems to demand it. Indeed, Antony not only "goes forth" in search of this wisdom, but is not prepared to "go back to his own place" unless he receives something of what he seeks. Devotion to place, in other words, is shaped by a willingness to enter onto and begin walking a path. Here it is "the road [*hodos*] to virtue" that Antony seeks to travel, a road long familiar to readers of Jewish and early Christian Wisdom literature. In the present instance, traveling that road clearly means engaging in actual physical movement, seeking out the help and advice of other ascetics living nearby. But it is also a moral, spiritual path involving ever deeper levels of engagement with the self and God.

There is a distinct forward momentum to Antony's life in this place. Although he goes forth from and returns to the same place, in truth he is moving further and further out (and in) each time. This is in part because his perspective is upon what lies ahead: "He would not look back" on the things he had left behind, says Athanasius, a

[12] *VA* 3.4–5; Gregg, 32.
[13] *VA* 3.2; Gregg, 32.

clear indication of the importance he attributes to freeing himself from the attachments of his former life and living fully and completely into his new life. It becomes clear that "remaining" in this place means reckoning with the competing claims of past and future, what lies behind and what lies ahead. Spatial language here helps to clarify the meaning of the ascetic's struggle, the state of his heart. When Athanasius invokes Paul's word about "forgetting what lies behind and straining forward [*epekteinomenos*] to what lies ahead" (Phil 3:13), he draws upon the language of forward momentum to articulate the role of desire in the ascetic's life. "Neither the way [*hodos*] of virtue nor separation from the world [*anachoresin*] for its own sake ought to be measured in terms of time spent," he says, "but by the aspirant's desire and purposefulness."[14]

Seen from this perspective, the dwelling place of the monk—whether understood metaphorically in terms of the "way" of virtue adopted or more literally in terms of the posture of marginality taken up in the act of "separation from the world"—will become stagnant, Athanasius suggests, unless it is filled with authentic desire for the infinite. Such desire leads the monk ever forward or, to use the language Athanasius employs elsewhere in the work, upward or inward. There is, in other words, a dynamism inherent in the ascetic life that drives one forward even as one comes to dwell ever more deeply in a particular place. This is the significance of the rhythm of departure and return that recurs in the early stages of *Life of Antony*: to respond to the touch of God upon the soul is to be "called forth," to transcend the confines of the domestic sphere and enter into an ever widening, ever deepening circle of self-knowledge and knowledge of God. But it is also to learn what it means to dwell in a place. It is to return again and again to the discipline of the place or, as Athanasius expresses it, "the place of discipline."[15]

THE SPACE OF SOLITUDE: THE TOMBS

The movement from the household to the place of discipline, the attention to place and movement within the ascetic regime, the sense of space and place as interior and exterior dimensions of reality—all this unfolds within the first few chapters of the *Life of Antony* and sets the stage for the ascetic struggle and the remarkable journey still to come. At this stage Antony has hardly begun the ascetic life. Nor has he journeyed far from his home village. But as Antony begins to

[14] *VA* 7.10; Gregg, 36.
[15] *VA* 4.2; Gregg, 36.

encounter resistance, this soon changes. Place becomes more important as Antony's ascetic struggle deepens, defining the context in which that struggle unfolds, providing the language for articulating temptation and the resistance to temptation, and suggesting the symbolic significance of ascetic life in the desert.

Antony's ascetic rigor threatens the devil who, in response, attempts "to lead him away from the discipline." This he does by raising before Antony's mind "a great dust cloud of considerations"—including memories of his possessions, his responsibilities toward his sister, the pleasures of food and money. In other words he attempts to lead Antony away from the place of discipline by luring him back into the domestic sphere. Athanasius describes the devil as wishing "to cordon [Antony] off from his righteous intention"; but Antony, we are told, "passed through these testings unharmed."[16]

This is only the beginning of Antony's struggles with the demons. But here already the spatial, topographical terms of that struggle are defined. The devil wants to *lead Antony away* from the ascetic path he has embarked upon, which in fact means leading him *back* to a place he has long since left. The devil also seeks to *cordon Antony off* from his righteous intentions, to divide him from himself. Even Antony's initial, tentative victory over these temptations is put in spatial terms: he *passes through* the temptations, emerging safely on the other side. All of this is consistent with Athanasius' sense of the struggle over space taking place between the devil and the ascetic. The enemy, says Athanasius, "was apprehensive that Antony might before long fill the desert with discipline."[17]

It is no coincidence that the devil's apprehension increases just as Antony is withdrawing farther into the desert. Having resolved to make himself "pure of heart and prepared to obey [God's] will, and no other," Antony "went out to the tombs that were situated some distance from the village . . . entered one of the tombs and remained alone within, his friend having closed the door on him."[18] Here the connection between Antony's devotion to the discipline and the occupation of a particular space becomes clear. Antony's decision to move to the tombs arises directly from his deepening awareness of the need for purity of heart; the change of location is the outward expression of a transformation that has already begun to take hold within him. The increased solitude of the tombs is also significant in this regard. For Antony not only moves further *out*; he also moves further *in*—into

---

[16] *VA* 5.2; Gregg, 33; *VA* 5.6; Gregg, 34.
[17] *VA* 8.2; Gregg, 37.
[18] *VA* 8.1; Gregg, 37.

solitude, into himself. Just prior to his departure for the tombs, we hear that Antony had become convinced that, like Elijah, "the ascetic must always acquire knowledge of his own life."[19] With this in mind, "he entered one of the tombs and remained alone within." This is only the second time the word *monos* occurs in the *Life of Antony*; it is the first time it is used to signify a solitude chosen within the context of ascetic practice. It marks a threshold in Antony's experience, the movement into a new space, the space of the self in solitude. Although this is a radically interior space, not susceptible to any clear mapping, the drama unfolds in a particular place, the tomb. The tomb locates and symbolizes the next step in Antony's journey—into the desert, into himself, into God.

It becomes immediately apparent that the withdrawal into the solitude of the tombs will be costly to Antony, for his own more concentrated attention to the discipline elicits ferocious resistance from the demons. He imagines the tomb to be a place of security, where he can give himself to ascetic practice in solitude. What he discovers is that it is a terrifying, liminal space, open to a withering array of competing forces. The demons invade the tomb and beat Antony with such force that when his friends come to look for him, they discover him "lying, as if dead, on the ground."[20] As if the place has become, once again, an actual tomb. Fearing for his safety, his friends carry Antony back to the village in the hopes of nursing him back to health. But Antony, upon waking later than night, insists on returning to the tombs. He is so weak that he has to be carried back by a friend. "As before, the door was closed. Again he was alone inside."[21]

One senses in this description of Antony's desire to return to the tombs the same kind of urgency that made it impossible for him to remain in the village church after having heard the reading of the gospel. The village, a place of safety and security, cannot hold him. Once again, he is drawn forth to a liminal space, open to the terrors of the demons but also open to his own heart and to God. This openness or porousness becomes a crucial dimension of Antony's subsequent experience of the tombs. Alone in his tomb, Antony seeks to maintain and deepen the integrity of his discipline, to become more secure in self-knowledge and purity of his heart. Yet this security is repeatedly threatened by the attacks of the demons. They violate the space of the tomb with shocking ease and in doing so threaten the integrity of Antony's inner life.

[19] *VA* 8.3; Gregg, 37.
[20] *VA* 8.3; Gregg, 37.
[21] *VA* 9.1; Gregg, 38.

> When it was night time, they made such a crashing noise that that whole place seemed to be shaken by a quake. The demons, as if breaking through the building's four walls, and seeming to enter through them, were changed into the forms of beasts and reptiles. The place immediately was filled with the appearance [of them].[22]

Antony reels from the assaults of these creatures, says Athanasius, and feels the pain of their blows in his body. But "being in control of his thoughts," his soul remains unmoved.

The violation of this space by the demons is thus severe but limited: they threaten its physical integrity, gain access to its interior, and fill it with wild and venomous creatures who inflict great harm on Antony (Athanasius, it should be noted, says that all of this *seems* to have happened, or that it seems to have happened in this way—an indication more of the ambiguity and psychological complexity of the experience he is describing than of its unreality). Clearly Antony is shaken by the assault on the tombs. Yet, at the deepest level he remains secure, the space inviolable. Athanasius attributes this to two factors: Antony's ascetic discipline and the saving power of Christ. The crucial elements of Antony's discipline in the present case are his "watchfulness of soul" and his "vigilance of mind." Both expressions convey a posture of alertness, a capacity to notice and withstand unwanted intrusions. Which is, apparently, just what Antony does in the case of the demons. They gain entry to a certain point but no further. They do not violate his interior space.

This is not only because of Antony's vigilance, however. It is also because he is possessed of a deep faith in Christ. As this particular round of attacks draws to a close Antony tells the demons why they have been unable to gain entry into the deepest places of his soul: "Faith in our Lord is for us a seal and a wall of protection."[23] Antony soon receives palpable evidence of this. "For when he looked up he saw the roof being opened, as it seemed, and a certain beam of light descending toward him. Suddenly the demons vanished from view, the pain of his body ceased instantly, and the building was once more intact."[24] What is the meaning of this beam of light? Elsewhere in Athanasius' writings it has clear christological significance. Here it does too, expressing the presence of Christ in the midst of Antony's struggles. The opening of the roof through which the light descends suggests a different, more beneficent structural permeability than was the case with the earlier invasion of the demons. Then, the tomb was cast in

---

[22] *VA* 9.5–6; Gregg, 38.
[23] *VA* 9.10; Gregg, 39.
[24] *VA* 10.1–2; Gregg, 39.

shadows. Now it is suffused with light, a saving light that reverses the effects of the attacking demons: not only do the demons themselves vanish, but Antony is restored to physical well being and the building itself, at one time at risk of coming apart, is "once more intact."

All of which reminds one just how ambiguous, highly charged, and porous Antony's space of solitude really is. Here he learns how vulnerable he really is to the assaults of the demons. Seen here in an almost cartoon-like simplicity, they assault Antony and his dwelling with raw physical force. Still, there can be no doubt that even here their assaults are expressions of profound interior struggles. In subsequent reflections on such experience, Antony notes:

> When they come, their actions correspond to the condition in which they find us; they pattern their phantasms after our thoughts. Should they find us frightened and distressed, immediately they attack like robbers, having found the place unprotected. Whatever we are turning over in our minds, this—and more—is what they do.[25]

It is the "unprotected place"—the soul full of fear and uncertainty—that is most vulnerable. But only by opening oneself to that vulnerability—with vigilance and faith—can the soul arrive at a place of security and peace. This realization is at the heart of Antony's apprenticeship in the tombs. By the time he arrives at this realization he is ready, finally, to enter the desert.

TO THE EDGE OF THE DESERT: THE FORTRESS

Or at least he thinks he is ready. Emerging from his recent struggles in the tombs "even more enthusiastic in his devotion to God," Antony approaches another ascetic living nearby to ask whether he will go with him to live with him "in the wilderness." The other declines because of his old age and because there is not yet a tradition of monks living in the desert. So instead, "Antony set out immediately for the mountain."[26] Very likely this is Mount Pispir, just east of the Nile River approximately fifty miles to the south of Memphis. Athanasius does not say why Antony goes there or how he knows of the place. But his journey to the mountain and the time Antony spends nearby mark further and significant, if provisional, steps in Antony's encounter with God in the desert. It is here that he will serve his final apprenticeship in solitude and prepare himself for the challenges and joys of the "inner desert."

---

[25] *VA* 42.5–6; Gregg, 63.
[26] *VA* 11.1–2; Gregg, 39–40.

Even before arriving at Mount Pispir, Antony must face significant challenges. Here the way or path *(hodos)* to the place becomes as much the means of testing as the place itself. Whereas earlier it is the act of settling into the tomb that stirs up the resistance of the demons, now it is the act of setting out for the mountain that provokes them. First the devil tries to thwart Antony by throwing "in his path *[hodos]* the apparition of a great silver dish."[27] Antony is immediately suspicious and begins asking questions of himself. His questions are not introspective in character but are rather focused outward, on the details of the scene. What is a silver dish doing here in the wilderness, Antony wonders? Where could it possibly have come from? The path has not been traveled, he notes; there is no trace of any travelers. What is more, it is large: if it fell, surely it would have been noticed. Or if not, the one who lost it would certainly have found it upon his return—"since this place is a desert." In other words, Antony concludes, what he is seeing is . . . impossible. It can only be a trick of the devil. As soon as realizes this, the dish vanishes, "like smoke from a fire."[28] Here Antony's attention to the landscape and finely honed sense of local knowledge contribute significantly to his unmasking of the illusion. Continuing on his way, Antony next encounters not an illusion, "but actual gold thrown in his path." Athanasius notes that "Antony marveled at the amount, but as one stepping over fire he passed it without turning. Indeed he hurried at such a pace that soon the place was hidden to view and unseen."[29]

Here again, spatial language defines the terms of Antony's ascetic work. Earlier, confined to his tomb, Antony struggles to stay put. Now he seeks to keep moving—to put even greater distance between himself and his village and to give himself to what he hopes will be a more demanding and rewarding solitude. Yet his path, the way forward, is blocked—by money. This emphasis on wealth as a primary impediment to the ascetic life is not unique to Athanasius; it appears throughout the early monastic literature. Still, it is significant that Athanasius locates these episodes here just at the point when Antony is taking his crucial step into the desert. In doing so, David Brakke suggests, "Athanasius marks the boundary between world and desert not with sex or food, but with money."[30] Antony has already divested himself of his property. In the early stages of his ascetic life, he has struggled with memories of his possessions. Now, standing at the threshold of a

---

[27] *VA* 11.2; Gregg, 40.
[28] *VA* 11.2–5; Gregg, 40.
[29] *VA* 12.2; Gregg, 40.
[30] Brakke, *Athanasius and the Politics of Asceticism*, 235.

more complete and radical withdrawal from his life in the world, he must confront the issue again. His response, especially to the gold, is remarkable and telling. It is the only thing standing between him and the mountain, that is, between his old way of life and the new life at the edge of the desert. He is attracted to it (he marvels at the amount)—a reminder that he has not yet lost his capacity to feel the allure of wealth and comfort, that he might even now be turned back by the sight of it. But he manages to pass by ("as one stepping over fire") and seems to find new momentum in doing so. He hurries *away* from the place where he saw the money, until it is hidden from view. And, Athanasius says, "Intensifying more and more his purpose, he hurried *toward* the mountain."[31]

Wealth does not disappear from Antony's ascetic life; it remains an enduring temptation. But in stepping over the gold in his path Antony effectively crosses a threshold and enters a new world. Taking up residence in a deserted fortress beyond the river, he gives himself over to an even more radical solitude than before, remaining "alone in the place, neither going out himself nor seeing any of those who visited."[32] Receiving bread twice a year from a nearby household, he maintains some contact with the surrounding community. Still, his solitude is now almost total, his devotion to the discipline unwavering.[33] Once again, the demons object, sensing that their own place is about to be supplanted by the work of this ascetic: "Get away from what is ours! What do you have to do with the desert?"[34] But Antony resists this plea to give this place back to the demons and instead spends nearly twenty years in the place pursuing the ascetic life by himself. When, at the urging of friends and admirers, he finally emerges, "as though from some shrine," he is, says Athanasius, physically whole, serene, and possessed of the power to heal, cast out demons, console those who are mourning, and mediate disputes. Antony's presence is so striking, his eloquence regarding the meaning of the solitary life so persuasive, that many are drawn to emulate him. So much so, says Athanasius, that "from then on, there were monasteries in the mountains and the desert was made a city by monks."[35]

One could well imagine this last, triumphalist statement being the final word of the *Life of Antony*. There seems little left for Athanasius' hero to say or do. Antony has been transformed, the demons van-

---

[31] *VA* 12.2–3; Gregg, 40.
[32] *VA* 12.5; Gregg, 41.
[33] *VA* 14.1; Gregg, 42.
[34] *VA* 13.2; Gregg, 41.
[35] *VA* 14.7; Gregg, 42–3.

quished, and the desert completely "colonized" by monks. In a sense, at least in the mythic terms of Athanasius' text, all of this is true. The next major section of the work entails relatively little action or movement. Instead it is didactic in character, with Antony speaking at length about the meaning and purpose of the ascetic life. It represents a kind of consolidation of all that has come before. This is particularly true in regard to the theme of the monastic dislocation of the demons: "I no longer have a place—no weapon, no city," says Satan. "There are Christians everywhere, and even the desert has filled with monks."[36]

However, Antony's own situation remains precarious, his journey into the desert unfinished. Indeed for all Antony's success, he has hardly begun to venture into the desert. He remains on the edge of the Nile valley, within easy reach of those living in the towns and the valleys nearby. Soon this becomes problematic, as his own devotion to God in solitude becomes hopelessly compromised by the almost unceasing demands made upon him by friends and supplicants. Antony realizes that he himself "no longer has a place," and that if he is to continue attending faithfully to God, he must find a new place.

THE PLACE OF THE HEART: TOWARD THE INNER MOUNTAIN

The Antony we meet subsequent to his emergence from the fortress is shown as teaching, preaching, and healing those who come seeking help—ordinary people, dignitaries as well as the growing number of monks who are following his example. He even travels to Alexandria at one point, Athanasius says, to support those who are being martyred there. But there are hints at the midpoint of this narrative that Antony is wearying of this activity, that he is seeking to recover a more radical solitude. One expression of this is the sudden increase in use of the term *anachoresis,* or withdrawal.

Even before going to Alexandria, Antony is said to have withdrawn by himself to his own cell in order to "intensify his discipline."[37] After the persecutions ended, he left Alexandria and "withdrew once again to his cell," subjecting himself "to an even greater and more strenuous asceticism."[38] Subsequent to this, he "withdrew and decided to spend a time in which he neither went out nor received any visitor."[39] These resolutions have little effect, for visi-

[36] VA 41.4; Gregg, 62.
[37] VA 45.1; Gregg, 65.
[38] VA 47.1; Gregg, 66.
[39] VA 48.1; Gregg, 67.

tors continue to come and Antony continues to respond to them. It comes as little surprise, then, to hear Athanasius relate that when Antony "saw that he was disturbed by many people and was not allowed to withdraw as he intended and wished . . . he considered carefully and struck out, departing into the upper Thebaid, in the direction of people who did not know him."[40]

This intensive focus on the notion of withdrawal is striking. In the previous forty-four chapters the term *anachoresis* is used only twice in relation to Antony's ascetic life. Suddenly it appears four times within five chapters. Athanasius seems to suggest that only now, as the demands on Antony increase, does the idea of *anachoresis* really take hold. As the clamor around him grows louder, Antony withdraws more regularly, more profoundly, into solitude. But it soon becomes apparent that the place itself is not sufficiently remote. It is too accessible. Which is why, when he realizes his aspirations for solitude will forever be frustrated in this place, Antony makes plans to depart for the upper Thebaid, a place where no one knows him, a place where he believes he will be able to give himself more fully and completely to the discipline. Yet, his decision to go into the upper Thebaid is, it seems, ill conceived. As Antony sits by the river waiting for a boat that will take him up the Nile, he hears a "voice from above" asking him where he is going and why. The voice convinces Antony that, in terms of solitude at least, he will find the upper Thebaid no better than the place he is in now, perhaps worse. The place he is seeking lies elsewhere. "If you truly desire to be alone," he is told, "go now into the inner desert." Antony needs no persuading. His only question is how to find the place. "And who will show me the way?" he asks.[41]

This exchange marks a crucial turning point in the narrative. Having responded to successive promptings to enter ever more deeply into the practice of the discipline and into a life of solitude, Antony now stands at the threshold of a new world. To cross that threshold means leaving behind him his life on the edge of the Nile valley and embarking on a journey across a wild, unfamiliar desert landscape. It means breaking, more completely than he has done up until now, with the social structures that have formed his life. And it means plumbing more fully the radical depths of his soul, confronting more honestly

---

[40] *VA* 49.1; Gregg, 67 [m].

[41] *VA* 49.4; Gregg, 68 [m]. Gregg translates Antony's destination as "the inner mountain," perhaps from a desire to maintain consistency with Athanasius's later descriptions of the place (cf. e.g., *VA* 82.1; Gregg, 90). In fact, in the latter part of the work, desert and mountain are often nearly synonymous, it being understood that the "inner mountain" is in the heart of the desert.

the world of the demonic, and relinquishing himself with greater abandon to the mystery of God.

The relationship between place and spirit, outer and inner landscape, is rendered here in delicate and subtle terms. An interior aspiration drives the action: Antony desires greater solitude in order to give himself over to the work of prayer and purification to which he feels himself called. But this aspiration is realized, symbolized one might say, only through a change of location. This is consistent with what we have seen already of Athanasius' portrayal of Antony's ascetic quest. In response to either the word of God or to a prompting deep within him, Antony has been called forth from certain places and led into other places: from house to church, from church to the edge of his village, from the edge of his village to the tombs, from the tombs to the deserted fortress. In Athanasius' skillful hands, the language of place becomes a supple and expansive medium for understanding the meaning of Antony's ascetic quest. Now, at the midpoint of his life (and at the midpoint of Athanasius' narrative), it does so again. Here, as much as anywhere else in the work, the language of place and the language of longing take on real density and depth. In Antony's journey to the interior desert, in his discovery of the mountain, and in his subsequent life in that remote place, topography shapes and gives meaning to the soul's deepest aspirations.

Athanasius appears to be far less interested in Antony's journey than in his destination. Antony's actual trip to the interior desert seems an almost perfunctory, routine affair. In answer to Antony's question, "Who will show me the way?" some Saracens appear who are "about to travel that way" and invite him to join them. Antony journeys with them for three days and three nights, "into the desert" eventually arriving at his destination.[42] It could not have been an easy journey; elsewhere in the narrative we hear of the "rigor" of such a trip, of the oppressive heat and lack of water that could imperil travelers in this part of the desert, and even of the possibility of death for those who ventured forth into this region carelessly or unprepared.[43] Perhaps this accounts in part for Antony's expression of uncertainty and need: "Who will show me the way? I have no knowledge of that

---

[42] VA 49.6; Gregg, 68.

[43] Travel in this region could be demanding: Antony is described in one place as making provisions to give visitors "a little relief from the rigor of a hard trip" (VA 50.7; Gregg, 69). Nor were heat and aridity insignificant factors; thus we hear of a case where for some travelers "the heat became oppressive and the water ran out along the way" (VA 54.2; Gregg, 71). Once, for lack of water, a visitor died on the way to Antony's mountain (VA 59.5; Gregg, 75).

[place]," he says. Is it possible that this confession also carries with it a trace of anxiety at the prospect of leaving behind the Nile valley and disappearing into the *terra incognita* of the inner desert? One can only speculate. What seems certain though is that Antony would have had little sense of what to expect. Nor does the reader of Athanasius' account have much idea of what to expect.

Thus we share in Antony's astonishment when we read that, after having traveled for three days across a dangerous, arid landscape, he comes upon a very high hill beneath which there is "water—perfectly clear, sweet and quite cold, and beyond [which] there [a]re plains, and a few untended date palms."[44] One can well imagine Antony wondering whether his eyes were deceiving him. Could such a place exist? Especially here in the inner desert? Apparently, against all expectation, it did exist. Athanasius tells us that, faced with this astonishing scene, "Antony, as if stirred by God, fell in love with the place."[45]

Nowhere else in the work do we hear anything comparable to this almost ecstatic expression of love for place. Not in Antony's first place of retreat near his village; not at the tombs; and not even in the deserted fortress which was the site of some of his most arduous struggles and most profound transformations. One wonders: what is it about *this* place that evokes such a powerful response from Antony? Also, what does this place and Antony's response to it signify within the larger story Athanasius is telling? The entire narrative moves toward and turns on Antony's discovery of the inner mountain; from this point forward the mountain is *the* point of reference for everything that happens. This remains true even though Athanasius later questions whether it is appropriate to treat the mountain as a sacred place. Still there is no question that for Antony as for Athanasius the mountain holds immense significance.

In terms of Antony's response to the place, the sheer beauty of the landscape, not to mention its utter improbability, may well have contributed to his feelings of astonishment and wonder. It is not at all difficult to imagine such a response when, after several days of hard travel in the desert, Antony happened upon that cluster of palms and cool spring and looked up to see those jagged peaks etched against an azure sky. It is a place full of allure and power, enough to make any desert traveler swoon with delight.

But one wonders if there might not have been something else that prompted his heart to overflow at the sight of this place, something having to do with his own chronic sense of displacement. Did Antony's

[44] *VA* 49.7; Gregg, 68.
[45] *VA* 50.1; Gregg, 68.

delight at arriving at the inner mountain arise at least in part because of his sense that after years of movement he might finally have discovered the place for him, his final resting place? It is hard to know. Certainly, within the terms of Athanasius' narrative, Antony's pilgrimage across time and space has a positive and constructive value: his growth and development in the ascetic life—from the time he leaves home until the moment he arrives in this place—is accompanied by, even seems to necessitate, movement, change. Yet, it is also true that within that continuous movement there is a profound desire for stability, rootedness. Antony seeks to dwell deeply in the places he inhabits, to "remain" in these places, even when the demons threaten to drive him out. He seeks also to move *within* these places, "forgetting what lies behind and straining forward to what lies ahead" (Phil 3:13).[46] Place and the movement between places stand in continuous tension with one another throughout the narrative. There is a restlessness in Antony that leads him ever forward and a restlessness that leads him to seek the place where he can give himself fully and completely to God.

Which is why it is both surprising and fitting to hear, immediately following Antony's expression of love for this place, that he looks upon it "as his own home."[47] It is surprising in that this is almost the first mention of home since the earliest moments of the narrative. Surprising too in that the idea of home now takes on a completely different meaning. Then, it was the place *from* which Antony was called, the place he had to renounce, put behind him in order to devote himself to the discipline. Nor, during his subsequent years of ascetic work, did the allure of home grow dimmer; again and again Antony had to struggle, for the sake of his own soul, not to "turn back." How utterly surprising and unexpected then to discover here in a remote corner of the desert, years and miles removed from that childhood home, a place that he recognizes immediately and embraces completely as "his own home."

This rediscovery of home represents an important moment in the development of Antony's ascetic quest. It is, after all, Antony's recognition of the place as "home" that convinces him to stay "in that place" from this point forward. After a lifetime of movement away from the domestic space, of ever deeper levels of detachment from its all-consuming demands, Antony "comes home again." He comes to know his dwelling place not simply as a place along the way, but as "his own home," the place to which he will give himself for the remainder of his days. This is not simply a rhetorical move on Athanasius' part, a way

[46] VA 7.11; Gregg, 37.
[47] VA 50.2; Gregg, 68.

of infusing this remote and forbidding place with the familiarity and comfort of the domestic sphere. Here in this place, from the depths of his solitude, Antony forges deeper, more intimate relationships with the wider community than he has ever known before. An intricate economy of exchange develops in this place, with Antony receiving material support from those outside and offering them in turn "provisions from the mountain"—his words and assistance.[48] No longer is home the place of inappropriate and consuming attachments. It has become the place of Antony's heart. And, because of his life there and his commitment to the discipline it has become a place of power, a healing center out of which pours forth an immensity of grace.

Antony's growing attachment to this place from this point forward is apparent. Repeatedly, we hear that he "remained on the mountain alone."[49] It is for the sake of the discipline, for the sake of prayer and the "contemplation of divine realities," that he does so.[50] Here more than ever before he begins to taste the reality of deep intimacy with God. Because of this he ventures forth from this place only reluctantly. Still the demands on him are considerable and often to attend to the needs of those who have come to see him. After doing so, however, he always returns to the mountain immediately, eagerly.[51] According to Athanasius, Antony "loved more than everything else his way of life in the mountain."[52]

Love transforms the mountain into a place of power. Certainly this is true for those making the long, hard journey to this remote place seeking healing or cleansing. None of them came away disappointed. But the power is not strictly speaking localized: it radiates forth from the mountain to touch even those in distant places through Antony's prophetic, even clairvoyant, powers: "Frequently," Athanasius says, "when he was in the mountain he saw even the things that took place in Egypt."[53] Such was the case when, from his place in the mountain, he "saw" two brothers lost in the desert, one already dead and the other near death. Seeing this, he sent two brothers to their aid—they

---

[48] *VA* 54.6; Gregg, 71. Cf. Brakke, *Athanasius and the Politics of Aceticism*, 232–8, on this exchange.

[49] *VA* 50.1; Gregg, 68. See also: *VA* 51.1; Gregg, 69.

[50] *VA* 84.3; Gregg, 92.

[51] After a few days attending to the needs of the monks in the outer cells, "he returned once more to the mountain" (*VA* 55.1; Gregg, 72). On another occasion, Antony "rejoiced as he set out for the mountain, which was his own home" (*VA* 71.3; Gregg, 83); "After he came and delivered a few statements about salvation and remarks pertaining to those who required help, he hastened to return" (*VA* 85.1; Gregg, 93).

[52] *VA* 84.6; Gregg, 92.

[53] *VA* 82.3; Gregg, 90.

buried the one and revived the other. Such visionary power was available to Antony, says Athanasius, because "while sitting in the mountain, he kept his heart alert."[54]

This last comment serves as a reminder of how important it was to Athanasius that Antony's prophetic power be seen not as a kind of magic nor as a result of the power associated with the place but rather as an expression of Antony's long, exacting discipline. Antony could see such things, Athanasius suggests, because his heart had become pure. Thus while the mountain is indeed a place of power—it is while Antony is "sitting in the mountain" that he sees such things—the power of the place is set within a larger framework of Antony's ascetic work. Indeed Athanasius not only relativizes the power of the place by situating it clearly within the context of Antony's ascetic work of purification of heart; he also relativizes Antony's ascetic work by situating it clearly within the context of Christ's saving work. For Athanasius, it is Christ working through Antony and not Antony himself who is the source of this power.

CONCLUSION: THE PLACE OF THE HEART

This is one reason, perhaps the primary reason, for the surprising turn the narrative makes toward the end: Athanasius calls into question the meaning and significance of place, in particular the place known as the inner mountain. His motivation for this appears to be twofold: his concern that Antony's accomplishments might be seen in isolation from the saving work of Christ and his concern that Antony's place might be turned into a shrine, might be seen as having greater significance than the ascetic's work there. Thus we hear of an instance in which a much sought after healing occurs only after those seeking Antony's help have *departed* from the mountain. This is to demonstrate, says Antony, that "this good deed is not mine . . . rather her healing is from Savior who works his mercy *everywhere*."[55] Here we see a clear attempt to relativize the significance of place and the work of the ascetic in order to preserve a christocentric focus to the work.

Perhaps the most striking expression of this relativization of place is found in the discussion over what to do with Antony's body after he dies. It was a common practice in Egyptian households—including many Egyptian Christian households—to display the bodies of the deceased on low beds in the homes. Athanasius objected to this practice, at

[54] VA 59.6; Gregg, 75.
[55] VA 58.4; Gregg, 74 (emphasis mine). See also Antony's warning against placing too much hope in a place: "A place does not prevent them [demons] from planning treachery" (VA 28.5; Gregg, 52).

least partly on christological grounds: such a practice, it seemed to him, deflected attention from the central importance of "the body of the Lord."[56] Antony shares this concern. Fearing that some of his followers might try to take his body from the mountain and return it for display in the village, Antony withdraws into the heart of the inner mountain, staying there with two of his closest followers. As the time of his death draws near, he instructs them specifically: "Do not permit anyone to take my body to Egypt, lest they set it in the houses . . . perform the rites for me yourselves, and bury my body in the earth. And let my word be kept secret by you, so that no one knows the place but you alone."[57]

No one knows the place. In the end, Antony disappears. And so, in a sense, does Antony's place. This is an intriguing, ironic coda to a work that is, as we have seen, nothing if not a sustained meditation on place. It seems unlikely that Athanasius wants to undermine all that has gone before, to suggest that in the end place has no significance in the life of the ascetic. But one cannot escape the feeling that here at the end of the narrative Antony's disappearance has real significance. If nothing else, perhaps we have here a note of caution aimed at helping the reader avoid a kind of reification of place and understand the hard won sense of place that emerges, gradually but surely, throughout the course of Athanasius's narrative.

After all, Antony's tenacious exploration of the desert and of his own heart teaches him to refuse all simple reductions, to cultivate an encompassing vision. Nowhere is this more true than in his relationship to place. Thus he learns not only about the importance of dwelling in a place, but also about the necessity of movement and change. He learns to pay attention not only to the shape and texture of the places he inhabits and the roads he travels but also to the shape and texture of his own heart. He withdraws from home and family into the darkness and obscurity of his solitude and emerges to embrace the larger community with healing compassion. He contends courageously with the demonic forces that beset him and bathes serenely in the saving light of Christ. He acquires profound self-knowledge and relinquishes himself ever more deeply into the mystery of God. In the end it is this back and forth rhythm—between place and journey, the exterior and the interior worlds, retreat and engagement, light and darkness, knowing and unknowing—that best characterizes Antony's sense of place. Perhaps it is this that leads Athanasius to highlight Antony's disappearance. As if to say to his readers: this is not the place of the heart. At least not for you. That place you have to discover for yourself.

[56] *VA* 90.5; Gregg, 96.
[57] *VA* 91.6–7; Gregg, 97.

Christ as Virtue in Didymus the Blind

PLACID SOLARI, O.S.B.

> My Didymus, however, who has the vision of the bride of the Song of Songs and those eyes which the Lord has commanded to be raised to the white shining fields, gazes yet higher still and delivers to us the ancient rule, so that he may be called the "Seeing Prophet."[1]

These words in the introduction to the Latin translation of Didymus' treatise *On the Holy Spirit* by his sometime-pupil and admirer Jerome offer some idea of the esteem which Didymus enjoyed during his lifetime. This esteem, however, was destined to be eclipsed by the controversies of subsequent centuries. With the exception of portions of a polemical treatise *Contra Manichaeos*, Jerome's above-mentioned Latin translation of the treatise *De spiritu sancto*, and some fragments from the exegetical chains, the works of this once-celebrated teacher were lost.[2] In 1941, some sixteen centuries after his death, a chance discovery during excavations for a munitions dump in Tura, Egypt, brought to light a cache of papyrus manuscripts which turned out to be works of Origen and Didymus. Although these newly-discovered papyrus texts lacked an author's name, the *Commentary on Genesis* (GenT), the *Commentary on Job* (JobT) and the *Commentary on Zachariah* (ZachT) were quickly identified as the works of Didymus on the basis of a comparison with fragments from the exegetical chains, or, in the case of the latter work, the close parallel with Jerome's commentary on

---

[1] Jerome, prologue to the Latin translation of *De spiritu sancto*, ed. Louis Doutreleau, Sources chrétiennes 386 (Paris: Cerf, 1992) 140.

[2] *Contra Manichaeos*, PG 39:1085–110. *De spiritu sancto*. Fragments cf. CPG 2544–64. For a list of all Didymus' works, see Louis Doutreleau, *Sur Zacharie* I, Sources chrétiennes (Paris: Cerf) 17–9, 119–28. The authenticity of the *De Trinitate* previously attributed to Didymus (*PG* 39:269–992) has been called into question by the Tura Commentaries.

the same biblical book which, by his own admission, was based on a work he had acquired from Didymus.

The attribution to Didymus of the other two major works, the *Commentary on the Psalms* (PsT) and the *Commentary on Ecclesiastes* (EcclT), required more investigation. Unlike the other commentaries, these two works represented the stenographic record of oral lectures given by Didymus for his disciples and evidently not intended for the general public. A careful study of these two commentaries has revealed not only the close relationship between them, but also the identity in thought and exegetical method with the authentic commentaries. On this basis, it is almost universally agreed that these two latter commentaries are to be included among the authentic works of Didymus.[3] In addition to these major works, fragments from other works of Didymus found at Tura have been collected and published.[4] A major contribution to the restoration of Didymus' works was made by the publication of a critical text of fragments of his exegesis on the Psalms from the exegetical chains (PsalmCat).[5]

These works have restored Didymus to some of his former prominence, and it is on them that this study will be based. They now represent one of the larger collections of patristic exegetical commentaries still in the original Greek. Furthermore, they introduce to us an important Christian thinker of the fourth century and the last major representative of the Alexandrian School of exegesis and spirituality begun by Origen. The Tura Commentaries are surprising in their witness to Didymus' complete fidelity even to the more audacious theories of his master, Origen, at a time when the Alexandrian Church was beginning to distance itself from these same theories. They give some insight into the rich diversity of the Egyptian monastic world where Didymus stands as a representative of a more traditional current Origenism in comparison to his contemporary Evagrius.

In his writings, Didymus makes little use of the term "purity of heart." The concept, however, is an important one, for Didymus sees

---

[3] A. Gesché, *La christologie du "Commentaire sur les Psaumes" découvert à Toura* (Gembloux: Éditions J. Duculot, 1962) 331–51, 409–17. A. Kehl, *Der Psalmenkommentar von Tura Quaternio IX, Papyrologica Coloniensia I* (Cologne: Verlag, 1964) 39–47. Wolfgang Bienert, *"Allegoria" und "Anagoge" bei Didymos dem Blinden von Alexandria*, Patristische Texte und Studien 13 (New York: Walter de Gruyter 1972) 23, 26–8. For a contrary opinion: P. Nautin, "Didymus the Blind," *Encyclopedia of the Early Church*, vol. I (New York: Oxford University Press 1992) 950–2.

[4] B. Kramer, ed., *Kleine Texte aus dem Tura-Fund*, Papyrologische Texte und Abhandlungen 13 (Bonn: Habelt Verlag, 1985).

[5] E. Mühlenberg, ed., *Psalmenkommentare aus der Katenüberlieferung*, 3 vols, Patristische Texte und Studien 15, 16, 19 (Berlin: Walter de Gruyter 1975, 1977, 1978).

the heart as the central part of the human being caught in a conflict between the flesh and the spirit. Following a brief biographical sketch of Didymus, this work will first examine Didymus' anthropology to illustrate how he alternately describes the human being as a reality composed of either body and soul, or body, soul, and spirit, depending on the perspective from which this being is considered. Next, we will consider Didymus' teaching on virtue, identified as participation in Christ, which provides the way to ascend to the state of perfect image of God in which the human being was first created.

DIDYMUS' LIFE

Didymus' life spanned almost the entire fourth century and was spent at Alexandria or its environs. In spite of the loss of his sight at an early age, he attained a remarkable erudition in religious as well as secular learning.[6] In particular, Didymus gained renown as an interpreter of the Scriptures, and it was this fame which attracted his two best-known disciples, Rufinus and Jerome. Rufinus, who together with his patron Melania remained a faithful friend of the Origenist monks in Egypt, attests that he was with Didymus for a total of eight years over two different occasions.[7] Jerome, although he remained with Didymus not quite a month, continued to study the Alexandrian's exegesis and requested from Didymus commentaries on Osee and Zachariah, which served as a basis for his own works on these books.[8] He also translated into Latin Didymus' treatise *On the Holy Spirit*. In the course of the subsequent Origenist Crisis, however, Jerome took care to distance himself from his mentor.

An intriguing note of Didymus' biography, mentioned by Rufinus and repeated by others, is that he served in an official teaching capacity at Alexandria.[9] Although this has sometimes been taken as an indication that Didymus was head of the famous Alexandrian Catechetical School founded by Origen, the history of this school and Didymus' possible connection with it remain an enigma. There is no compelling

---

[6] H. E. Rufinus, *Apologia* XI.7: "sed et in ceteris sive dialecticae seu geometriae, astronomiae quoque vel arithmeticae disciplinis ita esset paratus, ut nullus umquam philosoforum . . . optinere eum vel concludere quiverit." Palladius, *Hist. Laus.* IV. Jerome, *De vir. inl.* 109; *Chron.* an. 372.

[7] Rufinus, *Apologia* II.15.

[8] Ibid. Jerome, *Contra Rufinum* III.28; Ep. 71.5; 84.3; 112.4; *Comm. in Is.* prol.; *Comm. in Osee,* prol.; *Comm. in Zach.* prol.; *Comm. in Matt.* prol; *Comm. in Ep. ad Eph.* prol.

[9] Rufinus, *Apologia* XI.7: *Ita brevi deo docente in tantam divinarum humanarumque rerum eruditionem ac scientiam venit, ut scholae ecclesiasticae doctor existeret, Athanasio episcopo ceterisque sapientibus in ecclesia dei viris admodum probatus.*

reason to doubt Rufinus' description of Didymus as "scholae ecclesiasticae doctor," but it is likely that this is simply an indication that he continued the explanation of the Scriptures according to the tradition which had been synonymous with the theology of the Alexandrian Church for nearly two centuries. There is no evidence in the surviving commentaries or elsewhere that Didymus ever instructed catechumens. Furthermore, the connection between Didymus and Athanasius attested by Rufinus and others does not necessarily imply an "official" appointment. The fact that Didymus was "approved by Athanasius" could merely signify that his exegetical work and teaching was in keeping with the tradition of the Alexandrian Church and was clearly anti-Arian.

Of greater interest here is Didymus' association with the Egyptian monastic movement. He was known to Palladius, Rufinus, and Melania, and Anthony is reported to have visited him. In an account preserved by Jerome and Rufinus, Anthony is said to have consoled the blind exegete over his loss of sight by reminding him to rejoice in possessing the "eyes which angels have and by which God is seen."[10] Palladius, too, gives a report as to how Anthony had offered the prayer during one of their meetings in Didymus' cell.[11] The study of S. Rubenson on the letters of Anthony, which firmly sets them in the Origenist matrix of the Alexandrian tradition, strengthens the possibility of ties between Anthony and Didymus.[12]

Of interest, too, is the relationship between Evagrius and Didymus, two of the most eminent Origenist monks in Egypt at the close of the fourth century. Not only were they related through mutual acquaintances (e.g., Melania and Rufinus), but it is also clear that they knew one another. Evagrius praises Didymus as the "great and gnostic teacher" and cites his advice: "constantly exercise for yourself the things concerning providence and judgment . . . for nearly all trip up in these."[13] Furthermore, the editors of Evagrius' *Praktikos* consider that Evagrius is referring to Didymus when he speaks of the "most proven monk in the camp of the gnostics" who teaches on the unity of virtue.[14] While the relationship between these two monks merits closer

---

[10] Rufinus, *Apologia* XI.7. Jerome, *Ep.* 68.2. For a dating of this visit to 337, see S. Rubenson, *The Letters of St. Antony* (Lund: Lund University Press, 1990) 175, n. 1.

[11] Palladius, *Hist. Laus.* IV.

[12] Rubenson, *The Letters of St. Antony*.

[13] Evagrius, *Gnostikos* 48, ed. Antoine and Claire Guillaumont, Sources chrétiennes 356 (Paris: Cerf, 1989).

[14] Evagrius, *Praktikos* 98 with note, ed. Antoine and Claire Guillaumont, Sources chrétiennes 171 (Paris: Cerf, 1971) 706–8. For a possible influence of Didymus on Evagrius' *Ad Monachos*, see J. Driscoll, *The "Ad Monachos" of Evagrius Ponticus*, Studia

attention, it appears that Didymus represents a more "traditional" continuation of Origen's patrimony.

It was precisely his fidelity to Origen which would bring condemnation down upon Didymus. His death at the close of the fourth century spared him from the bitterness of the Origenist Crisis which arose shortly thereafter. His works continued to be read and esteemed for more than a century. However, in spite of the acclaim in which his person and teaching had been held during his lifetime, he was condemned along with Origen and Evagrius in the sixth century and his works consigned for the most part to oblivion until the fortunate discovery at Tura.[15]

ANTHROPOLOGY

The scriptural doctrines of the human being's creation in God's image and likeness and of the resurrection form the twin poles around which Didymus' anthropology revolves. He draws principally on his Christian predecessors at Alexandria, especially Origen, and it is largely through them that he takes over the elements from classical philosophy, especially Middle and Neoplatonism, and Stoicism, and from Philo, which provide the vehicle for his explanation of the fundamental data from Scripture. In considering Didymus' anthropology, it is important to realize that he moves on different levels unencumbered by the constraints of any systematic presentation.

One current of speculation in the ancient world on the relation between the human and the divine found expression in the concept of 'ομοίωσις, a process of becoming like unto the divine. From the beginning, this process was linked with the practice of virtue and purification.[16] Not only, then, did this idea form a part of the general intellectual milieu of Didymus' world, but came to him even more directly through its acceptance into the works of his Alexandrian predecessors Philo, Clement, and Origen.[17] That Didymus identified with

---

Anselmiana 104 (Rome: Benedictina, 1991) 156; 191, nn. 13, 14; 350. The term "gnostic" here refers to one who, by virtue, study, and ascesis, has advanced in perfection in Christian life and is able to penetrate the spiritual meaning of the Scriptures.

[15] For a review of the Origenist Controversy see E. Clark, *The Origenist Controversy: The Cultural Construction of an Early Christian Debate* (Princeton, N.J.: Princeton University Press, 1992). H. Crouzel, "Origenism," *Encyclopedia of the Early Church*, vol. II (New York: Oxford University Press 1992) 623–4.

[16] H. Merki, ΟΜΟΙΩΣΙΣ ΘΕΩ, Paradosis 7 (Freiburg: Paulusverlag, 1952) 1–5, 17–22. H. Louth, *The Origins of the Christian Mystical Tradition* (Oxford: Clarendon Press, 1981) 2–25.

[17] H. Merki, ΟΜΟΙΩΣΙΣ ΘΕΩ, 35–64.

this tradition is clear from a passage in the *Commentary on Ecclesiastes* where he alludes directly to the idea of becoming like unto God to the extent possible.[18] He thus accepts a dynamic idea of perfection as the realization of a likeness unto God through a process of growth in virtue. This idea finds expression elsewhere in the *Commentary on Ecclesiastes* when Didymus cites the famous aphorism "know thyself" (EcclT 238.7ff.). According to Didymus, the human being's knowledge of himself begins with the understanding of having been made for the reception of virtue, continues through the realization of the proper order between soul and body, visible and invisible realities, and finally "arrives at the goal so as to know God as He is" (EcclT 238.26). This traditional idea becomes the vehicle of a specifically Christian concept in Didymus inasmuch as likeness unto God is connected with participation in the Holy Spirit and knowledge of the Trinity.[19]

For Didymus this philosophical tradition of "likeness unto God" was fused into a system founded on the Scriptures. In this view, the words of Gen 1:26-27 provided divine authority for the fact that human beings are created in God's "image and likeness." On the basis of this Genesis text which speaks in verse 26 of human beings according to "image and likeness," but in verse 27 only according to "image," Didymus' predecessors at Alexandria had developed a spirituality based on the distinction between the "image" and the "likeness" of God in human beings.[20] This allowed them to render an account of the biblical narrative while both explaining the present imperfect state of human beings and freeing God from responsibility for evil. The aspect of "image" was for them a given constituent of the human soul, while that of "likeness," lost by the Fall, was a reality acquired as a result of the "imitation of Christ as well as through the sacraments [baptism and Eucharist] and moral striving."[21] Didymus explicitly accepts this distinction in his *Commentary on Genesis* (GenT 62.6-11) and it becomes

---

[18] EcclT 99.6–7: The soul can be perfected to the extent that it is attainable for it, can become like unto God to the extent possible. (The Tura Commentaries are cited according to the page and line numbers of the papyrus sheets.)

[19] JobT 288.14–22: Also those outside the preaching of the Truth understand concerning the soul that it is immortal. This immortality is clear from what happens to it; it participates in the Holy Spirit, receives knowledge of the Trinity, becomes like unto God to the extent possible.

[20] Clement Alex., *Protrep.* XII.122.4; *Strom.* II.22.131.6. Origen, P.A. III.6.1.; *In Ioh.* XX 22(20). W. Völker, *Der wahre Gnostiker nach Clemens Alexandrinus,* Texte und Untersuchungen 54 (Berlin: Akademie Verlag, 1952) 112–4. J. Daniélou, *Origène* (Paris: La Table Ronde, 1948) 289–90.

[21] P. Th. Camelot, "La théologie de l'image de Dieu," *Revue des Sciences Philosophiques et Thèologiques* 40 (1956) 461. H. Crouzel, *Théologie de l'image chez Origène* (Paris: Aubier, 1956) 67–9, 217–9.

the foundation for the entire enterprise of the moral life.[22] It is important to note that Didymus sees this process as involving the νους, or the core of the human person; an aspect which will be treated below. Didymus continues to make this distinction between image and likeness the cornerstone of his anthropology and doctrine on perfection at a time when the bishops of Alexandria appear to have abandoned this aspect of their church's tradition.[23]

The reality of the incarnation added a new element for consideration and the fundamental Genesis text was nuanced by the words of Paul in Col 1:15 according to which "He [Christ] is the image of the unseen God." Furthermore, the Alexandrians had accepted Philo's view that only the *logos* is God's image, while human beings are "according to the image" or "the image of the image."[24] In his exegesis of Gen 1:26-27, Didymus makes this interpretation his own, citing Col 1:15 as a supporting text.[25] In connection with this idea of the son as the image in which we are created, Didymus introduces another traditional Alexandrian theme, that of the titles of Christ, into his anthropology. Through this use of titles, as we shall see, Didymus develops his idea of Christ as virtue.

Didymus is opposed to any materialist or anthropomorphic concept of God's image as well as to any current of thought which would see God's image reflected in the human being as a composite of body and soul. Since God is a spiritual being, God's image must likewise be spiritual. It is to be found in the soul[26] or the "inner human being," to use the term frequently adopted by Didymus. In particular, the seat of

---

[22] GenT 58.27–59.1, 4-5: The *nous* which has come to the service of God is first characterized "according to the image" and subsequently, by progress toward perfection, becomes "according to the likeness" of God . . . since we are already "according to the image," we hope to become "according to the likeness."

[23] R. Bernard, *L'image de dieu d'après saint Athanase* (Paris: Aubier, 1952) 27. W. Burghardt, *The Image of God in Man according to Cyril of Alexandria*, Studies in Christian Antiquity 14 (Washington, D.C.: Catholic University Press, 1957) 6–8.

[24] Philo, *Opif.* 25; *Let. all.* III.95–96; *Spec. leg.* III.83. For a study of Philo's influence in Didymus see D. Ruina, *Philo in Early Christian Literature* (Leiden: E. J. Brill, 1993) 197–204.

[25] GenT 58.3-4, 13-16: The image of God is his only-begotten Son. Paul teaches this when he writes: "He is the image of the invisible God" (Col 1:15); a substantial and unchangeable image. "The one who has seen me has seen the Father" (John 14:9). Therefore it is not said: "Let us make the human being an image" but "according to the image," which is to be formed according to that image and to imitate it. For the human being is made capable of containing the image.

[26] JobT 273.22-27: In Genesis it is said, "God made the human being, according to the image of God He made him." The body is not according to the image, but the soul; God is not in a human form. Cf. PsT 199.32–200.7. PsalmCat 984.II.234.1-3. (Citations from Mühlenberg's edition give the entry number, followed by the number of the volume, followed by the page and line numbers.)

the "image" is the higher part of the soul, the νους, as will be explained below. The soul, as the seat of God's image, is both immortal and rational. To be more precise, since human beings are actually created in the "image of the image," i.e., in the image of the *logos*, it is as a rational being *(logikos)* that human beings exemplify the image in which they are created. From this, it follows for Didymus that human beings are essentially good and are created for virtue.[27]

Though Didymus clearly situates the image of God in the human soul, his belief in the incarnation and resurrection required that he render an account of the body's fate as well. He did this by claiming the body as an essential component of the human being, but a component whose quality varied directly with the moral state of the soul. To support this claim, he made use of the teaching on the "dual creation" of the human being, which arises from the three instances of creation in Gen 1:26-27; 2:7; and 3:21. The initial impetus for this teaching is provided by the two Greek words for "to make" used in Gen 1:26-27 (ποιειν) and in Gen 2:7 (πλαττειν). In keeping with Alexandrian tradition,[28] Didymus interprets the two different verbs as referring to two different acts of creation. The first account (ποιειν) is connected with the soul, or the interior human being, the second (πλαττειν) with the body, or the exterior human being.[29] A second stage of the question arises, however, from the fact that Didymus clearly interprets Gen 3:21 (creation of the "garments of skin") as referring to the heavy earthly body (GenT 106.8–108.15; JobT 277.26–278.6). The question then remains as to the identity of the body of Gen 2:7.

Didymus resolves this difficulty by following the direction of Origen, who assumed that a certain light and ethereal body has always been a permanent and essential component of the human being, even in the initial stage of creation as rational intellects. Although this teaching is not found explicitly stated in the surviving works of Origen, it follows clearly from his discussion of the bodies of angels, humans, and demons, from his view of the nature of the resurrected body, and,

---

[27] PsalmCat 725.II.85.12-16 (Ps 69). For they all have come into being according to the image and likeness of God and upright, having the innate notions concerning God sown within . . . they remember the good of which they have an innate notion according to their nature since they have come into being as rational and according to the image of God. Cf. PsalmCat 963; PsT 19.8-12; ZachT 206.3-9; JobT 141.19-33; 304.7-14.

[28] Philo, *Leg. all.* I.31, 53, 88. *Opif.* 69.134. Origen, *Hom. in Gen.* I.13; *Comm. in Cant.* prol.; *Hom. in Jer.* I.10; *Comm. in Matt.* XIV.16; *Comm. in Ioh.* XX.22(20); *Disp. cum Herac.* 15.28–16.10. H. Crouzel, *Théologie de l'image de Dieu chez Origène* (Paris: Aubier, 1956) 54–5, 148–53.

[29] JobT 273.15-22, 27–274.1; 275.31–276.5, 9-11. PsT 177.24-27; 178.26-28; ZachT 323.23-29. In JobT 273.32-33 πλαττειν is applied to the flesh (σερξ) rather than to the body.

in particular, from his repeated insistence that only the Trinity is absolutely incorporeal, while all created realities are found in some type of body as an aspect of their created condition.[30] This doctrine of "dual creation" as found in Didymus is divided into two instances, the first of which is articulated into two parts. The first instance includes the events represented by both Gen 1:26-27, the creation of the soul—or more exactly the νους—in God's image, and Gen 2:7, the creation of the light, ethereal body which is always associated with the soul. The two events are logically, not "temporally" distinct. The second instance is represented by the one fall in preexistence and results in the light body taking on the quality of its dense, earthly state as represented by the garments of skin of Gen 3:21. Although the papyrus sheets of the *Commentary on Genesis* containing the exegesis of the pertinent parts of the opening chapters of Genesis are missing, it is clear from his interpretation of Gen 3:21 that, before receiving the body of flesh, there was a prior body with which the soul was endowed.[31] Furthermore, he notes that, while Adam and Eve did not dwell in paradise in their dense bodies, they nevertheless had a body adapted to that region.[32]

In keeping with the traditional understanding that the final status of creation mirrors the initial status, Didymus also brings in his belief in the resurrection of the body to complement his teaching on its creation. Although Didymus clearly and explicitly holds the doctrine of the preexistence and fall of souls—a point which need not be examined here[33]—he is clear as to the fact that the body did not come into existence together with the Fall, but preexisted it. As an essential component of the human being, it is destined for resurrection.[34] The difference

---

[30] Origen, *P.A.* II.2.2; IV.3.15; IV.4.8. H. Crouzel, M. Simonetti, *Origène: Traité des Principes,* Sources chrétiennes 253 (Paris: Cerf, 1978–84) 138–41. H. Crouzel, *Origène* (Paris: Éditions Lethielleux, 1985) 128, 269, 279, 283.

[31] GenT 107.4-7: It was said first that the human being came to be "according to the image," which indicates the immaterial quality. But since he came into another state so as to need something he might use, he needed the body as an instrument. Now they also become "of skin." (It is important to note that the quality of "according to the image" is described as *immaterial* and not *incorporeal.* The spiritual image thus appears to have had a bodily instrument before the "now" of the creation of the skin garments.)

[32] GenT 108.5-7, 14-15: We do not say that in paradise they had the dense bodies and thus were expelled, for it is not possible to dwell there with a body of this sort. . . . Through these words it [Scripture] establishes that it was not possible for dense bodies to dwell there. GenT 118.13-16: We preserve what has been said above concerning the clay as indicating the bodily substance. This body was obviously adapted to the sojourn in paradise.

[33] The clearest expressions of this teaching are found in JobT 56.20–58.16 and EcclT 14.2–15.7.

[34] PsT 129.1, 4-6: On both accounts, both according to the soul and according to the body resurrection takes place. . . . A resurrection of the body also takes place, for the

between the earthly body and the resurrected body is explained by drawing on the distinction in 1 Cor 15:42-44 between the ψυχικον σωμα and the πνευματικον σωμα, a distinction realized initially in the risen body of the Savior.[35]

In order to explain this process of the change in quality of the body, Didymus, again following Origen, had recourse to a concept originally of Stoic origin. According to this concept the material substance, which is an essential part of every rational creature as a sign of its created, and thus mutable, status, is characterized by a certain amorphous substrate (ὑποκειμενον αποιον). This substrate, itself without quality, always receives its quality from the status of the immaterial rational soul to which it is linked. Thus the quality of the material substance of the body varies from the light, ethereal substance of paradise and the resurrection to the heavy, earthly body after the Fall.[36]

The importance of this doctrine of "dual creation" with its affirmation of the body as an essential component of the human being is twofold. First, it illustrates the fundamentally Christian inspiration of Didymus' work which has led him to modify the philosophical systems of his intellectual milieu and impart to them a distinctly Christian character. Second, it has given him a way of explaining how the bodies of rational creatures are capable of assuming different qualities in keeping with the moral status of those creatures, and thus to understand the resurrection of the body. This concern with moral status and striving is a fundamental concern of Didymus and governs the last aspect of his anthropology which must be considered, namely, his view of the human being as a dynamic rather than a static reality.

It is clear that Didymus considers the human being a composite of body and soul and that he has found a way to explain the essential and enduring character of the body. More important for Didymus' anthropology, however, is his view, taken over again from Origen, of the human being as a three-fold reality composed of body (σωμα), soul (ψυχη), and spirit (πνευμα). The justification of this view for both Ori-

---

making of it was not a fall, but the ruin after the making. On this account, it also rises. Cf. EcclT 348.4-7; JobT 379.38–380.1; PsT 71.17–72.2; 259.3-16; 328.23–329.9.

[35] PsT 71.17–72.1. The main treatment of this distinction is found in PsT 328.23ff. Cf. GenT 149.1-5; EcclT 348.4-7; 353.5-8; ZachT 231.11-20; 334.6-14.

[36] PsT 197.21-24; 263.25-27; EcclT 103.5-6, 11-12. Origen, *Peri Euch.* 27.8; *P.A.* III.6.7 with notes (SCh 268.250/ SCh 269.144-145); *Comm. in Ioh.* XIII.21; *CCels.* III.41 with notes (SCh 136.94-98), IV.56-57 with notes (SCh 136.326-332). H. Crouzel, "Doctrine origénienne du corps ressuscité," *Bulletin de Littérature Ecclésiastique* 81 (1980) 192–4, 242–5. H. Crouzel, *Origène* (Paris: Éditions Lethielleux, 1985) 279, 326–7. A. Le Boulluec, "De la croisance selon les stoïciens a la résurrection selon Origène," *Revue des Études Grecques* 88 (1975) 145, 149, 151–5.

gen and Didymus is to be found in the text of 1 Thess 5:23: "May the God of peace Himself make you holy and perfect; and may your spirit, soul and body be kept irreproachably whole and entire in the presence of Our Lord Jesus Christ." Since he believed that every detail of the scriptural text is a result of an intentional inspiration by the Holy Spirit, Didymus interprets these three terms "spirit, soul, and body" to refer to three distinct elements of the human being. It is important to keep in mind, though, that in employing these three aspects of the human being, he is not using them in a static—one might say ontological—point of view, but as part of a dynamic process which sees the human being as constantly in tension between the opposing forces of spirit and flesh. It remains, then, to look more closely at each of these components in Didymus' dynamic anthropology.

It has already been demonstrated above that the body (σωμα) is for Didymus an essential component of the human being from the first moment of existence and is the aspect that defines the human being's status as a creature. As used in the context of this three-fold anthropology, the reference is to the moral state of the body as it varies according to the status of the soul, as in the distinction between the ψυχικον and the πνευματικον σωμα.[37] In particular, in this dynamic anthropology, it refers to the body which has become heavy and flesh as a result of the Fall. In this state, it has an affinity to the material and transient elements of this passing world and, unless kept in check, serves as a weight which tends to drag the soul to adhere to these elements. Not only would Didymus find such a state of affairs disastrous because of his fundamental Platonic outlook, but he would also find this outlook buttressed by the scriptural text, endlessly repeated in the Alexandrian tradition, of 2 Cor 4:18: "For we look not to the things which are seen but to the things which are not seen; for the things which are seen are temporary, but the things which are not seen are eternal."

With regard to the soul in this dynamic anthropology, it is important to note that Didymus accepts the Platonic tradition of the three powers of the soul: the rational (λογιστικον), the passionate (θυμικον), and the appetative (επιθυμητικον). Among these three powers, the rational is to rule the passionate and the appetative, and any reverse of this order results in evil.[38] Among these powers, Didymus explicitly

---

[37] GenT 104:18-20; ZachT 231.19-20; 334.11; 405.27. Staab, *Pauluskommentare aus der griechieschen Kirche* (Münster: Aschendorff, 1933) 10.1-13; 27.23-29, 31-36.

[38] EcclT 238.11-12, 13, 14: And again it is the case in the soul that the rational power rules and the passionate and appetative powers are ruled. If the reverse of this happens, it is a very great evil . . . and if the rational power is ruled by the passionate power or by the appetative power, this rule is unlawful. Cf. PsT 262.9-11.

identifies the rational power with the νους.³⁹ Indeed, since it appears that Didymus agreed with Origen's idea of the initial creation of all rational beings as equal, then the νους and the soul are virtually identical, since νους comes to be in the state of soul (ψυχη) when it departs from the fervor of its contemplation of God.⁴⁰ Didymus' concept of νους is central to this study for, in addition to referring to the νους by the Stoic term ἡγεμονικον, he also identifies the νους by the scriptural term "heart" (καρδια).⁴¹ It is the νους as the core or center of the human being which is the focal point of this dynamic anthropology of creation, Fall, and return to God.

Before going further, however, it is necessary to examine Didymus' concept of "spirit," which forms the final element of his three-fold anthropology. The matter is complicated by the varied use which Didymus makes of the term "spirit," ranging from the Holy Spirit, to evil spirits, to the soul, the νους and "the spirit in the human being." Although Didymus at times identifies the spirit with the soul or the νους, on numerous other occasions he quite clearly states that the spirit is distinct from the soul.⁴² The role of the spirit as a distinct and separate element must thus be explained. For both Origen and Didymus, the spirit is the created element by which the human being participates in divine life. Though Didymus clearly distinguishes between the Holy Spirit and "the spirit which is in the human being" (cf. 1 Cor 2:11), the two are so intimately related that the "spirit in the human being" can be seen as the human element which participates in the Holy Spirit.⁴³

---

³⁹ PsT 142.29; One would not miss the mark in calling the rational power the *nous*. Cf. PsT 142.24; 143.2-6; 100.27; PsalmCat 132 I.199.24–200.14; EcclT 337.18-19.

⁴⁰ PsT 35.2-4; 139.27-31; PsalmCat 1113 II.287.2-8; Origen, *P.A.* I.3.8; I.4.1; II.8.3-4. Crouzel, *Origène*, 267–74.

⁴¹ PsT 53.18-20; 84.24-25; 100.27-101.1; 179.14-15; 276.26-28; 289.13-16; EcclT 33.1-2; 44.15-19; 337.19f.; ZachT 260.5-6.

⁴² PsT 139.2-3, 9-11: . . . his spirit is the one joined to the soul, about which it is said, "Whole and entire your spirit, soul and body" (1 Thess 5:23). . . . It is called, as I said, some rational power joined and as though inseparable in order that it might be the teacher of the soul. PsalmCat 545 I.374.1-2: And in these words he speaks of the spirit in both ways, either as the holy ruler and governor or as the spirit of the human being which is in him and is other than the soul of the human being. *De spir. sanct.* 242.7-9: Sicut enim alia est anima et corpus aliud, sic et aliud est spiritus ab anima, quae suo loco specialiter appellatur. Cf. ZachT 337.7-10; 323.5-29; PsT 42.9-11; 21-28; EcclT 124.22-26; 225.22-25; 315.16-19.

⁴³ EcclT 34.21-25: Just as the Holy Spirit, now according to the one who sends him, now according to the one who receives him, is called the spirit of Daniel, the spirit of Isaiah, then the Spirit of God, thus can it also be with wisdom . . . now it is called Wisdom of God, now of the one who receives it. To the extent that it is sent, it is of God. To the extent that he receives it to whom it is sent and partakes in it, it is called his [wisdom]. EcclT 315.16-17: The spirit who bears witness to the human being is the angel who

As the point of contact between God and the soul, or more specifically the νοῦς, the seat of one's free will, the spirit becomes the impetus for one's ethical striving.

This three-fold anthropology of spirit-soul-body thus represents Didymus' view of the human being as constantly involved in spiritual combat. The following description of Origen's anthropology by Henri Crouzel can also be applied to his faithful disciple Didymus:

> . . . it is oriented by the perspective of spiritual combat. Origen is not primarily a metaphysician nor even a theologian: his metaphysic and his theology are hardly set forth for their own sake, but are contained in his spiritual doctrine. . . . These three notions of spirit, soul, and body do not designate three elements which, arranging themselves together, would form the single substance which is the human being. However, the human personality is essentially in the soul: the spirit and the flesh (or the body) designate the two poles between which the soul is contested.[44]

The struggle, then, is between the flesh and the spirit. Although the term σάρξ in Didymus can mean simply the body of flesh as one component of the human being, its more frequent connotation, drawing on Rom 8:3-9 and 7:14, is that of an attraction to the lower things in connection with the lower powers of the soul.[45] It must be remembered that it is actually these lower powers of the soul added to the νοῦς which give it the quality of being "soul," i.e., νοῦς oriented toward a body. The νοῦς, however, created in God's image, is also the point of influence of the spirit through which the human being has contact with the Holy Spirit and thus a return to the original state of God's image and likeness. The tendencies represented by the flesh, or the body, and the spirit are diametrically opposed and thus the soul finds itself in a constant state of tension between the two.[46] The more the

---

is with him or the participation in the Holy Spirit. Cf. S. C. Reynolds, *Man, Incarnation and the Trinity*; unpublished dissertation. Harvard University, 1966, 19–23.

[44] H. Crouzel, "L'anthropologie d'Origène dans la perspective du combat spirituel," *Revue d'Ascétique et de Mystique* 31 (1955) 365.

[45] EcclT 219.25–220.1: With regard to the text at hand, I am not speaking in a literal sense but in the sense of ethical instruction as though in a tropological sense. I say this, that that human being is on the earth who "goes about according to the flesh," according to the text, "you will all die like human beings." This one is on the earth not only in his body but also in his heart. Cf. GenT. 152.26–153.14; JobT 347.25-26; PsT 261.6-9; 232.29-35; 269.27-30; EcclT 213.12- 19; ZachT 41.26–42.5.

[46] PsT 261.9-15: The flesh is spoken of distinct from the spirit. It calls the spirit judgment and the flesh the thing distinct from judgment. When someone thinks the things of the flesh and handles and lives according to them, he is far from the spirit. But when he follows the spirit, right judgment and above all participation in the Holy Spirit, then he brings the flesh to nothing. Concerning this type of flesh and the spirit distinct from

soul tends toward those desires attached to its lower powers, the more the body takes on the characteristics of the flesh and becomes that psychic body indicated by the Apostle (1 Cor 15:44-46) as being sown in corruption and not yet fit for the resurrection. To the contrary, the more the soul follows the lead of the νοῦς under the attraction of the spirit, the more it becomes wholly pneumatic, until it finally becomes "one spirit" (1 Cor 6:17) with God.

Thus do we find in Didymus the concept of the "pure heart," or as he more likely calls it, the "pure νοῦς." As the central, core aspect of the human being, it was created in God's image and likeness. Following the Fall, however, it is constantly pulled in opposite directions by the desires of the flesh connected with the body, now of flesh, and by the attraction of the spirit for the things of God. If, through the work of the Holy Spirit, it becomes "pure," it will "see God" (cf. Matt 5:8).[47] Now this purity which leads to the vision of God is the work of the Holy Spirit who leads the νοῦς to be perfected in virtue, which is identified with Christ.

TEACHING ON VIRTUE

The investigation of Didymus' concept of virtue presents certain difficulties. In keeping with contemporary trends, his ethical theory displays a mixture of elements drawn from Platonic, Stoic, and Peripatetic sources. Although the frequency with which Didymus cites classical authors gives evidence of contact with representatives of a variety of schools of thought, it is questionable whether he had a strong attachment to any one of them. It is far more likely that his acquaintance with these philosophers was a somewhat superficial one gained through *florilegia* or handbooks rather than a profound initiation attained through serious study. In the realm of virtue as in all other areas, it is Origen who links Didymus with the prior Alexandrian tradition of Philo and Clement, and it is primarily Origen's thought that our blind exegete strives faithfully to reproduce.

A particular difficulty in studying the theme of virtue derives from the fact that, though the question of virtue occurs constantly through-

---

it, he says, "You are not in the flesh but in the spirit" (Rom 8:9). Indeed they were in the flesh and weighed down with the body. In their disposition they had come to be outside it. And just as someone moving about on earth can have his mode of life in heaven, so also someone still in the flesh comes to be outside it when he follows the spirit. Cf. PsT 55.6-12.

[47] GenT 210.11-19; JobT 73.2-11; PsT 53.18–54.1; 84.24-25; 93.1-2, 5-8; ZachT 180.15-20; 194.6-12; 259.6-12; PsalmCat 887 II.171.19-21.

out Didymus' writings, nowhere in his surviving works does he dedicate a treatise specifically to this topic. The existence of a hitherto unknown work on virtue was revealed by the *Commentary on Zachariah* from Tura, where Didymus states that in his work *On the Virtues* he had demonstrated at length that the virtues are means and their excesses and deficiencies are vices.[48] It is regrettable that this treatise is no longer extant. The goal of this present study, however, is not to present a complete outline of Didymus' teaching on virtue. Instead, that part of his teaching which relates virtue specifically to Christ will be treated under the ideas of the goodness and unity of virtue, the distinction of virtue with special reference to justice, and the goal of virtue.

Didymus makes a connection between ethics and ontology. Virtue is good and only the good really exists. Virtue is always good, it is not a relative good.[49] Most often, Didymus makes this point in a negative fashion by stressing that evil does not exist in itself,[50] but is something accidental, something which derives from a good thing, and can only exist when practiced by someone.[51] Virtue, as a good which exists, has the foundation of its existence in God.[52] This identification of virtue with God is the core of Didymus' theory of virtue.

To emphasize the unity of virtue, Didymus turns to ideas deriving ultimately from the Stoic tradition, in particular the teaching of the concatenation or interdependence of the virtues. This teaching had its origin in Stoic anthropology's unitary vision of the soul whereby virtue or vice were seen as states which conditioned the entire soul. To be virtuous in one respect was necessarily to be virtuous in all; there was no question of degrees of virtue. Although this does not correspond

---

[48] ZachT 333.10-12.

[49] EcclT 82.29–83.1: No one says concerning virtue that it is good on occasion, nor concerning evil that it is bad on occasion. It is always base, and the good is always good and to be pursued. JobT 132.24-28, 31-32: If Paul writes concerning love, the words do not fit love but the one who has it. For he says, "Love does not boast, is not puffed up . . . love never fails." Virtue does not fail, but the one who has it does.

[50] JobT 281.17-21: See whether it is not fitting to understand the passage in this manner: Evil is non-being, thus those who participate in it are said to be non-being. JobT 220.33-34: Evil is insubstantial. JobT 393.2-10; 405.1-5; PsT 141.7; 288.22-24. *C. Man.* II *PG* 39, 1089A; PsalmCat 26 I.132.1-4; 69 I.160.19-21. For evil is not some substance but a quality.

[51] PsT 56.1-2: The one who falls away from the right teaching and prophecy is the tail; for evil is something which follows from the good. EcclT 334.6, 11-13: But evil, if one does not practice it, does not exist. . . . "His sin will be sought out and was not found in itself." "It is not found in itself." It is not one of the substances, it is an accident and is able to be set aside. Cf. PsT 78.14-17; 250.16-22; JobT 114.31–115.15.

[52] EcclT 334.3-6: Some who hold for the consemination of the soul say that virtue is like this; it does not exist apart from the one who practices it. This is false. It has its existence in God and it is from there that we draw it out.

to Didymus' anthropology, it must be kept in mind that, on the one hand, the later Stoics had modified their view of the soul under the influence of the Platonic three powers of the soul, and that, on the other, the theory of the interdependence of the virtues was an idea already domesticated by Didymus' Christian predecessors. The idea of the interdependence of the virtues is a commonplace of Didymus' teaching without strict attachment to a particular philosophical school. He uses this teaching, however, to express his specifically Christian approach to virtue as connected with God and Christ, and employs the Beatitudes from the Sermon on the Mount to illustrate the interdependence of the virtues.[53] His purpose is to emphasize that the virtues are compatible with one another, lead to becoming one with God, and are connected with "right faith" which leads to unity of heart and soul.[54]

Although Didymus seems more intent on following the Platonic-Stoic emphasis on the unity of virtue, he is also acquainted with the Peripatetic distinction of virtues, though he does not give a systematic treatment of this idea. He knows the four cardinal virtues, which he lists according to the Stoic tradition (courage, justice, temperance, prudence).

In other instances, however, Didymus' distinction of virtues seems to betray a completely different approach. One distinction he makes is the contrast between specific virtues (αι κατ' ειδος αρεται) with virtue in general ('η καθολου και γενικη αρετη), usually identified with justice.[55] In this identification of justice as virtue in general, Didymus is taking up the Platonic tradition which connected the virtues with the three powers of the soul, with justice as the moderator preserving harmony among them. In this instance, his teaching on virtue reflects his anthropology.

---

[53] GenT 26.116–21: Virtue is unifying inasmuch as it has an interdependence. For the one who is temperate is also courageous and prudent and just, and the one who has one virtue has the rest of them. Just as in the case of the Beatitudes in the gospel, the one possessing the capacity of one Beatitude has also the capacities for the others. JobT 5.16–35; PsT 186.22-27.

[54] For vice is not unifying, but rather divisive. We say that there is an interdependence of the virtues, but not of the vices. . . . For all who take virtue up perfectly are one and become one with God. For example, all believers according to the right faith have one heart and one soul, while the base do not have this.

[55] PsT 59.3-7: God "led" [my soul] "along the paths of justice." The paths of justice are the specific virtues or the practices of the virtues. Often in the divine teachings the name justice signifies virtue in general. There is also a specific virtue thus called justice. If we say that there are four specific virtues, courage, justice, temperance and prudence, one of the virtues is called justice. Cf. JobT 393.14-19; PsT 101.10-15; 231.2-6; PsalmCat 1146 II.296.15-17; 1261 II.350.26-28; ZachT 106.24-31; 267.14-17. A. Gesché, *La Christologie du "Commentaire sur les Psaumes" découvert à Toura* (Gembloux: Éditions J. Duculot, 1962) 369.

What is important to notice in Didymus' description of justice is how he connects justice with practical virtue and faith in Jesus Christ.[56] Furthermore, he identifies justice with Christ himself on the basis of 1 John 2:29 and 2 Cor 5:21.[57] Here again, Didymus' foundation of virtue in God provides the key for the interpretation of his thought. If his purpose were simply to present a description of virtue, the reader would be left with a contradiction. For if he is contrasting virtue in general with specific virtues, he is speaking in terms of a relation of the whole to a part. If this is the case, he cannot at the same time hold for the unity of virtue and the interdependence of the virtues, for in such a relationship the distinction between general and particular disappears.[58] His real intention, however, is to demonstrate the connection between human virtues and their foundation in divine virtue. His connection of virtue with Christ is the way he mediates between the one virtue of God and the many expressions of this virtue in human beings. With this in mind, the question of virtue as general and specific is not something opposed to the unity of virtue, but merely the treatment of the same topic from a different point of view.

It was fundamentally Didymus' spirituality which led him to turn to the Aristotelian tradition rather than the Stoic for certain aspects of virtue. As already noted, the unitary vision of the human person in Stoic anthropology does not correspond to Didymus' divisions of the soul. Furthermore, the Stoics' unitary approach to both the human person and to virtue led them to the doctrine that divine and human virtue is one and the same, and that one either is virtuous or is not; there are no degrees. Therein lies the problem for Didymus. For him, God is the source of virtue. Humans are virtuous not by nature but by participation. Thus human virtue is a habit, a quality. It is by acquiring all the virtues perfectly that one comes again to be "like unto God." In the wake of Clement and Origen, Didymus was particularly sensitive to the different levels of perfection or virtue, of progress or

---

[56] The name "just one" is sometimes used for each just person, sometimes for the one justified "through faith in Jesus Christ." I say that practical virtue is often justice; "Learn to do justice you rulers of the earth; the godless one has been brought to an end." As I said, right belief is also called justice, the fitting comprehension of pious teachings. Cf. PsT 45.1-3; PsalmCat 42 I.141.8-16; 124 I.196.11-15; 955 II.348.8-17; ZachT 123.22–124.1; 163.27–164.4.

[57] 1 John 2:29: Everyone who does justice has been born from him. 2 Cor 5:21: He made the one who did not know sin to be sin for our sake, in order that we might become the justice of God in him. Cf. GenT 213.18-20; PsT 205.7-12; 234.6-9; ZachT 100.10-15; 107.23–108.2.

[58] J. H. Horn, "Antakoluthie der Tugenden und Einheit Gottes," *Jahrbuch für Antike und Christentum* 13 (1970) 7.

regress, which were the result of the exercise of free will. He thus avoided a theory of virtue which allowed no gradations in favor of one which made room for individual choice and differences. In attempting to reconcile the various theories of virtue, the important factor is not an attachment to any particular philosophical tradition. Rather it is Didymus' Christian anthropology and his concern for degrees of progress in perfection based on freedom which provide the key to his teaching on virtue.

In considering the question of the end, or goal, of virtue, we come to the heart of Didymus' teaching. It is necessary to see how he accepted the contemporary understanding of virtue and used this to express his view of life as a constant process toward a recovery of the image of God according to which people had originally been created and from which they had fallen by sin. The connection of virtue with the "image" is made in the section of the *Commentary on Genesis* which treats of the central verses Gen 1:26-28. Didymus explains that the soul, by participating in God, becomes God's image, just as the one who participates in virtue becomes an image of virtue.[59] The important point here is the parallel between God and virtue. This parallel is continued in the explanation of the text at Gen 3:6-8 where Adam and Eve hide from God's face. Didymus notes that, before their transgression, God used to walk together with them not as something "outside of them, but was with them." After their transgression, however, he points out that the one who leaves God behind does so not in a local sense, but as one "turning away from virtue."[60] This brings us to the heart of Didymus' theory on virtue, according to which virtue exists essentially in God and humans have virtue through participation in the Trinity. This is stated most clearly in the *Commentary on the Psalms*.[61] Thus the fundamental dynamic of Didymus' anthropology, the passage from the state of "image" of God to the state of "likeness,"

---

[59] GenT 57.26-29: We have said before that the human being is principally the *nous* and the soul. The latter, participating in God, by the very participation becomes the icon of Him, just as we say that virtue forms into its image the one who participates in it. Cf. JobT 141.19-33; PsT 19.8-12; 67.18-21; 205.7-12, 18-20; PsalmCat 725 II.85.12-16.

[60] GenT 87.2-4, 13-15: Before the transgression, he did not walk about with them as something outside of them, but was with them. . . . Thus the one who deserts God brings about his own hurt, for he deserts Him not as though in a place, but turning away from virtue. Cf. PsT 228.18-20.

[61] PsT 77.21-24: Again some say either out of ignorance or pretended knowledge that it is so with virtue that it has its existence in something else. But this is not true. It exists essentially in God, in the Trinity. By participation in the Trinity human beings have the good and the just and virtue. Even if these separate from virtue, it exists. It exists in God, this virtue according to which the virtuous become thus. Cf. PsT 53.14-16.

is accomplished through the acquisition of virtue. Virtue is able to bring this about because virtue is essentially identical with divine life and participation in virtue is the same as participation in God. Perfection in virtue thus brings one to a state of perfect likeness to God.

Didymus' treatment of the relation between God and virtue is more nuanced than the mere statement of an identity between them. More precisely, it is through Christ as mediator that this participation takes place. In this, Didymus is once again following Origen's lead. For Origen, virtue is properly predicated of Christ, whom he calls "complete animated and living virtue."[62] Although Didymus does not have so explicit a statement regarding the identity of Christ and virtue anywhere in his surviving works, it is clear that he made the same connection. Of particular importance in the question of Christ as virtue is the dual operation of Christ on the individual believer. As Crouzel points out, Christ not only *forms* the individual according to virtue, but, as virtue himself, *is formed* in us.[63] A passage from the *Commentary on the Psalms* has a similar idea with regard to Christ as "life" and "light," who both enlivens the individual and lives in him.[64]

This identification of Christ with virtue represents a greater precision of the general connection of virtue with God, and is connected with the son's status as image of God and humans beings as an "image of the image." At one point in the *Commentary on Genesis* Didymus states that the soul, "participating in God, becomes his image by the very participation, just as we say that virtue forms into an image the one participating in it." He then uses Gal 4:19 "until Christ is formed in you" to connect this process of forming according to the image with Christ, implicitly identifying virtue and the image of God with Christ.[65] Again, in the same section regarding Gen 3:6-8 where Adam and Eve hid from the face of God, this face is identified as the "only-begotten Son, being His image," and hiding from the face of God is

---

[62] *Comm. in Ioh.* XXXII.11. *C. Cels.* V.39. For an extensive presentation on Origen's teaching of Christ as virtue, see Crouzel, *Théologie de l'image de Dieu chez Origène*, 228–30.

[63] Crouzel, *Théologie de l'image de Dieu chez Origène*, 228.

[64] PsT 147.12-14: The one who understands that Jesus is life–for he says, "I am the life," and is the living Son of the living Father; "I live through the Father"—they do not ever forget him. For he is present to their understanding and ever enlightens them so that each one can say, "Christ lives in me." Such a one is in Christ and has Christ living and working in himself. Cf. Crouzel, *Théologie de l'image de Dieu chez Origène*, 227–8.

[65] GenT 57.27–58.2: [The soul] participating in God becomes His image through the very participation, just as we say that the one who participates in virtue is an image of virtue. Paul, who spoke in Christ, understood this and said to those he was exhorting to be formed into the image of Christ, "Until Christ is formed in you," teaching that the true understanding about Christ, when it has come into the soul, gives it the character of Christ and forms it into his image.

connected with not practicing virtue. In this case, too, there is the implicit identity of virtue with Christ.[66] Continuing with the same episode from Genesis 3, Didymus explains that Adam's response of hiding himself out of fear because he was naked shows that he had lost virtue, which is divine clothing. He then explains immediately this divine clothing of virtue by means of two citations of Paul: Rom 13:14, "Be clothed in Christ Jesus," and Col 3:12, "Be clothed in heartfelt mercy," which is interpreted as "the way of life according to Christ."[67]

The procedure of associating the various titles of Christ given in Scripture with different manifestations of his relationship with the soul is perhaps the chief way in which Christ is identified with virtue in Didymus' works. The basis for this procedure is the fact that intelligible realities, such as Christ or the human soul, can be understood under a variety of dispositions and names. Furthermore, Didymus adopts the Origenist doctrine that the *logos* adapts himself to the capacity of each individual so that, while remaining substantially the same, he acts on each person in the way best adapted for that person's progress. As was seen above, one of the chief titles connecting Christ and virtue is the title "justice." In addition to the verses given above, Christ is identified with justice on the basis of 1 Cor 1:30, "Who has become for us wisdom from God, justice and holiness and redemption." Didymus states in several instances, chiefly in the *Commentary on the Psalms*, that Christ does not *have* justice, but *is* justice.[68] Didymus identifies justice as "complete virtue." It is by sharing in virtue through participation in Christ, who is justice and complete virtue, that the individual virtues come into existence in us.[69] This concept of virtue ac-

---

[66] GenT 89.16-18, 24-25: The phrase, "And they hid from the face of God," can be taken in another sense when we understand that "face" is His only-begotten Son, who is his image. . . . For the one who hides himself from God's face so as not to practice virtue, but to give the appearance, is hiding himself under hypocrisy. Cf. PsalmCat 1002 II.241.8-13.

[67] GenT 92.10-14: He [Adam] says that the cause of his fear is the nakedness, which comes from having lost the virtue which was his covering. For virtue is a divine garment. Thus Paul exhorts, "Be clothed in Christ Jesus," and, "Be clothed in heartfelt mercy," adorn yourself with a merciful conduct and a way of life in conformity with Christ.

[68] For the connection with 1 Cor 1:30: GenT 5:12–6:11; PsT 156.3-5; 195.31–196.1; 277.10-11. For the identification of Christ as justice: PsT 4.10-12: And just as he [the Word] is not called just because he has justice, but because he is justice itself, so also he is not king from ordination, but is very king from king, as God from God. Cf. PsT 53.11-14; 137.30–138.1; PsalmCat 75 I.165.7-9; 268 I.264.17-19; 1244 II.342.25-30.

[69] PsT 199.22: But justice, which is closely pursued, is complete virtue. PsT 48.17-18: He [Jesus Christ] is the giver of the virtues, it is he, by participation in whom the virtues come to be. PsalmCat 981 II.232.21-23: The Lord is all these things which have been said,

counts for Didymus' description of virtue according to the seemingly contradictory images of the Stoic interdependence of virtues and the Peripatetic concept of general and specific virtues.[70] Since Christ is perfect virtue, humans, to the extent that they participate in Christ, show forth specific virtue or different aspects of virtue. After passing through all the degrees of progress, they eventually come to identity with Christ in perfect virtue. What allows Didymus to make this step is the concept of "focal meaning" applied to virtue. This is illustrated in Plotinus' discussion in *Enneads* I.2.2 as to the meanings of "likeness," whereby he distinguishes between the likeness of copy to copy and the likeness of archetype to copy.[71] The virtue in the archetype, Christ, which causes virtue in others, is not the same as in those who participate in the archetype. Yet, once perfected, the images come to be one with the archetype. It is in this procedure of adopting contemporary philosophical models and filling them with Christian content that Didymus displays his true interest and inspiration and reveals the fundamental role of his spirituality in forming his intellectual concepts.

For Didymus, then, Christ is the center both of his anthropology and of his teaching on virtue and perfection. Just as Christ is the image according to which humans are created in God's image, so also is Christ the perfect and complete virtue, through participation in which humans regain the status of likeness to God. This drama of creation, Fall, and return is the basis of a dynamic process which determines Didymus' entire anthropology and doctrine of stages of perfection. This dynamism leads him to elaborate a view of the human being as composed of body, soul, and spirit. In this view, it is the νους, also identified as the heart, which is in constant tension between the opposing realities of the heavy body of flesh and the spirit. Once it has

---

seeing that he is true God, not being true God in the possession of the aforementioned virtues but he is the source and substance of them. Cf. PsT 81.10-13; ZachT 100.32–101.7.

[70] H. J. Horn, "Antakoluthie der Tugenden und Einheit Gottes," *Jahrbuch für Antike und Christentum* 13 (1970) 26: Jesus Christus ist vollkommene Tugend. Durch Angleichung an ihn bewegt sich der Mensch auf Gott zu. ὁμοίωσις und Antakoluthie zeigen sich hier in einer christlichen Umdeutung. Die Vollkommenheit der wechselseitig miteinander verbundenen Tugenden führt nicht mehr zu einer Gottheit, die ihrerseits in antakoluthen Bezügen zahlreicher Hypostasen besteht, sondern sie ist die eine Kyrios, in dem sich ihre verflochtene Vielheit eint.

[71] Plotinus, *Enneads* I.2. J. Dillon, "Plotinus, Philo and Origen on the Grades of Virtue," *Platonismus und Christentum: Festschrift H. Dörries*, ed. Horst-Dieter Blume and Friedhelm Mann (Münster: Aschendorffsche Verlagsbuchhandlung, 1983) 96–101. K. Demura, "Ethical Virtues in Origen and Plotinus," *Origeniana Quinta*, ed. Robert J. Daly (Leuven: University Press, 1992) 299. For an erudite discussion of the concept of "focal meaning" see G.E.L. Owen, *Logic, Science and Dialectic: Collected Papers in Greek Philosophy* (London: Duckworth, 1986) 180–99.

been purified by the work of the Holy Spirit from any inclination to vice and attachment to passing, material realities, it can be reformed by virtue and regain its original state of perfection. Although the surviving works of Didymus do not give any indication of having been composed specifically for a monastic audience, they resound nevertheless with the important monastic concerns of the understanding of the Scriptures and the way of perfection. They preserve for us a witness to the continued legacy of Origen in the attempt to draw on all areas of human erudition to give an understanding of faith.

Basil of Caesarea and Purity of Heart

HARRIET A. LUCKMAN

In her 1969 article continuing the study of purity of heart, Juana Raasch turned her attention to the early ascetical movements which were most influential in the formation of later monastic theology and practice.[1] The fourth century was ripe with ascetical writings and movements. Some of these movements would fade with time, others would continue on and eventually become models for later forms of monastic lifestyles. Among the most well documented of ascetical writers of this period is Basil of Caesarea (330–79), founder of a community of ascetical Christians and bishop of Caesarea.

Scholarship on Basil has not been lacking in the past thirty years with monographs and articles discussing his ascetical works almost as much as his doctrinal. Among this proliferation of studies on the thought and actions of Basil of Caesarea, the only voice to date which has discussed his concept of purity of heart—the concept that influenced and sustained at a very fundamental level Basil's convictions and subsequent writings on both asceticism and doctrine—has been that of Juana Raasch. In gratitude for her work in this area of Basil's thought the following essay is dedicated to her memory. Her research on the topic will be brought forward as well as new insights and scholarship done on Basil's thought since the time of her writing.

In the space given me in this volume, I will briefly discuss the background to Basil's ascetical practices and the underlining purposes of those practices in his mind. I will close by examining Basil's concept of the ideal Christian as being one in whom the Holy Spirit dwelt and acted. It was this "Spirit-bearer" who realized the truth of right belief which consisted also in right action, and who indeed, as a consequence, was "pure of heart."

[1] See Juana Raasch, "The Monastic Concept of Purity of Heart and Its Sources, IV," *Studia Monastica* II (1969) 269–314.

BASIL'S ASCETICISM: BACKGROUND AND PURPOSE

While the entire *Asceticon*[2] of Basil may appear in large part as little more than a penal code of rules and regulations governing behavior, it is in fact a document which supposed the supernatural solidarity of the ascetics living within the community. Community prayer is used at the most important moments of its life, and mutual obedience is seen as quite another thing than a mere organizational tool. If Basil is less than enthusiastic about the eremitical life, it is without doubt because the ascetic enjoys within the community the many kinds of helps, supports, and various gifts of his or her brothers and sisters.[3]

Juana Raasch noted that among ascetic and monastic writers of the first four centuries of the common era there were certain conditions of life which were considered favorable if not essential for the attainment of purity and simplicity of heart. This concept can be found as early as the exhortation to avoid duplicity as found in the *Shepherd of Hermas*[4] and the "Two Ways" doctrine of the *Community Scroll* of Qumran[5] and the *Epistle of Barnabas*.[6] These ascetical disciplines—fasting, celibacy, separation from the "world," vigils, etc.—were best seen as conditions rather than ends in themselves. These disciplines only provided the ascetic with the atmosphere and surroundings considered necessary for him or her to receive the true agent of purification—the Holy Spirit—and so attain to purity of heart which is the equivalent to charity.[7]

Emmanuel Amand de Mendieta, whom Juana Raasch followed closely in interpreting Basil's asceticism, argued that for Basil purification and custody of the heart is the essential exercise of asceticism.[8]

---

[2] The questions concerning dating and translations of what has come down to us as the "Long" and "Short" Rules of Basil of Caesarea will not be dealt with in this article for reasons of economy. For the most recent assessment of discussions surrounding the dates of Basil's *Asceticon* see Phillip Rousseau, *Basil of Caesarea* (Berkeley: University of California Press, 1994) 354–9.

[3] *Regulae Fusius Tractae* 7 (PG 31.927C). See *The Long Rules*, q. 7, *Saint Basil: Ascetical Works*, trans. Monica Wagner (New York: Fathers of the Church, 1950) 247–52.

[4] See especially *The Shepherd of Hermas*, Mandates 10 and 11, in *The Apostolic Fathers: Greek Texts and English Translations of Their Writings*, 2d ed., trans. J. B. Lightfoot and J. R. Harmer; ed. and rev. Michael W. Holmes (Grand Rapids, Mich.: Baker, 1992) 401–10.

[5] See *The Community Rule (1QS)*, especially II, in *The Dead Sea Scrolls in English*, rev. and extended 4th ed., trans. and ed. Geza Vermes (Baltimore: Penguin Books, 1995) 71–2.

[6] See *The Epistle of Barnabas*, esp. chs. 1–5, in *The Apostolic Fathers*, 275–327.

[7] See Raasch, "The Monastic Concept of Purity of Heart," 269.

[8] See Emmanuel Amand de Mendieta, *L'ascèse monastique de S. Basile* (Maredsous: Éditions de Maredsous, 1948) 117. Mendieta's work on Basil is monumental and remains one of the major European voices on Basilian asceticism. However, not only is Mendieta's work dated in the areas of philosophy, but it is also clear he accepted the common

What neither Mendieta nor Juana ever mentions is the fact that Basil quotes Matt 5:8, "Blessed are the pure of heart for they shall see God," only once in the entire corpus of his works. That singular quote is to be found in Letter 8, a letter dedicated to a discussion of the Trinity and right belief. "Blessed are the pure of heart" is therefore used to refer to those who hold the right and proper understanding of God, an understanding capable only to those who live pure lives.[9] Basil considered this "blessedness" as consisting in the true contemplation of the realities which the Holy Scriptures brought forth, a contemplation which concerned the "inner man." In this vein, Basil considers the "kingdom" of heaven as being located within the human person. Following this statement on the pure of heart he quotes Luke 17:21, "for the kingdom of heaven is within you."[10] This aspect of Basil's understanding of purity of heart will be covered in the section on the Christian as a bearer of the Holy Spirit. In this particular section on Basil's asceticism as such, a word needs to be said about Eustathius of Sebaste, whose concepts of ascetical discipline influenced the young Basil in very significant ways. It is also possible that the ecclesiastical reactions against Eustathian asceticism could have focused Basil's stress on purity of heart and purification as a communal virtue and one that presupposed right belief. It could also be in a sense Basil's reaction to the exaggerated emphasis on external practices accompanied by the rather self-righteous elitism of the followers of Eustathius. Basil's one-time infatuation with Eustathius—a well-known philosopher who was gaining fame and followers among some groups of ascetics during the 330s—when Basil was himself a young student in

---

presuppositions of the early twentieth century which desired a dichotomy between moral and ethical behavior over against doctrinal. Such presuppositions lead Mendieta into focusing on Basil's ascetical works as something "other" than his doctrinal, and in effect opposing the moral sphere against the intellectual. Mendieta's life at the time of this writing on Basil was also that of a Benedictine monk of Maredsous. His concept of what was in effect "monastic" in Basil is indeed viewed through this early-twentieth-century Western European prism. Juana Raasch followed Mendieta's lead quite innocently. Her work consequently suffers from wishing to see these artificial dichotomies in patristic thought and in a concept of monasticism that would not have been shared by Basil in the fourth century.

[9] "But I trust in God that you, because of your pure lives, will bring forth fruit thirty, sixty, and a hundred fold. For it is said, 'Blessed are the pure of heart, for they shall see God.' And, brethren, consider not the kingdom of heaven as aught other than the true contemplation of the realities, which the Holy Scriptures call blessedness; 'for the kingdom of heaven is within you,'" *Epistle 8*. See *St. Basil: The Letters,* trans. Roy J. Defarrari, Loeb Classical Library 190 (Cambridge, Mass.: Harvard University Press, 1972) 89. (*PG.* 32.245C–267B).

[10] *Epistle 8*, see note 9.

Athens is all too evident in Letter 2, and may in fact have been the driving force behind Basil's sojourns into Egypt.[11]

Eustathius of Sebaste (ca. 300–ca. 378) practiced a radical form of ascetical life which eventually prompted the calling of the Council of Gangra in 355.[12] Eustathius and his followers would not eat meat, would not celebrate the liturgy in the homes of married clergy, shunned mainline Church functions and regulations, forbade marriage as unworthy of the true follower of Christ, wore extravagant outfits that caused attention in the marketplaces, insisted that the female members dressed as the men and cut their hair very short. They also scorned the sacraments and claimed that they had all the spiritual help they needed via prayer.[13] Eustathius' group was seen as a threat to the unity of the Church and his notions were often censured by the ecclesiastical authorities of his day.[14] Nevertheless Eustathius' own reputation for holiness and upright conduct, as well as his heroic asceticism, put him in many ways above the reproach of his censors in matters of personal conduct. Around 350 to 355 Eustathius became a close friend to Basil's family, who wrote to Basil—then in studies in Athens—of Eustathius' heroism. Basil resolved to meet him and in Letter 2 one reads of his almost "breathless" search to catch up with Eustathius who had then traveled into Egypt. As Charles Frazee has suggested it seems clear from reading Letter 2 that Basil's journeys into Egypt were not to observe and be edified by Egyptian hermits and ascetics but rather to find Eustathius.[15] It also seems clear that Basil then adopted an Eustathian lifestyle once he returned home and set up his own retreat on the family estate at Pontus. It was at Pontus where he and Gregory Naziansus would spend the next ten years in solitude, prayer, reading of Scripture, and the study of Origen's *Philokalia*.

---

[11] For interesting studies on the influence of Eustathius of Sebaste on the young Basil see Charles A. Frazee, "Anatolian Asceticism in the Fourth Century: Eustathios of Sebastea and Basil of Caesarea," *The Catholic Historical Review* 66 (1980) 16–33; and J. Gribomont, "Saint Basile et le monachisme enthousiaste," *Irénikon* 53:2 (1980) 123–44.

[12] For information and translation of the Canons of the Council of Gangra, see O. Larry Yarbrough, "Canons from the Council of Gangra," *Ascetic Behavior in Greco-Roman Antiquity: A Source Book*, ed. Vincent L. Wimbush (Minneapolis: Fortress Press, 1990) 448–55.

[13] Ibid.

[14] What the exact practices and beliefs of Eustathius were we cannot know for certain. Reports of his conduct and beliefs survive only via texts written by his opponents. These antagonists were in fact bishops who felt Eustathius was wielding too much influence and consequent discord among their flocks. Eustathian asceticism and the entire context of the fourth-century debates concerning ascetical lifestyles would be well served by more in-depth study.

[15] See Frazee, "Anatolian Asceticism in the Fourth Century," 21.

It seems during this retreat period Basil began writing what would later be called his "Long" and "Short" Rules (365–370), which are in fact collections of questions and answers between himself and his brethren concerning the smooth running of communities of devout Christians. It is important to note at this point that Basil never calls those in his communities "monks." He refers to them, as will Macarius after him, simply as "Christians." While there may be different theories as to why Basil did this, it seems most reasonable to conclude that Basil did not want his ascetics to consider themselves an elite or special group, somehow separate from or "apart" from the larger Church community.[16] This could be due in large part to Basil's wanting to avoid the censures which befell Eustathius who indeed wanted his community to be considered "apart" and in many ways "above" the ecclesiastical Church. It could also be, as Paul Fedwick would like to show, Basil's own notion that such ideals should animate the entire body of the Church.[17] True holiness—or in Basil's mind the true fruits of the presence of God's Spirit within the faithful and worthy person—consisted in building up the body of Christ (the Church) by sharing the gifts of the Spirit with one another and so helping one another attain to salvation. Chapter 9 of his *De Spiritu Sancto* is a classic example that the fruits of holiness—the Spirit dwelling within the worthy Christian—were shown by acts of kindness and by aiding and abetting one another. Basil would write:

> Through His [the Holy Spirit] aid hearts are lifted up, the weak are held by the hand, and they who are advancing are brought to perfection. Shining upon those that are cleansed from every spot, He makes them spiritual by fellowship with Himself. Just as when a sunbeam falls on bright and transparent bodies, they themselves become brilliant too, and shed forth a fresh brightness from themselves, so souls wherein the Spirit dwells, illuminated by the Spirit, themselves become spiritual, and send forth their grace to others.[18]

The type of community Basil would envision and found for those who were so illumined by the Spirit was not strictly a "monastery" in the sense of a Pachomian Koinonia, or what in the West has become

---

[16] For major works concerning Basil's concept of the Church see Paul Fedwick, *The Church and the Charism of Leadership in Basil of Caesarea*, Studies and Texts 45 (Toronto: Pontifical Institute of Mediaeval Studies, 1979); and Herman Dörries, *De spiritu sancto: Der Beitrag des Basilius zum Abschluß des trinitarischen Dogmas*, Abhandlungen der Akademie der Wissenschaften in Göttingen, Philologisch-historische Klasse 3, ser. 39 (Göttingen: Vandenhoeck & Ruprecht, 1956).

[17] See Fedwick, *The Church and the Charism of Leadership*, 97–100.

[18] *De Spiritu Sancto* 9.23. SC 17.147 (PG 32.107A–110C).

associated with the Rule of Benedict. Nor would Basil have considered those who lived in his communities "monks" as we would understand the term today. Rather, Basil's aim, and indeed one of his greatest achievements, was to reconcile the two types of ascetical life. He would attempt to combine the eremitical style of St. Antony and the desert hermits of Egypt with the communal styles of Pachomius and the Syrian community which composed the *Liber Graduum*.[19] By so doing, he would effectively bring them into the very heart—and episcopacy—of the Church. Basil's communities would be responsible for building and running orphanages, hospitals, and charitable enterprises of all sorts open not only to fellow ascetics, but to any person in dire need.

Basil saw the ascetical life as having one aim: the soul's salvation.[20] This salvation was to be gained by humility and by a "cleansing of the Royal image" within us, hence making space for God to dwell.[21] Basil saw sanctification coming not from geographical separation as the Egyptian ascetics had, but rather solely in living and being in the Holy Spirit.[22] He wanted a withdrawal of the passions as had been taught by ascetics—Christian as well as non-Christian—before him. However, he saw this "withdrawal" worked out most successfully in community with others, especially in the observance of love and mutual support.[23] It was in this way one would grow in the Holy Spirit. Detachment was also a large part of the person's sanctification[24] and the community should be governed by the bonds of peace.[25] In *Morals 60.1* Basil speaks of the necessity of sharing our gifts with one another and

---

[19] For information concerning the document known to us as the *Liber Graduum* (the Book of Steps) see Robert Kitchen, "The Gattung of the Liber Graduum: Implications for a Sociology of Asceticism," *IV Symposium Syriacum 1984: Literary Genres in Syriac Literature*, ed. H.J.W. Drijvers, R. Lavenant, C. Molenberg, and G. J. Reinink (Rome: Pont. Institutum Studiorum Orientalium, 1987) 173–82. I am also indebted to Mr. Kitchen of Oxford University for the gracious sharing of his yet unpublished translation of the *Liber Graduum*. See also Arthur Vööbus, *History of Asceticism in the Syrian Orient I*, Corpus scriptorum Christianorum orientalium 14 (Louvain: Secretariat du CorpusSCO, 1958) 178–84. Dr. Deirdre A. Dempsey discusses the Syrian concepts of purity of heart and asceticism in this volume. I refer the reader to her article for more information on the subject of Syrian theology, sources, contemporary scholarship, etc.

[20] See "Ascetical Discourse," *Saint Basil: Ascetical Works*, 217.

[21] *De Spiritu Sancto* 9.23. SG 17.147, PG 32.107A–110C.

[22] *De Spiritu Sancto* 26.62. SG 17.228, PG 32.181C–182C.

[23] See note 3 above.

[24] *Reg. Fus. Tract.* 32. PG 31.994D–995C. Also *The Long Rules*, q. 32, *Saint Basil: Ascetical Works*, 295–6.

[25] *Reg. Fus. Tract.* 34. PG 31.999B–1002D. *The Long Rules*, q. 34, *Saint Basil: Ascetical Works*, 298–301.

inasmuch as the gifts of the Spirit are varied and one individual cannot receive them all, nor all receive the same gift, everyone should soberly and thankfully remain content with the gift granted to him and all should be in accord with one another in the charity of Christ, as are the members of the body.[26]

Basil also sees the harmonious ordering of the Church as a gift of the Holy Spirit,[27] and it was also by obedience to lawful and worthy superiors—including worthy bishops—that one was united to the Holy Spirit who operates to bring us back to paradise and so win for us the adoption of sons.[28] In consonance with the apocalyptic Syrian ascetical traditions before him, Basil also saw his communities participating in the heavenly choirs, standing as the watchers before the throne of God.[29] All the practices and aims of the ascetical lifestyle were to bring salvation to the individual soul—including a right belief—and to share those gifts for the building up of the Church. Ascetical practices were intended to facilitate in the Christian the cleansing and purifying of the "inner man" and hence allow one to become a true vessel for the indwelling of the Holy Spirit.

THE PURE IN HEART AS BEARERS OF THE SPIRIT

The end of the fourth century was beset not only with discussions concerning asceticism but also among other things by the question concerning the divinity and consubstantiality of the Holy Spirit. This debate was waged against the pro-Nicene party by proponents of what came to be known as Macedonianism, which later developed into Pneumatomochianism.[30] The task of the pro-Nicenes was to defend

---

[26] *The Moralia* 60. *PG* 31.793B–796A. *The Morals* 60, *Saint Basil: Ascetical Works*, 144-145.
[27] *De Spiritu Sancto* 14.39. *SC* 17.181; *PG* 32.139D–142B.
[28] *De Spiritu Sancto* 15.36. *SC* 17.171; *PG* 32.127D–128D.
[29] In *De Spiritu Sancto* 9.23. *SC* 17.147; *PG* 32.109A–110C. Basil speaks of our heavenly citizenship and our place in the chorus of angels. The concept of standing as "Watchers" before the throne of God can be found in Syrian ascetical/liturgical material prior to Basil as echoing Daniel, the books of Enoch, as well as the Sibylline Oracles and the Testament of the Twelve Patriarchs. See *The Old Testament Pseudepigrapha*, vol. 1, ed. James H. Charlesworth (Garden City, N.Y.: Doubleday, 1985). For a study of angelology in Jewish apocalyptic see Ithamar Gruenwald, *Apocalyptic and Merkavah Mysticism* (Leiden: Brill, 1980).
[30] See Emmanuel Amand de Mendieta, *The "Unwritten" and "Secret" Apostolic Traditions in the Theological Thought of St. Basil of Caesarea*, Scottish Journal of Occasional Papers 13 (Edinburgh: Oliver & Boyd, 1965) 23–4. Among the opponents of this new doctrine which in effect reduced the Holy Spirit to either a creature or an impersonal active power within the divine being were Athanasius, Cyril of Jerusalem, Basil of Caesarea, Gregory of Nazianzus, Didymus the Blind, Hilary of Poitiers, Ambrose of Milan, as well as a number of anonymous writers. See Pia Luislampe, *Spiritus vivificans:*

the divinity, consubstantiality, and activity of the Holy Spirit on the basis of Scripture, tradition, and liturgical practice. They were also concerned with applying this doctrine to the practical and pastoral needs of their respective communities.[31]

The role of the Holy Spirit in prophecy and teaching had been an element in the Church long before it became a doctrinal issue in the fourth century. The *Shepherd of Hermas* allots a role of great importance to those considered "possessed of the divine spirit"[32] and the thread continues especially strong in ascetical writings of the subsequent centuries.[33]

The biography of Antony of Egypt, the *Vita Antonii* of St. Athanasius written sometime around 357, provided a prominent example of the practical and pastoral application of the doctrine concerning the Holy Spirit and the spiritual power of the "holy man."[34] Under the pen of Athansius, Antony was portrayed not only as a "man of God"—a follower of Christ—but also as a humble "pneumatophor" whose life was in fact a spiritual "pneumatophony."[35] Antony became through his life of ascesis the means of revelation of the Holy Spirit for the whole world. Through his life of prayer and fasting, this simple "illiterate" Egyptian monk—to use the polemic of Athanasius—became the "pneumatophor" through whose struggles and victories over the demons the power of the Holy Spirit dwelling within him became evi-

---

Grundzüge einer Theologie des Heiligen Geists nach Basilius von Caesarea (Münster: Aschendorff, 1981) 11–23. Also de Mendieta, *The "Unwritten" and "Secret" Apostolic Traditions*, 21–5.

[31] See Paul Fedwick, *The Church and the Charism of Leadership*, 77–100.

[32] See *The Shepherd of Hermas*, Mandate 11:7-10, in *The Apostolic Fathers*.

[33] The notion of an indwelling of the Holy Spirit comes out especially strong in Aphrahat's *Demonstrations*, especially *Demonstration VI, "Of Monks."* See Aphrahat, *Nicene and Post-Nicene Fathers*, vol. 13, 2d series, ed. Philip Schaff and Henry Wace (Peabody, Mass.: Hendrickson Publishers, 1995).

[34] See Athanasius, *The Life of Antony and the Letter to Marcellinus*, Classics of Western Spirituality, trans. and intro. Robert C. Gregg (New York: Paulist Press, 1980).

[35] The term "pneumatophoros" goes back to the hermetic writings and in adjectival form to the Old Testament prophets, such as in Hos 9:7 and Zeph 3:4. In the Christian tradition the term was first used in *The Shepherd of Hermas*, Mandate 11:16. Translators have experienced difficulties in rendering "pneumatophoros" into English. For example Benedicta Ward's translation *The Sayings of the Desert Fathers: The Alphabetical Collection* (Kalamazoo, Mich.: Cistercian Publications, 1975) 6 reads, "Some say of St. Anthony that he was 'Spirit-borne' that is carried along by the Holy Spirit, but he would ever speak of this to men. Such men see what is happening in the world as well as knowing what is going to happen." Kirsopp Lake translates Mandate 11:16 of *The Shepherd* as, "Test then, from his life and deed the man who says that he is inspired." See Kirsopp Lake, *Apostolic Fathers*, vol. 2 (Cambridge, Mass.: Harvard University Press, 1992). For a recent and most insightful analysis of "Spirit" and "prophecy" in the first century of the common era, see John R. Levison, *The Spirit in First-Century Judaism* (Leiden: Brill, 1997).

dent. Antony's holiness as this "pneumatophor" was apparent also in such charismatic gifts as the reading of hearts and prophecy.[36] In the same century as Antony and Athanasius in Egypt, many forms of communal ascetical life were taking root in Syria and the Mesopotamian regions as the *Liber Graduum* and various texts on other ascetical groups reveal.[37]

It is against this previous ascetical background that Basil's moderation can be appreciated. It also serves to highlight Basil's own grasp and development of pneumatology and the ascetical goals of the Christian, all of which were directed toward purity of heart. Basil saw the human person as an image of God and a bearer of the Holy Spirit through the prism of ascetical perfection.[38] This was so because the ascetic ideally sought nothing more than to become a perfect Christian, not only in virtue and deed, but also in a proper understanding of the Scriptures and of the mysteries of the Christian faith.

In Basil's ascetical writings, the ascetic is portrayed as a "pneumatophor," that is, as an active vessel and distributor of the Holy Spirit with all the accompanying gifts. Basil also appreciated the activity of the Holy Spirit in the life of the smaller ascetical community as well as in the Church as a whole, as can be seen in his legislative, polemical, and dogmatic writings. As Fedwick notes, while Egyptian Christians desirous of working out their salvation and sanctification were advised to abandon—by physical and emotional withdrawal—the world of human relationships to seek in the wilderness the ideal environment in which to attain "holiness," Basil proposes instead a seeming paradox. According to Basil, the "ambiance" or the "place" (χώρα) of Christian sanctification and worship is not to be found in any physical or geographical location, but essentially consists in living and being in the Holy Spirit who is the "place" (χώρα) of those being

---

[36] As to how "illiterate" and "simple-minded" Antony really was see Samuel Rubenson, *The Letters of St. Antony: Monasticism and the Making of a Saint*, Studies in Antiquity and Christianity (Minneapolis: Fortress Press, 1995). From Rubenson's study and translation of these letters we have a much different Antony than the one Athansius presents. See also David Brakke, *Athanasius and the Politics of Asceticism* (Oxford: Clarendon Press, 1995) for an excellent study on the literary style and motivations of Athanasius.

[37] For the most complete evaluation on the *Liber Graduum* I am indebted to the yet unpublished translation and introduction to the *Liber* by Robert Kitchen, Oxford. Also, see Columba Stewart, *"Working the Earth of the Heart": The Messalian Controversy in History, Texts, and Language to A.D. 431* (Oxford: Clarendon Press, 1991) for an excellent study of the movement condemned as "Messalianism," an issue Basil would not have been ignorant of.

[38] See D. L. Balás, "The Unity of Human Nature in St. Basil's and Gregory of Nyssa's Polemics against Eunomius," *Studia Patristica* 14 (Berlin: Akademie-Verlag, 1976) 275–81.

sanctified.³⁹ For Basil, the withdrawal of the passions and the subsequent quiet (ησυξια) are precisely intended to facilitate this contact and even entry of the soul into the "ambiance" or "place" of the Holy Spirit.⁴⁰

The influence of Neoplatonism on Basil of Caesarea has been studied in depth,⁴¹ and it appears clear that Basil followed an ascending notion of purification as was common among the Platonic traditions as well as among the Jewish apocalyptic literature so influential among the early Syrian ascetics. Basil also is no exception to the rule among early Christian asceticism that it was the passions of the human body that kept us for the most part from union with God. Such an understanding appears particularly acute in his work on the Holy Spirit. Basil writes:

> Now the Holy Spirit is not brought into intimate association with the soul by local approximation. How indeed could there be a corporeal approach to the incorporeal? This association results from the withdrawal of the passions which, coming afterwards gradually on the soul from its friendship to the flesh, have alienated it from its close relationship with God. Only then, after one is purified from the shame whose stain he took through his wickedness, and has come back to his natural beauty, and as it were cleansing the Royal Image and restoring its ancient form, only then is it possible for him to draw near to the Paraclete.⁴²

While Basil viewed the human body in terms that appear particularly negative to modern readers, he is nonetheless well aware that the greatest renunciations—the most important and often most painful battles—take place unseen within the human heart. These battles are played out on the field of charity and in attaining a proper perception of reality and of the faith.

Basil's concept of purity as evidenced in his moral and ascetical writings appears to be located in the heart in the sense of the scriptural purity of heart concerned with the inner impulses and "thoughts." As noted in Letter 8, the purity of heart that would see God is also situated in right and proper belief concerning the Scripture teachings and

---

³⁹ *De Spiritu Sancto* 26.62. SC 17.228, PG 179B–186C. See Fedwick, *The Church and the Charism of Leadership*, 31.

⁴⁰ *De Spiritu Sancto* 26.63. SC 17.229, PG 183B–186C. See Fedwick, *The Church and the Charism of Leadership*, 31.

⁴¹ For an interesting study on Basil's debt to Plotinus and the *Enneads* concerning the question of passions and ascending purification, see John M. Rist, "Basil's Neoplatonism: Its Background and Nature," *Basil of Caesarea, Christian, Humanist, Ascetic: A Sixteen-hundredth Anniversary Symposium*, ed. Paul Fedwick (Toronto, Ont.: Pontifical Institute of Mediaeval Studies, 1981) 207.

⁴² *De Spiritu Sancto* 9.23. SC 17.147, PG 32.107A–110C.

our understanding of God. The two cannot be separated in Basil's mind. He also sees sin and evil originating not from "outside" the human person in the sense of demons attacking from "without," but rather it is the evil thoughts cultivated in the heart which are essentially the sources of sin. These evil thoughts and sins arise when the natural seeds of goodness are neglected and left uncultivated.[43] According to the thought of Basil—following his early and ever present teacher Origen—the human spirit is created in order to "remember" God. Material things have, in their own manner, been destined to evoke in the human spirit this very remembrance. Such is their true nature. This was the situation in paradise before the Fall. However, Adam turned this "remembrance," his thoughts and yearnings, away from God and directed them instead to the things of creation. This in turn served to make created and perishable things in effect gods and ends in themselves. By "remembering" God, we can return to the contemplation of true lasting beauty and again become "intimate" with God. By taking part in the death of Christ symbolized by the purification of baptism, the human person is united to the Holy Spirit and it is "this Spirit who operates to re-establish Paradise, the ascent to the kingdom of heaven, the return to God through the adoption of sons."[44] Fantasizing and empty imaginings which did not include or relate to God were in Basil's mind to be avoided as lacking reality, and as such considered unworthy of a true disciple of Christ. Hence custody of the heart was primarily a mental effort in order to maintain the constant remembrance of God, for it is thus "that we can excel in the love of God."[45] Philip Rousseau has rightly remarked that the sense of God's presence provided the environment for religious action, and indeed was itself the very source of such action.[46] Basil taught that one should do everything as if God were watching every move, trusting that such an awareness would promote correct behavior.[47] The implication here was that even amidst great and distracting activities one could remain in an abiding stillness. Basil had highest praise for the one who was ὅμοιος ἀεὶ αὐτὸς ἑαυτῷ διαμένων (roughly translated as "always remaining the same within himself"). Achieving such stillness within the heart depended to some extent on the ability to focus one's life and thoughts, just as one might focus attention on a psalm verse.[48] Basil

[43] *Regulae brevius tractatae* 75 (*PG* 31.1273A-B).
[44] *De Spiritu Sancto* 15.36. *SC* 17.171, *PG* 32.127D–128D.
[45] *Regulae fusius tractatae* 5.2 (*PG* 31.921B); *Saint Basil: Ascetical Works,* 243.
[46] See Philip Rousseau, *Basil of Caesarea* (Berkeley: University of California Press, 1994) 126–8.
[47] *Regula brevius tractatae* 294 (*PG* 31.1289B–1292B).
[48] Ibid., 279 (*PG* 1279A).

writes in Epistle 293 that "Neither losses nor illness nor the other inconveniences of life shall touch the virtuous man [τοῦ σπουδαίου] so long as he keeps his mind on God."[49] This concentrated stillness which one built around oneself came to constitute a place, a sanctification, the preservation of which consisted in "clinging wholly to God without interruption at all times, and studying to please him."[50] It was, however, a quiet and a type of peace that was to be shared. According to Rufinus' Latin translation, it was a stillness that had a social effect, and the closeness of God's presence was thus made visible to all.[51]

This notion of stillness and purity of heart being achieved via the remembrance of God can be seen echoed in letters, ascetical and otherwise. Returning to Letter 2, we can see how having achieved a continual remembrance of God one can soar to the heights of prayer and virtue. Basil writes:

> Prayer is to be commended, for it engenders in the soul a distinct conception of God. And the indwelling of God is this—to hold God ever in memory, His shrine established within us. We thus become temples of God whenever earthly cares cease to interrupt the continuity of our memory of Him, whenever unforeseen passions cease to disturb our minds, and the lover of God, escaping them all, retires to God, driving out the passions which tempt him to incontinence, and abides in the practices which conduce to virtue.[52]

In Letter 22 Basil warns the Christian not to be "easily drawn away by anything from the remembrance of God and from His will and judgments." He admonishes that there "should be no clamor, or any scene or commotion wherein anger is expressed, or any other elation of the mind which draws us away from the full assurance of God's presence."[53] We can find the most poignant summary of this doctrine in Basil's letter to a distant friend:

> I exhort you to cleave zealously to the salvation of your soul, moderating all the affections of the flesh by reason, and constantly keeping the thought of God firmly established in your soul, as in a most holy temple; and in every word and in every deed hold before your eyes the judgement of Christ, so that, when all your several activities have been

---

[49] *Epistle* 293 (PG 32.1034D–1036B).
[50] Rufinus' Latin translation of the Rule of Basil reads: *"adhaerere deo ex integro et sino aliqua intermissione in omni tempore sollicitum esse et studium genere placendi ei."* Basil *regula: A Rufino latine versa,* Corpus scriptorum ecclesiasticorum latinorum, ed. Klaus Zelzer (Vindobonae : Hoelder-Pichler-Tempsky, 1986) 173.
[51] Basil *regula: A Rufino latine versa.* CSEL 86.174.
[52] *Epistle* 2.4 (PG 32.230B).
[53] *Epistle* 22.1 (PG 32.288B).

brought before that strict and terrible scrutiny, they may bring you glory on the day of reward, when you are accounted worthy of praise in the presence of every creature.[54]

The love of God achieved via continual remembrance of God was the vehicle as well as the end of "purity of heart" and in effect the entire monastic life. It is a love that is efficacious, "the love of God, which simultaneously arouses us to carry out the commandments of God and is itself perpetually and constantly guarded by them."[55] Since Christ has indicated that keeping his commandments is the best indication of love for him, and the best means of remaining in this love, this should be the aim of all the actions of the sincere Christian. Basil would write: "We have set one goal and one single rule for our actions: to keep the commandments of God in a manner pleasing to him."[56]

Basil would be in harmony with the Syrian tradition of prayer as found in Aphrahat that a pure heart is a heart that has but one purpose and aim.[57] It is a heart in the sense of the mind and inner-most part of the person, that is directed to God and to the keeping of the commandments of love in all activities. That is in itself the best sacrifice and is itself a pure and continual prayer. Basil would write: "We must be careful not to think that every prayer consists of audible syllables; it is rather from a purpose of the soul, from virtuous actions which include all of life, that prayer will take on its full meaning."[58]

Basil sees this intention of continual prayer as what could be termed "purity of heart." He would write, "Who is the pure in heart? He who has not to blame himself for spurning the commandment of God or leaving it undone or neglecting it."[59] There is a totality about the Christian's obligation to keep the commandments. When they are kept in their totality, purity of heart—which includes the entire self as well as thoughts and impulses—is achieved. Basil gives its highest expression to the insistence of the early monks on the Christian's obligation to carry out all the commandments of Christ without exception in a combination of literal fidelity and a certain liberty of spirit. For Basil it was a means of establishing the Gospel as the norm of the Christian life.[60]

[54] *Epistle* 146 (*PG* 32.595B).
[55] *Regulae fusius tractatae* 5.2 (*PG* 31.919B); *Saint Basil: Ascetical Works*, 243.
[56] *Regulae fusius tractatae* 5.3 (*PG* 31.919C); *Saint Basil: Ascetical Works*, 243.
[57] Aphrahat, *Demonstration* IV, "On Prayer," *The Syriac Fathers on Prayer and the Spiritual Life*, intro. and trans. Sebastian Brock (Kalamazoo, Mich.: Cistercian Publications, 1987) 5–28.
[58] *Homily 5 in Martyrem Iulittam* 3 (*PG* 31.244A).
[59] *Regulae brevius tractatae* 280 (*PG* 31.514B); *Saint Basil: Ascetical Works*, 337.
[60] See Raasch, "The Monastic Concept of Purity of Heart," 311.

In the mind of Basil the obligation to keep the commandments in their totality is binding on those in all stages of the Christian life, beginners as well as the more advanced. However, it is possible to fulfill all the commandments out of a slavish fear of punishment or a mercenary hope for reward. Such dispositions did not constitute the pure of heart. The heart in Basil's mind was not pure unless the commandments were fulfilled completely, not only by omitting none of them, but also in the sense of carrying them out in an integral and perfect manner so as to please God. In *De Baptismo,* the question is asked as to whether it is safe for one who has not freed his heart from a consciousness of iniquity to perform sacerdotal functions. The answer interprets Lev 21:16, 17, 21 in the sense that a "blemish" is taken to mean "a commandment partially or incompletely observed or fulfilled in a manner not pleasing to God, some human consideration such as a wound or leprosy, manifesting itself in the observance."[61]

It was charity and the manner with which one carried out the commandments that determined whether a person's heart was pure and hence freed from all sin and imperfection. Basil would write: "For indeed when a man does the will of God but not as God wills, nor with a disposition of love towards his neighbor, his zeal for good works is fruitless, according to the will of our Lord Jesus Christ (Mt. 6:5; 23:5, I Cor. 13:3)."[62] Juana Raasch noticed the similarity between Basil's concept of the natural innateness of this love with certain Stoic teachings.[63] She would note that the seeds of this love are as natural and as innate as the Stoic *spermatikos logos* which grows and develops spontaneously "in the school of God's commandments."[64] She cites Basil on this point where he writes: "For nothing is so characteristic of our nature as to associate with one another, to need one another, and to love our kind."[65] Purity of heart for Basil can then be seen as a type of single hearted disposition toward the keeping of all the commandments of Christ for no other reason than love: love of Christ and love for one an-

---

[61] Basile de Césarée, *Sur le baptême,* Source chrétiennes 357, ed. U. Neri; trans. with intro. and notes by Jeanne Ducatillon (Paris: Cerf, 1989) 211.

[62] *Regulae fusius tractatae* prol. (PG 31.896); *Saint Basil: Ascetical Works,* 223.

[63] Raasch, "The Monastic Concept of Purity of Heart," 311–2. Juana recognized certain similarities between Basil and the Stoics, especially with regard to the Stoic concept of innate knowledge. What remains to be examined further are similarities in Basil's thought concerning ethics as well. While it is not possible to cover the matter in detail within this essay, I would nonetheless refer the interested reader to Martha Nussbaum's careful and accessible study of Stoic ethics in her *The Therapy of Desire: Theory and Practice in Hellenistic Ethics* (Princeton, N.J.: Princeton University Press, 1994) 316–483.

[64] *Regulae fusius tractatae* 2.1 (PG 31.908B); *Saint Basil: Ascetical Works,* 233.

[65] *Regulae fusius tractatae* 3.1 (PG 31.917A) (917A); *Saint Basil: Ascetical Works,* 239.

other. In this way, Basil sees the commandment to love as being twofold wherein the second commandment "to love one another as I have loved you" (John 13:34) is as great as the first and the distinctive mark of the true Christian.[66] The perfect flowering of charity is in effect the basis for all action.[67] Basil criticized the eremitical lifestyle for this very reason: the loner cannot carry out all the commandments, especially the law of love.[68] Basil never ceases to write that Christians must live a communal—or perhaps better put a social—life in order to be fully in agreement with the Gospel. In this well-known teaching of Basil it holds true that the hermit—while having the theory of the Christian life—does not have the practice. Basil would write:

> Whose feet will you wash? Whom will you care for? In comparison with whom will you be last if you live by yourself? What about the good and pleasant thing—brothers living together in harmony—which the Holy Spirit compared to the perfumed ointment flowing down from the High Priest's beard? How can this be achieved in the solitary life?[69]

Basil would hold that the eremitical ideals of the Egyptian deserts limited the purification and custody of the heart to a personal sanctification. This concern with personal holiness falls far short in Basil's mind of the demands insisted upon by the Gospel teachings of loving one's neighbor. Basil would consider it impossible to achieve purity of heart which consists of keeping all the commandments out of love in a life that was only devoted to self-purification in isolation.

On the other hand, Basil also was not unaware of the sin of his neighbor. In the *Shorter Rules* Basil counseled that purity of heart involved not a blindness to the weaknesses and failings of another, but rather required a hatred if not an outright horror of sin in oneself and in others. Basil would write:

> How can the soul be persuaded that it is pure from sin? By a hatred and horror of sin in oneself and in others. Towards sinners the pure in soul feels a certain fearful sympathy, that is a fear of similar tendencies in himself that could lead him to do likewise.[70]

---

[66] *Moralia* 80.22 (*PG* 31.867C–D); *Saint Basil: Ascetical Works*, 203.

[67] *Regulae fusius tractatae* prol. (*PG* 31.896). As Juana Raasch notes this is the characteristic teaching of Clement of Alexandria and of Origen concerning the perfect Christian life as one of liberty, spontaneity, and love. Clement certainly took much of this from the Stoic notion of the "wise man" as well as from New Testament writings, particularly the Pauline letters. Interesting to note is that while Clement makes perfect action depend on *gnosis*, Basil defines it as moved by love (αγαπε). See Juana Raasch, "The Monastic Concept of Purity of Heart," 312, n. 224.

[68] *Regulae fusius tractatae* 7 (*PG* 31.928-933); *Saint Basil: Ascetical Works*, 246.

[69] *Regulae fusius tractatae* 7.4 (*PG* 31.933B); *Saint Basil: Ascetical Works*, 252.

[70] *Regulae brevius tractatae* 96 (*PG* 1290).

This horror of sin and contamination would cause Basil to shun the company of others who may not have measured up to his particular standards of perfection. It was a practice of his that often lead to his own self-imposed isolation and sense of intense loneliness which he would come to lament. In an early and somewhat idealistically naïve letter, Basil would write, "The friend refrains from nothing, not even that which gives pain."[71] Yet some years later in a condescending and insensitive letter written to an allegedly offensive layman, Basil, now a bishop, betrayed more pain on his own part "for forgetfulness of friends" and that "haughtiness which is engendered by power."[72] Apparently his own capacity for friendship had been called into question. It was also an element of his personality that would receive attention by Gregory Nazianzus in his funeral oration for the great Basil, his onetime friend.[73] These citations sum up the sad irony of Basil's own personal experience: that of a man dependent at all times on the affection of others and deeply hurt when they failed to match his expectations and demands. Yet also a man who was seemingly unaware of the pain he himself would inflict on others through his rigid standards of behavior and often through his own indifference to their situations.[74] It is a sad irony in the life of a man who was so insistent upon the communal aspects of love and charity for one another as the mark of a true Christian.

CONCLUSION

In her study of Basil's notion of purity of heart, Juana Raasch brought into focus a concept that was foundational to the ascetical and doctrinal understandings of the great bishop of Caesarea. It is a concept seldom if ever treated in works on Basil, yet it was one that focused his attention on the concrete, active love of a heart centered constantly on the memory of God's presence in all of creation. Basil was by all accounts, with the exception of his years spent in the solitary retreat in Pontus, a man of action for whom the demands of the Gospel required intensive involvement with the world around him and the people with whom he came into contact. Where Juana may

---

[71] *Epistle* 20 (*PG* 32.283D–286C).

[72] *Epistle* 56 (*PG* 32.403C–405B).

[73] See Gregory of Naziansus' funeral oration for Saint Basil in *Funeral Orations of Saint Gregory Nazianzen and Saint Ambrose*, Fathers of the Church 22, trans. Leo P. McCauley (New York: Fathers of the Church, Inc., 1953). Also *PG* 36.493-605.

[74] For an excellent study on Basil and the tragedy of his friendships see Philip Rousseau, *Basil of Caesarea* (Berkeley: University of California Press, 1994) 233–69.

have fallen under the spell so prevalent during the time she was writing of some dichotomies between "morals" and "doctrine" in the patristic period, she nonetheless brought into focus an aspect of Basil's thought hitherto largely neglected. Had she stayed with the original texts she may have avoided some of the unfortunate conclusions concerning these dichotomies. Her work, nevertheless, remains admirable and provides the interested reader with a ferreting out of some of Basil's most poignant statements on charity and mutual sharing within community.

While the influence of Stoicism and Neoplatonism in the spirituality of Basil has not been treated in this essay, it remains to be said that Basil was able to assimilate the spirit of the times into a Christian understanding and praxis. Having been educated in Athens and considered one of the most brilliant thinkers of his day, Basil was not unaware of the theories and ascetical practices of the Stoic or Neoplatonic sage and wiseman. The rigorist practices of Eustathius of Sebaste would influence him greatly as would the liturgical and apocalyptical spiritualities of the Syrian ascetics prior to his time. The canons of the Council of Gangra would also place retraints upon certain forms of ascetical practice and attitudes in his time, directives and opinions Basil clearly tries to accept and adopt in his own legislation for his communities. Basil was a man of the fourth century, a century in so many ways foreign to modern thinkers and often not only hard to understand but in may ways inaccessible to twentieth-century minds. The movements and instincts of the human body would remain threats to Basil's understanding of what would constitute a holy and "pure" heart. Basil's own demise at the age of forty-nine would bear tragic witness to a life spent in constant denials to the often quite legitimate demands of an undernourished and ailing body. Yet it was clearly the love with which one lived one's Christian witness that was the mark of the true Christian in Basil's eyes. For Basil, purity of heart consisted not in an isolated existence concerned and preoccupied with self-perfection or even with the attainments of the lofty heights of prayer and mystical experiences. Basil would leave no in-depth teachings on prayer, nor would he recount any personal experiences of what we could consider mystical states or stages of union with God. For Basil union with God was seen by one's behavior toward one's fellow Christians, and one's work and unity for and with the larger Church community. The separation between an "intellectualist" tradition and an "experiential" tradition in prayer and spirituality would have been a separation unthinkable in Basil's mind or indeed in the thoughts of any of his contemporaries. Worthiness of life was what would determine an advanced stage of union with God, a worthiness of life made apparent by the ability to see God's presence in all of creation—particularly in one's own heart—and by the ability to live in humble loving harmony with one's brothers and sisters.

Juana Raasch has done a great service to all those who would study the mind and thought of Basil's asceticism by bringing to light the centrality of Basil's thoughts on purity of heart, even though the actual use of Matt 5:8 appears only once and that in regards to proper understanding of the Trinity. The studies of Juana Raasch have left us with areas in Basil's thought that are not only central to him, but also in many ways revolutionized the role of the ascetic in the Church. Prior to Basil's episcopacy, ascetical lifestyles remained for the most part among fringe groups within the larger Church community. With the rise of Basil to episcopal power and responsibility, the role of the ascetic became the defining light of the true Christian and the lifestyle of those most capable of assuming episcopal responsibilities. The predominate Christian virtue was purity of heart, and this was made manifest by the love and care one showed to one's fellow human beings. The ability to live and work in community taught, and made almost exclusive to true Christianity, by Basil removed the individualistic concerns for self-sanctification which were divorced from the responsibilities to one's fellow human companions that Basil saw far too prevalent in the eremitical quest for holiness in his time. The true Christian for Basil was indeed an ascetic, but he or she was an ascetic who by disciplinary practices was able to make space within the mind and heart for the Spirit of God to dwell. This would be the means of attaining purity of heart. The fruit of purity of heart was nothing less than unselfish love in a clear mind and heart living in reality, centered and focused always on God.

Temple and Throne of the Divine Glory:
"Pseudo-Macarius" and Purity of Heart, Together with Some Remarks on the Limitations and Usefulness of Scholarship

HEIROMONK ALEXANDER GOLITZIN

I am grateful that the editors of this volume asked me to write this essay if only because the assignment obliged me to read Sr. Juana Raasch's five articles in *Studia Monastica* on "The Monastic Concept of Purity of Heart and Its Sources,"[1] and I look forward to the publication of these studies within a single cover. Even after certain notable developments in the scholarship of the past thirty years—of which more anon—Sister Juana's analysis of the literature bearing on purity of heart in the first four Christian centuries retains great value. To the best of my knowledge her study is unique in English, and her treatment of the subject both comprehensive and careful. Nonetheless, three decades of scholarly endeavor since the publication of her articles have led to developments in the ways that some of her source materials are today perceived, and this applies with peculiar force to the subject I have been asked to consider, the several collections of monastic sermons and correspondence which have come down to us under the name of Macarius the Great of Egypt, but which are now agreed to have been the work of an unknown ascetic from somewhere near the borders that the late-fourth-century Roman Empire shared with

---

[1] Juana Raasch, "The Monastic Concept of Purity of Heart and Its Sources," *Studia Monastica* 8:1 (1966) 7–33; 8:2, 183–213; 10:1 (1968) 7–55; 11:2 (1969) 269–314; and 12:1 (1970) 7–41.

Sassanid Persia.² For the sake of convenience, and to avoid the unpleasant prefix "pseudo," I shall continue to refer to him as Macarius.

Sister Juana devotes well over twenty pages to Macarius, more than for any of the other writers whom she covers save, quite rightly, Origen of Alexandria.³ This is all the more striking in that the *Macarian Homilies* figure so little in pre-Reformation, Western Christian spirituality and, subsequent to the sixteenth century, appear chiefly in the works of Protestant pietism.⁴ It is not therefore accidental, I think, nor especially surprising that Macarius should end up the target of the sharpest criticism Sister Juana has for any of the ancients whom she examines. He is, in her reckoning, overly subjective, courting the overthrow of sober moral discipline in favor of an undiscerning "short cut to the mystical,"⁵ and, incidentally, guilty on occasion of "pure Platonism."⁶ The homilies represent a "school" of Eastern Christian spirituality which, in exalting the heart, places too a great a stress on experience, on feeling,⁷ and which in consequence blurs the fine New Testamental line between the present age, where baptismal reception

---

² The *Macarian Homilies* do not enjoy any one definitive critical text. They have been handed down to us in several collections. To date, three of those collections have been published in the Greek in relatively critical form: Collection I in *Reden und Briefe [von] Makarios/Symeon. Die Sammlung I des Vaticanus Graecus 694 (B)*, ed. Heinz Berthold (Berlin: Akademie-Verlag, 1973); Collection II in *Die 50 geistlichen Homilien des Makarios*, ed. Hermann Dörries, Erich Klostermann, and Matthias Kröeger (Berlin: W. de Gruyter, 1964); and Collection III in *Neue Homilien des Makarios/Symeon*, ed. Erich Klostermann and Hermann Berthold (Berlin: Akademie-Verlag, 1961). The last has also been more recently edited by V. Desprez, *Pseudo-Macaire, Oeuvres spirituelles*, vol. 1: *Homélies propres à la Collection III*, Sources chrétiennes 275 (Paris: Cerf, 1980). Macarius' "Great Letter" was edited first by Werner Jaeger, *Two Rediscovered Works of Ancient Christian Literature: Gregory of Nyssa and Macarius* (Leiden: E. J. Brill, 1965), and then by R. Staats, *Makarios-Symeon: Epistola Magna* (Goettingen: Vandenhoeck & Ruprecht, 1980). In referring to the homilies below, I shall begin with large Roman numerals to indicate the collection, lower case for the homily, and then Arabic numerals for the subsections. Of some interest, perhaps: the "Symeon" referred to in several of the titles above was one Symeon of Mesopotamia, named as a Messalian by some of the ancient heresiologists and credited by H. Dörries as the real author of the homilies. See the latter's *Symeon von Mesopotamien: Die Überlieferung der messalianischen "Makarios"-Schriften* (Leipzig: J. C. Hinrichs, 1941). The name still appears on occasion attached to the homilies, chiefly by German scholars. They seem to like that sort of thing.

³ Raasch, "The Monastic Concept of Purity of Heart," 10:1, 24–55 on Origen, versus 12:2, 7–31, on Macarius.

⁴ See the brief sketch of the Macarian trajectory in G. Maloney's introduction to his translation of Collection II, Pseudo-Macarius, *The Fifty Spiritual Homilies and the Great Letter*, Classics of Western Spirituality (New York: Paulist Press, 1992) 20–7.

⁵ Raasch, "The Monastic Concept of Purity of Heart," 12:1, 30.

⁶ Ibid., 12:27.

⁷ Ibid., 12:13–14, 16.

of the Holy Spirit constitutes merely the earnest of God's kingdom, and the world to come, hence Sister Juana's accusation, along with "pure Platonism," of "gnostic de-eschatologizing."[8] Hence, too, I think, the suggestion of a rather ominous link between Macarius and the enthusiasms of American Pentecostalism.[9] Macarius emerges thus as a species of Protestant *avant la lettre*. He is much too much the individualist and enthusiast.[10]

The echoes of Reformation and Counter-Reformation polemic that I believe in part underlie Sister Juana's treatment of Macarius are certainly nothing new, and were as certainly more common earlier this century than, thankfully, they are today. Neither is the use of an early first-millennium, Eastern Christian writer as cannon fodder for later second-millennium, Western Christian controversies without precedent. Just because a procedure is not new, however, does not mean that it is just or, put more neutrally, helpful. I suggest, though, that Sister Juana was led, even in fact betrayed, by the prevailing scholarship of her day into an interpretation of the Macarian texts which was actually at variance—or at least in tension—with much of her own work, both on Macarius himself and regarding his relation to the preceding objects of her study. Scholarship between her day and ours would have cleared up much, if not all, of her difficulty—but more on that in a moment as I should like first to elaborate somewhat on my last point.

The five essays in *Studia Monastica* trace the course of the notion of purity of heart from its origins in the Hebrew Scriptures and the thought of Greek philosophy, chiefly Stoicism, through the New Testament and Apostolic Fathers (essay one), to the second- and third-century figures of the Apologists, Irenaeus of Lyons, and Methodius of Olympus (essay two), then to the thought of the great Alexandrians, Philo the Jew, Clement and Origen the Christians (essay three), on to the age of monastic foundations in the fourth century as represented by Aphrahat of Persia, the *Vitae* of Anthony and Pachomius, the purported letters of both Anthony and his disciple, Ammonas, and the monastic legislation of Basil the Great (essay four), concluding with writings of Macarius, Evagrius of Pontus, and John Cassian, and the late fifth-century collection of earlier monastic lore, the *Apophthegmata Pateron* (essay five). It is an impressive sweep and impressively handled. Three things struck me, however. There was first

---

[8] Ibid., 12:30–31, 8–9.

[9] Ibid., 12:29.

[10] The notion of Macarius as pietist was warmly embraced by H. Dörries in the latter's posthumous monograph, *Theologie des Makarios/Symeon* (Göettingen: Vandenhoeck & Ruprecht, 1978). See esp. 253, n. 247; and—"not far from Luther"—456.

of all the curious fact that, while virtually everything Sister Juana had to say about Macarius' predecessors, from Stoic custody of the heart and the piety of the Jerusalem Temple cultus (the "clean hands and pure heart" of Psalm 24), through the interiority of the prophets and the New Testament teaching of the Spirit's presence as love within the believer's heart, to the hoary language of the "two ways,"[11] to Origen's "inner man" and spiritual fire, and down to the pneumaticism of the early monks, turns up—all of it—in spades in the *Macarian Homilies*, yet Macarius is still represented as less a summary of all that had gone before him, as the author of an extraordinary (if not always consistent) blending of ancient Jew and Greek and paleo-Christian with, moreover, striking affinities to his contemporaries in Coptic Egypt (including the great Anthony himself),[12] than as a dangerously unbalanced innovator. Secondly, the core of his innovation is said to lie in his insistence on the experience of God as available now, in this life. His view that the "soul," in Sister Juana's paraphrase of one of the homilies, "having become pure . . . sees with pure eyes the Sun of justice in the depths of its heart, [and] . . . even now . . . [may be] rapt out of this world into heaven," that "the purified intellect can see the glory of Christ" is an example of Platonism.[13] Certainly it is true that Sister Juana is nervous throughout her five essays about anything concerning the *visio dei*. The Psalmist's talk about "seeing God" is a metaphor;[14] the theophanies of the Old Testament are "symbolical";[15] while in Christian writers of the fourth century, "the phrase, 'to see God,' is always metaphorical."[16] God's statement to Moses in Exod 33:20, "None can see My face and live," is held up as determinative.[17] Yet, thirdly, she cannot help noting elsewhere the appearance among early Christians of what appears to be an affirmation of at least the possibility of the vision of God in this life, thus Irenaeus on the light of Christ,[18] Clement on the ascent to heaven to see the angels

---

[11] Raasch, "The Monastic Concept of Purity of Heart," 12:1, 10–2. For the "two ways" theme in Macarius, see I.xviii.4; xxvii.2; xxxiii.3–4; xxxiv; III.iv; and xiii.1–2.

[12] Raasch, "The Monastic Concept of Purity of Heart," 12:16–19.

[13] Ibid., 12:27. For a like treatment of the "light" theme in the homilies, see also H. V. Beyer, "Die Lichtlehre der Möenche des vierzehnten und des vierten Jahrhunderts, eroertet am Beispiel des Gregorios Sinaites, des Evagrios Pontikos, und des Makarios/Symeon," *XVI Internationaler Byzantinistenkongress, Akten 1:2, Jahrbuch des öesterreichischen Byzantinistik* 31:1 (1981) 473–512. I shall have occasion to note below that Macarius (and Evagrius) was likely drawing on sources other than just the Platonists.

[14] Raasch, "The Monastic Concept of Purity of Heart," 8:1, 11.

[15] Ibid., 8:12.

[16] Ibid., 11:2, 306, n. 200.

[17] Ibid., 8:1, 12.

[18] Ibid., 8:2, 188; citing Irenaeus, *AH* IV.xx.5.

and God,[19] and even Aphrahat—no "Platonist" at all, but instead a representative of "primitive Christianity"—writing on the ascent to heaven in such a way as to lead Sister Juana to look for a parallel in the pre-Christian, apocalyptic text of I Enoch.[20] In Macarius, though, where the same possibility of the *visio dei* is held out to the reader, we are asked to take alarm at the unlikely combination of modern Pentecostalism with ancient Platonism. What can explain these discrepancies?

Now we arrive at the matter of that scholarly betrayal I spoke of above. Sister Juana was the unfortunate heir to nearly a half century of Macarian scholarship which had stressed the homilies' connection with the late-fourth-, early-fifth-century monastic "heresy" of Messalianism. The "heresy"—my reasons for the quotation marks will appear shortly—of these "praying ones,"[21] condemned at several local councils in the late fourth century and at the Ecumenical Council of Ephesus in 431, appears to have been an extreme charismaticism that was felt to threaten the sacraments and thus the hierarchy of the Church. Two later, more detailed lists of condemned Messalian propositions include: the denigration of sacramental efficacy in favor of private prayer, the co-indwelling of God and the devil in the soul, a crudely physical notion of this "mingling" of substances with Manichaean overtones, the claim to see the Holy Spirit with physical eyes, shiftlessness, sexual immorality, and perjury resulting from a purported liberation from the thrall of the passions through mingling with the Spirit. In 1920, L. Villecourt pointed to the fact that several of the Messalian propositions had been lifted, in some cases verbatim, from the *Macarian Homilies*.[22] Six years later M. Kmosko published the complete anti-Messalian dossier in the introduction to his edition and translation of the late-fourth-century Syriac text, the *Liber Graduum*, whose shared expressions and themes with both the *Macariana* and Messalianism were also noted.[23] From the 1920s through the 1980s Macarius was thus linked indissolubly with Messalianism, and thereby with formal "heresy." To be sure, there was debate about the degree or intensity of his ties to these "heretics," but nothing could shift the linkage.[24]

---

[19] Raasch, "The Monastic Concept of Purity of Heart," 10:1, 22–23.

[20] Ibid., 11:2, 281–2.

[21] "Messalian," Syriac *meṣalyane*, is derived from the Syriac verb, ṣloʾ, "to pray."

[22] L. Villecourt, "La date et l'origine des 'Homélies spirituelles' attribuées à Macaire," *Comptes rendus de l'Académie des Inscriptions et Belles-Lettres* (Paris: n.p., 1920) 250–8.

[23] *Patrologia Syriaca*, vol. 3: *Liber Graduum*, ed. Michael Kmosko (Paris: Firmin-Didot, 1926) clxxii–ccxciii.

[24] See Dörries, *Theologie des Makarios/Symeon,* esp. 11–3 on Macarius as "anti-Messalian." See also J. Meyendorff, "Messalianism or Anti-Messalianism? A Fresh Look at

This is the general background to Sister Juana's treatment of the homilies,[25] but more specifically still I must underline the influence on her of one of the great pioneers in the field of Eastern Christian spirituality, the late Fr. Irenée Hausherr. While the latter's contributions were massive and invaluable, he was unfortunately at his magnificent worst when, in the first volume of *Orientalia Christiana Periodica,* the periodical he had been instrumental in creating, he published two enormously influential articles, "Les grands courants de la spiritualité orientale" and "L'Erreur fondamentale et la logique du Messalianisme."[26] The first article attempts a taxonomy of Eastern Christian spirituality, which Hausherr breaks down into six currents or "schools." He begins with the "primitive spirituality" of the New Testament and early Church, which rested in the liturgy and strove for the moral perfection of charity,[27] then moves to the overly "intellectualist school" of the Alexandrians and later of Evagrius Ponticus, which focused on the contemplation of the divine light as its essentially Platonist goal,[28] takes up briefly the curious case of Dionysius Areopagita as an inconsequential anomaly,[29] and then describes the "school of mystical feeling" which appears on the Christian scene with Messalianism generally, and Macarius in particular, and whose defining feature is its insistence on the sensible perception of grace.[30] Fifth, and as a kind of antidote to the preceding, Hausherr offers the "school of obedience," which he associates particularly with Basil the Great and which he heartily approves for its sober stress on morality, obedience, and fraternal charity.[31] The sixth "current," the Hesychast spirituality of later Byzantium, combines the unfortunate Platonism of the "intellectualist school" and its mysticism of light with the excesses of the "school of sentiment," in order to produce the "fatal" theological developments associated with Gregory Palamas (+1359), and thus also contributing to the anti-intellectualism and "paramysticism" of the contemporary Orthodox Church.[32]

---

the Macarian Problem," *Kyriakon: Festschrift Johannes Quasten* (Muenster: Aschendorff, 1971) 2:285–90; and, for a recent equation of the homilies with Messalianism, see Andrew Louth, *The Origins of the Christian Mystical Tradition* (Oxford: Clarendon Press, 1981) 113–25.

[25] Raasch, "The Monastic Concept of Purity of Heart," 12:1, 8–9.

[26] I. Hausherr, "Les grands courants de la spiritualité orientale," *OCP* 1 (1935) 114–38; and "L'erreur fondamentale et la logique du Messalianisme," *OCP* 1 (1935) 328–60. It would be difficult to overstate the influence of these articles for over two generations of scholars.

[27] Hausherr, "Les grands courants," 116–20.

[28] Ibid., 121–4.

[29] Ibid., 124–5.

[30] Ibid., 126–8.

[31] Ibid., 129–31.

[32] Ibid., 130–6.

The polemic is obvious, even if Hausherr is aiming it at a target considerably to the east of Augsburg, Geneva, and the Azusa Street revival. What is perhaps not so obvious is his superimposition of a medieval and post-medieval Western spiritual map onto what he characterizes as the trackless "virgin forests" of Eastern Christian spirituality. Hausherr is quite explicit about this. Whereas, he argues, different schools of spirituality in the West were carefully distinguished by the establishment of the religious orders, the East is not so obliging and, in consequence, his article will seek to blaze some paths for inquiry and provide a compass.[33] Yet it is clear, to me at least, that the contours of his proposed spiritual geography turn out to be suspiciously familiar. One can surely catch the echoes of Eckhart's intellective versus Bernard's affective mysticism, or even of Dominican piety in contrast to Franciscan, in the opposition of the "schools" of intellect and feeling, as well as the resonance of good, solid Benedictine sobriety (and maybe Jesuit, too) in the "school of obedience," though of course there is nothing in the Catholic West to match the delusions of the schismatic Hesychasts. This is, finally, the map that Sister Juana humbly accepted as her guide through the first four Christian centuries. It appears everywhere in her essays.[34]

Polemic, and its unfortunate effects on Sister Juana's treatment of "Macarius," applies with even greater force to the second of Hausherr's articles, arguably the most wretched thing he ever wrote (and which I understand he regretted in later life), "L'erreur fondamentale." The latter amounts in effect to a kind of screed against the errors of the *Macarian Homilies*, here held up to the reader as "authentically representative" of the heretical Messalians.[35] Indeed, the homilies embody a compendium of heresies. Manicheism lurks beneath the notion of an indwelling demon and the language of "mingling,"[36] while "deistic positivism" and "naturalistic mysticism" are concealed in the Messalian (i.e., Macarian) confusion of grace with the conscious experience of grace.[37] The equivalent of Pelagianism is embedded in the insistence—Hausherr calls it the exclusivism—of prayer and the hope of deliverance from the passions *(apatheia)*,[38] while a dangerous credulity

[33] Ibid., 114–6.
[34] Sister Juana follows Hausherr's taxonomy. Macarius is too much the advocate of feeling, likewise in "The Monastic Concept of Purity of Heart" we find her writing on the "primitive" spirituality of the early Church (8:1, 22–32), the intellectualism of the Alexandrines (10:1, 13–55), Basil's sober moral thrust (11:2, 308–14), and again Evagrian intellectualism (12:1, 31–4).
[35] Hausherr, "L'erreur fondamentale," 332.
[36] Ibid., 333–4.
[37] Ibid., 337–8.
[38] Ibid., 343 and 352.

regarding visions of light leads to "full quietism" and undiscerning confidence.[39] Along the way, Hausherr simply brushes aside as mere posing all of "Macarius'" careful distinctions and qualifications.[40] When we then turn to Sister Juana's work on "Macarius," it is scarcely surprising that we find her careful observations, made on the basis of her own reading, running side by side and not always harmoniously with the negative judgments she has taken primarily from Hausherr. It is almost as if she feels called to take time out every page or two in order to make a bow in the direction of her "authority." Early on, she makes explicit her deference to the great man's judgment: "The excellent study of Macarian and Messalian spirituality published by Fr. Irenée Hausherr discusses these matters so thoroughly and perceptively that it leaves little to be added except, perhaps, the implications of the Jewish and Qumranian origins of the 'Two Spirits' theme."[41] She was ill-served by her expert, for in her modest "except perhaps" regarding links with ancient Jewish thought, as well as in the affinities she finds between Macarius and contemporary Coptic and Syriac-speaking ascetics, and in her brief but pregnant reference to ties between the fourth-century Aphrahat and Second Temple Jewish apocalyptic, she was in fact pointing toward paths of inquiry vastly more helpful and potentially illumining than that roadmap Hausherr had supplied three decades earlier whose tracings she felt obliged to follow. The thirty years since her articles appeared have done much to vindicate her intuitions, and quite as much more, I think, awaits vindication.

In the space remaining to me, I should like first to touch on some of these recent scholarly contributions pertaining to Syriac-speaking Christianity and asceticism, particularly as they affect our appreciation of the *Macarian Homilies*. Secondly, I would like to point very briefly to some of the avenues opened up by recent advances in the study of apocalyptic literature. I will conclude by at last moving on to Macarius himself. What will begin to emerge, I think, is that the homilies do in fact represent that remarkable coalescence of a number of themes and currents which, taken together, Sister Juana's essays suggest, but which she was unable fully to develop because of her deference to the construction that others, ostensibly more "expert" than she, had placed upon them.

Up until a generation ago, the literature of Syriac-speaking Christianity had been treated as something of a stepchild beside the vastly better-known volumes of the Greek and Latin Fathers. It was of inter-

---

[39] Ibid., 356–7, referring to *Macarian Homily* II.viii.3.
[40] E.g., ibid., 351.
[41] Raasch, "The Monastic Concept of Purity of Heart," 12:1, 16.

est chiefly for Scripture scholars working on textual criticism, or for students of Church history and doctrine bent on ferreting out witnesses to Greek theology preserved uniquely in Syriac translation, for example the writings of a Theodore of Mopsuestia or of a Severus of Antioch. True, there were those who loved and worked with the Syriac texts for their own sake. One thinks of the lexicographical labors of the Payne Smiths, father and daughter, of Fathers Nau and Graffin in the creation of the *Patrologia Orientalia*, or, later in this century, of Arthur Vööbus' tireless quest for manuscripts to edit, as well as of his two volumes on Syrian asceticism,[42] or of Dom Edmund Beck's groundbreaking editions and translations of Ephrem Syrus for *CSCO*,[43] to name but a few. Several studies appeared in the 1960s and 70s which made substantial use of Syriac sources in order to shed new light on the very ancient origins of Christian asceticism, perhaps in particular the works of G. Kretschmar, G. Quispel, M. Harl, A. Guillaumont, J. Amstutz, P. Nagel, and F. E. Morard.[44] Harl, Guillaumont, and especially Morard provided, in fact, solid ground for reading the Greek Christian use of the word, *monachos* (monk), as a calque on the Syriac theological term *ihidaya*. But it was really not until the work of two English scholars that, beginning in the mid-1970s, the world of Syriac-speaking Christianity began to acquire a real shape in its own right and evoke interest in circles outside the narrow bounds of professional Syricists. Robert Murray's *Symbols of Church and Kingdom* in 1975, together with the nearly innumerable books, articles, and texts written or edited by Sebastian Brock, have put the Christian world "east of Byzantium" definitively on the scholarly map as a third universe at once in relation to yet distinct from the better-known Greek

---

[42] A. Vööbus, *A History of Asceticism in the Syrian Orient*, 2 vols. (Louvain: Secretariat du CorpusSCO, 1958 and 1960).

[43] See also Beck's many articles on Syrian asceticism, e.g., "Ein Beitrag zur Terminologie des aeltesten syrischen Moenchtums," *Studia Anselmiana* 38 (1956) 254–67.

[44] Georg Kretschmar, "Ein Beitrag zur Frage nach dem Ursprung fruechristlicher Askese," *Zeitschrift für Theologie und Kirche* 64 (1961) 27–67; Gilles Quispel, *Makarius, das Thomasevangelium, und das Lied von der Perle* (Leiden: E. J. Brill, 1967); M. Harl, "À propos des *logia* de Jésus: Le sens du mot *monachos*," *Revue des études grecques* 73 (1960) 464–74; A. Guillaumont, "Le nom des 'agapètes,'" *Vigiliae christianae* 63 (1969) 30–7; A. Guillaumont, "Monachisme et éthique judeo-chrétienne," *Recherches des science religeuses* 60 (1972) 199–218; A. Guillaumont, "Perspectives acutelles sur les origines du monachisme," *Aux origines du monachisme* (Maine & Loire: Abbaye de Bellefontaine, 1979) 215–27; F. E. Morard, "Monachos, moine: histoire du terme grecque jusqu'au IVe siecle," *Zeitschrift für Philosophie und Theologie* 20 (1973) 332–441; Joseph Amstutz, *Haplotes: Eine begriffsgeschichtliche Studie zum jüdisch-christlichen Griechisch* (Bonn: P. Hanstein, 1968); Peter Nagel, *Die Motivierung des Askese in der alten Kirche und der Ursprung des Mönchtums* (Berlin: Akademie-Verlag, 1966).

and Latin Christian literature.[45] The value of this "third world" for the light it can shed not only on Christian use of ancient Jewish traditions, but on hitherto unnoticed elements in the Greek and Latin Fathers has only just begun to be exploited.

In the case of the *Macarian Homilies,* and with regard to the vexed matter of Messalianism, very considerable light, indeed, was recently shed by Fr. Columba Stewart's splendid study *"Working the Earth of the Heart."*[46] Stewart carefully analyzes the ancient documents on Messalianism and the latter's background in Syrian ascetical traditions, then combines this with a close examination of three key Macarian terms, assurance *(plerophoria),* perception *(aisthesis),* and experience *(peira),* the Macarian language of mingling and mixture (e.g., *kerannymi, mignymi*), and then sets this lexicon against its appearance in both prior Greek patristic usage and the deployment of equivalent terms in such Syriac works as Aphrahat's *Demonstrations,* Ephrem's homilies and hymns, and the *Liber Graduum.* The result, as Stewart remarks one-third of the way through his study, is interesting in view of what I had to say about the directions in which Sister Juana's essay might have gone: "[Macarius] was engaged in quite an interesting task. Formed, or at least profoundly influenced, by Syriac Christian symbols and poetic traditions, this anonymous teacher was interpreting and translating aspects of the Syriac tradition for a Greek-speaking audience." It follows thus that the Greek bishops' "categorical denunciations of Messalian errors may be seen to rest largely on the misunderstanding of unfamiliar terminology, and culture joins with (and perhaps supplants) doctrine as the basis of controversy"[47]—thus, too, the quotation marks around the "heresy" of Messalianism. I would add that Stewart's verdict of a culture clash as at the root of the controversy applies just as aptly to Macarius' modern critics as it does to those troubled Greek ecclesiastics who excerpted from the homilies in order to compile their lists of "Messalian errors." Indeed, given the quite profound influence that Macarius would enjoy in the Christian

---

[45] Robert Murray, *Symbols of Church and Kingdom: A Study in Early Syriac Tradition* (New York: Cambridge University Press, 1975); Robert Murray, "An Exhortation to Candidates for Ascetical Vows at Baptism in the Ancient Syrian Church," *New Testament Studies* 21 (1974) 59–80. For S. Brock, the following sampling must suffice: "Clothing Metaphors as a Means of Theological Expression in Syriac Tradition," *Typus, Symbol, Allegorie,* ed. Margot Schmidt and Carl Friedrich Geyer (Regensburg: Pustet, 1982) 11–38; "Early Syrian Asceticism," *Numen* 20 (1973) 1–19; and *The Syriac Fathers on Prayer and the Spiritual Life* (Kalamazoo, Mich.: Cistercian Publications, 1987).

[46] Columba Stewart, *"Working the Earth of the Heart": The Messalian Controversy in History, Texts, and Language to A.D. 431* (New York: Oxford University Press, 1991).

[47] Ibid., 69, and see also his conclusions, 234–40.

East in following centuries, we might also apply Stewart's model of cross-cultural miscommunication to the anti-Hesychast polemic in the early Hausherr and, forty years later from a Lutheran perspective, in Herman Dörries' posthumous monograph on the *Makariana*.[48]

Sister Juana's brief allusion to 1 Enoch and "apocalyptic visionaries" in connection with citations from Aphrahat's sixth *Demonstration*[49] leads me to a second arena of modern scholarship, the reevaluation of apocalyptic literature in biblical studies whose first significant landmark was, perhaps, the collection of articles edited by John Collins for the journal *Semeia* in 1979.[50] This development is linked in turn to new directions in the fields of Christian origins and rabbinic studies, with all three disciplines promising—and, to a certain extent, already delivering as a result of their cross-fertilization—freshly illumining insights into long-studied texts and movements, for example the remarkable books on the origins of Gnosticism by Alan Segal and Jarl Fossum.[51] While none to my knowledge have as yet pushed their inquiries along these lines much beyond the third century A.D., there is nothing in theory that should prevent one from doing so. In fact, I suggest that to extend inquiry from pre-Christian apocalyptic into the fourth century and beyond, particularly into the texts of early monasticism, will prove as fruitful as it has already begun to prove for earlier periods. Obviously, such cannot be the task of this essay, but I think I can at least point to some ways in which the Macarian language of vision, of light, and glory shining within the purified "temple" of the heart or intellect, hitheto characterized as a platonizing corruption of primitive Christian piety,[52] draws instead on most ancient Christian and pre-Christian Jewish sources, with deeper roots still in the liturgy of the First Temple and the prophetic revelations. Remarkably, Sister Juana anticipated this as well, beginning her discussion of purity of heart with Psalm 24 and the cultic piety of the Jerusalem

---

[48] Thus Dörries' caricature of Byzantine Hesychasm in *Theologie des Makarios/Symeon*, 249–53.

[49] Raasch, "The Monastic Concept of Purity of Heart," 11:2, 279–81, citing Aphrahat, *Demonstrations* 6.1, 14; 9.4 (Parisot, *Patrologia Syriaca* I:251, 263–6, and 414).

[50] John J. Collins, ed., *Apocalypse: The Morphology of a Genre*, Semeia 14 (1979).

[51] Alan Segal, *Two Powers in Heaven: Early Rabbinic Reports about Christianity and Gnosticism* (Leiden: E. J. Brill, 1977); Jarl Fossum, *The Name of God and the Angel of the Lord* (Tübingen: Mohr, 1985). For our purposes, i.e., the relation to mysticism, see also Gilles Quispel, "Ezekiel 1:26 in Jewish Mysticism and Gnosis," *Vigiliae Christianae* 34 (1980) 1–13, and again Jarl Fossum, "Jewish-Christian Christology and Jewish Mysticism," *Vigiliae Christianae* 37 (1983) 260–87.

[52] Thus Raasch above, n. 13, together with Hausherr, "Les grands courants," 122 and 134; Dörries, *Theologie*, 252–3; and Beyer, "Die Lichtlehre," esp. 498ff.

Temple.[53] In order to take up her hint, however, I must first devote some space to the relevant aspects of the reevaluation of apocalyptic.

What has occurred in the work of Collins and others is an awakening to the mystical element in many of the apocalypses. The older reading of this literature had stressed its purely eschatological aspect, one which was seen as including a deterministic view of history (the divine plan), *ex eventu* prophecy, a preoccupation with the signs of the endtimes, and a pronounced ethical dualism—light versus dark, good versus evil, God versus the devil and his angels. These elements have usually been accompanied by speculation about the literature's sociological and psychological functions, together with often smug and patronizing remarks about the "decline of prophecy" and the perception of an increased distance between God and humanity as opposed to prophetic "inwardness."[54] While there is doubtless some truth to the older approach, it is also true that any definition of apocalyptic as a genre which focused exclusively on the characteristics just listed would necessarily exclude many works which all agree must be included. This applies first and foremost to the grandfather of the genre, the *Book of the Watchers,* i.e., the first thirty-six chapters of 1 Enoch, which dates back at least to 200 B.C.[55] While this text does feature some naughty angels, the fallen "watchers" of the title, one will look in vain for much in the way of historical determinism, signs of the end, *ex eventu* prophecy, or that cosmic struggle between good and evil which shows up with such force two generations later in Daniel. What 1 Enoch 1–36 is interested in, together with such other apocalypses as the Jewish 2 Enoch and the Christian ascension of Isaiah, is the seer's ascent to heaven, his vision of the Glory of God on the celestial throne and of the angelic hosts, and his initiation into the contours of that heavenly geography which includes the secrets of nature and the rewards and punishments to be allotted the righteous and the reprobate.[56] Thus, as Christopher Rowland remarked sixteen years ago, "To speak of apocalyptic . . . is to concentrate on the theme of the direct communication of heavenly mysteries."[57] Collins presents a somewhat

---

[53] Raasch, "The Monastic Concept of Purity of Heart," 8:1, 11–2.

[54] For an able example of this earlier approach, see David S. Russel, *The Method and Message of Jewish Apocalyptic* (Philadelphia: Westminster Press, 1964), perhaps esp. ch. 3: "The Decline of Prophecy and the Rise of Apocalyptic," 73–103.

[55] See E. Isaac's introduction to 1 Enoch in *The Old Testament Pseudepigrapha,* ed. James H. Charlesworth (Garden City, N.Y.: Doubleday, 1983) 1:5–12, esp. 6–7.

[56] See John J. Collins' introduction to the *Semeia* collection: "Towards the Morphology of a Genre," *Semeia* 14 (1979) 1–20.

[57] Christopher R. Rowland, *The Open Heaven: A Study of Apocalypse in Judaism and Early Christianity* (New York: Crossroad, 1982) 14.

more circumspect and prosaic definition of the genre in his introduction to the essays in *Semeia*, but one still clearly inclusive of at least the possibility of the mystical: "Apocalypse is a genre of revelatory literature with a narrative framework in which a revelation is mediated by an otherworldly being to a human recipient, disclosing a transcendent reality which is both temporal, insofar as it envisages eschatological salvation, and spatial, insofar as it envisages another, supernatural world."[58]

As "Apocalyptic in Rabbinic Literature," an essay included in Collins' *Semeia*, suggests, this opening to the mystical element in the genre owes much to the labors of the great scholar in Jewish mysticism, Gershom Scholem.[59] It was Scholem's thesis that a line of continuity ran back from medieval kabbalism to the authors of the apocalypses. To provide linkage between these two literatures, separated by over a millennium and by the rise of rabbinic Judaism, he successfully demonstrated the antiquity of the *hekhalot* texts, dating them in the period of the Talmud's compilation (ca. A.D. 200–ca. A.D. 600). The term *hekhalot* is the plural of *hekhal*, palace or temple. In this literature of the Talmudic era the palaces (or temples) in question signify the heavens of the angels and, in the highest heaven, the chariot throne, *merkabah*, of the divine glory which Ezekiel had seen on the banks of the Chebar.[60] These are specifically mystical texts, purporting to show the way, or at least describe the ascent (and return), to heaven of one or another of the great sages of the Mishnah, usually Rabbi Akiba or Ishmael.[61] Thanks to Scholem, they have been recognized as genuinely representative of the apocalyptic genre, and it is precisely because of that recognition, despite the fact that these texts are generally innocent of eschatology, that the genre as a whole has had to be reevaluated in such a way as to include the, as it were, "good news" of apocalyptic, that is, that some have gone up to heaven, to the palace or temple on high, to receive the secrets of the celestial realm.

---

[58] Collins, "Toward the Morphology of a Genre," 9.

[59] See in particular, Gershom Scholem, *Major Trends in Jewish Mysticism*, 3d rev. ed. (Jerusalem: Schocken Publishing House, 1973) esp. 40–79; Gershom Scholem, *Jewish Gnosticism, Merkabah Mysticism, and Talmudic Tradition*, 2d ed. (New York: Jewish Theological Seminary of America, 1965). See also Ithamar Gruenwald, *Apocalyptic and Merkavah Mysticism* (Leiden: E. J. Brill, 1980), and, for a more sceptical view of the continuities, David Halperin, *Faces in the Chariot* (Tübingen: Mohr, 1981).

[60] For the link between Ezekiel's chariot-throne and later apocalyptic and *merkabah*, see Gruenwald, *Apocalyptic and Merkavah Mysticism*, 29–72; and J. Dan, "The Religious Experience of the Merkabah," *Jewish Spirituality* 1:289–307.

[61] See A. J. Salandini, "Apocalypses and 'Apocalyptic' in Rabbinic Literature and Mysticism," *Semeia* 14 (1979) 187–205.

"Temple" points to another aspect or current in apocalyptic recently underscored by Martha Himmelfarb's study *Ascent to Heaven in Jewish and Christian Apocalypses*.[62] She begins her book by citing 2 Enoch 22:8-10 where the patriarch, having ascended to the throne of the Glory, is stripped and anointed with the oil of glory in order to be made "like one of the glorious ones," that is, an equal of the angels. Himmelfarb understands this procedure, common to eight Jewish and Christian apocalypses composed between 200 B.C. and A.D. 200, as a kind of priestly investiture, set against the background of the heavenly palace as the great temple whose priests are the angels.[63] Her first chapter analyzes the development of this idea, beginning with God enthroned in the sanctuary of the preexilic temple, moving to the different adjustments made by the Deuteronomist and the Priestly source to the Babylonian destruction, and focusing on Ezekiel's mobile throne as the primary inspiration for 1 Enoch 1–36 and subsequent apocalypses, with their transposition of the earthly temple to heaven and the transformation of the former's human priests into the latter's angels. Likewise, the linen vestments prescribed for the high priests in Lev 16:4 become angelic vesture in Ezek 10:2ff. and provide the basis for the shining robes of the Glory enthroned and of his heavenly clergy in the apocalypses.[64] Thus, to fill out the "gospel" implicit in some apocalypses, there is Himmelfarb's second chapter which develops the notion of the ascent to heaven as including participation in the heavenly priesthood.[65] This is to say that not only did certain ancient apocalypses preach that some—be it only a few—had gone up to stand before the throne of the Glory, but that they had also been transformed through investiture with the robes of glory and thus clothed with angelic status.[66]

The relevance of this material and of these themes—the *visio gloriae*, ascent to heaven, transformation and participation in the liturgy of heaven—together with their scriptural roots in the prophetic visions

---

[62] Martha Himmelfarb, *Ascent to Heaven in Jewish and Christian Apocalypses* (New York: Oxford University Press, 1993).

[63] Ibid., 3–4.

[64] Ibid., 9–28.

[65] Ibid., 29–46.

[66] For perhaps the most extraordinary account of transformation in the *merkabah* literature, see the late (sixth-century?) text, 3 Enoch, ch. 15 (Charlesworth, *The Old Testament Pseudepigrapha*, 1:267). Relatedly, see also C.R.A. Morray-Jones, "Transformational Mysticism in the Apocalyptic-Merkabah Tradition," *Journal of Jewish Studies* 43:1 (1992) 1–31, esp. 18ff. Compare Morray-Jones' remarks (30) on the echoes of this tradition in 2 Cor 3:18 and Eph 4:13 with the frequency of these two texts in Macarius, below nn. 68 and 71.

of Ezekiel (and, certainly, Isaiah 6) and the glory theophanies at Sinai and Zion (e.g., Exodus 19, 24, 33–34, 40; 1 Kings 8), to the Macarian corpus should be on the way toward becoming clear. Since Macarius is a Christian writer, I am also obliged at least to note the appearance of these themes in the New Testament. Here, too, there is support to be found in the works of a number of recent scholars.[67] Certainly, the particular New Testament texts which bear on these themes, and which appear repeatedly in the homilies, testify to the link that Macarius himself understood as existing between the ancient accounts of theophany and transformation, and the Gospel of the Word incarnate, crucified, and risen. It will have to be enough for my purposes here merely to list the most important scriptural loci. These must begin with St. Paul's ascent to the third heaven and hearing "ineffable words" in 2 Corinthians 12, and his discussion of Exodus 34 in 2 Cor 3:7–4:6, with its notes of transformation into glory *(metamorphoumetha apo doxes eis doxan)* and the illumination of "the knowledge of the glory of God in the face of Christ" which is to shine within the Christian heart.[68] Still, within the Pauline corpus I should note the apostle's mention of incorporation into the body of Christ's glory in Phil 3:21, and his statements about the Christian as "temple of God" or "of the Holy Spirit" in 1 Cor 3:16 and 6:19-20.[69] The Transfiguration narrative of the Synoptics appears with some frequency, as do the theophanies of fire, glory, and light in Acts' accounts of Pentecost, the vision of Stephen, and Paul's own conversion experience on the Damascus road.[70] We should also include Macarius' frequent use of Eph 4:13, "the stature of the fullness of Christ," as well as his occasional references to Revelation 3 and 21 (the celestial city, inscribed divine name, and glory), to 2 Peter 1:4 and Christians as "partakers of the divine nature," and to the

---

[67] See, for example, James Tabor, *Things Unutterable: Paul's Ascent to Paradise* (Lanham, Md.: University Press of America, 1986) esp. 11–21 and 83–7; Alan Segal, *Paul the Convert: The Apostolate and Apostasy of Saul the Pharisee* (New Haven, Conn.: Yale University Press, 1990) 9–11, 58–64, and 152–7; and, most recently, C.R.A. Morray-Jones, "Paradise Revisited (2 Cor. 12:1-12): The Jewish Mystical Background of Paul's Apostolate," *Harvard Theological Review* 86:2–3 (1993) 177–217 and 265–92.

[68] For a sampling only of 2 Cor 3:7–4:6 in Macarius, see I.x.3, xxviii.2, lviii.2; II.v.5, xxv.3; III.iii.2, and xxviii.2; for 2 Corinthians 12: I.x.3, xxviii.2, l.2; III.xvi.2, and xxiii.2.

[69] For example, I.xxix.1 for 1 Cor 6:19-20, and I.lviii.2 for Phil 3:21. However, for the soul (or heart or *nous*) as temple, *naos*, see: I.iii.2, 3, v.2, vii.18, x.4, xxv.1, xl.1, lii.7; II.xi.1, xxvii.19, xxxii.5, 6, xlvii.14; III.xxii.2, and xxviii.4. This sample list does not include the related terms applied to the soul or "inner man": throne *(thronos)*, house *(oikos)*, dwelling place *(katoiketerion)*, palace *(palation)*, and church *(ekklesia)*.

[70] For example, I.xviii.4 (on the reality of the divine light) and lviii.2 (on Paul's conversion as related in Acts). For references to the Transfiguration: I.x.3; II.iv.13, viii.3, and xv.38.

"unapproachable light" of God's dwelling place in 1 Tim 6:16.[71] The Gospel of John's emphasis on divine indwelling also appears frequently, in particular Christ's promises to "manifest himself" and take up his dwelling in the believer (14:21, 23), and to give the "glory" that he had with the Father to his followers (17:5, 22-24).[72] On a few occasions groupings of these texts appear as a kind of catena in support of the *visio dei/gloriae* within the heart.[73]

It is not my place to argue whether or not the New Testament writers intended these passages to signify an actual vision of light, though I believe that in several instances they did (the Lucan accounts of Paul's conversion are certainly explicit enough). However, I can safely say that Macarius was convinced that they did and that, in addition, he believed that the share in divine glory they promised was at once the fulfillment of the promises and manifestations of the Old Testament and the heart of the Good News accomplished in Christ and now made available to the believer in the Holy Spirit. The Gospel according to Macarius might be summed up as a kind of extended paraphrase of St. Paul's argument in 2 Cor 3:7–4:6. The Glory of God appeared to Israel on Sinai (Exodus 19, 24, 33–34) and came to dwell in a special way in the sanctuary of the Temple in Jerusalem (see 1 Kings 8). In the latter it was accessible in the cultus, especially to the high priest on the occasion of his yearly entry into the holy of holies (cf. Leviticus 16–17), and appeared there to the prophets (e.g., Isaiah 6, Ezekiel 10–12 and 43:2-5).[74] But this accessibility was limited, hence the cloud and smoke of Sinai, the temple curtain, and the veil over Moses' shining face. In Christ, the Glory of God came veiled by the flesh (cf. John 1:14 and Heb 10:19-20), was manifested hiddenly on Golgotha

---

[71] For Eph 4:13, see I.ii.6.5, iii.5.5 and 6, xiii.2.5, xxix.2.10, xxx.6, xxxvii.3.2, xxxviii.2.9, xl.3.8, xlv.4.1, lxiv.9; II.iii.5, xv.41, xviii.14, xxxvii.7; III.i.2, vi.2, xii.2, xvi.2, xxi.1, and xxviii.4. For 2 Pet 1:4, see I.xiv.23, l.1.8, liv.5.6; II.xxv.5, xxxiv.2, xxxix, xlix.9; III.viii.2, and xviii.1.

[72] For a sampling of Macarius' use of the Johannine texts, see I.iv.7, xviii.4; xxii.2, xxix.1, xxxv; II.xv.38; III.xvi.4, and xxviii.2.

[73] See, for example, esp. I.lviii.2, and also xxix.1 (from Ezekiel 1 to 1 Cor 6:19-20 to John 14:21 and 23), and xviii.4.

[74] For discussion of the glory or *kabod* tradition in the Old Testament, see Tryggve D. N. Mettinger, *The Dethronement of Sabaoth: Studies in the Shem and Kabod Theologies,* trans. Frederick H. Cryer (Lund: CWK Gleerup, 1982) esp. 80–123. In the New Testament and Church Fathers, see respectively Gerhard Kittel, *"Doxa," Theological Dictionary of the New Testament,* trans. and ed. Geoffrey W. Bromiley (Grand Rapids, Mich.: Eerdmans, 1968) 3:233–53; and P. Deseille, "Gloire de Dieu," *Dictionnaire de spiritualité ascétique et mystique* (Paris: G. Beauchesne et ses fils, 1967) 6:421–63. For the use of the term doxa in Macarius, see I.ii.1, x.3, xxv, lviii.1; II.xii.8–9, xv.38, xx, xxv.3, xlvii.1; III.ii.1, iii.3, xxviii.4, and *Great Letter* 36.

and openly on Tabor. Through the resurrection of Christ and gift of the Spirit, the same glory is implanted through baptism as, in Macarius' language, a kind of seed of the eschaton within the believer,[75] specifically in the heart or "inner man" or—since Macarius is not greatly concerned with terminology here—in the soul or intellect.[76] Thanks to that baptismal seed, the Christian heart—or, again, "inner man" or soul or intellect—thus becomes the potential successor to Sinai and Zion.[77] The heart is, potentially, the locus of theophany, and that potential is quite real. Macarius insists on the substantial character of the divine light within. It is a *phos hypostatikon* and not a created thing or mere product of the intellect *(noema)*, but uncreated, foreign *(xenon)* to our nature as creatures, a true inhabitation of the divine presence and, on occasion, truly perceived by the "eyes of the heart" (or soul or mind, etc.).[78] There are, therefore, some even now alive who have seen it, including "Macarius himself," and it is the vocation of all Christians to see and know it, whether now and in the world to come, or in the latter alone.[79] Then, at the eschaton, the body as well will share openly in this transformation, and Macarius comes back often—*pace* Hausherr

---

[75] See I.xlii on baptism as seed, and for the sacrament as earnest *(arrabon)* see I.xxv.2; III.xxviii.3; and *Great Letter* 3.

[76] Macarius certainly makes frequent use of "heart" as equivalent to the "inner man," thus I.iii.2, iv.30, xxvii.2, xxxix, liv.2, 3; II.iv.4, v.5, viii.3, x.1, xi.9–13, xiii.1, xv.8, 20, 28, 33, 34, xix.7, xxiv.2, xxvi.21, 22, xxxii.3, xliii.3, 7; III.iii.2, xx.2, xxviii.4; *Great Letter* 6, 22, 34, 40, and 42. But see above, n. 69 on *naos*, where the "temple" within is almost without exception identified with the soul *(psyche)*, or "inner man," or occasionally the intellect *(nous)*. On the central importance of the "inner man"/soul, see, for example, I.iii.3, v.2, xviii.7 (the "inner man" = the *imago dei*), xxiii.2, xxiv (the soul as key to the spiritual reading of Scripture), xxv.1 (the soul as locus of interior warfare), xl.1, liv.2, 3, lxii (the *nous* called to rule over the passions), lxiv; II.xxviii.1, xxx, xxxvii.1, xliii.7 (the *nous* as the "eye" of the heart, thus cf. II.vi.8, where the *nous* is the "eye of the soul"), xlvii.2–14; III.xviii.2, xix.1 (the soul as the city made for God), xxi.3, xxvi.4, 7 (the soul as *imago* again), and xxviii.2. "Heart" for Macarius seems in short to be the simple equivalent of soul or "inner man," hence caution is in order when confronting the very frequent assertions regarding the "affective" emphasis of the homilies, or the too frequent contrasts drawn between, say, the Evagrian *nous* and the Macarian *kardia*.

[77] See the glory reflected from Moses' face in Exodus 34 as the type of the Christian in II.xii.14 and xlvii.1 (recall above, n. 68, on related use of 2 Corinthians 3–4); the body as the altar in parallel with Elijah's Carmel (1 Kings 18) in II.xxxi.5; the implied parallel between the soul and Jerusalem (the Temple) in I.xxiv and II.xxviii.1, together with n. 69 above, the soul as temple, and, nn. 103ff. below, as the chariot-throne with echoes of the *merkabah* tradition.

[78] See esp. I.xvii and lviii.1–2, together with II.vi.5–7 and Macarius' witness to his own experience in II.viii.6. Note Macarius' insistence in II.vi.5–7 that the gifts, the throne and crowns, are not created things, but the Holy Spirit itself.

[79] See again II.viii.6 with reference to Macarius himself. For *apo tou nyn*, see, for example, I.xxxiii.3, xxxiv, l.2, liv.4, lviii.2; II.xvii.4; III.xvi.4.

and Sister Juana—to the contrast between "now" (hiddenly, within) and "then" (openly, in the body).[80] Likewise, he is not careless about these experiences. There are criteria for discernment between demonic illusion and the true light of heaven, of which meekness, humility, and the non-judgmental love of the brethren are vastly the most important. The devil, he declares, can never counterfeit the great virtues.[81]

The note of demonic opposition brings me to the nature of the "veil" and so to the cleansing of the heart or "inner man." Taking his cue, I think, from St. Paul's interpretation of the veil over Moses' face as the Israelite's lack of faith and hardness of heart, Macarius expands the allegory to make of the veil a symbol of the demonically inspired tumult of the passions which has "darkened" the human soul since the Fall. The first humans lost their share of the divine glory in exchange for the clothing of the devil's darkness.[82] At this point Macarius introduces the long tradition of both pagan Greek and Christian teaching about the struggles of the soul with the drives, impulses, and thoughts (*logismoi/dialogismoi*) which impel the human being to evil deeds.[83] There is nothing particularly original about the substance of his thinking here. Sister Juana provides ample precedent for it in her first four essays, particularly (though not exclusively) in the article devoted to the Alexandrians, and one can it find nearly everywhere among Macarius' monastic contemporaries.[84] I would, though, like to point out two distinctive elements in his treatment of the thoughts and of the human contribution he expects from his readers and advisees, since both elements bear on the note of controversy surrounding the homilies, while the second carries with it as well echoes of the ancient themes of temple and transformation, though now in a specifically and even ecclesiastically Christian language.

The first item is the seriousness of the struggle and its depth. Macarius is fierce in asserting the importance of the human will. Nei-

---

[80] For the opposition "now" (*nyn*) versus "then" (*tote*), see I.xviii.6, xxiv, xxviii.1, lviii.3; II.ii.5, v.7–12, xi.1, xv.38, xvii.4, xxxiv.2; III.ii.1.

[81] See, for example, I.ii.10 (on the virtues as criteria), v.3, vi.3 (for the need of discernment), xxix.1 (on avoiding trust in mental images); II.xii.3–5, xv.8 (humility necessary), xxvii.14 (love), xxxviii.4–5 (perfection not in this life).

[82] Thus see, for example, I.ii.2-3, xxxv (Adam's loss of the glory), l.1 ("mingling" of the soul with the passions); II.ii.2–3 (the dark veil of the devil), xv.25 (Adam's loss of mastery over the thoughts); and III.xxvi.5.

[83] See again II.xv.25, together with I.lxi.1–2; II.xxxi.3, and the references to Macarius' use of *synago* for the gathering of the "thoughts," n. 94 below.

[84] See Raasch, "The Monastic Concept of Purity of Heart," 8:1, 9–10 and 13–5, on the "thoughts" in Stoicism and the later prophets; 8:2, 212, on Methodius of Olympus; 10:1, 27–33, on Origen; 11:2, 283–4, in Ammonas; 309–10 for Basil; and 12.1, 31–2, on Evagrius.

ther grace nor sin is ever compelled, *anangkastike*,⁸⁵ but the ascetic way does require that one force oneself—literally, do oneself violence *(biazesthai heauton)*, an ascetic reading of Matt 11:12 with a history already old in the fourth century.⁸⁶ The homilies thus make much use of another hoary set of images from the Christian and pre-Christian, Jewish past: the military language of battle and warfare with its roots in the holy war tradition of the Old Testament.⁸⁷ In the spite of the prominence accorded the will, however, Macarius repeats over and over that at bottom, in the very deepest regions of the human heart or soul, the presence of evil cannot be eradicated by any human effort. Here is the place of the "hidden" or "incurable passions" *(krypta/aniata pathe)*, the bubbling spring of evil impulses—Sister Juana is altogether right in noting here the presence of the ancient Jewish motifs of the evil *yetzer* and the "two ways"—whose quenching is beyond our powers.⁸⁸ The Holy Spirit's inhabitation, the divine fire (or rain or sun) is required to dry up (or moisten or thaw—the images come thick and varied) the wounded terrain of the innermost man. The cosmic struggle of apocalyptic literature is played out on this interior landscape. Christ descends with his angels into the soul as into hell, there to do battle.⁸⁹ Baptism marks the beginning, the seed of salvation. It establishes the divine presence within the soul, but it does not wholly reform us all at once—a question of some controversy for those who came after Macarius.⁹⁰ The Christian soldier is rather given the weapons and armor for the fight which he or she then must wage in preparation for that last and definitive divine intervention whose radiance may, from time to time, be glimpsed even in this life.⁹¹

---

⁸⁵ Citing II.xxvii.10–11. For the importance of the *autexousion*, the capacity for self-determination, in Macarius, see I.xli, xlii; II.xv.23, 36, xix.1ff.; III.xxv.2, 5, and xxvi.3.

⁸⁶ See Irenaeus, *AH* IV.xxxvii.7, and *pace* Hausherr ("L'erreur fondamentale," 339) who sees Macarius' use of this verse in an ascetic context as "Pelagianism"!

⁸⁷ See esp. I.l.4, with its use of Deuteronomy 20. For the ancient elements, originally Jewish and then ascetic Christian, at work here, *via* in particular citations from Aphrahat, Ephrem, and still earlier sources, see Murray, "An Exhortation to Ascetical Vows." In Macarius, see also I.lx.1–2; II.xi.14, xv.28, 33, xxi; III.xxiii.5.

⁸⁸ For the "spring" of the passions within, see I.vi.3; II.xv.48, xx.4; and III.xxv.5; and for the "hidden" or "incurable passions," I.ii.10, xxv.1, lxiii.3; and III.xxv.1.

⁸⁹ See esp. II.xv.33, and for other reminiscences of the cosmic warfare of apocalyptic now transferred to the soul, see the language of the two ways, two kingdoms, light and dark, etc., in the texts cited above, n. 11.

⁹⁰ See above, n. 75, and on the controversy, K. T. Ware, "The Sacrament of Baptism and the Ascetic Life in the Teachings of Mark the Monk," *Studia Patristica* 10 (1970) 441–52.

⁹¹ On the equipping of the Christian soldier, see I.l.4, lx.2; and III.xxiii.5.

The role for human action and the necessity of divine grace, together with the mention just above of baptism, take us to my second distinctive set of images, one which also bears on the ancient theme of the Temple, as well as on Macarius' effort to articulate the importance of the Church's public liturgy for ascetics who were concentrating exclusively on the inner life. Put briefly, he understands the eucharistic liturgy and ecclesiastical assembly as a revealed allegory—or, perhaps somewhat better, iconography—of the soul's life in grace.[92] This does not mean that he rejects or belittles the reality of Christ's presence in the consecrated bread and wine, for he is quite specific that he does recognize it.[93] Rather, he takes the specific terminology of gathering (*synaxis, synago*) and change (*metaballo, metabole*) traditionally associated with the liturgical assembly and the transformation of the eucharistic elements,[94] and then applies them, respectively, to the labors of ascesis, the gathering of the *logismoi*, and the action of the Holy Spirit which alone transforms.[95] For example, in an allusion to the (clearly eucharistic) Gospel narrative of the feeding of the five thousand, Macarius states: "He who changes [*metaballon*] the nature of the five breads into many . . . the Same can change this soul into His own goodness by the Spirit."[96] The equation of soul with Church is elsewhere made explicit: "Church is said with regard to both the many and to the single soul. For that soul which gathers [*synagei*] all its thoughts is also the Church of God."[97] The macrocosm of the Church and microcosm of the soul reflect each other, and it is the former, Macarius tells us in a homily devoted exclusively to this subject, which was set up for the latter's sake: "The whole depiction [*diatyposis*] of the icon of the Church [came to pass in order] that the intelligible beings of faithful souls might . . . be made again and renewed and, having accepted transformation [*metabole*], be enabled to inherit life everlasting."[98] The consecration of the eucharistic elements, in other words, is at once an anticipation and an image of the eschatological transforma-

---

[92] See I.xxii.2, xxvi, and lii.2.

[93] See below on I.lii, together with Dörries, *Theologie*, 387–409.

[94] For the liturgical echoes of *synago, synaxis, metaballo*, and *metabole* see Geoffrey William Hugo Lampe, *A Patristic Greek Lexicon* (Oxford: Clarendon Press, 1961) 848.2–850.1 and 1295.1–1296.1.

[95] This is particularly the case in Homily I.lii (discussion below), but for Macarius' other, like use of *synago/metaballo* with respect to the soul's gathering of the thoughts and transformation by grace, see I.iv.7, xxi.2, xxii.1, xxvi, lxiii.4; II.xxiv.2, xxxi.1, 2, xxxiii.1, xlix.2, 5, 8, 9; III.vii.1, 2, xviii.2, xxii.2, xxv.5, and xxvii.5, 6.

[96] II.xliv.2.

[97] II.xii.15; cf. xxxvii.8–9.

[98] I.lii.1.6.

tion of the believer. Even the sequence of the liturgy, the *synaxis* proper (or "Liturgy of the Word" in today's parlance) as followed by the consecration *(anaphora)*, and the spatial ordering of clergy and congregants, proceeding from the episcopal throne in the east end down through the nave to the church porch outdoors, are "an illustration [*hypodeigma*] of what [is occurring] in the soul by grace."[99] Just as the *synaxis* and *anaphora* are incomplete without each other, so is ascetic labor useless without the grace of the Spirit which, however, will not come to us without those labors, and, just as there is a progression in the visible arrangement of the church's architecture from the church porch to the sanctuary, and in authority from the catechumen outside the doors to the deacons and priests around the bishop's throne, so the soul is to progress from its struggle for the virtues to promotion and "spiritual rank" *(axioma)* in order to be "inscribed among the perfect workers and with the blameless ministers [*leitourgoi*, likely a reference to deacons] and assistants [*paredroi*, literally, 'those beside the throne, *edra*', thus the priests] of Christ."[100]

There is a remarkably similar treatment of the soul's relation to the liturgy in the twelfth *mimro* or discourse of the contemporary *Liber Graduum*. Without any of the philosophical lexicon that Macarius deploys, the *Liber* develops the same idea by speaking of the "three churches": the church in heaven, the church on earth, and the "little church" of the heart, where it is the middle church, the earthly liturgy, which mediates between heaven and the inner life.[101] But the *Liber* was never translated into Greek, so it was Macarius whose version of the allegory of the liturgy was to contribute substantially to the thought of Dionysius Areopagita (ca. 500), Maximus the Confessor (+682), Symeon the New Theologian (+1022), and Gregory of Sinai (+1340)—a thousand years of Greek Christian thought.[102] One can say that in this idea alone, the correspondence obtaining between the inner and outer liturgies, he made a vital contribution to the reconciliation and balance of charismaticism and institution, of the mystical and the ecclesial, which has obtained—generally—in the Eastern Church to the present day.

He did so in the service of traditions of theophany and of human participation in God which were carried on from the New Testament,

---

[99] I.lii.2.1.

[100] I.lii.2.2–8.

[101] See Kmosko, *Liber Graduum* XII, cols. 285–304. ET: Brock, *The Syriac Fathers on Prayer* (Kalamazoo, Mich.: Cistercian Publications, 1987) 45–53.

[102] See Alexander Golitzin, *Et Introibo ad Altare Dei: The Mystagogy of Dionysius Areopagita* (Thessalonica: Patriarchikon Idryma Paterikon Meleton, 1994) 402–13, for a sketch of this trajectory.

and which in fact, in their pre-Christian forms, helped shape the New Testament writers themselves.

Nowhere is Macarius' fidelity to ancient currents and readiness to express it in terms drawn from both those hoary sources and from contemporary culture more evident than in the opening sections of the first homily in the better-known collection of fifty homilies. He begins by paraphrasing the vision of Ezek 1:1-28, and then moves to its explanation:

> What the prophet saw he truly and assuredly did see, but [the vision] also suggested something else, and it depicted beforehand something secret and divine, a mystery truly hidden from eternity and, after generations, made manifest in the last days with the appearance [lit., epiphany] of Christ. For he [i.e., Ezekiel] beheld the mystery of the soul that is going to receive its Lord and become His throne *[thronos]* of glory. For the soul which has been made worthy of fellowship with the Spirit of His light, and which has been illumined by the beauty of His ineffable glory after having prepared itself for Him as throne *[cathedra]* and dwelling place, becomes all light and all face and all eye.[103]

The reference to "faces" and "eyes" deliberately recalls the four faces and many eyes of the angelic bearers of the chariot throne, and Macarius goes on to make explicit his identification of the "living creatures"—the *hayyot* of Ezekiel and later on the focus of much of the rabbinic *merkabah* lore—with the Christian soul:

> The four living creatures which carry the chariot were also bearing a type of the four governing faculties [lit., "thoughts", *logismoi*] of the soul . . . I mean the will, the conscience, the intellect *[nous]*, and the power to love *[agapetike dynamis]*, for through them the chariot of the soul is steered, and God takes up His rest *[epanapauetai]* upon them.[104]

He who rides and directs these steeds of the soul is the same, Macarius stresses a few lines later, as the one who rode upon Ezekiel's cherubs, "Who holds the reigns and guides with His Spirit."[105]

What we therefore find in this remarkable passage, and in others like it in the homilies, is what Gershom Scholem himself, in an offhand remark concerning Macarius that has never to my knowledge been taken up by scholars of the homilies, called "a mystical reinterpreta-

---

[103] II.i.2.

[104] II.i.3. For other recollections of the *merkabah* tradition in Macarius, esp. the soul as equated with the angelic "living creatures," the *hayyot*, see also II.i.9, xxxiii.2; I.xxix.2; and III.xiii.2. For a straight borrowing of the *Phaedrus* chariot and charioteer, see II.xl.5. For other echoes of the apocalyptic tradition, see I.xxxiii.3 and II.xiv.4–5.

[105] Ibid.

tion of the *Merkabah.*"¹⁰⁶ It is also clearly a stunning marriage of Ezekiel with the *Phaedrus,* save that Plato's rider and charioteer, the *logistikon* (roughly equivalent to the Macarian *nous*), has been bumped out of the driver's seat in favor of Israel's God, and placed in harness, that is, demoted to the status of the other faculties of the soul. Certainly, there is Platonism here, but it is hardly "pure." Macarius makes the soul locus of theophany. This is precisely what his exact contemporaries in Egypt, Evagrius and Ammonas, are doing with the very same Old Testament materials, Evagrius in particular with the Sinai theophany and Ammonas with, again, Ezekiel.¹⁰⁷ All of them are engaged in what I choose to think of as "the interiorization of apocalyptic." The ascent to heaven, the vision of the throne of the glory, the initiation into the mysteries of God's purposes: all of these now reside within the soul, because, as Macarius remarks elsewhere, "with Christ everything is within" *(endon).*¹⁰⁸ This is no surrender of the Gospel to the Hellenes, but the buckling into harness, like Plato's *logistikon* just above, of the great Greeks in the service of the Gospel beatitude: the pure in heart shall see God. Macarius is not at all the systematizer that Evagrius is, but as regards this *logion* at least, they are on the same wavelength. Purity of heart for both means the cleansing of the inner man, the temple within, in order to receive the glory of God, the substantial light of the Trinity, upon the altar of the human spirit or *nous.* The contradistinction of "intellect" and "feeling," mind and heart, is at bottom false. Sinai and Zion, Carmel and Tabor and the Jerusalem to come are, for both Macarius and Evagrius, present reality as well as future hope, for Messias has come and breathed his Spirit within. The last things have begun, and those on high are joined with those below.

To turn back one last time to Sister Juana, almost all of the points I have just made are present in embryo in her essay: the links to ancient Jewish traditions, to Aphrahat, to the Egyptian monks, and indeed—an area I have not touched upon—to the great Cappadocians. Where might she have taken these connections had she not been burdened with the faulty map and misleading polemic that were handed her as authoritative guides? Perhaps the greater wonder is that she did so well.

---

¹⁰⁶ Scholem, *Major Trends,* 79.
¹⁰⁷ For Ammonas, see his Ep. XIII, *Patrologia Orientalis* XI:612–4. For Evagrius on the interiorization of Sinai, see Nicholas Sed, "La Shekinta et ses amis araméens," *Cahiers d'Orientalisme* 20 (Geneva: P. Cramer, 1988) 233–47, esp. 240–2; and for the light in Evagrius, see A. Guillaumont, "Un philosophe au désert: Évagre le Pontique," *Revue de l'histoire des religions* 181 (1972) 29–56, esp. 51–6; and A. Guillaumont, "La vision de l'intellect par lui- même dans la mystique évagrienne," *Mélanges de l'Université Saint Joseph* 50:1–2 (Beirut: n.p., 1984) 255–62.
¹⁰⁸ III.viii.1.

A Reflection on the Use of "Heart" in Select Prayer Texts in Early Christianity

MARY ANTHONY WAGNER, O.S.B.

One of the *Sayings from the Desert Fathers of the Fourth Century* became an appropriate icon for me as I began to reflect on the early Christian liturgies insofar as they are luminous with petitions for purity of heart.

Abbot Lot came to Abbot Joseph and said: Father, according as I am able, I keep my little rule, and my little fast, my prayer, meditation and contemplative silence; and according as I am able to strive to cleanse my heart of thoughts; now what more should I do? The elder rose up in reply and stretched out his hands to heaven, and his fingers became like ten lamps of fire. He said: Why not be totally changed into fire?[1]

Taking my cue from this advice of Abbot Joseph, I realized that "fire" and "prayer" and the "heart" are integrally related to one another in the prayer texts of early Christianity. Therefore, previous to identifying references to "purity of heart" in the early Christian liturgies, I knew that I needed to see, at least, some of the significantly key references to "fire" in Scripture. This seemed especially imperative to me as I also became aware of the Semitic roots of the Syrian liturgies and writings.

A core passage in Scripture which associates God's relationship with the people of Israel is that of the burning bush and other references to fire. For example, as Moses is speaking to the people of Israel and urging them to be faithful to the covenant that God made with them, he says:

---

[1] *The Wisdom of the Desert: Sayings from the Desert Fathers of the Fourth Century*, trans. Thomas Merton (Norfolk, Conn.: New Directions Books, 1960) LXXII, 50.

> Did any people ever hear the voice of a god speaking out of the midst of the fire, as you have heard, and still live? . . . To you it was shown, that you might know that the Lord is God; there is no other besides him. Out of heaven he let you hear his voice, that he might discipline you; and on earth he let you see his great fire, and you heard his words out of the midst of the fire (Deut 4:33, 35-36).[2]

The prophets also speak in terms of fire. Isaiah speaks of the Lord whose glory will purify like "a burning fire" (10:16). Jeremiah, warning the false prophets that they cannot continue in their lies, tells them that God's "word is like a fire" (23:29). Ezekiel, chastising the people for being unfaithful to their covenant with the Lord, says: "You profaned your sanctuaries; so I brought forth fire from the midst of you; it consumed you, and I turned you to ashes upon the earth in the sight of all who saw you" (28:18).

The evangelist Matthew puts into the mouth of John the Baptizer: "Every tree that does not bear good fruit is cut down and thrown into the fire" (3:10). Likewise, when John is clarifying his own identity relative to Jesus, he says: "He will baptize you with the Holy Spirit and with fire. . . . the chaff he will burn with unquenchable fire" (Luke 3:16-17). And Luke puts into the mouth of Jesus: "I came to cast fire upon the earth; and would that it were already kindled!" (12:49). Peter, comparing the testing of faith to that of gold, speaks of being "tested by fire" (1 Pet 1:7).

Besides the implication of purification by fire, scriptural writers speak of the wholeness of the heart, the purity of the heart, and of the uncircumcised heart. Speaking about the people of Israel changing their ways, the Lord Yahweh says: "If then their uncircumcised heart is humbled and they make amends for their iniquity; then I will remember my covenant" (Lev 26:41).

In Deuteronomy, "wholeness" is combined with the "circumcised" heart: "The Lord your God will circumcise your heart . . . so that you will love the Lord your God with all your heart and with all your soul, that you may live" (30:6). The Lord assures them that "[if you] will seek the Lord your God, and you will find him, if you search after him with all your heart and with all your soul" (Deut 4:29), they will be saved. We know how essential this was to the covenant and how Jesus accepted it as the first of all the commandments, from the rich young man who sought to follow him (Luke 10:25).

---

[2] All Scripture quotations are from *The Holy Bible: Revised Standard Version / Catholic Edition*, ed. Bernard Orchard and R. C. Fuller (Collegeville: The Liturgical Press, 1966). This writer took the liberty to modify the quotations to fit the flow of the manuscript, and on occasion for inclusive language.

Promising to gather the people of Israel together, through the prophet Ezekiel, the Lord says: "I will take the stony heart out of their flesh and give them a heart of flesh" (11:19). Later Ezekiel exhorts: "Cast away from you all transgressions which you have committed against me, and get yourselves a new heart and a new spirit!" (18:31). The Lord's plans are for welfare and not for evil: "You will seek me and find me; when you seek me with all your heart, I will be found by you" (Jer 29:13). From our own liturgy for Lent, we know well the exhortation of the prophet Joel: "Return to me with all your heart . . . and rend your hearts and not your garments" (2:12-13). The psalmist knows that God "knows the secrets of the heart" (44:21) and that it is God who "creates a clean heart" and "puts a new spirit" within us (51:10). God is good to "those who are pure of heart" (73:1). So the psalmist prays with confidence: "Search me, O God, and know my heart!" (139:23), and also knows that a place is secured in God's tent for those who "speak the truth from the heart" (15:2) and have "clean hands and a pure heart" (24:4). With confident joy, the psalmist prays: "I give thanks to thee, O Lord my God, with my whole heart" (86:12); and since the invitation has been extended to seek the Lord, the psalmist says with trust: "My heart says to thee, 'Thy face, Lord, do I seek, hide not thy face from me'" (27:8).

The New Testament writers extend the significance of the pure heart, describing God as wholehearted and tender-hearted. Luke presents Mary, the mother of Jesus, as humbly acceptant of her relationship with her divine child, "keeping all these things in her heart" (2:51). Jesus describes himself as "gentle and lowly in heart" (Matt 11:29). He speaks in one of his parables about those who receive the word of God "in an honest and good heart" (Luke 8:15). Speaking of the conversion of Lydia, the seller of purple goods, Luke writes that "the Lord opened her heart to give heed to what was said by Paul" (Acts 16:14). In speaking to the Ephesians about their faith in the Lord Jesus and their love toward one another, Paul prays that the "eyes of their hearts may be enlightened, that they may know what the hope is to which they have been called" (1:18). Exhorting Timothy about his mission in Ephesus, Paul says: "The aim of our charge is love that issues from a pure heart and a good conscience and sincere faith" (1 Tim 1:5). Peter, writing to the exiles of the dispersion, encourages: "Having purified your souls by your obedience to the truth for a sincere love of the brethren, love one another earnestly from the heart" (1 Pet 1:22). One translation says "deeply" from the heart, which stresses Peter's telling those exiles "to have unity of spirit, sympathy, love of the brethren, a tender heart and a humble mind" (1 Pet 3:8). Writing to the

Romans, Paul firmly clarifies the true meaning of circumcision when he writes: "He is a Jew who is one inwardly, and real circumcision is a matter of the heart, spiritual and not literal" (2:29). Finally, the disciple John, being overwhelmed with the reality of our being the children of God and having the joy of coming to know God directly, says: "Every one who thus hopes in God purifies himself as he is pure" (1 John 3:3).

The liturgies of the early Christian West give rich evidence of strong Christian assemblies and a deep commitment to their eucharistic celebrations. There is evidence, for example, in the early accounts of Christians being arrested, during the Roman persecutions, for attending their gatherings in secret places. When asked why they had done so, some of the accounts indicate that the simple, firm reply was: "I had to go. I am a Christian!" To be a Christian meant commitment to the Christ who had sacrificed himself for them. This was "purity of heart" at its depth.

Many of the early liturgical documents of the Western Church are testimonials to belief in the reality of the "flesh and blood of Jesus" being present to them as they were giving "eucharist" (thanksgiving) to God. The bond between Christians was evidenced not only in their gatherings for the Eucharist but also in their carrying the Eucharist to those who were absent and in their care for the needy. There were domestic rituals as the Eucharist, carried home from the Sunday celebrations, was also part of the daily prayers in the home.[3] These documents also testify to the early replacement of the Sunday, the day of the Lord's resurrection, for the Sabbath, even when followers of Jesus were "attending the temple together and breaking bread in their homes, they partook of food with glad and generous hearts, praising God" (Acts 2:46-47). We also learn how the ministries were performed by various members of the assembly, about their belief in the Father, Son, and Spirit, and about their veneration of the blood of martyrs who had been empowered to profess Christ through the Eucharist. In the *Didache*, known also as *The Teaching of the Twelve Apostles*,[4] there is explicit reference to "confessing your sins so that your sacrifice may be pure. Anyone at variance with his neighbor must not join you, until they are reconciled, lest your sacrifice be defiled" (14:1-2).

---

[3] There is explicit mention of this in the *First Apology of Justin* (150 C.E.) and in the *Apostolic Tradition* attributed to Hippolytus (ca. 215 C.E.). There is an extensive treatment of this, and of other references within this article, in Nathan Mitchell's *Cult and Controversy: The Worship of the Eucharist Outside of Mass* (New York: Pueblo Publishing Co., 1982).

[4] The text used for these references to the early liturgical documents is *Early Christian Fathers*, trans. and ed. Cyril C. Richardson (New York: Macmillan, 1970).

Martyrdom and the Eucharist were integrally united. It was through the Eucharist that the Christian was empowered to stand firm in the faith. It was once told that the icons of martyrs were often imaged with reddened cheeks to indicate that the martyrs had been fortified by the Eucharist in their final struggle: being one with Christ in his death and resurrection. Cyprian encouraged his North African community of Carthage, especially when threatened by persecution, to "drink the chalice of the Blood of Christ so that they themselves may also be able to shed their blood for Christ."[5] Saint Basil of Caesarea (+379) similarly recommends this for solitaries in the desert, from the Eucharist they had received at the eucharistic assembly.[6] There is a further identification of martyrdom with the Eucharist, remarkably portrayed in the description of the martyrdom of Saint Polycarp, the Bishop of Smyrna (155), by fire:

> When he had concluded the Amen and finished his prayer, the men attending the fire lighted it. And when the flame flashed forth, we saw a miracle, we to whom it was given to see. And we are preserved in order to relate to the rest what happened. For the fire made the shape of a vaulted chamber, like a ship's sail filled by the wind, and made a wall around the body of the martyr. And he was in the midst, not as burning flesh, but as bread baking or as gold and silver refined in a furnace, and we perceived such a sweet aroma as the breath of incense or some other precious spice.[7]

Finally, we have the remarkable self-proclamation of Ignatius, Bishop of Antioch, in his letter *To the Romans* (4:1–2) as he was on his way to be thrown to the beasts in the Roman coliseum: "Let me be fodder for wild beasts—that is how I can get to God. I am God's wheat and I am being ground by the teeth of wild beasts to make a pure loaf for Christ."[8]

Thus, within several centuries after Paul gave the Christian world what he said he had "received from the Lord" and passed on to us—the command of Jesus to "Do this, as often as you drink it, in remembrance of me" (1 Cor 11:23-24)—apostles, martyrs, and thousands of unknown saints were sanctified and turned into pure sacrifices to God.

---

[5] *Letter* 58.1, in *St. Cyprian: Letters* 1–81, trans. Rose Barnard Donna in *Fathers of the Church,* vol. 51 (Washington, D.C.: Catholic University of America Press, 1964) 163.

[6] St. Basil, *Letter* 93, in William H. Freestone, *The Sacrament Reserved,* Alcuin Club Collections XXI (London: A. R. Mowbray and Co., 1917) 41.

[7] *The Martyrdom of Saint Polycarp, Bishop of Smyrna, as Told in the Letter of the Church of Smyrna to the Church of Philomelium 15:1-2* in Richardson, *Early Christian Fathers,* 154–5.

[8] Richardson, *Early Christian Fathers,* 104.

It is in the Syriac Christian Aramaic tradition of the Middle East that we have a uniquely valuable image of Semitic Christianity. It is replete with references to the image of the heart, in continuity with the Semitic scriptural tradition.[9] The heart is centered in the whole person: at times reflecting gladness, sadness, disappointment, impatience, fear, anger, hatred, courage, stubbornness, wisdom, and plans and intentions for the future. That the Lord could replace a stony heart with a new heart, a heart of flesh (Ezek 11:19), and that in Christ the love of God has been poured forth into our hearts (Rom 5:5) fulfills Isaiah's prophesy that God's Spirit would be poured out upon us from on high (32:15).

To pray with "purity of heart" is expressed and described in various ways in the Syriac liturgies. One term repeatedly used is that of the "altar of the heart"—the body being the temple and hidden within is the altar, the inner church, the spiritual center on which self-offerings are made to God. John of Apamea, a solitary in Syria, writing in the *Letter to Hesychius,* exhorting Christians to learn from the gospel, wrote: "Your service to the Lord of all is performed in the mind, in your inner person, that is where the ministry to Christ takes place" (#28).[10]

In the *Book of Steps*, a fourth-century anonymous set of homilies, we find terms like: "a hidden self-emptying of the heart" (*Discourse* xii.i),[11] "there is a hidden fasting of the heart, fasting from evil thoughts. . . . The body is become a hidden temple and the heart a hidden altar for ministry in the spirit" (*Discourse* xii.i);[12] and in another passage on tears at prayer: "The heart does not become pure, then, unless hidden sin has disappeared from it . . . when we have become open-faced in the presence of our Lord" (*Discourse* xviii.4).[13] The heart as altar has the interior liturgical role to offer prayers made upon it. As the epiclesis transforms the bread and wine of the Eucharist, so is prayer made "by means of the heart, gathered in deep-felt groaning," in which the body itself does not toil.[14]

In Syrian spirituality and worship, the heart is the altar inside the sanctuary of the body/temple, on the altar of which prayer is contin-

---

[9] I am indebted to Stephen J. Bonian, S.J., whose writings were published in *Diakonia* 22:2, 121–6, on "Purity of Heart in Syriac Prayer" and his review of the Sebastian Brock book *The Syriac Fathers on Prayer and the Spiritual Life*.

[10] Sebastian Brock, *The Syriac Fathers on Prayer and the Spiritual Life* (Kalamazoo, Mich.: Cistercian Publications, 1987) 88.

[11] Ibid., 45.

[12] Ibid., 46.

[13] Ibid., 57.

[14] Ibid., "General Introduction," xxvii.

uously offered. In the *Book of Steps* we read that "the body is become a hidden temple and the heart a hidden altar for ministry in the spirit" (*Discourse* xii.i).[15] Likewise, Isaac of Nineveh speaking of texts on prayer says: "Many of the early Fathers—I refer to some of the great solitaries—did not even know the psalms, yet their prayer ascended to God like fire, as a result of their excellent ways and the humility of mind which they had acquired" (4.19).[16] Frequent mention is made of hearts, free of hidden sin and evil thoughts, which "become open-faced in the presence of our Lord." The heart is the spiritual center of the human person. Ephrem the Syrian speaks of both the body and the heart as the bridal-chamber for Christ the bridegroom.[17] In order to remain faithful to the only-begotten bridegroom, the heart must be "single" *(ihidaya)*, that is single-minded, undivided, in its loyalty to Christ.[18] Aphrahat, prominent in the fourth-century Christian Church in the Persian Empire, in his homilies entitled *Demonstrations*, speaks of this "inner chamber" where there is need for purity of heart for prayer to be acceptable to God.[19]

Another significantly descriptive term for the heart that is pure is that it is luminous, indicative of the divine indwelling. An anonymous Syriac mystic wrote: "A pure heart (is one) in which the light of the vision of you shines out."[20] This is true because, after our baptism, we live in the light of Christ. Ephrem the Syrian, after speaking of the heart as a luminous object, an eye, and a mirror, writes in one of his Hymns on the Church (xxix.9): "Let our prayer be a mirror, Lord, placed before your face; then your fair beauty will be imprinted on its luminous surface."[21] Ephrem also applies the "luminous eye" to Abraham, Isaac, and Ezekiel in his *Hymn on the Church* (ii.4).[22]

In *The Prayers of Sarapion of Thmuis*, a fourth-century bishop and friend of Antony the hermit and of Athanasius of Alexandria, purity of heart is associated with a clean conscience. We read: "Sanctify also the deacons so that they may be pure in heart and body and may be able to serve with a pure conscience. . . . Receive this people. Grant that they may become entirely genuine and live entirely blamelessly and

---

[15] Ibid., "I Book of Steps," 46.
[16] Ibid., "Isaac of Nineveh 4," 290–1.
[17] Ibid., "General Introduction," xxv.
[18] Ibid.
[19] Ibid., "Aphrahat #2," 6.
[20] Ibid., "On Prayer from the Teaching on the Solitaries," 184.
[21] Ibid., "General Introduction," xxx.
[22] Sebastian Brock, *The Luminous Eye: The Spiritual World Vision of Saint Ephrem* (Kalamazoo, Mich.: Cistercian Publications, 1985) 73.

purely."[23] Likewise, incorporating the concept of circumcision to denote purification, in his Hymn on Virginity Ephrem wrote:

> With a circumcised heart
> uncircumcision becomes holy;
> in the bridal chamber of such a person's heart
> the Creator resides (44:20).[24]

The seventh-century Martyrius stressed

> wakefulness and attentiveness in prayer especially during the holy mysteries of the Eucharist "standing firmly before God with wakefulness of heart in spiritual service" (218). And at the gospel, "Let us incline our ear toward him, and purify our hearts with its words, so that we may hear his living voice with the ears of our minds, and behold with the eyes of our hearts his great beauty" (221).[25]

The pure heart, purified from all evil, is capable of gazing on all things "considering (all) from God's point of view," according to Isaac of Nineveh.[26] He also relates in a poignant fashion the role of a pure heart at the liturgical celebration of the sacred mysteries: "Stir up within me the vision of your Mysteries so that I may become aware of what was placed in me at holy baptism. You placed within me a Guide: may he show me your glory at all times" (#14).[27] And in a prayer attributed to Joseph the Visionary we read: "Create in me a pure heart so that your holy power may reside within me, so that through the power of your Spirit I may in a spiritual fashion inhale your salvation."[28]

That this "inhaling of salvation" was not to take place in a vacuum, however, is clear from the important and insistent instruction given to the people not to absent themselves from the Christian assembly, "Since you are members of Christ, you should not scatter yourselves from the church by not assembling; for you have Christ for your head, as he himself promised: for you are partakers 'with me'" (ii.59).[29]

It is eminently clear from these many texts, which have been culled from the various Syriac writers on purity of heart and its effectiveness within the Christian worshiper, that it is God's work more than that of

---

[23] Maxwell Edwin Johnson, *The Prayers of Sarapion of Thmuis* (Ann Arbor, Mich.: UMI Dissertation Services, A. Bell and Howell Company, 1994) 91, 95.

[24] Quoted in Brock, *The Luminous Eye*, 128.

[25] Stephen Bonian, review of Sebastian Brock's *The Syriac Fathers on Prayer and the Spiritual Life*, in *Diakonia* 22:2, 65–8.

[26] Brock, "Isaac of Nineveh," *The Syriac Fathers*, 294.

[27] Ibid., "Prayers of the Mystics," 351.

[28] Ibid., 357.

[29] *The Liturgical Portions of the Didascalia*, intro., selection, and trans. Sebastian Brock and Michael Vasey (Bramcote: Grove Books, 1982) 17.

the person so gifted. A final quotation from John of Apamea's *Letter to Hesychius* evidences such confidence promised to the one praying:

> Purify the movement of your thoughts; if you have to struggle with them, be persistent in your struggle and do not give up. When God sees your persistence, then all of a sudden grace will dawn in you, and your mind will find strength as your heart burns with fervour and your soul's thoughts shine out.[30]

It is obvious that in the understandings of these early Christian writers and spiritual directors that purity of heart surpasses all verbal utterances. As Aphrahat, writing on prayer, said: "Purity of heart constitutes prayer more than all the prayers that are uttered out aloud, and silence united to a mind that is sincere *[sincerity of heart]* is better than the loud voice of someone crying."[31]

To return to the desert father with whom I began these reflections, I think that Abbot Joseph would feel that these early Roman and Syriac Christians did indeed give testimony in their liturgical and private prayers to hands raised on high with fingers "like ten lamps of fire."

---

[30] Brock, "John the Solitary," *The Syriac Fathers*, 96.
[31] Ibid., "Aphrahat, Demonstrations IV, On Prayer," 5.

Apatheia and Purity of Heart in Evagrius Ponticus

JEREMY DRISCOLL, O.S.B.

INTRODUCTION

Seizing a particular word in the biblical text, as the genre of scholia requires, Evagrius comments on the word "gift" in the following text from the book of Proverbs: "He that has pity on the poor lends to the Lord; and he will recompense to him according to his gift" (Prov 19:17). Evagrius says, "Here he calls 'gift' purity of heart, for it is in proportion to our passionlessness *[apatheia]* that we are judged worthy of knowledge."[1] This text contains in a condensed form virtually all I would like to speak about in the present study. Here we find the expression "purity of heart" in apposition with the technical term *apatheia*; both are related to knowledge *(gnosis)*, Evagrius' term for the final goal of the monastic life.

It is commonly observed that Evagrius was especially influential in introducing this word of Stoic origins, *apatheia*, into the monastic vocabulary, or at any rate of firmly establishing it there.[2] Jerome was unmeasured in his criticism of Evagrius on this point.[3] It is often claimed

---

[1] In Prov 19:17 (G 199) SC 340, 294. The translations of Evagrius' texts in what follows are my own. In the translations of a scholion, a word in quotes indicates that this word is found also in the biblical text on which Evagrius is commenting.

[2] Evagrius takes this from Clement. See Antoine Guillaumont, "Le gnostique chez Clément d'Alexandrie et chez Évagre le Pontique," *Alexandrina: Hellénisme, judaïsme et christianisme à Alexandrie: Mélanges offerts au P. Claude Mondésert* (Paris: Cerf, 1987) 198. Praktikos, 103. For Clement see Juana Raasch, "The Monastic Concept of Purity of Heart and Its Sources, III. Philo, Clement of Alexandria, and Origen," *Studia Monastica* 10 (1968) 13–24.

[3] Letter 133. CSEL 56, p. 246. Most scholars agree that Jerome has not correctly understood Evagrius on this point. Nonetheless, his letter was influential in promoting a misunderstanding among Latin readers.

that for this reason Cassian, who transposed much of Evagrius' teaching into a Latin key and did not hesitate to transliterate Greek terms, intentionally avoids the use of *apatheia* and regularly replaces it with the expression "purity of heart."[4]

This "common knowledge" is correct in its main lines, but it requires some nuance. Mark Sheridan has shown that Cassian's use of *puritas cordis* and other such terms to express what Evagrius' intends by *apatheia* is probably not so much motivated by a desire to avoid a term that Jerome—and also Augustine!—had not looked favorably upon, but rather by the fact that he, Cassian, was very familiar with Latin philosophical vocabulary and that there were other terms available to express what the Greeks expressed with *apatheia*.[5] Sheridan's study is an important contribution to reading Cassian with a keener eye fixed to spot his own reliance on traditional Latin terminology and for coordinating this with the biblical expression *puritas cordis*. But it also suggests to me a line of investigation worth pursuing in this present study; namely, with what other vocabulary does Evagrius express what he also expresses in his use of the word *apatheia*? In fact, it is a mistake to think that Evagrius speaks of the particular phase of spiritual progress that *apatheia* is concerned with only by using this one particular Stoic term. This could be the impression left if one were to know him on the issue only through his work *The Praktikos*, the main subject matter of which is precisely *apatheia*, where the term itself is used many times and where all of the chapters serve to fix with clarity what Evagrius means by it and what its role is in the context of the larger spiritual journey the monk undertakes. But in other works of Evagrius there are an ample number of texts which show that he uses also other vocabulary, more biblical and including "purity of heart," to express *apatheia*. These are the texts I propose to examine here.

The examination can unfold in three steps. First, I will summarize Evagrius' teaching on *apatheia* as it is found in *The Praktikos*. His precise vocabulary in this work will provide us with a set of eyeglasses for recognizing the same things expressed with other terminology. Second, I will examine texts from Evagrius' scholia on the biblical

---

[4] Salvatore Marsili, *Giovanni Cassiano ed Evagrio Pontico. Dottrina sulla carità e contemplazione*, Studia Anselmiana 6 (Rome: Editrice Anselmiana, 1936) 115, n. 1; Praktikos, 103, n. 6; C. Stewart, " From λογος to verbum: John Cassian's use of Greek in the Development of a Latin Monastic Vocabulary," *The Joy of Learning and the Love of God: Essays in Honor of Jean Leclercq* (Kalamazoo, Mich.: Cistercian Publications, 1995) 20–1.

[5] M. Sheridan, "The Controversy over ἀπάθεια: Cassian's Sources and His Use of Them," *Studia Monastica*, 39 (1997) 287–310. Juana Raasch, "The Monastic Concept of Purity of Heart and Its Sources, V. Symeon-Macarius, The School of Evagrius Ponticus, and The Apophthegmata Patrum," *Studia Monastica* 12 (1970) 32.

book of Proverbs. This will be an exercise in accumulating relevant texts, in the random order that they occur, following the same random order that the genre of scholia creates. A particular word or phrase of the biblical text is chosen and commented on. Finally, I will examine the use of both *apatheia* and other terminology for the same in Evagrius' *Ad Monachos,* a work in which he locates much of his spiritual vocabulary within a textual structure that shows clearly the relation of one term to another.

In 1970 Juana Raasch wrote, "Evagrius makes little use of the Scriptural term *heart* but prefers to speak of *katharotes* as a quality of the *psyche* or the *nous.*"[6] When she wrote, primarily summarizing S. Marsili's studies of 1936, as she says, some of the important critical texts of Evagrius' work which have since been published were not yet available. And little attention had been given by scholars to his letters or to his *Ad Monachos,* considered to be of minor importance within the whole corpus. Nearly thirty years later we are in a much better position to understand Evagrius on this precise question.[7] Thus in all three steps of this study we shall focus especially on the terms "heart," "purity of heart," and *"apatheia."* Although our main purpose here will be to know Evagrius on the question, we will see, in relation to the earlier remark about Cassian's use of Evagrius, that Cassian not only had other Latin philosophical terminology available to him, but he also had in Evagrius himself an extensive use of "purity of heart" to signify *apatheia.*

APATHEIA IN *THE PRAKTIKOS*

There are major studies on Evagrius' understanding of *apatheia* in *The Praktikos.* Thus, our purpose here will be only to summarize with a view to fixing precisely the meaning of the term.[8] The Platonic threefold division of the soul is a major dimension of Evagrius' anthropology. These are the rational part (λογιστικόν), the irascible part (θυμικόν), and the concupiscible part (ἐπιθυμητικόν). The spiritual

---

[6] Raasch, "The Monastic Concept of Purity of Heart and Its Sources, V. Symeon-Macarius, the School of Evagrius Ponticus and the Apophthegmata Patrum," in *Studia Monastica* XII (1970) 32.

[7] I refer the reader to the critical editions listed at the end of these notes by the Guillaumonts and P. Géhin, to the long introduction of G. Bunge in his translation of the letters and to his studies in general, and to my own *The "Ad Monachos" of Evagrius Ponticus, Its Structure and a Select Commentary,* Studia Anselmiana 104 (Rome: Editrice Anselmiana, 1991).

[8] For thorough studies, see A. and C. Guillaumont, SC 170, 98–112, together with individual comments on the various chapters in the whole of Sources chrétiennes 171. Also G. Bunge, *Evagrios Pontikos, Praktikos oder Der Mönch, Hundert Kapitel über das geistliche Leben* (Köln: Luthe-Verlag, 1989).

struggle of the monk is conceived as a battle for establishing virtue in these various parts. Different virtues are suitably established in a part of the soul to which they correspond, while various vices can also be identified as trouble in one or another part of the soul.[9]

For Evagrius there are two major divisions of the spiritual life: *praktiké*, where the concern is purifying the passionate part of the soul;[10] and knowledge, where the rational part of the soul devotes itself to contemplation and knowledge.[11] Thus, the monastic life as conceived by Evagrius is the entire struggle to rid oneself of *evils* (related to the passionate part) and *ignorance* (related to the rational part) and to establish in the soul *virtue* (related to the passionate part) and *knowledge* (related to the rational part). For Evagrius there can be no knowledge in the higher part of the soul without virtue first being established in the passionate part of the soul. The technical term for virtue established in the passionate part of the soul is *apatheia*, or passionlessness.[12] It is not a final goal, but an intermediary one.

The Praktikos (TP) is Evagrius' principal work devoted to this stage of the spiritual life. It can be seen there that *praktiké* basically consists in doing combat with evil thoughts. The text analyzes eight principal evil thoughts (also called demons) and offers sage advice for how to defeat them. The advice is structured according to the three parts of the soul (TP 15); locating the problem as being in the rational, the irascible, or the concupiscible parts; and speaking of the virtues which must be in those parts instead (TP 15–33). This advice is followed by six chapters which speak about the passions (TP 34–9), that is, a general meditation on what moves evil thoughts in the irascible and concupiscible parts, together called the passionate part of the soul.[13] Evagrius observes that it is possible to make progress over the passions of the body to such an extent that one is eventually no longer troubled by them. However, the struggles of the soul, that is, those concerning relations with other people (TP 35), will continue until

---

[9] The classical expression of this in Evagrius is *The Praktikos* 89, where the various parts of the soul are clearly identified along with the corresponding virtues. This clear statement can function for all other occurrences of the terms in the writings of Evagrius. See also *Praktikos* 15.

[10] Thus, *The Praktikos* 78: "*Praktiké* is the spiritual method which purifies the passionate part of the soul." SC 171, 666.

[11] Cf. *The Praktikos* 89. There are divisions within the realm of knowledge also.

[12] This literal English translation of the Greek term is useful once this clear meaning is established; namely, that it signifies no longer being troubled by the passionate part of the soul. Thus, in what follows where the English "passionlessness" or "passionless" are used, it will always be for the Greek ἀπάθεια or ἀπαθής.

[13] Cf. *Praktikos* 38, 49, 78, 84.

death (TP 36). After this, a sort of demonology is presented with advice on how to conduct oneself in their presence, how to recognize and guard against their wily devices by observation, asceticism, and prayer (TP 40–53).

In their study of the structure of this text the Guillaumonts see the material I have discussed thus far as constituting a first part of the text. The second part, which extends from chapters 54 to 90, is devoted to the question of passionlessness, at which state the monk progressively arrives by his victory over the demons or passions.[14] There are a number of signs by which the condition of passionlessness can be detected: in the dreams the monk has (TP 54–6), when the mind sees its own light at the time of prayer and is calm in the face of distractions (TP 63–70), when each of the three parts of the soul acts according to nature (TP 71–90). In other words, these are all indications that some spiritual progress has been made. And indeed, there are degrees and nuances to the progress such that Evagrius distinguishes between a perfect and an imperfect passionlessness.[15] The text reaches a conclusion of the development with chapter 90, a chapter which prepares the way for the meditations on knowledge that follow in the next two works of the trilogy.[16]

Perfect passionlessness means that health is established in the two passionate parts of the soul, the concupiscible and the irascible. Then these two parts work together to maintain the soul in this state and to leave it free for its higher part, the rational, to function for knowledge. The concupiscible part *desires* virtue and knowledge. The irascible part *fights* the evil thoughts which attack all three parts of the soul. In the passionless soul, thoughts from the passionate part no longer mount up to darken the mind,[17] and thereby is the rational part ready to pass into knowledge.

This summary can serve to provide us now with what I earlier called a set of eyeglasses to discern other ways and other terms which Evagrius uses to speak about this same reality.

THE SCHOLIA ON PROVERBS

When the language is taken from the philosophical tradition, it allows for a clear and precise articulation of the various dimensions of the spiritual journey. In Evagrius and most others who function in

---

[14] A. and C. Guillaumont, SC 170, 118.
[15] Cf. *Praktikos* 60 and the comments of A. and C. Guillaumont in SC 170, 108–10.
[16] *The Gnostikos* and *The Kephalaia Gnostica*.
[17] Cf. *The Praktikos* 74.

similar theological traditions, this philosophical language does not contaminate the Christian content but makes it possible to think about it more profoundly. Thus, the distinction of the rational, irascible, and concupiscible parts of the soul, together with *apatheia* as a term describing health in the latter two parts, all enable a clear understanding of particular issues that must be dealt with in order to reach the ultimate goal of contemplative knowledge of the Holy Trinity.

In what follows we shall see how Evagrius ponders these issues also under the influence of biblical language. His philosophical framework allows him to penetrate the biblical text more deeply. At the same time the biblical language is itself decisive, enabling him to make connections and shape insights that would not be possible to him if left to the philosophical tradition alone. Perhaps nowhere is this so clear as in what Evagrius says of the ubiquitous biblical word *heart*.[18] He does not use it as a simple biblical code word for one or another part of the soul, as this is conceived by Greek philosophy. Instead, we shall find him using it across all three parts and beyond.[19] With this term he is able to show the dynamic and inextricable interconnections that exist between all the various dimensions of the inner life. We can see this now by what I called above an exercise in the accumulation of texts from his biblical scholia.

---

[18] The word "heart" is rarely used in a metaphysical sense in classical Greek writing, as Juana Raasch shows in "The Monastic Concept of Purity of Heart and Its Sources, I" *Studia Monastica* 8 (1966) 9–11. Evagrius' frequent use of this word is due to his saturation in the biblical language. In general I find Raasch's studies to be too suspicious of what she calls "Hellenism," contrasting this with a pure Gospel tradition which the former gradually contaminates. Examples of this suspicion would be the following: "The Monastic Concept of Purity of Heart and Its Sources, II. Among the Second-Century Apologists and Anti-Heretical Writers and in the Literature of the Third Century, Not Including the Alexandrians," *Studia Monastica* 8 (1966) 87–8; "The Monastic Concept of Purity of Heart and Its Sources, III. Philo, Clement of Alexandria, and Origen," 54–55; "The Monastic Concept of Purity of Heart and Its Sources, IV. Early Monasticism," *Studia Monastica* 11 (1969) 271, 293, 308; "The Monastic Concept of Purity of Heart and Its Sources, V. Symeon-Macarius, the School of Evagrius Ponticus and the Apophthegmata Patrum," in *Studia Monastica* XII (1970) 27.

[19] More often than not, "heart" indicates the soul, as Evagrius understands this; but it should not be thought that this is a hard and fast rule. It is in fact the duty of the gnostic—Evagrius' term for one who is passionless and enjoys contemplation—to teach others how particular texts in Scripture are to be understood as referring to one or another part of the soul, or one or another stage of spiritual progress. Cf. *The Gnostikos* 18, 19, 20. Thus, in one place Evagrius can say, "The Scripture applies many other names to the soul and its representations, of which it is only possible to list a few which apply to the soul: mind, soul, heart. . . ." In Prov 25:26 (G 317). SC 340, 408. Evagrius goes on to list twenty-two other scriptural names. And yet, elsewhere he can say, "It is in fact a habit of the divine Scripture to say 'heart' in place of 'mind.'" In Ps 15:9. PG 12.1216A.

The Scholia on Proverbs

In Prov 19:17 (G 199). It will be useful to look again at the scolion with which this study opened. This short saying yields a rich meditation for the reader who is familiar with the discussion of *apatheia* from *The Praktikos*. Commenting on a verse from Proverbs, Evagrius says, "Here he calls 'gift' purity of heart, for it is in proportion to our passionlessness [ἀπάθεια] that we are judged worthy of knowledge."[20] The biblical verse is bound to inspire Evagrius, for it speaks of "having pity on the poor." For him this would fall into the category of *praktiké*, and in fact he considers such a practice of major importance in establishing virtue in the irascible part of the soul.[21] The Proverbs text goes on to say that God will recompense the one who helps the poor according to his gift. Evagrius often will take one particular monastic practice or one particular biblical word and let it stand for the whole. So he does here with the word "gift." If the Scripture speaks of "recompense according to the gift," such recompense could only mean for Evagrius knowledge. And he makes that point explicit in this short explanation. But he also wants to explain "according to his gift," and thus does so within the logic of his understanding of passionlessness, since in a general way he knows that it is "in proportion to our passionlessness" that we come to knowledge.[22] Worthy of note for the scope of this present study, Evagrius rather spontaneously introduces the expression "purity of heart" as another way of saying passionlessness. The scholion thus lines up very nicely purity of heart, *apatheia,* and knowledge.

I have chosen to comment on this particular scholion first because I think it immediately pries loose too narrow an understanding of Evagrius as a monastic thinker who only uses philosophical categories and vocabulary on the issue that this whole collection of studies is considering. In this case "purity of heart" stands directly for what also is expressed by the term *apatheia.* But if we examine other texts now, we will see that the word *heart* itself does not stand for just one or several parts of the soul which Evagrius' philosophical language allows him to distinguish. It moves across a wide spectrum.

---

[20] In Prov 19:17 (G 199) SC 340, 294.

[21] "The rich man purifies his irascible part through almsgiving. . . ." In Prov 22:2 (G 234). SC 340, 328. "The monk who gives no alms will himself be in need, but the one who feeds the poor will inherit treasures," AM 25. "He who is merciful to the poor destroys irascibility," AM 30.

[22] Recall the distinction between imperfect and perfect passionlessness that was noted in *The Praktikos*. The expression "judged worthy of knowledge" (καταξιούμεθα γνώσεως) in this scholion is similar to a second title to Evagrius' work *The Gnostikos*, found in some manuscripts. This work is concerned with those who have reached perfect passionlessness. Cf. A. and C. Guillaumont, SC 356, 20.

In Prov 3:15 (G 30). "She [wisdom] is more valuable than precious stones; no evil thing shall resist her." It is the second half of this verse that Evagrius feels required to explain: "It is only in front of wisdom that the demons are powerless because they are not able to throw evil thoughts into the heart of one who has become wise. For the mind [νοῦς] that is touched by the contemplations of wisdom becomes unreceptive to impure thoughts."[23]

Although the word *heart* is not in the biblical text being commented on here, it comes naturally to mind for Evagrius to express his thought. It is a commonplace in his teaching to speak of the battle against evil thoughts; and if in *The Praktikos* he speaks of such thoughts troubling one or another part of the soul, named according to the classical Platonic division, here he speaks more generally of thoughts in the heart. But also of considerable interest in this text is the fact that *heart* stands in virtual apposition to the word *mind* (νοῦς), Evagrius' technical term for our fundamental instrument of contemplation.[24] Purity is at issue here, expressed negatively. In one moment the talk is of evil thoughts in the heart, in the next of impure thoughts in the mind—two ways of saying the same thing.

In Prov 17:24 (G 168). "The countenance of a wise man is sensible; but the eyes of a fool go to the extremes of the earth." "The heart of 'a fool' is an 'extreme' evil."[25] The exegetical tradition within which Evagrius works, which of course derives its general lines from Origen, often has a tendency to move quickly from references to some dimension of the material world to an interior sense relevant to the human condition. That is the case here, where "earth" and indeed its "extremes" are rather naturally taken in this text as representing extreme evil, since it is a fool that is being spoken about here. For the purposes of this present study, we want to notice that Evagrius effects the passage to this interior sense by means of the word "heart." The literal sense of the verse is something to the effect that the "material" eyes of a fool wander all over the place. For Evagrius, the spiritual sense refers to the heart. So, here "heart" becomes a general word for the interior, which can either be in evil, indeed an extreme evil, or—unsaid here but certainly implied—in wisdom or knowledge.

In Prov 19:7 (G 191). "A good thought [ἔννοια] will draw near to those that know it [τοῖς ἐιδόσιν], and a prudent man will find it." "Here he has called the knowledge of God a 'thought' and 'those who

---

[23] In Prov 3:15 (G 30). In SC 340, 124.

[24] For what I hope is a useful summary of Evagrius' understanding of this term, see my *The "Ad Monachos" of Evagrius Ponticus*, 8–11.

[25] In Prov 17:24 (G 168). In SC 340, 264.

know it' are the pure of heart."[26] In the biblical text Evagrius finds two words whose general sense fits well his understanding of the goal of monastic life, ἔννοια and εἰδόσιν. In this scholion he simply renders that explicit by using his preferred and more precise term, knowledge of God, τὴν τοῦ Θεοῦ γνῶσιν. Wanting to explain who it is that will know this, he adds that it will be the pure of heart, an expression that seems to come rather naturally at this point, as a means of expressing what he does so often; namely, the intimate relation between *praktiké* and knowledge. The pure of heart (= *praktiké*) will have the knowledge of God. Once again, then, we have the expression "pure of heart" put directly in relation with the whole goal of the monastic quest, knowledge of God.

In Prov 21:20 (G 228). "A desirable treasure will rest on the mouth of the wise; but foolish men will swallow it up." "The wisdom of the Lord 'will rest' [ἀναπαύσεται] in the heart of 'the wise,' but 'foolish men' [ἄφρονες] will destroy it."[27]

The exegetical method used here is a quick and simple movement to the spiritual level of the text, repeating the scriptural verse and substituting for the literal sense of "treasure" the spiritual sense "wisdom," for the literal sense of "mouth" the spiritual sense "heart." There is a logic to these substitutions. Evagrius could not have failed to be struck by two words in the biblical text, ἀναπαύσεται and ἄφρονες, both of which have precise meanings in his theological vocabulary.

The word ἄφρονες is the opposite of φρόνιμος or φρόνησις (prudence), a virtue which Evagrius so consistently associates with wisdom that when one is mentioned, the other is implied, if not also explicitly mentioned. In *The Praktikos*, where so much of the discussion is based on the three parts of the soul, Evagrius locates, as has been said, various virtues in these different parts. Wisdom and prudence are placed together in the rational part of the soul.

> The task of prudence is to command [the battle] against the opposing powers and to protect the virtues and to throw up a front against vices; also it regulates what is neutral according to the circumstances. [The task] of intelligence is to arrange harmoniously everything which contributes to our goal. [The task] of wisdom is to contemplate the reasons for the corporeals and the incorporeals.[28]

What is interesting in this conception is how virtues in the rational part of the soul are looking in different directions, as it were. Wisdom

---

[26] In Prov 19:7 (G 191). In SC 340, 286.
[27] In Prov 21:20 (G 228). In SC 340, 324.
[28] *The Praktikos* 89. SC 171, 682–4.

contemplates and is directed toward knowledge, while prudence is directed toward *praktiké*, commanding the battle against the demons. Intelligence manages some harmony between the two. Another text from *The Praktikos* confirms this interpretation, and in it the other word which concerns us, ἀνάπαυσις, is also used.

> Rest [ἀνάπαυσις] is wisdom's, but work is yoked to prudence. For there is no procuring of wisdom without war, and there is no successful war without prudence. For prudence has been entrusted with opposing itself to the irascibility of the demons, forcing the powers of the soul to act according to nature and preparing the way for wisdom.[29]

Within the logic of such vocabulary, one could almost say that Evagrius could not have explained the expression "a desirable treasure will rest" any other way than by taking it to mean "wisdom will rest." But what about the substitution of the word "heart" for "mouth"? It could, of course, simply be a word with which Evagrius expresses the interior meaning of the text. Yet as we seek in this present study to understand the relation between Evagrius' use of *apatheia* and his use of the heart, another text sheds some further light on the question. In *Ad Monachos* Evagrius says, "In the gentle heart, wisdom will rest; a throne of passionlessness: a soul accomplished in *praktiké*."[30]

The vocabulary of this proverb as well as the general idea expressed in it is based on the Lord's words, "Come to me, all who labor and are heavy laden, and I will give you rest [κἀγὼ ἀναπαύσω ὑμᾶς]. Take my yoke upon you, and learn from me; for I am gentle and lowly in heart [πραΰς εἰμι καὶ ταπεινός], and you will find rest for your souls [καὶ εὑρήσετε ἀνάπαυσιν ταῖς ψυχαῖς ὑμῶν]" (Matt 11:28-29). It is not only the terms "gentle" and "rest" which Evagrius borrows from the gospel passage; the way he uses the terms "heart" and "soul" also reflects their use in the gospel. The gentle heart of the proverb stands in relation to the gentle heart of the Lord in the gospel passage. The monk will learn to have a gentle heart by learning from the Lord.[31] The Lord promises rest for *souls*, and the proverb from *Ad Monachos* connects soul with passionlessness. That in the proverb *wisdom* is said to rest in the gentle heart is a formulation based on another dimension of the gospel passage; namely, "learn from me."

---

[29] *Praktikos* 73. SC 171, 660.

[30] AM 31. I comment on this proverb at length in *The "Ad Monachos" of Evagrius Ponticus*, 199–209.

[31] Evagrius cites this gospel text in a passage where he lists examples of gentleness. He mentions Moses, David, and "even the Savior himself [who] commanded us to be imitators of his gentleness, saying, 'Learn from me, for gentle am I and humble in heart and you will find rest for your souls.'" Mal. Cog. 14. PG 79.1216 D.

In all the passages examined here, a number of similar questions continue to turn up with different vocabulary: the relationship between *praktiké* and knowledge, the role of wisdom and prudence in relation to these, the heart and the soul as the place for both the battle that prudence undertakes and the place where wisdom will rest, passionlessness as the link between these two. Evagrius himself can be used to summarize all this:

> The soul which has rightly done *praktiké* with God and has loosed itself from the body reaches those places of knowledge where the wings of passionlessness bring it to rest and from where it receives those wings of the holy dove which it spreads out wide through the contemplation of all the aeons and then comes to rest in the knowledge of the adorable Trinity.[32]

In Prov 22:20 (G 247). "And you inscribe them [the words of the wise] three times in yourself, in view of counsel and of knowledge, on the breadth of your heart."

> The one who has enlarged his heart by purity will understand the reasons of God, reasons which concern *praktiké,* and natural contemplation and theology. For all the material of the scripture is divided into three parts: ethics, natural contemplation, and theology. Proverbs corresponds to the first, Ecclesiastes to the second, and the Song of Songs to the third.[33]

This is an important scholion for our present investigation because in it we find purity of heart associated not only with *praktiké* but also with two levels of knowledge which Evagrius regularly distinguishes: natural contemplation and theology.[34] The biblical trilogy of Solomon's books—Proverbs, Ecclesiastes, and the Song of Songs—is associated with these three dimensions of spiritual progress.[35] Thus, here "heart"—the enlarged heart, the pure heart—has for its object every dimension of the monastic life, from its beginnings in *praktiké* to its highest levels in knowledge of theology.

If this accumulation of various texts is acquainting us with a certain frequency of the concept "purity of heart," this is the first time we

---

[32] Mal. Cog. (Long) 29, Muyldermans 52. The Greek for "rest" in this passage is based on καταπαύειν. The passage draws its use of the dove image from Ps 54:7. Cf. In Ps 54:7. A similar distinction in a rest associated with *praktiké* and another associated with knowledge is found at KG III, 68.

[33] In Prov 22:20 (G 247). SC 340, 342.

[34] By "natural contemplation" Evagrius means knowledge of the created world. By "theology" he means knowledge of the Holy Trinity. Cf. *The Praktikos* 1–3.

[35] Much could be said on this point. I speak of it at greater length in "Spiritual Progress in the Works of Evagrius Ponticus," *Spiritual Progress: Studies in the Spirituality of Late Antiquity and Early Monasticism,* Studia Anselmiana 115, ed. J. Driscoll and M. Sheridan (Rome: Editrice Anselmiana, 1994) 50–4.

have encountered the idea of an enlarged heart. The immediate inspiration for Evagrius on this particular occasion comes from the biblical text itself. "Breadth of your heart" (ἐπὶ τὸ πλάτος τῆς καρδίας) becomes in his comment "the one who has enlarged his heart" (ὁ πλατύνας . . . τὴν καρδίαν αὐτοῦ). However, the image of an enlarged heart occurs frequently in Evagrius, as well as enlargement as a general concept, and is regularly used to refer to the realms of knowledge.[36]

In Prov 24:27 (G 291). "Prepare your works for your exodus, and equip yourself [to go] into the field."

> Our Lord in the Gospels called the world a "field,"[37] and now Solomon calls the contemplation of the world a "field." But the "field" in the Gospels is that of man composed of body and soul, for it is of the senses; while the "field" spoken of here is of the mind alone, for it is intelligible and composed of the reasons of this world. This is the "field" into which the pure of heart enter.[38]

Again the reader is struck in this scholion by the close association between purity of heart and the goal of knowledge. It is worth untangling how Evagrius arrives at such a conclusion. He begins by employing an exegetical device common to the Alexandrian tradition; namely, interpreting a word in one part of the Scripture with a clearer explanation of it from another part. In this case, he proceeds by citing the highest authority, the Lord himself, who explicitly begins an explanation of one of his own parables by saying, "The field is the world." That will definitely establish, at least in general terms, how the word "field" in the Proverbs text is to be understood, but on observing the two texts closely Evagrius notices a difference. The world of the Gospel parable is clearly the world of this present life and the present human condition, where man is composed of body and soul; for in this world of the parable, weeds are sown by the Evil One and are allowed to grow along with the good wheat until harvest time.

Looking at the Proverbs text, Evagrius reasons that it cannot be the same world that is spoken of there. The language of "preparing works" makes him think in general terms of *praktiké*. The exodus spoken of makes him think of the passage from *praktiké* to knowledge. ("Here he calls the soul's exit from evil and ignorance an 'exodus.'")[39] In the proverb's second line, therefore, going into a field (i.e., a world)

---

[36] Cf. In Prov 1:20-21 (G 12); 18:16 (G 184); In Ps 4:2; 17:37; 80:11; 118:32, 96; AM 135.
[37] Matt 13:38.
[38] In Prov 24:27 (G 291). In SC 340, 282, 284.
[39] In Prov 1:20-21 (G 12). In SC 340, 102. For similar interpretations of "exodus" see also In Prov 8:3 (G 99); KG IV, 64; V, 6, 21, 30, 36, 68, 71, 88; VI, 47, 49, 64; AM 21, 54. On these texts from AM, see my *The "Ad Monachos" of Evagrius Ponticus*, 190–1; 221–3.

cannot be the world where the Evil One still sows weeds but must be the world that one enters in the exodus from evil and ignorance. That world is an intelligible one, which the "mind alone" can know. A mind still immersed in the struggles of body and soul cannot enter that intelligible world.[40] But a concise way of referring to the world where such struggles are past would be "pure of heart." It is not a world of the senses but "the contemplation [θεωρία] of the world."[41] Thus, the pure of heart will enter into the intelligible world and its reasons, which the mind alone can perceive.

In Prov 27:8 (G 332). "As when a bird flies down from its own nest, so a man is brought into bondage whenever he estranges himself from his own place." "The 'place' of the heart is virtue and knowledge; and if a man 'estranges himself' from it, he falls into evil and ignorance and becomes a slave since 'Everyone who commits sin is a slave of sin' (John 8:34)."[42]

Evagrius moves immediately to a spiritual sense of the literal meaning of the text, expressing the interior sense of "place" as "heart." And here his application covers the whole range of the interior life, the two main realms of virtue and knowledge, whose opposites are evil and ignorance. Thus, "heart" here serves to express the proper place of the one who lives the monastic life. Going away from the heart—from virtue and knowledge—is to be a slave to sin.[43]

PURITY OF HEART IN THE *AD MONACHOS*

We have seen that *The Praktikos* offers a neat and orderly exposition of Evagrius' teaching on *apatheia*. In the biblical scholia the discussion on the same comes as it may, according to the order of the biblical text and the words found therein. This genre does not permit an orderly presentation of Evagrius' thought. Now, however, having trained our eye to spot the issue of *apatheia* as it is exposed in biblical language, particularly with the use of the word "heart," it is possible to conclude

---

[40] It should be noticed that Evagrius is carefully using the language with which he describes the various conditions in which rational creatures find themselves after the fall: body, soul, mind. The mind alone is at the root of the original creation, and it will also describe the final condition.

[41] In the strong sense of θεωρία, "seeing through" the world of the senses. What is seen are the "reasons of the world," also spoken of in the scholion, of which the intelligible world is composed.

[42] In Prov 27:8 (G 332). SC 340, 420, 422.

[43] This examination of proverbs has not been exhaustive on the proverbs from *The Scholia on Proverbs* that relate to this theme. Other relevant texts would be the following: In Prov 6:27-28 (G 82); 8:5 (G 100); 16:33 (G 152); 17:23 (G 166); 22:15 (G 244); 20 (G 312); 26:23 (G 328).

this study by referring to another Evagrian text that does permit an orderly presentation; namely, the *Ad Monachos*.

I have spoken of this text elsewhere at length and have argued that its structure contains a secret which Evagrius expects the careful reader to uncover.[44] Its 137 proverbs unfold in an order of spiritual progress which begins with faith, the first virtue of *praktiké*, and concludes with the mind presented before the Holy Trinity, the goal of the entire monastic life. The particular place within this structure where a specific issue—a virtue, a vice, a level of knowledge—is treated is a key to how Evagrius conceives that issue in relation to the whole. The language of *Ad Monachos* is heavily biblical. This is clear, among other ways, in the abundant use of the word "heart" in the text. Thus, in this text the reader has, as it were, the best of both worlds: an orderly presentation similar to what is found in *The Praktikos*, and a heavily biblical language similar to what is found in the scholia.

Evagrius uses the word "heart" evenly throughout the entire text. Therein it is closely associated with *apatheia*, but it has other functions and references as well. A brief review of these uses, always following the order which is a key to understanding them, will serve to summarize in an orderly way all that we have seen so far.[45]

> Anachoresis in love purifies the heart;
> anachoresis in hate agitates it (AM 8).

This first appearance of the word "heart" in the text speaks of its purity. This saying is part of the first chain of proverbs with which Evagrius moves his reader from meditations on faith, the first of the virtues, to love, the goal of *praktiké*. Thus love, here meaning practical charity toward others, is what purifies the heart.

> Where evil enter in, there also ignorance;
> but the hearts of holy ones will be filled with knowledge (AM 24).

Here, interestingly, "heart" is referred to the final goal of monastic life, knowledge. As we have already seen in some of the scholia, it is a term that can at one and the same time refer to the life of *praktiké* and the purification that must be worked there, and to the life of knowledge. The same is true in a proverb that follows closely after:

---

[44] Jeremy Driscoll, "A Key for Reading the *Ad Monachos* of Evagrius Ponticus," *Augustinianum* 30 (1990) 361–39; Driscoll, *The "Ad Monachos" of Evagrius Ponticus*; Jeremy Driscoll, *The Mind's Long Journey to the Holy Trinity: The* Ad Monachos *of Evagrius Ponticus* (Collegeville: The Liturgical Press, 1993).

[45] I have already commented more amply in *The "Ad Monachos" of Evagrius Ponticus* on all the texts that I will cite here.

> An ornament for the head: a crown;
> an ornament for the heart: knowledge of God (AM 27).

Or again,

> In the gentle heart, wisdom will rest;
> a throne of passionlessness: a soul accomplished in *praktiké* (AM 31).

In this tightly constructed proverb the whole range of monastic life is exposed in its two basic phases. As noted above in the commentary on In Prov 21:20, "wisdom resting" is a standard way with which Evagrius expresses a dimension of the life of knowledge. Of course, no one enters that rest without the work of *praktiké*, expressed in three different phrases here, each of which summarizes the goal in a different way. Passionlessness is equivalent to the soul accomplished in *praktiké*. And a more biblical way for saying the same is "gentle heart." With this expression Evagrius often summarizes the goal of *praktiké*, a particular version of what he means by a pure heart.[46]

The heart is the place of struggle for the monk, as in the following:

> Like a strong south wind on the sea,
> so is irascibility in the heart of a man (AM 36).

> Better a fast with a pure heart
> than a feast in impurity of soul (AM 44).

This is a clear example of the parallel sense of *heart* and *soul*, the question of purity being always at issue. And purity is always a struggle against evil thoughts, as the proverb that follows immediately in the text shows:

> He who completely destroys evil thoughts in his heart,
> he is like the one who dashes his children against the rock (AM 45).

An angelic dream gladdens the heart, while a demonic one agitates it (AM 52). The heart is made to glow after the struggle with listlessness, the most oppressive evil thought of them all (AM 55). And again, evil thoughts should never be allowed to linger in the heart (AM 58), even if it is temptations that test the heart of a monk (AM 60). In a strategically located proverb that treats of pride, "the original evil," Evagrius warns, "Do not give your heart to pride" (AM 62).

At the center of the text of *Ad Monachos* Evagrius has placed a chain of ten proverbs which in this placement functions as a hinge for the movement from *praktiké* to knowledge. Each of the ten proverbs treats

---

[46] Cf. Jeremy Driscoll, "Gentleness in the *Ad Monachos* of Evagrius Ponticus," *Studia Monastica* 33 (1990) 295–321.

this theme (AM 63–72). At the center of this center are three proverbs which treat *apatheia* or passionlessness (AM 66–68), thereby expressing its crucial role in the whole of spiritual progress. In the first of these three proverbs, the word "heart" appears once again:

> Without milk, a child is not nourished
> and apart from passionlessness, a heart will not be raised up (AM 66).

The word "heart" continues to be used in the text, but hereafter the references consistently refer the heart to knowledge. The monk who "keeps his heart" will be filled with knowledge (AM 94). Humiliation of the irascible raises up the heart (AM 100). "Without knowledge the heart will not be placed on high" (AM 117).

In the final movement of the text, Evagrius constructs proverbs that move in a crescendo toward the final proverb which speaks of the mind being presented before the Holy Trinity. Along this way, the heart and its purity remain at issue.

> The wisdom of the Lord raises up the heart;
> his prudence purifies it (AM 131).

Here once again are the twin virtues of wisdom and prudence, which operate in the rational part of the soul. In this proverb their object is the heart. The heart raised up by wisdom is the heart that enjoys contemplation of "the reasons for the corporeals and the incorporeals."[47] The prudence that purifies the heart is the work of *praktiké*, where we saw the task of prudence is "to command [the battle] against the opposing powers and to protect the virtues and to throw up a front against vices."[48]

Finally, in the proverb that immediately precedes the "mind presented before the Holy Trinity" (AM 136), one reads,

> Contemplations of worlds enlarge the heart;
> reasons of providence and judgment lift it up (AM 135).

Here one encounters again what was noted as a frequent image in Evagrius: the enlarged heart.[49] It is precisely contemplation that does so. Thus, the heart is not just something purified in *praktiké*, but in some sense the very instrument of contemplation, enlarged, lifted up by knowledge of different kinds.

---

[47] As according to *The Praktikos* 89, cited above in the comment on In Prov 21:20.
[48] Also according to *The Praktikos* 89, cited above in the comment on In Prov 21:20.
[49] In the commentary on In Prov 22:20. See n. 36 for other references.

CONCLUSIONS

Examination of the scholia on Ecclesiastes and on the Psalms would continue to build the case that is unfolding before us, as would many passages from Evagrius' letters.[50] The case briefly stated is this: Evagrius makes frequent use of the expression "purity of heart"; by it he expresses in biblical language what he also expressed with precision in a term borrowed from the philosophical tradition through Clement, that is, *apatheia* (passionlessness). Purity of heart or passionlessness are different ways of saying the same thing. It is not the final goal of the monastic journey but the necessary intermediate threshold that must be passed on the way to contemplation and knowledge of the Holy Trinity.

Our examination has also shown that "purity" is one issue for Evagrius and the "heart" another. If the term *"apatheia"* has the advantage of expressing that dimension of things which concerns the concupiscible and irascible parts of the soul no longer being disturbed by the passions, the term "heart" allows Evagrius to speak more fluidly across various dimensions of the inner life. With it he sometimes refers to these parts of the soul, at other times to all three parts, then to one part only, but also to the mind, or the mind as it is united with the soul. Heart is certainly the object of purification in the work of *praktiké*, but it is also the instrument used for contemplation.

In explaining that it is ultimately the instrument for contemplation or knowledge that must be purified, Evagrius moves very naturally from what may first seem a more philosophical term, "mind" (νοῦς), to what may seem the more biblical term, "heart." But this natural movement only shows that the sharp distinction between philosophical and biblical is not made by Evagrius. It tends to be more our problem than that of these ancients.

> To be sure, it is not the mind itself which sees God, but rather the pure mind. "Blessed are the pure of heart, for they shall see God" (Matt 5:8). Note that he does not praise purity as blessed but rather the one seeing [i.e., contemplating]. Purity is passionlessness of the reasonable soul, but seeing [contemplating] God is true knowledge of the one essence of the adorable Trinity, which those will see who have perfected their conduct here and through the commandments purified their souls.[51]

Evagrius is extremely consistent in his talk about the inner life. His vocabulary is both philosophical and biblical, but he coordinates these two sources to speak just one language, which may be described as

---

[50] See, for example, In Eccl 5, 39, 44, 48, 63, 64, 68, 72; Letters 12:2; 14; 17:3; 25:6; 27:1; 39:5; 54:2; 56:2; 58:3.

[51] Letter 56:2, Frankenberg, 604.

Christian and monastic. One of the most characteristic dimensions of his thought is the division of the monastic journey into the two stages of *praktiké* and knowledge. Yet just as characteristic is his never losing an opportunity to unite these two, teaching in one moment that the purity of *praktiké* is not an end in itself, in the other that the knowledge which is the goal is not possible apart from purity. The biblical text itself instructs him to always keep in balance these two dimensions.

> I have faith in God that you will reap thirty and sixty and a hundredfold the fruit thanks to the purity of your lives. "For blessed are the pure of heart; they shall see God."[52]

> In the pure heart another heaven is imprinted, of which the vision is light and the place spiritual.[53]

> The state of prayer is the condition of passionlessness, which by a supreme love snatches up on high the mind in love with wisdom, the spiritual mind.[54]

[52] Ep Fid 36.
[53] Letter 39:5, Frankenberg, 592.
[54] Prayer 53. *PG* 79.1177C.

ABBREVIATIONS AND EDITIONS OF PRIMARY SOURCES CITED

AM	*Ad Monachos*, ed. H. Gressmann, "Nonnenspiegel und Mönchsspiegel des Euagrios Pontikos," *Texte und Untersuchungen* 39:4 (1913) 143–65.
Ant	*Antirretikos*, ed. W. Frankenberg, *Evagrius Ponticus*, Abhandlungen der königlichen Gesellschaft der Wissenschaften zu Göttingen, Phil.-hist. Klasse Neue Folge, Bd. XIII, 2 (Berlin: Weidmannsche buchhandlung, 1912).
Ep Fid	*Epistula Fidei*, ed. J. Gribomont, *Basilio di Cesarea*, vol. 1: *Le lettre* (Turin: n.p., 1983). Letter 8 (84–113) = Evagrius' *Epistula Fidei* and is cited with the line numbers of this edition.
Gnostikos	Evagrius Ponticus, *Le gnostique: Ou a celui qui est devenu digne de la science*, Sources chrétiennes 356 (Paris: Cerf, 1989).
In Eccl	Evagrius Ponticus, *Scholies a l'Ecclesiaste: Edition princeps du texte grec*, Sources chrétiennes 397, trans. Paul Géhin (Paris: Cerf, 1993).
In Prov	Evagrius Ponticus, *Scholies aux Proverbes*, Sources chrétiennes 340, trans. Paul Géhin (Paris: Cerf, 1987).
In Ps	*The Scholia on Psalms*, cited according to the key of Rondeau in "Le commentaire sur les Psaumes d'Évagre le Pontique," *Orientalia Christiana Periodica* 26 (1960) 307–48. (*PG* 12; *PG*

Abbreviations and Editions of Primary Sources Cited 159

	27; J. B. Pitra, *Analecta sacra spicilego Solesmensi*, v. 2 [Frascati, 1884], v. 3 [Paris, 1883].)
KG	Evagrius Ponticus, *Les six centuries des "Kephalaia Gnostica" d'Évagre le Pontique*, Patrologia Orientalis 28, trans. Antoine Guillaumont (Paris: Firmin-Didot, 1958) fasc. 1, no. 134.
Letter	*Letters*, ed. W. Frankenberg, *Evagrius Ponticus*, Abhandlungen der königlichen Gesellschaft der Wissenschaften zu Göttingen, Phil.-hist. Klasse Neue Folge, Bd. XIII, 2 (Berlin: Weidmannsche buchhandlung, 1912). With Greek fragments in C. Guillaumont, "Fragments grecs inédits d'Évagre le Pontique," *Texte und Untersuchungen* 133 (1987) 209–21. Paragraph numbers according to Evagrios Pontikos, *Briefe aus der Wüste, Eingeleitet, übersetzt und kommentiert von Gabriel Bunge* (Trier: Paulinus-Verlag, 1986).
Mal. Cog.	*De Diversis Malignis Cogitationibus* or *The Treatise on Evil Thoughts*, PG 79.1200–1233.
Mal. Cog. (Long)	*De Diversis Malignis Cogitationibus* with supplement by Joseph. Muyldermans, *A travers la tradition manuscrite d'Évagre le Pontique*, Bibliothèque du Muséon 3 (Louvain: Bureaux du Muséon, 1932) 47–60.
Praktikos	*The Praktikos*, ed. A. and C. Guillaumont, *Évagre le Pontique. Traité Pratique ou Le Moine*, Sources chrétiennes 170, 171 (Paris: Cerf, 1971).
Prayer	*De Oratione capitula* or *The Chapters on Prayer*, PG 79.1165–1200 with the edition of S. Tugwell, *Evagrius Ponticus: Practikos and On Prayer, translated by Simon Tugwell*, published privately by the Faculty of Theology, Oxford, 1987.
Skemmata	*Skemmata*, ed. Joseph Muyldermans, *Evagriana*. Extrait de la revue *Le Muséon*, v. 42, augmenté de *Nouveaux fragments grecs inédits* (Paris, 1931) 38–44.

Purity of Heart in the Life and Words of Amma Syncletica

MARY FORMAN, O.S.B.

INTRODUCTION

In Juana Raasch's comprehensive study of purity of heart she emphasizes the need for custody or guarding the heart, "the center of the emotions," as well as "the source of mental activities of thinking, planning and remembering, which God alone can see."[1] Since the heart represents the inner life of the person, the metaphor, purity of heart, "stands for the removal of inner defilement, that is, sin, in its very principle: the inner disposition."[2] Of major concern to biblical writers were the thoughts of the heart, which once "conceived in the heart and born as words and actions determine the quality and direction of a [person's] whole spiritual life."[3] Both evil thoughts (Septuagint: *logismoi kakoi*) and vain thoughts *(logismoi mataioi),* which according to biblical authors can defile the heart, became the subject of monastic writers.[4]

Jesus also viewed the heart as the place from which evil and defilement sprang. His parables teach that the heart is the ground (Luke 8:15) or the tree or treasure (Luke 6:44-45; cf. Matt 12:33-35) which brings forth good or evil. Furthermore, he orders his disciples to be vigilant against such thoughts and sentiments of the heart.[5]

---

[1] Juana Raasch, "The Monastic Concept of Purity of Heart and Its Sources," *Studia Monastica* 8 (1966) I:13. This series of articles was published in five parts over a four-year period. Hereafter, citations from her articles will be designated by *SM*, followed by volume number, date, series number (I through V), and page number.

[2] Ibid., I:13.
[3] Ibid., I:15.
[4] Ibid.
[5] Ibid., I:18.

Raasch stressed the connection between purity of heart, as found in the Bible and early Jewish writings, and freedom from evil thoughts, which recurs frequently in monastic literature, as follows:

> From the point of view of monastic spirituality, perhaps the most significant findings of this study of the place of purity of heart in the Bible and early Jewish writings are the fact of its origin and its importance within this tradition, its link with the coming of the Holy Spirit into the heart and with the vision of God, the idea of demons defiling the heart, and above all, the relation of purity of heart with freedom from evil thoughts and the frequent use of the actual word *logismoi*, certainly one of the most commonly recurring terms in ancient monastic literature. There can be no doubt . . . that the expression *logismoi tes kardias* in Eastern spirituality has been borrowed from the language of the Septuagint.[6]

The following reflection on the process of purification of the inner person from the *logismoi*, as described by the desert amma, Blessed Syncletica, is dedicated in memory of Sister Juana, as a tribute from one researcher of early monastic sources to another.

WHO WAS BLESSED SYNCLETICA?

Amma Syncletica, a fifth-century monastic foundress, is known mainly through the twenty-seven apothegms derived from the *Vita Syncleticae*, which are found in the alphabetical collection of the *Apophthegmata Patrum*.[7] The *Vita Syncleticae* is actually a didactic presentation of this amma's experiences of the ascetical life presented to her disciples. The main body of the work is surrounded by a few chapters, which open with a description of her life and virtues (chs. 1–21) and close with her final illness and death (chs. 104–13).[8]

---

[6] Ibid., I:21.

[7] See J.-P. Migne, *Patrologia Graeca* 65, cols. 421–8 for AP 1–18; also, J. C. Guy, *Recherches sur la tradition grecque des "Apophthegmata Patrum,"* Subsidia hagiographica 36 (Brussels: Societé des Bollandistes, 1962) 34–5 for AP 19–27. In English, there is "Syncletica," *The Sayings of the Desert Fathers: The Alphabetical Collection*, rev. ed., Cistercian Studies 59, trans. Benedicta Ward (Kalamazoo, Mich.: Cistercian Publications, 1984) 230–5.

[8] One French and two recent English translations of the *Vita Syncleticae* are available: *Vie de sainte Syncletique et Discours de salut a une vierge*, Spiritualité Orientale 9, trans. Odile Bénédicte Bernard, intro. Lucien Regnault (Maine-&-Loire: Abbaye de Bellefontaine, 1972); "Pseudo-Athanasius: The Life and Activity of the Holy and Blessed Teacher Syncletica," intro. and trans. Elizabeth A. Castelli, *Ascetic Behavior in Greco-Roman Antiquity: A Sourcebook*, Studies in Antiquity and Christianity, ed. Vincent L. Wimbush (Minneapolis: Fortress Press, 1990) 265–311; and Pseudo-Athanasius, *The Life of Blessed Syncletica*, Peregrina Translations Series 21, trans. Elizabeth Bryson Bongie (Toronto: Peregrina Publishing Co., 1995). Citations in English will be taken from the

Her unknown biographer,[9] who came by the sparse details of her life from her contemporaries (*VS* 3), states that her origins were in Macedonia but that her family had migrated to Alexandria (*VS* 4). Despite her parents' attempts to marry her off (*VS* 7), she devoted her life to the practice of virginity in her home (*VS* 9–10). Only when her parents died was she free to dispose of her property and take up the solitary life in the tomb of a relative, located some distance from the city (*VS* 11). After some time, during which she grew in ascetical training and virtues, some women came to her for help in living the ascetical life (*VS* 21). She and the women eventually formed a community (*VS* 100–1).

Toward the end of her life, that is, in her eightieth year, she was visited with bodily suffering, which lasted three and a half years (*VS* 106). Descriptions of her illness show a progression of an infection in the gums which lead to gangrene and bone deterioration (*VS* 111), and finally to her death (*VS* 113).

The bulk of the chapters (*VS* 21–103) of this holy amma's life is devoted to her teaching to the women disciples gathered around her, like an assembly *(syncletos)*.[10] The following topics—Syncletica's teachings on purity, her understanding of the heart, the treatment of the *logismoi* and the aim of monastic life—will all be examined in the following pages.

CONCEPT OF PURITY IN SYNCLETICA'S TEACHING

Not once in the *Vita* is the Greek phrase *katharos/katharsis tes kardias* (pure/purity of heart) ever found. Nor does Syncletica speak of *apatheia*, the term used most frequently by Evagrius to mean what Cassian would later translate as *puritas cordis* (purity of heart).[11] Even though Syncletica frequently draws on Evagrian concepts like the principal vices, the "practical life," and pure prayer,[12] nevertheless she

---

Bongie translation and cited as *VS*, followed by chapter number, Bongie, and page number. The Greek edition, source for the French and English translations, can be found in J.-P. Migne, *Patrologia Graeca* 28, cols. 1488–557; hereafter this work will be cited as *PG* 28, followed by column numbers.

[9] See Mary Forman, "Amma Syncletica: A Spirituality of Experience," *Vox Benedictina* 10:2 (Winter 1993) 199–200, who states that the attribution to Athanasius was made much later by the fourteenth-century Greek historian Nicephorus Calixtus. Some manuscripts ascribe the *Vita* to the ascetic Polycarp or to Blessed Arsenius of Pegades, both of whom are otherwise unknown (see the aforementioned article, 229–30, n. 5).

[10] *VS* 4, Bongie, 10 states: "Named for the heavenly assembly [i.e., *syncletos*], Syncletica has her origins in the land of Macedonia."

[11] See Raasch, *SM* 12 (1970) V:32: Cassian probably uses *puritas cordia* for Evagrius' terms *apatheia* and *katharotes* because he wished to avoid being connected with the Pelagian controversy.

[12] See Regnault, "Introduction," *Vie de sainte Syncletique*, x–xii.

appears reserved in her elaboration of purity, when compared to her predecessor Evagrius. The term *katharos* appears only three times in the amma's long discourse.[13] Each instance will be explored here that we may understand what this amma taught her disciples about purity.

The first instance of *katharos* appears in *VS* 28, where Syncletica explains the meaning of Matt 10:16, "Let us become *cunning as serpents and innocent as doves*," with respect to temptations.

> What, then, are we to do against this danger? Let us become *cunning as serpents and innocent as doves*, pitting against his snare all our intellectual resources. For the advice *Be cunning as serpents* has been given so that we may not fail to notice the onslaughts of the Devil; for *like* very quickly earns recognition from *like*. *Innocence of the dove* indicates purity of action *[to katharontes prazeos]*. Every good deed, then, will be a move away from something worse. But how are we to escape what we don't know. . . . At all times, therefore, there is a need for vigilance; for he wages war through external acts and wins victory through internal acts. And he accomplishes more through internal thoughts *[dia ton endon logismon]*, for, unseen, he keeps attacking by night and day [*VS* 28].[14]

Syncletica draws from the biblical aphorism a means of protection. The serpent's cunning symbolizes a form of discernment of demonic impulses, while the dove's innocence calls for purity of action. Both spiritual engagements—cunning awareness and purity of deeds—require vigilant attentiveness to one's internal thoughts, the *logismoi*.

Syncletica continues her teaching in chapter 29 with the suggestion of the two weapons by which the attacks of the evil one are defeated: by laborious ascesis and pure prayer *[askeseos epiponou kai katharas proseuches]*.[15] Although these tools provide "general protection against every destructive thought" *(epi pantos logismou olethriou)*, one can also employ some particular mental devices, that is, to offer against a most shameful thought *(aischistou logismou)* its opposite.[16] Elsewhere in *Vita Syncleticae* Syncletica proposes the remedies of opposites, including the virtue of *obedience* as a means to cure the malady of *disobedience* (*VS*

---

[13] See *VS* 28: *to katharon tes prazeos*, *PG* 28.1504C; *VS* 29: *katharas proseuches*, *PG* 28.1540D; *VS* 74: *to katharon*, *PG* 28.1529D. The verb *kathairein* is found in *VS* 80, *PG* 28.1533D. The word impurity is found as a plural *akatharsias* in *VS* 45, *PG* 28.1513C, and the singular *akatharsian* in *VS* 66, *PG* 28.1525D.

[14] *VS* 28, Bongie, 23–4; Greek: *PG* 28.1504C.

[15] *PG* 28.1504D.

[16] Ibid. The remedy of opposites had a long history going back to early Greek medicine practiced in the Aslepian temples of ancient Greece; see *contraria contrariis*, the remedy of contrary things for contrary illnesses, described in C. A. Meier, *Ancient Incubation and Modern Psychotherapy*, trans. Monica Curtis (Evanston, Ill.: Northwestern University Press, 1967) 69.

51) and humility as the remedy for pride (*VS* 56). Thus for Syncletica, the latter virtues serve as active agents against specific vices.

In the Evagrian system of spirituality, all the virtues ultimately culminate in *apatheia,* whose child is *agape.* Evagrius relates the intimate connection between these two qualities by means of the words spoken by desert elders to a young monk about to receive the habit, at the beginning of his *Praktikos,* as follows:

> The fear of God strengthens faith, my son, and continence in turn strengthens this fear. Patience and hope make this latter virtue solid beyond all shaking and they also give birth to *apatheia.* Now this *apatheia* has a child called *agape* who keeps the door to deep knowledge of the created universe. Finally, to this knowledge succeed theology and the supreme beatitude.[17]

In a few pithy sentences Evagrius is describing the process by which "the passions are expelled" from the heart "and *apatheia* or *katarotes* attained."[18] The next purification brings about "the elimination of 'simple thoughts' or discursive reasoning through the lower forms of contemplation."[19] Both of these purifications occur at the end of the *praktike.* "At this point charity, *agape,* arises as the result of *apatheia* or purity and as its positive aspect."[20] After this, the contemplative stage follows.

By contrast, Syncletica offers beginner-disciples of her community a different understanding of the virtues and their interrelationship with *agape* and poverty. For she says:

> Just as dreadful qualities are attached to one another . . . , so the opposite qualities of these vices are dependent upon love [*agape*]; I mean, of course, gentleness and patience, as well as endurance, and the ultimate good—holy poverty. It is not possible for anyone to acquire this virtue (I mean, to be sure love [*agape*]) apart from holy poverty, for the Lord did not enjoin love on one person, but on all. Those, therefore, who have resources must not overlook those who have needs.[21]

Throughout the next two chapters, Syncletica proclaims that almsgiving is "the beginning of love for those who do not know love." Just as physical circumcision prefigured the symbolic circumcision of the heart *(tes kardias),* "so also has almsgiving been established as a teacher of love [*tes agapes*]. For those, therefore, to whom love [*he agape*] has

---

[17] Evagrius, "Introductory Letter to Anatolius," *The Praktikos,* 14.
[18] Raasch, *SM* 12 (1970) V:31–2.
[19] Ibid., 32.
[20] Ibid.
[21] *VS* 72, Bongie, 45; Greek: *PG* 28.1529B–C.

been given by grace, almsgiving is superfluous. I am saying this not to belittle mercy, but to show the purity of holy poverty *[tes aktemosunes to katharon]*."[22] For Syncletica, *agape* is closely aligned with the purity *(to katharon)* of poverty, not with the *apatheia* of Evagrius. Moreover, poverty manifests an interior spiritual condition of the loving heart, much like "circumcision of the heart," whereas almsgiving is only a beginner's lesson in loving, much like physical circumcision. Thus the process of growing from almsgiving to the purity of holy poverty is one of the "graced" movements of love, acquired through the exercise of virtues.

The use of the imagery of "circumcision of the heart" *(peritome tes kardias)* is a biblical one, for Rom 2:29 states: "real circumcision is a matter of the heart, spiritual not literal" *(peritome kardias en pneumati ou grammati)*.[23] This reference to *kardia*, like all others in the *Vita*, is a result of Syncletica's either alluding to or directly quoting Scripture.[24] Two of these occurrences of *kardia* in the *Vita* will be the focus of our study.

"HEART" AS *KARDIA* IN THE *VITA SYNCLETICAE*

The most important quality of the heart, from the point of view of virtues to be cultivated, was humility. Humility was highly valued by Syncletica precisely because it was the very virtue of Christ, by which he fulfilled salvation for humankind. About this virtue, Syncletica teaches:

> Because humility is good and salutary, the Lord clothed himself in it while fulfilling the economy [of salvation] for humanity. For he says: *Learn from me, for I am gentle and humble of heart [tapeinos te kardia]*. Notice who it is who is speaking; learn his lesson perfectly. Let humility become for you the beginning and the end of virtues. He means a humble

---

[22] *VS* 73–4, Bongie, 45–6; Greek: *PG* 28.1529D.

[23] *VS* 73, *PG* 28.1529D. The Romans 2:29 verse is taken from *Greek-English New Testament*, Greek text *Novum Testamentum Graece*, editio XXVII, in the tradition of Eberhard Nestle and Erwin Nestle, ed. Barbara and Kurt Aland et al. (Stuttgart: Deutsche Bibelgesellschaft, 1981) 413. Hereafter this work will be cited as follows: Nestle-Aland, *G-E NT*, followed by page number.

[24] (1) *VS* 41 compares the monastic life with the life of the laity based on Syncletica's interpretation of Isa 1:5: *"Every head [is destined] for pain, and every heart for sadness"*; see *VS* 41, Bongie, 30, where heart *(kardias)* is used three times. (2) *VS* 49 addresses the temptations of the devil who so seduces the soul that it is not allowed to say: *"I will give praise to you, Lord, with all my heart" (en ole kardia mou)*; see *VS* 49, Bongie, 34, *PG* 28.1517B. (3) *VS* 83 takes up the vice of determinism, which Syncletica views as a form of foolishness, like that described in Ps 14:1: *"The foolish man said in his heart [en kardia autou] there is no God"*; see *VS* 83, Bongie, 51, *PG* 28.1536D. For further information on the vice of deter-

heart [*Phronesin . . . tapeinen*]; he refers not to appearance alone, but to the inner person [*ton entos anthropon*], for the outer person [*ho extos*] will also follow after the inner (*VS* 57).²⁵

Syncletica clearly teaches that humility of heart, based on Christ's own example, is the beginning and end of the virtuous life. The priority of place for humility among the virtues, in the lives of early desert monks, is affirmed by Douglas Burton-Christie, who writes:

> Humility was the starting point for the desert monks, both because it was the first commandment and because they knew that without the self-emptying which humility implied, the treasures for which they had come to the desert would forever elude them. The *Sayings* is filled with questions about the meaning of humility and about how to acquire and cultivate it: its importance was equaled only by its elusiveness. The monks' questions about humility focused on and drew upon various words of Scripture and in particular the witness of Christ. In pursuing humility, they were attempting to realize in their own lives the call to self-emptying exemplified in the words and witness of Jesus.²⁶

Not only does Syncletica attest to the importance of humility within the monastic heritage, but she also distinguishes that this Christian virtue par excellence must be manifested interiorly, that is, *ton entos anthropon*.²⁷ Could she be drawing her wisdom also from Eph 3:16, which states: "may [God] grant you to be strengthened with might through his Spirit in the inner person" *(eis ton eso anthropon)*?²⁸ If so, then, it is God's spirit at work interiorly, that is, in the soul, who ultimately brings about the attitude which was Christ's.

Later on, Syncletica advises the women of her community to "imitate this humility that he put into practice," rather than feigning humility through outward appearance so as to seek fame (*VS* 59). The latter group of people will be known by their fruits.²⁹ Once again, the amma stresses that the outward behavior of humility should coincide with the interiority of the virtue incarnated in their hearts.

---

minism, see Kevin Corrigan, "Syncletica and Macrina: Two Early Lives of Women Saints," *Vox Benedictina* 6:3 (July 1989) 252–3. (4) *VS* 57 quotes Matt 11:29 on a humble heart and *VS* 92 alludes to 1 Cor 14:14-15 on the heart being busy with distracting thoughts while the mouth speaks. Both of these later chapters will be examined in detail below.

²⁵ *VS* 57, Bongie, 38–9; Greek: *PG* 28.1521C.
²⁶ Douglas Burton-Christie, *The Word in the Desert: Scripture and the Quest for Holiness in Early Christian Monasticism* (New York/Oxford: Oxford University Press, 1993) 236.
²⁷ *VS* 57, Bongie, 38–9; Greek: *PG* 28.1521C.
²⁸ See Nestle-Aland, *G-E NT*, 508.
²⁹ *VS* 59, Bongie, 39.

Humility is again mentioned in chapter 92 as a virtue necessary among many others with which the virgin is to be clothed as she is "betrothed to the Heavenly Bridegroom."[30] The amma urges her followers "to wash away [apolousasthai] the filth of our sins with laborious ascesis, . . . let us make our souls bright with virtues," namely, with a crown of faith, hope, and charity (agape), the necklace of humility (tapeinophrosunen), the belt of self-control, the radiant garment of poverty, and to partake of the imperishable foods of prayers and psalms.[31] In addition, they are to "consider with the spirit what is being said. For often the mouth speaks, but the heart is busy with thoughts" (de kardia peri logismous).[32]

With this advice on the virtues, Syncletica reveals a creative rewriting of Eph 6:14-18 on the armor of God needed to withstand the schemes of the devil. The only virtue she shares in common with the Ephesians text is faith. She does mention prayer, which is also found in Eph 6:18.[33] While both writers are concerned about the armory of virtues needed to battle against evil, Syncletica chooses the virtues she considers most necessary for the particular combat in monastic life: humility, chastity and poverty.

The last admonition in chapter 92 warns against the heart being occupied with logismoi: "For often the mouth speaks, but the heart is busy with distracting thoughts."[34] This aphorism is a paraphrase of yet another biblical phrase, 1 Cor 14:14. There Paul is concerned about praying in a tongue, where the spirit prays but the mind, unable to interpret it, remains unfruitful. So he resolves this problem by stating in verse 15: "I will pray with the spirit [to pneumati] and I will pray with the mind [to noi] also."[35]

When Syncletica substitutes heart (kardia) for the mind (to noi), which can no longer consider what the spirit says because it is busy with the logismoi or evil thoughts, she also transforms the meaning of the biblical verses. Syncletica has changed Paul's concern, that of the distraction of keeping the mind and spirit attentive to what the tongue speaks, to a situation of a heart so preoccupied with logismoi it cannot receive the spirit of the words spoken.

---

[30] VS 92, Bongie, 57. The bridal imagery of betrothal, so highly developed in the Brautmystik of medieval mystical language, was used in early monastic vitae for the spiritual marriage of virgins with Christ.

[31] PG 28.1544D.

[32] VS 92, Bongie, 59; Greek: PG 28.1546A.

[33] Compare euchai of VS 92 (PG 28.1544D) with proseuches of the Greek New Testament (Nestle-Aland, G-E NT, 514).

[34] VS 92, Bongie, 57.

[35] Nestle-Aland, G-E NT, 463 for both English and Greek.

Throughout chapter 92 Syncletica is concerned about clothing the soul with spiritual virtues by washing away its sins and doing away with the *logismoi* of the heart. *Vita Syncleticae* 92 represents the only place in the *Vita* where the *logismoi* are linked directly with *kardia*, within a larger context of washing or purifying the heart.

TREATMENT OF THE *LOGISMOI* IN THE SOUL

Most frequently Syncletica, like Evagrius before her, prefers the term *psyche* to *kardia*.[36] The *psyche* or heart was for the desert monastics where the spiritual warfare took place, predominantly as a battle against the *logismoi akatharoi*, that is, impure thoughts or *logismoi*.[37] In 2 Cor 10:4 Paul speaks of the spiritual warfare of Christians living in the world: "for the weapons of our warfare are not worldly but have divine power to destroy strongholds. We destroy arguments" *(logismous)*.[38]

The *logismous*, understood pejoratively, was not so much a rational thought as it was a mental image; this image appeared in the lower level of the cognitive faculty or *dianoia*, where its attractiveness stirred the mind, either to bring about a "passionate movement . . . which incites the person to a secret decision against God's law, or at least to some sort of dialogue with this image, which presents itself as some sort of idol, and should instead be driven away."[39] Guarding the heart "from impassioned thoughts, impassioned words and evil actions" required "*prosuche* and *proseuche*, attentiveness and prayer," by which one repelled "intruding thoughts immediately."[40] Other practices, like abstinence and fasting, were also aids against such *logismoi* taking root in the heart or soul.

Much of Amma Syncletica's discourse focuses on recognition of the various *logismoi* that attack the souls of members, whether newly come to monastic life or engaged long in the struggle for purification of their hearts. In *Vita Syncleticae* 25 Syncletica warns against frequenting marketplaces because the licentious words heard there can cause "disgusting and virulent images to arise."[41]

Again in chapter 28, Syncletica warns of the need for vigilance because the enemy "wages war through external acts and wins victory

---

[36] Raasch, *SM* 12 (1970) V:32: "Evagrius makes little use of the spiritual term *heart* but prefers to speak of *katharotes* as a quality of the *psyche* or the *nous*."

[37] See Tomás Spidlík, *The Spirituality of the Christian East: A Systematic Handbook*, Cistercian Studies 79, trans. Antony P. Gythiel (Kalamazoo, Mich.: Cistercian Publications, 1986) 238; pp. 237–56 treat the topic of the *logismoi* in detail.

[38] Nestle-Aland, *G-E NT*, 486.

[39] Spidlík, *The Spirituality of the Christian East*, 239.

[40] Ibid., 243.

[41] *VS* 25, Bongie, 22.

through internal thoughts" *(dia ton endon logismon)*; actually by means of the latter, he can continue attacking day and night.[42] How then does one protect oneself from such attacks? As we saw earlier in the study of "purity" in *Vita Syncleticae* 29, one utilizes the weapons of laborious ascesis and pure prayer *(askeseos epiponou kai katharas proseuches)*, which are remedies against every destructive thought *(epi pantos logismou olethriou)*.[43]

Next Syncletica takes up again the topic of the *logismoi* (*VS* 45) by employing the analogy of the soul likened to a ship on rough seas.

> Like a ship our soul *[he psuche]* is sometimes engulfed by the waves without *[ezothen]* and is sometimes swamped by the bilge-water within *[endothen]*. Certainly we too sometimes perish through sins committed externally *[ektos]*, but we sometimes are destroyed by thoughts within us *[dia endon logismon]*. And so we must guard against onslaughts of spirits from outside us *[ezothen]*, and bail out impurities of thoughts inside us *[tas endon ton logismon . . . akatharsias]*; and we must always be vigilant with regard to our thoughts *[de gregorein pros tous logismous]*.[44]

In an elaborate word play on the *outer* waves of the sea, that is, external sins or spirits attacking the soul from outside, and the *inner* bilge-water, that is, inner thoughts or impure thoughts inside the soul, Syncletica portrays the soul caught in a storm. Vigilance against both forms of assault is necessary to keep the boat afloat. Here, as before in chapters 26 and 28, the biblical word for vigilance is stressed.[45] In *Vita Syncleticae* 26 the amma repeats the warning about guarding the thoughts of the mind: "Consequently, the mind must become painstakingly diligent with respect to its thoughts" *(pros tous logismous ten dianoian)*.[46]

The specific vice of pride is particularly deadly, in Syncletica's opinion, because it is so seductive (*VS* 49).[47] She asks, "What must one do, then, when such thoughts *[logismon]* are present?"[48] She responds by posing the remedy of meditation on certain scriptural verses, namely,

---

[42] *VS* 28, Bongie, 24; Greek: *PG* 28.1504D.

[43] *VS* 29, Bongie, 24; Greek: *PG* 28.1504D.

[44] *VS* 45, Bongie, 32; Greek: *PG* 28.1513C.

[45] Cf. *VS* 26: *Gregoreite* = Stay awake! *PG* 28.1501D; *VS* 28: *gregorein* = to be watchful, *PG* 28.1504C; and *VS* 45: *gregorein* = to be watchful, *PG* 28.1513C.

[46] *VS* 45, Bongie, 32; Greek: *PG* 28.1513C.

[47] *VS* 49, Bongie, 33–5, treats the vice of pride, by which the devil tempts the soul to think itself superior in fasting, or is seduced by comparing its heroic deeds to those of her associates, or deludes the soul with forgetfulness of its own mistakes and so it ceases to look to God for mercy, or suggests positions of authority, teaching posts, or healing gifts in order to deceive the soul.

[48] *VS* 50, Bongie, 35; Greek: *PG* 28.1517B–C.

Ps 22:6; Gen 18:27; and Isa 64:6. This process of offering biblical words as healing remedies against the *logismoi* is called *antirrhesis* or "counter-speaking," an art perfected by Evagrius in his *Antirrheticus,* a manual of biblical verses used to counter the eight principal vices.[49]

Syncletica continues with stating that any woman anchorite with *logismoi* of pride must enter a cenobium, where she will follow the daily regime of eating twice a day, to face censure, to perform acts of service, to hear stories of renowned lives of saints, and to see herself against the backdrop of community members practicing austerities.[50] These are all counter-remedies whereby she will soon realize she is no better than the cenobites with whom she resides.

Besides pride, other dangers to the soul include malicious talk and empty hearsay. Against these Syncletica gives this advice: "Prepare your soul *[ten psuchen]* without superfluity. For by entertaining the ill-smelling impurity *[akatharsian]* of words you will introduce stains to your prayer *[te euche sou]* through your thoughts *[dia ton logismon].*"[51] This particular counsel shows clearly that the *logismoi,* when taken in, bring about impurity to the soul, which, in turn, makes one's prayer stained, that is, impure.

One final chapter will be examined, which also addresses the issues of the *logismoi* creating stains on the soul and the need for prayer. In chapter 80 Syncletica draws a parallel between treating the soul in depth and cleaning a house of insects. Since in a monk or nun minor sins are readily recognized, no less than tiny insects in a clean house, it follows that

> we must, then, keep cleaning our "house" *[hemon kathairein ton oikon]* continually and be on the lookout lest any of the soul-devouring *[psuchopsthoron]* "beasties" slip past us into the storerooms of the soul *[en tois tes psuches tameiois].* And we must fumigate out places with the holy incense of prayer *[tes proseuches].* For just as the stronger fumigants drive out venomous creatures, so prayer *[euche]* with fasting chases out foul patterns of thought *[logismon rhuparon].*[52]

Notice that the activity of cleaning the house, the image for the soul, is described by the verb *kathairein,* which means "to purify." In this chapter, the focus is on the power of prayer, acting as a fumigant, to purify the soul of the *logismoi,* the small beasts that can devour the soul.

---

[49] Spidlík, *The Spirituality of the Christian East,* 243.
[50] *VS* 50, Bongie, 35.
[51] *VS* 66, Bongie, 42; Greek: *PG* 28.1525D.
[52] *VS* 80, Bongie, 49; Greek: *PG* 28.1533D, 1536A.

In comparing these last two chapters, one concludes that the *logismoi* are a source of impurity to one's prayer (*VS* 66), but also that one cannot even hope to purify one's soul without prayer (*VS* 80).

IS THE AIM OF THE MONASTIC LIFE CONTEMPLATION?

Amma Syncletica believes that her words are only suitable for those who choose the monastic life *(ton monere bion ethelousin)*.[53] For her, monastics are of two kinds: one is comprised of those who make much use of contemplation and spiritual knowledge *(hoi theorias kai gnosos emphoroumenoi)*; and the other, those who have a taste for asceticism and practices *(hoi asketikes kai praktikes apogeuomenoi)*.[54] What is interesting here is that the amma does not go on to specify which kind represents the anchorites and which the cenobites. She hints at the distinction of two kinds in the chapter previously examined in this study. There in chapter 50 she advises that a female anchorite still troubled by *logismoi* of pride should enter a cenobium.

Seemingly for her own community, Syncletica presents teaching overwhelmingly aimed at *praktike*, that is, the ascetical exercises which will root out the *logismoi* and eventually lead to purity of heart. "If *praxis* leads to *theoria*,"[55] as it did for many early teachers of asceticism, then, for Syncletica, this purification of the heart manifests itself in a contemplation of God closely bound to loving the neighbor. In chapter 71, she describes three categories of people: evil folks, courageous souls who desire to save the weak, and those in between. The courageous ones are "led into the height of contemplation" *(eis megethos theorias achtheisa)*.[56] Moreover, they behave like the Lord who ate with tax collectors and sinners. In acting from the motivation of brotherly love *(philautos)* they are willing to save sinners, even to the point of risking being scorched by the fiery insults of others. In so doing, "these are the guardians of pure love" *(outoi tes heilikrinous agapes hoi psulakes)*.[57]

Its value notwithstanding, one cannot rush headlong into contemplation *[pros theorian]*, Syncletica counsels, without first mastering the practical life *[praktikon bion]*.[58] She compares the acquiring of the rudiments of practice before going on to contemplation to the learning of the letter *alpha*, which requires effort and time in seeing the shape and learning its name, numerical value, and pitch, before one compre-

---

[53] *VS* 43, *PG* 28.1512D.
[54] *VS* 43, *PG* 28.1513A.
[55] Spidlík, *The Spirituality of the Christian East*, 335.
[56] *VS* 71, *PG* 28.1528D.
[57] *VS* 71, *PG* 28.1529B-C.
[58] *VS* 86, Bongie, 53; Greek: *PG* 28.1540B.

hends the Divine from merely pagan learning.[59] Amma Syncletica professes an innate caution with respect to *theoria* or contemplation, that is, desiring to understand the things of God before one is ready.

This caution is also reflected in her warning of the danger of people not yet formed by the experience of the ascetical life trying to teach others (*VS* 79). These may call followers to salvation, but end up doing them harm. Meanwhile "teaching that is based on ascetic experience, on the other hand, not even all eternity could destroy."[60] The souls of the latter kind have their rough edges chiseled away, so that "the word *[ho logos]* presents on the faithful the eternal image of Christ."[61]

Far more important than seeming to be a teacher of holy matters is the process by which one is transformed into the likeness of the Word. Such a transformation is brought about by many experiences of the rough edges of the soul being chiseled. As Syncletica has indicated several times throughout her work, this process is one of purification of the *logismoi*, in which over time, with the aids of prayer and ascesis and the grace of God, one gradually comes to reflect the image of the *logos*, the One who is love incarnate. Such, then, is the aim of the monastic life according to Amma Syncletica.

CONCLUSIONS

Amma Syncletica's teachings on the ascetical life were drawn from the wisdom she gained from her own encounters and battles with the *logismoi*. Her understanding of purity of heart was spoken to beginners of the monastic life and consequently her remarks are mostly limited to vigilance against evil thoughts. To counteract the *logismoi*, she suggested the tools of discernment, *purity* of action, laborious ascesis, and *pure* prayer. The remembrance and recitation of scriptural verses or the practice of holding opposing thoughts with respect to destructive suggestions were to act as counter-remedies to such *logismoi*.

Whereas Evagrius' system of purification of the heart lead from the *praktike* through *apatheia* to *theoria*, Syncletica was more cautious. She may have been aware of the controversies over the use of *apatheia*; at the same time, her disciples were cenobites still learning the basics of the monastic struggle for purity of heart. Rather than aligning *agape*, the culmination of a life of virtues, with *apatheia*, Syncletica associated *agape* with poverty. The latter manifested the interior spiritual condition of a loving heart.

---

[59] *VS* 86, Bongie, 53.
[60] *VS* 79, Bongie, 48.
[61] *VS* 79, *PG* 28.1533C.

The heart for Syncletica was most frequently understood as the *psyche*, except in instances where she quoted or alluded to biblical verses which employed *kardia*. The virtue most closely connected with the heart, for her, was humility, precisely because it was the very quality of Christ's heart or inner person. Humility, along with chastity and poverty, were the key virtues needed by her disciples as weapons in the struggles of the heart.

While her teaching was primarily focused on the *praktike* utilized to combat the *logismoi*, Amma Syncletica did not discount the possibility of someone attaining *theoria* or contemplation. However, the pursuit of contemplation tended to be reserved chiefly to anchorites. Cenobites, on the other hand, who mastered the *praktike* manifested the height of contemplation through their love of others, that is, they became "the guardians of pure love" (*VS* 71). These had undergone the transformation, through many experiences of the rough edges of their souls being chiseled, into the very image of the divine *logos*. It is these lovers who, experienced in the ways of the movements of their own souls, can lead others on the pathway to becoming an image of the divine.

Purity of Heart in St. Augustine

GERTRUDE GILLETTE, O.S.B.

The subject of purity of heart attracted Augustine from his early days as a priest in Hippo to his mature days as an aged bishop. Christ had taught him in the Gospels that the vision of God is reserved for those who are pure of heart: "Blessed are the pure of heart for they shall see God" (Matt 5:8), and Augustine burned to see the face of God. His desire to enkindle a like yearning in the hearts of his people led him to speak often of the means necessary to prepare oneself for the vision of God.

This essay will use broad strokes in attempting to give the main ideas surrounding Augustine's concept of purity of heart: first, what it is; then both what impedes and what helps attain it; finally, the primary role God plays in the attainment of purity of heart. The concept itself is expressed by Augustine in a number of ways: "purity of heart," "simplicity of heart," a "clean heart," and a "single" or "simple heart."[1] They are all attempts to express a state of soul, an inner disposition of the heart which is focused on God alone.

Since purity of heart is a disposition of the heart, Augustine sees that the starting place to obtaining this virtue is taking a closer look at one's own heart: "You are saying to me, 'show me your God.' I'm saying to you, 'Pay a little attention to your heart.'"[2] Alas, the task is not an easy one for any generation, for upon examination the human heart is found to be very different from God, and so Augustine: "Blessed are the pure of heart for they shall see God. Make this your business, give

---

[1] The following are examples of Augustine's terminology: *cor mundum* (Sermon 53, PL 38.366); *cor purum* (Enarrationes in psalmos 140.2.26, CCL 40.2026); *simplicitas cordis* (Ep. 147.23.54, PL 33.622); *cor simplex* (De sermone domini in monte 2.2.9, PL 34.1273); *cor singulum* (Sermon 216.5, PL 38.1079).

[2] Sermon 261.5: *Tu mihi dicis: Ostende mihi Deum tuum. Ego tibi dico: Attende, paululum ad cor tuum.* PL 38.1205.

yourself time for this, apply yourself to this task. What you want to see is pure, what you want to see it with is impure."[3] *What you want to see is pure . . .* the theological foundation for this virtue lies in God. God alone is pure; without the corresponding purity, one cannot hope to see God. Furthermore, the clarity of the vision is commensurate with the purification, even in this life.

Augustine actually wobbled on the question of whether it was possible to have a direct vision of God in this life, more inclined to the idea in his early life but then gradually abandoning it—at least as regards an intellectual vision of God—following St. Paul that "now we see dimly in a mirror, but then face to face" (1 Cor 13:12).[4] However, he never totally abandoned the possibility of seeing God even in this life with the eyes of the heart, a subject to which we will come shortly.[5] As regards the next life, when the faithful will experience the fullness of the vision of God and be filled with God to their capacity, they will not even then see the essence of God as it is known to himself.[6] The reason for this is that even after having been cleansed from all sin and defilement, the creature remains a creature, limited and incapable of comprehending fully the infinite God.

THE EYE OF THE HEART

Augustine has devoted many pages to the question of what the final vision of God will be. In the first place, he tells us, it will be totally unlike the Old Testament manifestations, which were visions not of God's essence but of a particular form perceivable by the senses, usually that of sight or sound. Since God is by nature spirit, he will not be perceived by the eyes of the body but by what Augustine likes to call "the eye of the heart."[7] By "eye" Augustine means that faculty which has the power to focus on and ultimately to pierce into the mysteries of God. This is the incredible potential which lies within the human nature created and re-created by God.

---

[3] Sermon 261.4: *Beati* mundo corde, quia ipsi Deum *videbunt* (Matt 5:8) . . . . *hoc habeto negotium, ad hoc te advoca, insta huic operi. Quod vis videre mundum est, immundum est unde vis videre.* PL 38.1204.

[4] See Frederick van Fleteren, "Augustine and the Possibility of the Vision of God in This Life," *Studies in Medieval Culture* XI (1977) 9–16.

[5] Mary T. Clark, "Augustine: The Eye of the Heart," *Spiritualities of the Heart*, ed. Annice Callahan (Mahwah, N.J.: Paulist Press, 1990) 23–32.

[6] De Genesi ad litteram 4.6.12 and 12.28.56.

[7] Augustine leaves open the possibility that the eyes of the resurrected body will be able to perceive something of God. See Epistula 147.52–54 and his more mature thought in De civitate dei 22.29.

As directed toward human acts, this "eye" is the intention with which we perform all our actions[8]—a kind of inner light that reveals to us whether or not we are performing an action for a good purpose.[9] When one acts for a wrong reason, then the inner light is eclipsed, deflected as it were toward the things of earth and dividing the heart.[10] The task of keeping the eye of the heart directed upward is a constant struggle but made easier by habit and desire.[11] The difficulty comes from the fact that although the human being was made to see the light which is God, sin has entered in and obscured the vision. In such a state, the whole human race is comparable to the man born blind, desperately in need of a cure: "That is what the eyes of the heart are cured for, for that they are opened, for that purified, to see the light which is God."[12] So important is the opening (or cleansing, purifying, healing—Augustine uses these terms almost interchangeably) of the eye of the heart that nearly everything else has been given to us for this reason:

> Brothers and sisters, what calls for all our efforts in this life is the healing of the eyes of our hearts, with which God is to be seen. It is for this that the holy mysteries are celebrated, for this that the word of God is preached, to this that the Church's moral exhortations are directed, those, that is, that are concerned with the correction of our carnal desires, the improvement of our habits, the renunciation of this world, not only in words but in a change of life. Whatever points are made by God's holy scriptures, this is their ultimate point, to help us purge that inner faculty of ours from that thing that prevents us beholding God.[13]

Augustine devoted a considerable amount of energy in expounding how one cleanses the heart to make it pure. But before taking up this

---

[8] De sermone domini in monte 2.13.45–48. Augustine is commenting on the verse: "If therefore your eye be single, your whole body will be full of light" (Matt 6:22).

[9] Ibid., 2.13.46.

[10] Ibid.

[11] Margaret Miles has pointed out that in Augustine's description of corporeal and spiritual vision, neither activity is purely passive. Just as "physical vision implies effort and selectivity on the part of the viewer," i.e., "concentration or focus is required before an object can be seen," in the same way, the will must actively focus its attention and energy on God in order to be able to see its divine object. Margaret Miles, "Vision: The Eye of the Body and the Eye of the Mind in Saint Augustine's *De trinitate* and *Confessions*," *Journal of Religion* 63 (1983) 125–42. The quotations are taken from 127.

[12] Sermon 136C.2: *Ad hoc enim oculi cordis sanantur ad hoc aperiuntur, ad hoc mundantur, ut videant lucem, quod est deus.* PL 2.795.

[13] Sermon 88.5: *Tota igitur opera nostra, fratres, in hac vita est, sanare oculum cordis, unde videatur Deus. Ad hoc sacrosancta mysteria celebrantur; ad hoc sermo Dei prae-dicatur; ad hoc exhortationes Ecclesiae morales, id est, pertinentes ad corrigendos mores, ad emendandas carnales concupiscentias, ad renuntiandum non voce tantum, sed mutata vita huic saeculo; ad hoc agunt quidquid agunt divinae sanctaeque Litterae, ut purgetur illud interius ab ea re quae nos impedit ab aspectu Dei.* PL 38.542.

important topic, let us first turn to what he believes are the hindrances that block the heart's clear perception of God.

DUPLICITY OF HEART

Since, following Augustine, we have defined purity of heart as one's single focus on God, then an impediment to that singleness of vision is anything which diverts the attention to another object. Whether the diversion is total or partial it produces duplicity of heart; for even in the case of total diversion, when we have completely lost the fear of God and act only for our own selfish motives, yet in our deepest self the heart is sadly divided for we still yearn for true and lasting happiness while trying to find it in transitory and false objects of happiness. Whatever, therefore, is desired apart from God, for its own sake, becomes a hindrance for finding God inasmuch as it diverts the natural desire of the heart for God and for happiness to objects which cannot satisfy it.[14] These other objects are temptations which try to deflect the faithful "from the road of their hearts"; they must stand firm and not deviate from their purpose.[15]

Augustine finds a scriptural example of simplicity versus duplicity of heart in the parable of the king who sits down to consider whether his army of ten thousand is sufficient to overcome his opponent's army of twenty thousand (Luke 14:31-32). Since twenty thousand is twice ten thousand, Augustine sees in the first king an instance of one who is single of heart, while his adversary represents those who possess duplicity. He concludes that the first king has the wherewithal to defeat the second because of the simplicity of heart with which he seeks God.[16]

What causes duplicity may be vices as flagrant as greed, love of money, avarice, pride, ambition, envy, or injustice; or less obvious faults such as love for temporal things[17] and reluctance to do one's duty; or even the more subtle deviants such as a desire to receive praise or some other benefit for one's good actions. Thus, if we desire to have others think well of us while we are giving alms, we allow our good intention to be mixed with impure motives.[18] It is not that being

---

[14] Enarrationes in psalmos 4.9.

[15] Sermon 4.9.

[16] Ep. 243.10.

[17] Sometimes Augustine contrasts the single-minded attention given to God to the dissipation of the soul caused by the many objects of desire in this world. "The cleansing of the eye of the mind urged by Augustine is the collection of the soul's central energy and affection which has been 'poured out' onto sensible objects of fear and love." Miles, "Vision," 133. See, e.g., Confessions 10.29.40.

[18] De sermone domini in monte 2.2.9.

praised by others for a good deed is an evil in itself; but an object does not have to be evil in order to debase a higher object. Augustine takes an example from the world of nature: if gold is mixed with pure silver, the silver debases the value of the gold. Silver is not vile in its own nature, but when mixed with gold, the composite substance reduces the worth of the higher metal. So too, "our mind is defiled by a desire for the things of the earth, although the earth itself is pure in its own class and in its own order."[19]

The difficulty of discerning its deviant character and perhaps also its widespread contagion led Augustine to denounce the poison of human praise again and again. As bishop, he was in a key position to know how easily human praise can turn the heart inward—even if momentarily—away from its gaze on God. "No one," he says, "has a single heart . . . unless he rises above human praise, . . . that is, unless his thoughts and his efforts to please are directed solely [to God]."[20] In all of these cases, turning toward what is not God not only directs a person away from God, it also causes a certain darkness in the heart because one is no longer looking directly into the light.

Duplicity is also present in contentiousness. Augustine had to deal with this problem on a pastoral level, warning his congregation not to argue with their neighbors and to avoid conceitedly taking issue with theological opinions not for the sake of truth but seemingly simply for the love of differing.[21] He saw clearly that any kind of a quarrelsome attitude was directly opposed to that peace which Scripture says leads to the vision of God.[22] Indeed, two persons quarreling are poking each other's eyes out so that they cannot see God![23] In the same camp are those who question others for the purpose of acquiring information in order to accuse them—like those in the gospel who laid snares for Christ by their questions (Luke 20:2-8). Augustine seems to be particularly irked by these deceitful pretenders with their double hearts.[24]

Apart from the temptations to evil which distract the heart from God, there is also the simple fact of having to live with a body in this world and to take care of its temporal needs. There is no denying that

---

[19] De sermone domini in monte 2.13.44: *ita et animus noster terrenorum cupiditate sordescit, quamvis ipsa terra in suo genere atque ordine munda sit*. PL 34.1289.

[20] De sermone domini in monte 2.1: *Non ergo habet simplex, id est, mundum cor, nisi qui transcendit humanas laudes, et illum solum intuetur, cum recte vivit, et ei placere nititur qui conscientiae solus inspector est*. PL 34.1270.

[21] For the latter, cf. Ep. 147.49.

[22] Heb 12:14: Strive for peace with everyone and for the holiness without which no one can see God.

[23] Sermon 23.18.

[24] Ibid., 308A.7.

feeding and clothing the body takes a certain amount of energy and mental activity which necessarily demands that attention be given to these practical considerations. Thus our very condition as humans diverts our attention to things of the earth. "The mind's occupation with what is needed for our present life often mars and sullies our inner eye and generally divides the heart."[25] What is to be done? Augustine is eminently practical. One can hardly stop eating or working—indeed to do so would be an evil.[26] Although the gospel instructs us not to worry about tomorrow ("Look at the birds of the air. They neither sow nor reap. . . ."),[27] Christ himself had a purse, and Paul collected money for the poor in Jerusalem and supported himself by tent weaving.[28] So the point cannot be that one should neglect the necessities of life. Yet, since these things are in their very nature distracting, is there no solution? Augustine finds a resolution to the difficulty in the continuation of the pericope from Matthew: "Seek first the kingdom of God and his justice and all these things shall be given you besides" (Matt 6:33). Augustine noticed that Christ did not say, "seek first the kingdom of God and then afterwards seek the other things," as if it were a matter of prioritizing one's needs in life. No, Christ said "seek *first* the kingdom . . . and *then* all these things will be *given* to you."[29] This means that the necessities of life will be given to a person if he or she performs them not for their own sake, that is, merely to have or enjoy them, but for the sake of the kingdom, to use them as means of attaining the kingdom. In other words, one must have a single, ultimate purpose or vision focused on the Lord—even while attending to things of this world.[30]

---

[25] De sermone domini in monte 2.12.43: *Saepe etiam cogitatio necessariarum rerum ad istam vitam pertinentium, sauciat et sordidat interiorem oculum nostrum; et plerumque cor duplicat. . . .* PL 34.1288.

[26] Augustine wrote a small treatise against some monks who thought they did not have to work, but only had to pray and all would somehow be given to them. See, De opere monachorum 17.20, translated into English as: *The Work of Monks* in *Treatises on Various Subjects*, The Fathers of the Church 16, ed. Roy J. Deferrari (New York: Fathers of the Church, 1952).

[27] Matt 6:26.

[28] De sermone domini in monte 2.17.57.

[29] Ibid., 2.17.56.

[30] Augustine's synthesis may be illustrated by drawing an analogy from modern technology. A camera lens can focus on any single object whether that object is close to it or far away. But as soon as there are two objects in the picture of varying differential distances, such as a person six feet away and a mountain many miles away, if the camera focuses on one of the objects, the other will be somewhat blurred. So too, as one focuses on God, the world begins to fade, or if one focuses on things of this world, God begins to fade or blur. If, however, one backs away from the closer object in the picture until both objects are in focus at the infinity setting, then one picture emerges with each object clear and unblurred. Furthermore, in this view, the closer object is better seen in

CLEANSING OF THE HEART

Such a pure vision is the task of a lifetime. Sins, the pleasures of this world, desire for praise, and all the impediments to purity of heart mentioned earlier do not disappear by a simple willing them away. The cleansing of the heart is hard work. Indeed, the very dignity of the reality which the heart is made to see requires a proportionate effort and solicitude in purifying its desires.[31]

Augustine mentions several ways of going about the purification. First of all, one must recognize and condemn one's own sins: "Condemn what you are, that you may deserve to be what you are not. . . . Crush [iniquity] and purify it; drive it from your heart."[32] Not only do actual sins have to be renounced, but even any lingering yearning for the sinful object or pleasure, whether one succumbs to it or not.[33] Thus the first step is to separate oneself completely from evil. When this has been done, the heart has been directed away from something, but not yet toward someone. What directs the heart's gaze toward God? *Faith*. And while faith points, it also purifies. Augustine's foundation for the latter is Acts 15:9 where Peter declares that God cleansed the hearts of the Gentiles by faith. The Bishop of Hippo is fond of quoting this verse continually in regards to obtaining purity of heart. It is therefore of fundamental importance for his understanding of how one obtains this virtue. Let us therefore try to probe more deeply into its significance.

First of all, Augustine holds as primary the idea that believing is a kind of seeing or understanding and that it must precede rational comprehension, following the Septuagint reading of Isa 7:9: "If you do not believe, you cannot understand." On the other hand, those who insist on seeing before believing "are like to blind men, desiring to see the physical light of the sun in order to be cured of blindness, whereas they cannot possibly see it unless they are first cured."[34] It is not God

---

relationship to the background. In other words, if we put some distance between ourselves and the world, even those necessary things of life, then they can be seen more clearly against the background of eternity. In this way a single vision is possible even while the objects are in different positions to the viewer. What this metaphor helps to do is to see that for Augustine there is one vision, one focus, one object into which everything else "fits." To have such a vision is to have purity of heart.

[31] De sermone domini in monte, int. 1.

[32] En. in ps. 99.5.50, 52–53: *Damna quod es, ut merearis esse quod non es. . . . Contere illam [iniquitatem] in corde tuo, et munda; expelle illam de corde tuo. . . .* CCL 39.1395. Also see Sermon 20.2.

[33] En. in ps. 99.5.

[34] Sermon 346.2: *Similes sunt hominibus caecis, qui corpoream lucem solis istius prius videre desiderant, ut a caecitate sanentur, cum eam videre non possint, nisi ante sanentur.* PL 39.1524.

who must change and become visible for the sake of unbelievers,[35] but it is they who must realize that their very salvation depends on a change of outlook and heart. They must be willing to prepare themselves to see before they see[36]—to step out in trust and accept as true what is not apparent. On the everyday level, this occurs when they trust in God's providence in whatever circumstances they may find themselves. Augustine deals with this topic often enough in his homilies, where he tells his people that they must be prepared to accept everything that happens without grumbling against God or resisting his will because contrariness makes the heart crooked before God.[37] In one homily, Augustine talks about discontent agitating the heart, making as it were clouds in the mind which prevent the light from penetrating.[38] The same theme occurs in another sermon where the bishop addresses those who become discouraged whenever they compare the sufferings the just often have to endure with the prosperity of the unjust. It does not seem "fair" to them. Besides, such folk would say, if this is the case, what is the point of being good? Augustine responds that if one is truly a Christian, one must say to oneself: "I will trust in God, he knows what he is doing, we cannot know the reason he chooses to do this."[39] Such a person is certainly purified of self-constructs as well as of the need to know the reasons for things which are not necessary to know. Augustine believes that those who live by this kind of faith understand the things of God in a deeper way, which may mean that their trusting hearts "see" or feel a certain *rightness* in doing God's will, even while not understanding what is being asked of them.

Another way the heart is purified is through suffering. God allows suffering because it enkindles in the faithful a desire for the future life.[40] As fire separates the dross from the gold in the furnace, so the soul is purified of its attachments to all that is not God through suffering.[41] Job passed the test with flying colors.[42] Even when the conscience is free of sin, God continues to keep it clean through the troubles which continue to afflict it.[43]

[35] En. in ps. 73.25.
[36] Ibid., 99.5.
[37] Ibid., 96.18.
[38] Ibid., 91.14.
[39] A paraphrase of En. in ps. 93.2.31, 32, 35–37: *Unusquisque christianus . . . si bonus fidelis est . . . dolet talia murmurantes, et dicit sibi: Deus novit quid agat, nos non possumus nosse consilium ipsius, quare parcit malis ad tempus, vel quare laborant boni ad tempus.* CCL 39.1302.
[40] Sermon 341.13.
[41] En. in ps. 61.11.
[42] Sermon 91.4.
[43] En. in ps. 33.II.18.

A third way of purifying the heart is given to the faithful in the Lord's Prayer. Augustine finds this prayer, especially the petition "forgive us our debts just as we forgive our debtors," particularly helpful for cleansing the soul of those numerous minor faults and sins which creep in on a daily basis. Don't say:

> "But they are only little ailments." Pile them up and they weigh you down. . . . What is more minute than drops of rain? Rivers are filled by them. . . . What you notice is that they are minor, and you don't notice that they are many. . . . But anyway, God has promised [through the Lord's prayer] a daily remedy [for them].[44]

FAITH WORKING THROUGH LOVE

Although we have already emphasized the importance of faith in the purifying of the heart, we must now nuance what Augustine means by faith. It certainly means more than a mere belief that God exists, for "the devils believe and tremble" (Jam 2:19) and it does them no good, as Scripture testifies. This distinction becomes clearer when one contrasts the way Peter and the devils proclaimed Christ to be the Son of God. Peter was commended, the devils condemned. Why? "The heart was different, although the voices were the same."[45] What kind of faith makes the heart pure? "Faith working through love" (Gal 5:6). "Unless [God] is loved by faith, the heart cannot be cleansed so as to be fit and ready to see him."[46]

Love of God then is the unspoken element in that trust of God and God's providence of which we spoke above, for it is love alone that changes the heart. Augustine clearly states that even if one has prophecy or one of the other gifts of the Spirit, these are not guarantees that the person is changed for the better. All they indicate for certain is that the Holy Spirit is working through a person, as happened with both Saul (1 Sam 19:20) and Caiaphas (John 11:50), who prophesied without it benefiting them. Only the highest gift, charity, promises that the Holy Spirit is actively dwelling within a person in a purifying and therefore sanctifying way.[47]

---

[44] Sermon 261.10: *Sed parvi morbi sunt? Congerie premunt. . . . quid minutius pluviae guttis? Flumina implent. . . . Tu attendis quia minora sunt, et non attendis quia multa sunt. . . . Sed plane quotidianum remedium dedit Deus.* PL 38.1207.

[45] Sermon 53.11: *Unde hoc, nisi quia vox par, et cor impar?* PL 38.369. For Peter see Matt 16:16; for the demons, Luke 4:34.

[46] De trinitate 8.4.6: *Nisi [Deus] per fidem diligatur, non poterit cor mundari, quo ad eum vivendum sit aptum et idoneum.* PL 42.951.

[47] Sermon 162A.2.

If it is love which changes the heart, it is love also which purifies us for the vision of God. By its very nature, the heart or will is directed toward the good. For Augustine, the human will is a single faculty of desire, whether the object perceived as good is a thing of insignificant value or the Supreme Good. It is necessary, therefore, to channel the will to the desiring of the true good and not to allow it to waste time and energy on lesser goods, or even on what may be evil:

> Cleanse your love: the waters flowing into the draught, turn into the garden; what desires it had for the world, the same let it have for the world's Creator. So we say to you: Love nothing? God forbid. Dull, dead, hateful, miserable you will be if you love nothing. Love, but look well what you love.[48]

Channeling our love is nothing else than learning to love God while renouncing or despising all else. The complete renunciation of all but God cannot be compromised if one desires to be pure of heart: "Where can you get hold of that perfect simplicity which is absolutely steady, and unshakable in its perseverance? . . . 'Whoever does not renounce all that he has, cannot be my disciple'" (Luke 14:33).[49] It is by despising the things of this world and loving God that the heart is purified of its attraction to what is not God.[50]

Augustine offers a measuring stick with which one can judge if one is beginning to possess a pure heart. "Question your own hearts when you pray to God: see how you utter the verse: 'Forgive us our debts as we forgive our debtors.'"[51] Forgiveness can only come from a pure heart animated by love. This love, reaching out to those who have hurt us, to those who are our enemies, is truly pure. Unlike the natural love of family and friends, which even the wicked possess, the love of one's enemies seeks no personal gain and therefore one's motives in loving are unmixed. This is the kind of love God has for all of us. Ours will not be pure until it is like God's—unconditional love, pure love from a pure heart.[52] Even more challenging are Augustine's words to the ef-

---

[48] En. in ps. 31.II.5.26–30: *Purga ergo amorem tuum; aquam fluentem in cloacam, conuerte ad hortum; quales impetus habebat ad mundum, tales habeat ad artificem mundi. Num vobis dicitur: Nihil ametis? Absit. Pigri, mortui, detestandi, miseri eritis, si nihil ametis. Amate, sed quid ametis videte.* CCL 38.228.

[49] Sermon 301A.2: *Ubi perfecta illa simplicitas, et omnino stabilis, atque inconcussissime perseuerans? . . . qui non renuntiat omnibus quae sunt eius, non potest esse meus discipulus.* MiAgI 83, line 2.

[50] Cf. also En. in ps. 84.9.

[51] Ibid., 103.I.19.34–37. *Interrogate, quando rogatis Deum, corda vestra: Dimitte nobis debita nostra, sicut et nos dimittimus debitoribus nostris.* CCL 40.1491.

[52] Cf. also Sermon 90.7.

fect that you can gauge if your heart is pure in whether or not your heart now finds *delight* in loving your enemy.[53]

In a very concrete way, Augustine had to deal with the love of his enemies, and this in turn affected the formulation of his sacramental theology. The Donatists were a group who had split from the Church about a hundred years before Augustine's day. In his effort to reunite the two churches, Augustine focused his attention and energy on one single point: schism was a sin against charity, a sin so serious as to impede the work of the Holy Spirit. Yes, he concluded in his work on baptism, the Donatists had valid sacraments; but the sacramental rite did not bring with it the sanctifying life of the Holy Spirit because their lack of love for their enemies—made evident in their desire to remain separated from the rest of their Christian brethren—blocked the operative grace of the Holy Spirit.[54] Purity of heart cannot abide separatism. Such purity was the driving force which impelled Augustine in his efforts to end the Donatist schism.

Love then perfects faith both by propelling us longingly toward God and by overflowing into concrete acts of love toward our neighbors.[55] The same single-mindedness with which we are to love our enemies must be present in our love for all our neighbors. The tendency to seek advantage for ourselves in our service to others is a continual temptation, but it is not the way of the pure. We ought to do good to others for the sake of their salvation, and not for the sake of our own temporal gain.[56] The very act which is performed with the proper intention perfects the initial purity in the heart and reflects it to others:

> The heart . . . is purified by behavior, by mode of life, by chastity, holiness, love, and by the faith which works through love. . . . [It] is like a tree that has its roots in the heart; deeds, after all, only proceed from the root of the heart. If you plant greed there, thorns proceed from it, if you plant charity, fruits proceed from it.[57]

These acts of genuine love for our neighbor purify the heart so that it can see God. "By loving your neighbor you cleanse your eye for seeing

---

[53] En. in ps. 39.21.
[54] De baptismo, 3.16.21, 5.8.9, and 7.45.89.
[55] Cf. En. in ps. 31.II.5.
[56] De sermone domini in monte 2.22.74.
[57] Sermon 91.5: *Cor . . . mundatur autem moribus, vita, castitate, sanctitate, dilectione, et fide quae per dilectionem operatur* (Gal 5:6) *. . . tanquam arbor est, quae radicem habet in corde: neque enim facta procedunt nisi de cordis radice; ubi si plantaveris cupiditatem, spinae procedunt; si plantaveris charitatem, fructus procedunt.* PL 38.569.

God, as John clearly says 'If you do not love your brother whom you see, how will you be able to love the God whom you do not see?' (1 John 4:20)."[58] But if love is purifying, it follows that one should be able to see God more clearly as one becomes more and more purified. As mentioned earlier, Augustine held out for the possibility of seeing God with the heart even in this life. He comes to this through the definition of God given in 1 John 4:16: "God is love." Since God is love, is God not present then in the love by which we love our neighbor? "Therefore, love your neighbor and look upon the source in you from which you love your neighbor, and there you will see, as far as you can, God."[59] The vision of God in this life begins with a laying hold of him through love: "The more ardently we love God, the more surely and serenely do we see him."[60]

This pure love for God and neighbor is, moreover, gradually realized through the repetition of concrete acts of virtue. In an interesting passage in his *De doctrina christiana*, Augustine teaches that it is necessary to remove certain hindrances in ourselves before we can interpret Scripture correctly. These hindrances are overcome through the cultivation of certain virtues, namely, those which are classically known as the gifts of the Holy Spirit. Augustine treats them in "reverse" order, beginning with fear of the Lord and ascending to wisdom. As one ascends the ladder, one's vision of God (as well as one's penetration into the meaning of Scripture) becomes clearer. The penultimate step is devoted to the virtue of understanding which Augustine relates to the love of one's enemies, for this act purifies the mind to an incredible degree: "When he arrives at the love of his enemy he ascends to the sixth step [i.e., to understanding] where he cleanses the eye through which God may be seen in so far as he can be seen by those who die to the world as much as they are able."[61] In order to ascend to the last step—

---

[58] Tractatus in Joannis Evangelium (Ev. Jn.) 17.8: *Diligendo proximum purgas oculum ad videndum Deum, evidenter Joanne dicente,* Si fratrem quem vides non diligis, Deum quem non vides quomodo diligere Poteris? PL 35.1531.

[59] Ev. Jn. 17.8: *Dilige ergo proximum: et intuere in te unde diligis proximum; ibi videbis, ut poteris, Deum.* PL 35.1532. See also De trinitate 8.5.12.

[60] De trinitate 8.9.13: *Quanto flagrantius diligimus Deum, tanto certius sereniusque videamus.* PL 42.960. Augustine could hold both: that the vision of God is reserved until the next life and that it was possible to have it with the eyes of the heart now. M. Miles believes Augustine's reasoning to lie in the difference between "glance" and "gaze": the one a momentary touch of God and the other the permanent fulfillment of the vision in the next life. See Miles, "Vision," 136. I suspect that Augustine allows for a "vision" of God in this life because of the way in which the affective faculties bring a certain "form" or quality to the mind which enables it to perceive or "touch" God.

[61] De doctrina christiana 2.7.11: . . . *cum pervenerit usque ad inimici dilectionem, ascendit in sextum gradum, ubi jam ipsum oculum purgat, quo videri Deus potest, quantum potest ab iis qui huic saeculo moriuntur quantum possunt.* PL 34.40.

to wisdom—one thing more is necessary: to abstain from any judgment of your neighbor or yourself in the light of the truth: "On this step he so cleanses the eye of his heart that he neither prefers his neighbor to the Truth nor compares him with it, nor does he do this with himself because he whom he loves is not like himself."[62] This state brings about peace and tranquility.

In the early Church there were three specific ascetical practices which were seen to be especially fruitful for keeping one's heart directed toward God. Augustine speaks often of these; they are prayer, fasting, and almsgiving.

PRAYER, FASTING, AND ALMSGIVING

As regards all three exercises considered together, Augustine says that they are, like forgiveness, helpful in purifying a person from daily sins. Minor faults and failings creep into us like water seeping into a boat; we must bail them out daily through fasting, praying, and almsgiving and saying with a pure heart: "Forgive us our debts, as we also forgive our debtors."[63] All three are likewise powerful aids in overcoming the many temptations which beseige the faithful.[64] Let us now consider Augustine's treatment of them individually, especially as regards their specific role in achieving purity of heart. We shall deal with them in the order of fasting, almsgiving, and prayer.

Since purity of heart is a heart totally focused on God, that which draws the attention to things of this world has to be overcome. The flesh belongs to this category for, although the mind tends upward, the flesh draws one to the earth. The flesh is, as it were, a burden weighing down the soul.[65] *Fasting* casts off the ballast of this earthly luggage so that the soul can fly more freely upward.[66] The body can also be compared to an untamed and excitable horse. The only way to bring it under control is to cease feeding it. Once subdued through weakness, it will then be less inclined to yield to illicit joys.[67]

---

[62] Ibid.: *In hoc autem gradu ita purgat oculum cordis, ut veritati ne ipsum quidem praeferat aut conferat proximum; ergo nec seipsum, quia nec illum quem diligit sicut seipsum.* PL 34.40. This passage was pointed out to me by Br. Philip Friel, O.C.S.O., in a paper which he delivered at the Patristic, Medieval, and Renaissance Conference, Villanova, 1995, entitled, "St. Augustine: The Vision of God and the Spiritual Body which will exist at the Resurrection of the Saints."

[63] En. in ps. 66.7.

[64] Sermon 207.1.

[65] Wis 9:15: The corruptible body weighs down the soul, and this earthly tent burdens the thoughtful mind.

[66] De utilitate ieiunii 2.

[67] Ibid., 3–5.

Besides bringing the body under control, fasting also "expands" the soul to desire God. Augustine seems to be saying that the experience of feeling the lack of food in the body is a reminder of how much the human creature is in need of God. But the link between craving for food and craving for God is not immediately evident. Theologically it might be true, but how can one prove that every soul hungering for food is at the same time in some way also increasing his or her conscious need and desire for God? Yet those who have fasted have experienced at least this much: give the body less and the mind is freer for God. So Augustine appeals to his audience: "If anyone understands this, he proves by experiment how usefully one fasts."[68]

The topic of fasting occurs frequently enough in Augustine's works, quite often in the course of a sermon where he mentions that since the congregation is fasting he will keep his words brief so as not to tax them beyond their strength. The material suggests that Augustine's congregation fasted regularly and sincerely. The fact that he does not harp on it as frequently as he does, for example, on almsgiving indicates that they knew the importance of fasting well enough not to need the same constant reminders.

Like any good work, it is possible to fast with mixed intentions, so Augustine felt the need to give a few caveats to a person fasting: one should not insist on it to the exclusion of other things,[69] nor fast to receive human praise,[70] nor should one ever judge someone else's fasting or lack of it, following Rom 14:3: "Let him who eats not despise him who eats not." Both Jesus and John were misunderstood, one eating and the other fasting (cf. Matt 11:18-19).[71]

Besides the obvious curbing of the appetites, fasting also cultivates positive fruits, such as inner joy[72] and unity. The not-so-obvious relation between fasting and unity is dealt with in Augustine's treatise *De utilitate ieiunii*. Of the eleven chapters which comprise this small work on fasting, six of them deal with the subject of unity. After explaining that fasting unifies the body by bringing the lower desires into subjection to the mind, Augustine goes on to say that all the members of Christ's body should love one another.[73] In other words, just as the restraining of one part of the body brings unity to the whole, so fasting done by individual members of Christ's body the Church has a like ef-

---

[68] Ibid., 3: *Si quis hoc sapit, etiam ipso experimento probat quam utiliter jejunetur.* PL 40.709.
[69] Ep. 36.26.
[70] De sermone domini in monte 2.12.40.
[71] Ep. 36.26.
[72] De sermone domini in monte 2.12.42.
[73] De utilitate ieiunii 6.

fect of unifying the whole body, all the more so if the purpose of the fasting is for the sake of loving one's neighbor. If we have understood Augustine's point correctly,[74] then we can conclude that since fasting purifies the love (the binding force of unity), the more sincerely one fasts for the sake of loving unity, the more effectively it comes about.

The saintly bishop may have in mind the unity between the Catholics and the Donatists.[75] The heart is the organ of love and, as we have seen, love of God is measured by the love of one's neighbor, especially one's enemies, so that the latter becomes the measuring stick of one's degree of purity. Any steps taken to overcome the division—so that the Donatists were not the enemy but again part of the body—were concrete expressions of purity of heart. Therefore, fasting for the purpose of unity is indeed a means of purifying the heart.

The second great means of purification is *almsgiving*. The very act of giving things away to another frees one from the distraction of ownership. Things are burdens; when a person lessens the burden he is carrying around by giving to someone in need, he is helping both himself and his needy neighbor at the same time.[76] Augustine is quite aware, however, that having riches is not in itself an evil, for some rich people are humble and some poor folk are proud. Evil lies in the heart. Besides, the very act of almsgiving may be—like fasting—an occasion of soliciting praise. Again he warns that one must act with a pure heart and seek no temporal advantage for oneself in the act of charity. Furthermore, although charity covers a multitude of sins, almsgiving should not be used as a kind of insurance, as if one could sin with impunity as long as one gives alms.[77] Nevertheless, with these caveats solidly in place, the practice of giving alms to relieve the lot of the poor was a topic dear to the heart of Augustine. The poor of Hippo used to remind the bishop on his way to the church to ask the congregation to be more generous with them than they had been, and he would respond to their request by reminding his people of their duty: "I'm

---

[74] The editor of this work in the Fathers of the Church volume believes that these chapters on unity are an unfortunate digression from the main topic. I am inclined to think that there is an underlying correlation which was more obvious to his congregation than to us. See the following note.

[75] The occasion for the composition of this treatise may have been a period of fasting when the division between the Catholics and the Donatists was still very strong, perhaps in the decade leading up to 411. It is possible and even probable that fasting was asked of the faithful before the decisive Catholic-Donatist Conference of July 411 to prepare for the bishops' debate. But without any clear reference to the Conference in the treatise, the possibility that this particular work was delivered as an incentive to fast for unity at that particular moment in history remains tentative.

[76] Sermon 61.12.

[77] Enchiridion 20.77.

begging you, I'm warning you, I'm commanding you, I'm ordering you. Give to the poor. . . ."[78] In one homily he told them that whatever they had which they did not need belonged to the poor.[79]

The subject of almsgiving is, furthermore, theologically important for reasons deeper than its mere moral application. Almsgiving has christological significance. First of all, Christ himself gave to the poor as can be gathered from the Last Supper scene recorded in John; the fact that Jesus' words to Judas were interpreted by the other apostles as an injunction to go give something to the poor shows that it was a common practice for the Lord.[80] More significantly, Christ is the perfect almsgiver because he gave himself totally to us in our need, even making himself our bread.[81] Several lessons can be drawn from this. First, we are to give because Christ gave, that is, in imitation of Christ. Second, we are to give *as* Christ gave, that is, totally, so that our abandonment of all that is not God, even of our own lives, may free us completely for him. Third, if Christ is the giver, we are the receivers. Indeed, in this respect, we are all God's beggars in need of everything.[82]

Finally, almsgiving and fasting both help to make us more fit for our third practice of *prayer*.[83]

> Through prayer, therefore, it is brought about that a heart is turned toward him who is always ready to give, provided that we are ready to accept whatever he may give. And in that change of heart there is a cleansing of the inner eye through the exclusion of the erstwhile longing for temporal things, and the gaze of the single heart is able to bear the single light divinely shining without any setting or motion. Not only is the single heart able to bear this light, but it is also able to abide in it . . . with joy. In this way, life is rendered truly and sincerely blessed.[84]

---

[78] Sermon 61.13: *Date ergo pauperibus: rogo, moneo, praecipio, jubeo.* PL 38.414.

[79] En. in ps. 147.12.27–29. "The superfluities of the rich are the necessities of the poor. You possess what belongs to others when you possess more than you need." *Superflua diuitum, necessaria sunt pauperum. Res alienae possidentur, cum superflua possidentur.* CCL 40.2148.

[80] En. in ps. 103.III.12.

[81] Sermon 207.1.

[82] Ibid., 61.8.

[83] Ibid., 207.3.

[84] De sermone domini in monte 2.3.14: *Fit ergo in oratione conversio cordis ad eum, qui semper dare paratus est, si nos capiamus quod dederit; et in ipsa conversione purgatio interioris oculi, cum excluduntur ea quae temporaliter cupiebantur, ut acies cordis simplicis ferre possit simplicem lucem, divinitus sine ullo occasu aut immutatione fulgentem: nec solum ferre, sed etiam manere in illa; non tantum sine molestia, sed etiam cum ineffabili gaudio, quo vere ac sinceriter beata vita perficitur.* PL 34.1275.

The cleansing of the heart which is realized through confession of sins, fasting, and almsgiving prepares the heart to be a dwelling place for God. Prayer is then not a directing of one's thoughts and attention outside of oneself, but a conversation, a relationship, and a union taking place within the heart, or center, of a person. Drawing on Matt 6:6, Augustine compares the heart to a secret chamber which a person enters to pray. It is necessary that such a person be at home there and at peace with himself. If not, he is like a man whose wife is wearisome; since there is no peace in his home, he prefers to spend his time elsewhere. One must, therefore, cultivate peace in one's heart by first ridding oneself of sin and creating a clean conscience. In this way, "the very cleanness of your heart will delight you" and will encourage you to pray: "Enter in, cleanse all. Lift up your eyes to God, and immediately he will hear you."[85] Let us note that the cleansing of the soul of every sin is a prerequisite for deep prayer.

Another requisite for achieving purity in prayer is an attitude of readiness before the Lord, which Augustine points out in the passage already quoted: "Through prayer, therefore, it is brought about that a heart is turned toward him who is always ready to give, provided that we are ready to accept whatever he may give."[86] This readiness necessary for those who wish to be pure of heart is taking his earlier injunction of trusting in divine providence a step further. Not only do we submit to God's will and make an act of trust once we are in a particular situation, but we even anticipate whatever his will might be and stand in calm readiness. Readiness adds an element of eagerness to one's prayer which helps one to remain truly intent upon God (and therefore not on oneself), even when one is suffering.

Even though God is the object of prayer, and union with God the final purpose of prayer, nevertheless, there is an aspect of desolation in prayer which Augustine considers to be of utmost importance. This comes out strongly in his letter to Proba, a rich widow seeking to know how to pray. Augustine insists that her wealth is not an impediment to prayer as long as she realizes her own need for God. It is not so much a matter of having or of not having, but of not needing.[87] Indeed, we should all have a spiritual widowhood within us in order to

---

[85] En. in ps. 33.II.8.24–31. The fuller passage reads: *Cum ibi coeperis gaudere, ipsa munditia cordis tui delectabit te, et faciet orare: quomodo si uenias ad aliquem locum, silentium est ibi, forte quies est ibi, mundus est locus. Oremus hic, dicis; et delectat te compositio loci, et credis quod ibi te exaudiat Deus. Si ergo loci uisibilis te delectat munditia, quare te non offendit immunditia cordis tui? Intra, munda omnia, leua oculos tuos ad Deum, et statim te exaudiet.* CCL 38.287.

[86] De sermone domini in monte 2.3.14. See n. 84 for the Latin.

[87] Ep. 130.2.3.

pray with that desolation and dependence which prayer requires. What is desolation? The sense of being absent from the Lord.[88] So important is this attitude that Augustine delicately hints that Proba must first feel desolate before she can pray correctly.[89] Desolation, then, adds another important element to the notion of purity of heart; it describes the heart's relationship to the Lord as belonging to him and yet longing for him because the soul does not yet have him fully.[90] It seems that the having and not having increases the desire and the desolation. Yet, it might be asked just how essential an element is desolation to purity of heart, since we shall certainly have perfect purity in heaven where we shall possess God fully. Perhaps Augustine would answer in this way: since even in heaven the longing will always continue, then too the sense of total dependence—that we do not have in ourselves that which is our goal—will certainly continue as a constitutive part of our prayer before the Triune God.

While we are still in the world and distracted by the necessities of life as well as by other things, fixed times for prayer bring the mind back to its first duty. Love and desire are enkindled by prayer, but they grow lukewarm by reason of cares and preoccupation with other things. We, therefore, call our mind back to prayer at fixed hours and press forward to what we desire.[91] Attention is kept alert by short prayers darted up to heaven—as the monks in Egypt practiced.[92] Prayer can be lengthened when one is free; which does not mean that many words are needed: "continual longing is not the same as much speaking."[93]

PURITY OF HEART IS GOD'S WORK

So far we have concentrated only on those texts which speak of what the individual should do to be pure of heart. This could lead to the idea that as long as *I* do this and that, as long as *I* fast and give alms and pray intent on doing God's will, then I shall be single hearted. Nothing could be further from the truth. In one way, making the heart pure is not our work at all. God alone is pure and if we are pure it is by God's grace. From this perspective, it can now be said that the heart

---

[88] Ibid., 130.16.30.

[89] Ibid., 130.2.6.

[90] It is in this context that the famous phrase "there is in us a certain learned ignorance" occurs. Ep. 130.15.28: *Est ergo in nobis quaedam, ut ita dicam, docta ignorantia.* PL 33.505.

[91] Ep. 130.9.18.

[92] Ibid., 130.10.20.

[93] Ibid., 130.10.19: *Aliud est sermo multus, aliud diuturnus affectus.* PL 33.501.

which is purified by faith is more specifically purified by faith in Christ.[94] Although we had been created to see God, that light which is continually shining, we could not because of our sins. Since the light was too much for us, God became human in order to heal our eyes which could not see him.[95] In the incarnate form of the Son of God, our eyes have something to look upon. Beholding his activity, which points beyond mere human activity, we come to realize that he is God.[96] Augustine goes so far as to declare that seeing Christ's humanity was not such a great thing, for some saw it and did not profit from what they saw.[97] Healing begins when one moves beyond his humanity to believe in his divinity.[98]

The question still remains what is the particular element within belief in Christ which enables the eyes of the heart to lose their blindness. Augustine may have had his own personal experience in mind when he writes that

> [believing in] the humility whereby God was born of a woman and was led through such great insults to his death by mortal men is the most excellent medicine by which the swelling of our pride may be cured and the exalted mystery by which the chain of sin may be broken.[99]

Reflecting on the incarnation and death of Christ, on he who dispossessed himself of all for us (cf. Philippians 2),[100] so that one accepts and believes, cures a person of pride and breaks the inner attraction and bondage to sin. The next step is to accept what God offers in order to be further purified. As presented in one sermon, Christ comes to us sick ones on our bed of pain. He offers the sick man a bitter cup of trials and temptations: "'Drink it,' he says, 'drink it in order to live.'" And if the

---

[94] This is clearly what separates Augustine's notion of purification from that of the Platonic philosophers. See below n. 99 and Robert A. Herrera, "Augustine's Concept of Purification and the Fool of the Proslogion," *Anselm Studies* 2 (1988) 253–9.

[95] Sermon 261.6–7.

[96] Ibid., 88.14.

[97] En. in ps. 109.12.50–52: "That you should not think it was anything great that that form should be seen, his friends saw it, his enemies saw it, and some who saw it, slew him, some who saw it not, believed." *Ne aliquid magnum putes uideri formam illam, uiderunt amici, uiderunt inimici; et quidam uidentes interfecerunt, quidam non uidentes crediderunt.* CCL 40.1612.

[98] Sermon 136C.1–5.

[99] De trinitate 8.5.7: . . . *humilitatem qua natus est Deus ex femina et a mortalibus per tantas contumelias perductus ad mortem, summum esse medicamentum quo superbiae nostrae sanaretur tumor, et altum sacramentum quo peccati vinculum solveretur.* PL 42.952. For the pertinent passages in the *Confessions*, see 7.18.24, 8.12.28–30, and 10.43.68.

[100] De agone christiano 33.35. It is the pure of heart who can comprehend the surpassing love of Christ on the cross (Eph 3:17-19).

invalid should cry out, "'I can't, I can't bear it, I can't drink it,' the healthy doctor drank it first, so that the invalid would not hesitate to drink it."[101]

The same lesson is made in other places from another perspective. The faithful make up the bride of Christ. Christ came to the bride while she was still ugly in her state of sinfulness. He hung on the cross, revealing his love and his mercy for her, drawing her into this love. Through his cleansing love, he brought her to a confession of her sins and made her beautiful.[102] "By loving we are made beautiful. . . . How do we become beautiful? By loving Him who is always beautiful. The more love increases in you, the more beauty increases; for love itself is the soul's beauty. 'We love because he first loved us'" (1 John 4:19).[103] Purifying and making beautiful is the work of God through love.

Allowing God's mercy to penetrate and dissipate one's sins must be so thorough that one forgets the past, as it were, and the sinful associations of the past.[104] In this insightful interpretation of Ps 44:10, "Forget your own people and your father's house," Augustine may have in mind those who accept God's forgiveness, while retaining an unhealthy memory of the sin. He is probably not referring to a lingering desire for the sin, for that is obviously an evil, but most likely to a fear that the sin will come back to haunt them, perhaps that what was private will become exposed. This kind of fearful memory is contrary to purity of heart which trusts the Lord totally.

The initiative God takes and the supernatural power God supplies in every morally good act performed by God's creatures is at the heart of Augustine's controversy with the Pelagians. For our purposes, it suffices to say that no one can make the slightest progress on his or her own without the assistance of the Holy Spirit, who "both helps our infirmity and cooperates with our strength."[105] With the aid of the Holy Spirit, one advances from inchoate love to more advanced love, to perfect love and to perfect holiness, which is "love from a pure heart, a good conscience and faith unfeigned" (1 Tim 1:5).[106]

---

[101] Sermon 88.7: *Bibe, inquit, bibe, ut vivas. . . . Non possum, non fero, non bibo: prior bibit medicus sanus, ut bibere non dubitaret aegrotus.* PL 38.543.

[102] En. in ps. 103.1.4–6 and elsewhere. For a fuller treatment of these texts, see my dissertation: "The Glory of God in Augustine's 'Enarrationes in psalmos,'" Ph.D. diss., The Catholic University of America, 1996. UMI, Ann Arbor ML 410–3.

[103] Tractatus in epistolam Joannis ad Parthos (Ep. Jn.) 9.9: *Diligendo pulchri efficimur. . . . Quomodo erimus pulchri? Amando eum qui semper est pulcher. Quantum in te crescit amor, tantum crescit pulchritudo; quia ipsa charitas est animae pulchritudo. Nos diligamus, quia ipse prior dilexit nos.* PL 35.2051.

[104] En. in ps. 44.25.

[105] De natura et gratia 70.84. Cf.: *. . . sed per Spiritum sanctum qui datus est nobis, qui et infirmitati nostrae opitulatur, et sanitati cooperatur.* PL 44.290.

[106] Ibid.

CONCLUSION

For St. Augustine, purity of heart is a heart which is singularly focused on God alone. This demands a certain detachment from all else, certainly from sin, but also from everything that can tempt and distract us from our single vision. When circumstances require that we turn a gaze to the necessities of life, then those things are to be done or enjoyed, not for their own sake but for the sake of God. Purity of heart is primarily the work of God within us, who asks us to respond humbly in faith to the love and mercy of Christ manifested in his incarnation and death. Trusting readiness to accept whatever the Lord has in mind must also be cultivated in our hearts for them to be pure. Practices which help us to become detached from things of this world so that we can better turn our attention to God are prayer, fasting, and almsgiving. A practical way we can know how pure or impure our hearts are is to discern to what extent we love our enemies. But above all, God's incredible love for us arouses in us a purifying love for God alone. "For if someone has love, he sees God, for 'God is love': and that eye is cleansed more and more by love to see that unchangeable Substance in whose presence he may always rejoice, which he may enjoy forever, joined together with the angels."[107]

---

[107] Ep. Jn. 9.10: *Nam si habeat dilectionem, Deum videt; quia* Deus dilectio est: *et purgatur ille oculus magis magisque delectione, ut videat illam incommutabilem substantiam; cujus praesentia semper gaudeat, qua perfruatur in aeternum conjunctus Angelis.* PL 35.2052.

The Beginning and End of Purity of Heart: From Cassian to the Master and Benedict[1]

BENEDICT M. GUEVIN, O.S.B.

While the Master and Benedict are ultimately indebted to John Cassian for their notions of purity of heart, the manner in which they appropriate his teaching on the subject is uniquely their own. The difference between Cassian, the Master, and Benedict is especially clear not only with respect to the beginning of purity of heart, that is, the practice of the virtue of discretion,[2] but to the end to which purity of heart leads.

The title of this essay will also serve as a means of dividing it. In the first part, "The Beginning of Purity of Heart," I will describe and trace the function of discretion from Cassian to the Master and Benedict. In part two, "The End of Purity of Heart," I will discuss the goal to which purity of heart leads in each of our three monastic authors. In both instances, I will argue, Benedict is closer to the thought of Cassian.

---

[1] I wish to thank my confrere, Fr. Placidus Riley, O.S.B., for reading my manuscript and for offering many helpful suggestions for its improvement.

[2] In his classic study, M. Olphe-Galliard examines the three foundations of Cassian's teaching on purity of heart: discretion, interior combat, and renunciation. See M. Olphe-Galliard, "La pureté du coeur d'après Cassien," *Revue d'ascétique et de mystique* 17 (1936) 28–60. Cassian also begins the process of achieving purity of heart with the "fear of the Lord" (cf. *Inst.* IV, 35.1, 39.1, 43.1; *Conlationes* XI, 13.2; XIV, 16.6, etc.). The "fear of the Lord" seems to be a more all-encompassing reality. But if purity of heart is achieved by eliminating vices and acquiring virtues, then discretion, as the "mother of virtues," comes first.

THE BEGINNING OF PURITY OF HEART[3]

Cassian

Most of the foundational material concerning discretion can be found in the last eight books of Conference I and in Conference II. In these two conferences we see Cassian and his companion, Germanus, "interviewing" Abba Moses. Of this venerable desert father, our two young seekers after monastic wisdom ask the following question: "What is the purpose and the end of monastic life?" Abba Moses replies, "The end [*telos*] of our profession is the kingdom of God or the kingdom of heaven; but the goal or *scopos* is purity of heart, without which it is impossible for anyone to reach that end."[4]

In Conference II, Cassian and Germanus ask Abba Moses about the most important virtue needed by a monk to arrive at purity of heart. By way of reply, the old desert monk recalls a meeting that he himself had attended at Thebaid many years earlier at which the renowned Abba Antony presided. The group of elders gathered around the blessed Antony spoke among themselves about this very question. Various answers were given. Some said, "the love of fasting and vigils," others "complete renunciation," a third group suggested "the desert life," and, finally, still others said "charity," meaning "hospitality." Then, it was the great Antony's turn to speak. While he recognized that all of the practices they had put forward were useful, one virtue in particular was able to lead the monk down the "royal road" to God,[5] namely, discretion, the "begetter, guardian and moderator of all virtues,"[6] "the source and root of all the virtues,"[7] and "the eye and the light of the body."[8]

---

[3] I originally presented part one of this essay, absent any discussion of the *Rule of St. Benedict*, as a paper entitled *"Puritas cordis:* From Cassian to the *Rule of the Master"* at the XXVI Incontro di Studiosi dell'Antichità Cristiana held at Rome's Augustinianum University, May 8, 1996. This paper, with some modifications, was published under the title "Discretion: From Cassian to the *Rule of the Master,"* in Il monachesimo occidentale dalle origni alla Regula Magistri. *Studia Ephemeridis 'Augustinianum'* 62 (1998) 169–78. It is to this paper that I refer the reader for a more complete account of discretion in the *Rule of the Master*. For an overview of Cassian's notion of purity of heart, cf. Columba Stewart, *Cassian the Monk* (New York/Oxford: Oxford University Press, 1998) 42–7.

[4] Cassian, *Conlationes* I.4. The English translations of Cassian's *Conlationes* are taken from *John Cassian: The Conferences,* Ancient Christian Writers 57, trans. Boniface Ramsey (New York: Paulist Press, 1997).

[5] The concept of "royal road" was common in monastic literature. It is based on Num 21:22.

[6] Cassian, *Conlationes* II.4.

[7] Ibid., II.9.

[8] Ibid., II.2.

In Conference I, Cassian and Germanus had already been introduced to the function of discretion in the attainment of purity of heart by Abba Moses. In order to understand the full import of what they learned there, we have to look at Abba Theodore's instruction in Conference VI.[9]

Abba Theodore's remarks to Cassian and Germanus are rooted in the fundamental belief that God created human beings with a free will. Free will allows one to remain united to God—whether God sends adversity or prosperity[10]—or to reject God. God sends adversity for three reasons: to test *(ad probationem)*, to purify *(ob emundationem)*, or to punish *(ob merita delictorum)*.[11] This triple proof of human responsibility and perfectibility is a call to go beyond oneself and to persevere in one's efforts without going backward. The will is especially engaged in this effort. The will is like a rower who must use all the strength of his arms to keep the boat from being carried backward by the current.[12]

By insisting on human freedom and responsibility, Cassian makes clear that purity of heart concerns essentially the will. It is the will that establishes even in this life that permanent union with God, destined to be perfected in heaven, which is called charity.[13]

An essential element in the attainment of purity of heart, then, is free will. The human being is a rational creature who, in spite of original sin and its consequences, is still capable of choosing to do the good.[14] A precondition of the exercise of free will—whether for good or for evil—is the spontaneous form of the natural activity of the mind, which is thought. Without thought, free will could not be exercised, for it is precisely the function of free will to accept or reject what the mind proposes for its deliberation.

To return to Cassian and Germanus, what they learned from Abba Moses in Conference I was that thoughts come either from God, the devil, or the memory. It is by a wise discretion *(sagaci discretione)* that one comes to know the origin, the cause, and the author of a thought in order to know whether it should be accepted or rejected by the will.[15] Abba Moses compares the role of discretion to that of the banker who examines carefully the quality of the metal of the coins in his care.

---

[9] Here I am following Olphe-Galliard, "La pureté du coeur d'après Cassien," 33.

[10] Thus, the monk is called upon to be ambidextrous, accepting, like Joseph, Job, and St. Paul, both happiness and sadness with patience and thanksgiving (cf. *Conlationes* VI.10).

[11] Cf. *Conlationes* VI.11.

[12] Cf. ibid., VI.14.

[13] Cf. Olphe-Galliard, "La pureté du coeur d'après Cassien," 33.

[14] Cf. *Conlationes* XIII.12.

[15] Cf. ibid., I.19.

Discretion assures that a particular thought or opinion is "gospel metal."[16]

Discretion, then, is the virtue that keeps the monk free of the danger of excess or deficiency in his monastic practices[17] by following the teachings of an elder.[18] Excess, according to Abba Antony, is virtue practiced presumptuously; it is exaggerated fervor that goes beyond the limits dictated by temperance.

Neither excess nor deficiency in monastic practice will lead the monk to purity of heart.

Do we find Cassian's notion of discretion in the *Rule of the Master*? Given the fact that the Master is steeped in the writings of Cassian and the *Vitae Patrum*, we can certainly respond in the affirmative, both with respect to a general theory of discretion as well as to its practical consequences.[19] If it can be asserted that discretion, as a general theory with practical consequences, can be found in the Master, does it serve the same function as in Cassian, namely, as a foundation for the attainment of purity of heart?

The Rule of the Master

Any discussion of discretion in the *Rule of the Master* must attend to the vocabulary he uses. Unlike Cassian, who frequently uses the noun *discretio*, the Master does not. What we do find in the *Rule of the Master* is four uses of the verbal form of *discretio*, namely, *discernere*.[20]

(1) In *RM* 2.16 the Master writes that the abbot is to "make no distinction [*discernatur*] of persons in the monastery." Here, the Master is referring to distinctions based on the social origin (slave or free) or moral character (sinners or the just) of those coming to the monastery.[21] Of course, the Master will make distinctions among the brothers, as we will see in subsequent pages. But these distinctions are based on a criterion other than that of social status and this, in imitation of the Lord who provides equal earthly benefits for both the just and the sinner.

---

[16] Cf. ibid., I.20, 21, 22; II.9.

[17] Ibid., II.16.

[18] Ibid., II.24.

[19] Cf. Adalbert de Vogüé, *La communauté et l'abbé dans la règle de saint Benoît* (Paris: Desclée de Brouwer, 1961) 380–1.

[20] Cf. *RM* 2.16 *(discernatur)*; 2.20 *(discernimur)*; 28.23 *(sustinendi sensu discreta)*; 42.4 *(in aliqua parte discretus)*. English translations of the *RM* are taken from *The Rule of the Master*, trans. Luke Eberle, Cistercian Studies Series 6 (Kalamazoo, Mich.: Cistercian Publications, 1973).

[21] Cf. ibid., 2.16–22.

(2) In *RM* 2.20 we read that "God marks us out *[in hac parte aput Deum discernimur]* only if we are found better than others in our deeds." Three verses earlier the Master states that the abbot is to share in this distinction: "Let him not love one more than another, unless he finds that one excells in good works."[22] Neither social class nor previous moral quality is to be the basis for loving one brother more than another. What matters is "good deeds."

(3) The third use of the verb *discernere* is found in *RM* 28.23. Here, the Master is speaking of fasting with respect to children. Children are to fast on Wednesday, Friday, and Saturday, but only in winter when the days are shorter. On other days, they may eat at the sixth hour. In summer, when the days are longer, they are to eat at the sixth hour; on other days at the third hour, "because at that age they lack strength . . . as also the proper understanding of endurance" *(sustinendi sensu discreta)*. But in subsequent verses, it is clear that it is the abbot who "discerns" this relaxation and not only for children, but for the old and the infirm.[23]

(4) The final use of the verb *discernere* is found in *RM* 42.4. In response to the question, "How are the psalms to be chanted at Compline?" the Master responds that, while the psalms of Compline are to be sung with antiphons, the third psalm is intoned with alleluia, "because the seven times a day the prophet says we must give praise to God are all sung in the same fashion, because of the sevenfold Spirit, who is not divided in any way" *(in aliqua parte discretus)*.

From this look at the Master's vocabulary, it is clear that the most important location for a general theory of discretion can be found in *RM* 2 concerning the abbot. For the Master, the abbot is the one person in the monastery who exercises the virtue of discretion. How does the Master paint his portrait of abbatial discretion?

In one of the most beautiful passages of his rule the Master writes:

> He [the abbot] should have such love and kindness toward all the brethren that he will not prefer one to another, and will combine in himself the characteristics of both parents for all his disciples and sons by offering them equal love as their mother and showing them uniform kindness as their father.[24]

It is in this description of the abbot's discerning recognition of and adaptation to the various sorts of monks in his monastery that we see the Master's notion of discretion at work.

---

[22] Ibid., 2.17.
[23] Cf. ibid., 28.19–26.
[24] Ibid., 2.30–31.

Let us now examine the manner in which this more theoretical notion of abbatial discretion is exercised in the concrete practice of the monastic virtue of obedience.

The Master begins chapter 7 of his rule with the lapidary phrase: "The first step of humility is obedience without delay."[25] But no sooner does he state this principle than he qualifies it. "But this kind of obedience is proper to the perfect, few in number, those who consider nothing more dear to them than Christ."[26] After discussing in more detail the obedience of these few,[27] the Master warns the many (whom he calls weak and indolent) who cannot give this kind of immediate obedience, not to be unduly alarmed or despaired, but to be inspired to do likewise.

Who are these many who cannot obey immediately? How does the Master characterize them? He writes that there are assorted kinds of misery to be found in the monastery: those possessed of a sluggish and lazy nature, of ears that do not understand, of minds that are distracted and wander off into a jungle of thoughts. For these, he says, "we . . . indulgently moderate the strictures of obedience."[28] Here, we see the practical application of abbatial discretion.

The Rule of St. Benedict

To the Master's four uses of discretion, we find eight corresponding instances in *RB*. Five of these are in the form of the verb *discernere*;[29] three appear in some form of the noun *discretio*.[30] There are only two points of contact between *RM* and *RB*; these are found in the first abbatial directory of each rule.[31] Six out of Benedict's eight uses of the notion of discretion are, therefore, independent of the Master. Let us first consider the two points of contact between *RM* and *RB*.[32]

In adopting the Master's chapter on the abbot, Benedict omits, adds, and retains material.[33]

Absent from *RB* 2 is the Master's requirement that the abbot be like God who "commands the elements to serve sinners as much as the just."

---

[25] Ibid., 7.1.
[26] Ibid., 7.2.
[27] Cf. ibid., 7.3-9.
[28] Ibid., 7.13.
[29] *RB* 2.16, 21; 63.1, 5; 64.17.
[30] Ibid., 64.18, 19; 70.6.
[31] *RM* 2.16 = *RB* 2.16; *RM* 2.20 = *RB* 2.21.
[32] See note 31 above.
[33] In what follows I am indebted to Terrence Kardong's analysis in *Benedict's Rule: A Translation and Commentary* (Collegeville: The Liturgical Press, 1996) 62–3.

Absent, too, are the Master's references to the humility of the abbot and his paternal and maternal love for the monks.[34] What we find in their place is the admonition to uproot vices harshly and immediately.

Benedict adopts, however, the Master's injunction to the abbot against making distinctions as well as his maxim concerning God's favor on those who are superior in good works (to which Benedict adds "humility"). It is in these two verses that we find repeated, and in similar terms, the Master's use of *discernere*. Here, as in *RM*, the meaning of *discernere* is one of discernment, an attitude which demands that the abbot measure his approach according to the personalities of each monk: "threatening and coaxing by turns, stern as a taskmaster, devoted and tender as only a father can be."[35]

The last revision that Benedict makes is his suppression of the Master's exaggerated thesis that if a monk obeys the abbot alone, the latter becomes fully responsible for both of them before God.[36] In place of the Master's stress on abbatial responsibility, Benedict discusses two different matters: the difficulty of governing souls and the need for the abbot to attend to spiritual matters more than to temporal ones.[37]

The overall effect of Benedict's omissions and additions is a portrait of the abbot that is less tender than that of the Master, and even quite harsh. This portrait will change substantially in Benedict's second abbatial directory.[38] There, we will see both meanings of discretion at work, namely, discernment and moderation.

After discussing the question of the abbatial succession in *RB* 64.1–6, Benedict turns his attention, in verses 7–22, to the qualities needed in an abbot. These verses, written without recourse to the Master, have a characteristic about them unique in the Rule: they entirely rework an earlier theme, in this instance the qualities of the abbot. Whether we owe this reworking to a greater lived experience on the part of Benedict and to his use of different scriptural and monastic sources,[39] or, as Adalbert de Vogüé hints, to a redactor other than Benedict,[40] this section remains a shining example of Benedict's prudence, charity, and knowledge of the human heart.[41]

---

[34] Cf. *RM* 2.26–31.
[35] *RB* 2.24. For a full description of what this means, see *RB* 2.25–29.
[36] Cf. *RM* 2.35–38.
[37] Cf. *RB* 2.31–36.
[38] Cf. *RB* 64.
[39] Cf. Kardong, *Benedict's Rule,* 540. See also André Borias, "S. Benoît au fil des ans," *Collectanea Cisterciensia* 50 (1988) 218–38, esp. 222–5.
[40] Cf. de Vogüé, *La communauté,* 382–3.
[41] Cf. Anselmo Lentini, *San Benedetto: La Regola,* 2d ed. (Monte Cassino: n.p., 1980) 585–6.

The first thing one notices about this chapter is Benedict's retrieval of a theme he had previously omitted from the Master in *RB* 2, that is, abbatial humility. He writes:

> Once in office, the abbot must keep constantly in mind the nature of the burden he has received, and remember to whom he will have to give an account of his stewardship. Let him recognize that his goal must be profit for the monks, not preeminence for himself. . . . He is to distrust his own frailty.[42]

The humble abbot will profit the monk by being learned in divine law; by being chaste, temperate, and merciful; by hating not the brothers but their faults; by being prudent and avoiding extremes, even while not allowing faults to flourish; by not crushing the bruised reed;[43] by being loved rather than feared.[44] If this were not enough, the abbot is not to be excitable, anxious, extreme, obstinate, jealous, or oversuspicious.[45]

Following this description of desirable abbatial qualities, we find in quick succession the three remaining references to discretion:

> [The abbot] must show forethought and consideration in his orders, and whether the task he assigns concerns God or the world, he should be discerning and moderate [*discernat et temperet*], bearing in mind the discretion of holy Jacob [*cogitans discretionem sancti Iacob*], who said: If I drive my flocks too hard, they will all die in a single day. Therefore, drawing on this and other examples of discretion, the mother of virtues [*Haec ergo aliaque testimonia discretionis matris virtutum sumens*], he must so arrange everything that the strong have something to yearn for and the weak nothing to run from.[46]

These explicit references to discretion, discernment, and moderation do not exhaust Benedict's use of this multifaceted theme. For we also find this theme implicit (and independent of the Master) in several other passages of the *RB*.

Benedict's concern for the temporal and spiritual well-being of his monks is nowhere better expressed than in *RB* 27. In his treatment of the excommunicated, the abbot must show the utmost care and concern. On their behalf, he is to use the skill of a wise physician and im-

---

[42] *RB* 64.7–8, 13.

[43] Cf. Isa 42:3. In Cassian's *Conlationes* II, entirely devoted to the theme of discretion, we read that an elder is also enjoined "not to crush the bruised reed" (see *Conlationes* II.13), as in *RB* 64.13.

[44] Cf. *RB* 64.9–15.

[45] Cf. ibid., 64.16.

[46] Ibid., 64.17–19.

itate the loving example of the Good Shepherd. In this ministry, he is not alone. *Senpectae,* that is, those whom the abbot discerns to be mature and wise, may be recruited to assist the abbot in his task of winning over the excommunicated brother.

This is neither the first nor the last time in the Rule that discretion and discernment are exercised by other than the abbot. The deans,[47] the cellarer,[48] the guestmaster,[49] the novice master,[50] and the infirmarian[51] all share in one way or another the abbot's burden of leadership and his charism of discretion and discernment. This sharing of the abbot's charism concerns not only the temporal affairs of the monastery, but even the more delicate matters of conscience for which both discretion and discernment are essential.[52]

While Cassian understands discretion mostly in terms of spiritual direction, the purpose of which is to help the monk sort out his interior thoughts in order to make progress toward purity of heart, Benedict extends this notion in *RB* 3. Here Benedict requires that the abbot consult the community on matters of importance, discerning from the expressed views of different persons what is good for the entire community.[53] Similarly, if the community discerns the need for a second-in-command, and the abbot judges it best, he can, with the advice of God-fearing brothers, choose a prior.

Before I turn to the end of purity of heart, let me summarize what I perceive to be the differences between Cassian's understanding of discretion and that of the Master and Benedict.

SUMMARY

Whatever particular differences there are between Cassian's use of the notion of discretion and that of the Master and Benedict stem from the fact that each is writing out of very different contexts. Cassian has in mind the relationship between a master and a disciple that obtained in Egyptian semi-eremitical monasticism, while the Master and Benedict are writing rules for cenobites who live under a rule and an abbot.

It is quite possible that this difference of context is not without its consequences for how our three authors treat the virtue of discretion. It is necessary for the inexperienced hermit to obey his abba in much the

---

[47] Cf. ibid., 21.1–4.
[48] Cf. ibid., 31.1–2, 7–15.
[49] Cf. ibid., 53.21–22.
[50] Cf. ibid., 58.6–8.
[51] Cf. ibid., 36.7.
[52] Cf. ibid., 46.5–6.
[53] Cf. Kardong, *Benedict's Rule,* 78.

same way as the cenobite obeys his abbot and with similar results, that is, freedom from a presumptuous self-will. But in the *Rule of the Master,* the authority of the abbot is experienced in a way that is not found in the desert tradition. In spite of, and oddly, perhaps because of, the Master's desire that the abbot show discretion, moderation, and forbearance in his dealings with the monks of his community, abbatial authority comes across as heavy-handed, ubiquitous, and, at times, casuistic.

Now one may argue that it is unjust to compare Cassian's use of *discretio* with the Master's and Benedict's. The former, after all, is describing the life of hermits; the latter two, that of cenobites. This argument would have merit if we did not have Cassian's writings concerning cenobites as found not only in the *Institutes* but in the *Conferences* as well. And what does Cassian say regarding *discretio* in the life of the cenobite? He describes hermits as those who had first lived for a long time in monasteries where they learned patience and discernment according to the rule *(omnem patientiae ac discretionis regulam diligenter edocti).*[54] Discretion is one of the lessons—along with patience, humility, renunciation, and the elimination of vices—that the cenobite learns before he moves on to the eremitical life.

The integration of the role of discretion in cenobitic monastic life is more satisfactorily achieved in the RB where the qualities of the abbot, present and future, are essentially those of prudence, moderation, and discernment.

Context is not the only consideration to which one must attend in determining the different uses of discretion in Cassian and the Master and Benedict. Another factor is their respective anthropologies.

Cassian and Benedict have a much greater appreciation for human perfectibility. While Cassian does not pretend that the monk can be entirely free from sin in this life, he still holds out the hope and the possibility of reaching purity of heart. Benedict is even more positive here. While adopting, along with the Master, Cassian's conclusion to the signs of humility,[55] Benedict, following the Master's lead, adds:

> Now, therefore, after ascending all these steps of humility, the monk will quickly arrive at that perfect love of God which casts out fear. Through this love, all that he once performed with dread, he will now begin to observe without effort, as though naturally, from habit, no longer out of fear of hell, but out of love for Christ, good habit and delight in virtue. All this the Lord will by the Holy Spirit graciously manifest in his workman now cleansed of vices and sins.[56]

---

[54] Cassian, *Institutes* V.36.
[55] Cf. ibid., IV.39, 3.
[56] *RB* 7.67–70 = *RM* 10.87–91.

The monk reaches purity of heart through his cooperation with the workings of the grace of the Holy Spirit.

From the Master and Benedict's shared expansion of Cassian's conclusion to the signs of humility, one would expect to be able to deduce a shared anthropology. But is this the case? In spite of their shared conclusion, I do not believe so.

On the whole, the Master has a more jaded—some might say realistic—view of the human person than Cassian or Benedict. If perfection does not mean an absence of spiritual weakness, it does not mean the presence of spiritual maturity either.[57] Spiritual maturity, as we have seen, is expected of the abbot, not the "perfect." By and large, the Master does not believe that his monks—be they the few or the many, the perfect or the imperfect—will achieve spiritual growth. The best that can be expected of them is docility. Perhaps this may explain the reason for the Master's need to add a lengthy eschatological discourse both at the end of his chapter on humility[58] and, earlier, at the conclusion of his chapter on the holy art.[59]

Finally, to return to a question I posed earlier in this essay: if it can be ascertained that discretion, as a general theory with practical consequences, can be found in *RM* and *RB*, and if, moreover, it can be maintained that discretion serves the same end as in Cassian but in a different way, that is, to free the monk from presumptuous self-will, can we conclude thereby that discretion serves the same function in *RM* and *RB* as in Cassian, namely, as one of the foundations for attaining purity of heart? At this point, I would have to answer negatively for the Master and positively for Benedict.

Even though the Master is willing to describe perfect monks as "pure of heart, cleansed from sin, who fear the everlasting fires of hell and seek the immortal treasures of eternal life,"[60] I find no discernible connection between that description and the virtue of discretion as a *habitus* of the monk. While these perfect monks may have learned something about discretion from the abbot's example, this is not clear from the Master's text. We are left to assume that if the monk attains to purity of heart, he owes it to the workings of the abbot's discretion and to divine grace.

As for Benedict, he shares Cassian's thinking that discretion is not only learned in the cenobium but can be exercised by other than the

---

[57] Cf. Terrence Kardong's "Perfection in the Rule of the Master," *American Benedictine Review* 48:1 (1997) 88–107.
[58] Cf. *RM* 10.92–120.
[59] Cf. ibid., 3.78–94.
[60] Ibid., 9.41; cf. 9.47.

abbot. Even though Benedict does not replicate Cassian's more systematic presentation of the connection between *discretio* and purity of heart, nonetheless, like Cassian, he calls *discretio* the "mother of virtues." While less systematic, perhaps, than Cassian, Benedict is clear that those who are making progress toward purity of heart are also those who have some measure of *discretio*.

THE END OF PURITY OF HEART

Now that we have discussed the virtue of discretion, the mother of virtues, it is time to turn our attention to the end to which purity of heart leads.

Cassian

In Conference I, Cassian and Germanus have been listening to Abba Moses talk about the goal *(scopos,* i.e., *destinatio)* and the end *(telos,* i.e., *finis)* of the monastic life.[61] Having described all of the difficulties that this life entails, the abba asks them: "What is your goal *[destinatio]* and what is your end *[finis]*, which drives you to endure all these things so willingly?"[62] To the abba's question, Cassian and Germanus respond that it is in view of attaining the kingdom of heaven that they are ready to endure.[63] Acknowledging the astuteness of their response concerning the end *(finis)*, Abba Moses begins to instruct them on the goal *(scopos)*, about which Cassian and Germanus had professed ignorance.

Abba Moses begins his instruction by telling them that all human activity needs a goal *(scopos)*. He calls this goal the "soul's goal" *(animae destinatio)* or the "mind's constant intention" *(mentis intentio)* in which one must faithfully persevere in order to arrive at "the longed-for fruit" *(ad finem desiderati fructus)*.[64]

Using a familiar example from the agricultural society in which he lived, Abba Moses proceeds to illustrate the relationship between goal and end. The farmer, he explains, achieves his end *(finis)*, which is to live peacefully amidst the abundance of a rich harvest, by first acting according to his goal *(destinatio)*. He does this by clearing the field of brambles and weeds, certain that his end, namely, peace, will not be achieved without this labor.

---

[61] Cf. Cassian, *Conlationes* I.2. For a good discussion of these themes see Stewart, *Cassian*, 40–2.
[62] Ibid., I.2.
[63] Cf. ibid., I.3.
[64] Cf. ibid., I.4.

There exists a similar relationship between goal and end in the monastic life as well. Abba Moses declares that "the end of our course [*finis*] is the kingdom of God. But we should inquire carefully into the nature of our goal [*scopos*]." A little further on in this chapter, Abba Moses explains that "the end [*finis*] of our profession . . . is the kingdom of God or the kingdom of heaven; but the goal or *scopos* is purity of heart, without which it is impossible for anyone to reach that end [*ad finem*]."[65]

Just as the farmer cannot achieve the peace that comes with an abundant harvest without first clearing the soil, so too the monk will not attain to the reign of God unless he has first achieved purity of heart. How is purity of heart acquired?

Purity of heart is arrived at by means of interior combat and renunciation as well as discretion. The monk who desires to achieve purity of heart must first practice renunciation, giving himself to a life of poverty and fasting.[66] But material renunciation is, of itself, insufficient. For the goodness or badness associated with material goods, which are neutral in themselves, stems from the free choices, good or bad, one makes in using them. Therefore, if the monk is truly to become a spiritual person, he must practice a second kind of renunciation, namely, that of the will. It is from the will, that is, from the interior self, that springs the vices which, unlike material goods, are a feature of the monk's interior life. The renunciation of the monk's will is the active life, or *praktikè*,[67] which is oriented not only toward the elimination of vices, but also toward the acquisition of virtues. When, like the farmer's field, the monk's soul has been cleared of vices and purified by means of the virtues, the queen of which is charity, that is, when he has reached *puritas cordis*, only then is he ready for the third kind of renunciation, namely, from contemplating the visible in order to contemplate the invisible. With this, the active life culminates in the contemplative life, or *theoria*.[68]

Cassian provides yet another description of the movement involved in acquiring purity of heart in the conclusion of Book IV of the *Institutes*. Here, Cassian summarizes what he has taken pains to develop in the preceding forty-two chapters concerning the formation of those who have renounced the world. He writes:

---

[65] Ibid.

[66] For the characteristics of this first form of renunciation, see ibid., III.6; IV.19; VIII.5; XXI.8–9; etc.

[67] *Praktikè*: cf. ibid., XIV.1.3; 2.1; 4.1; 8.1; 8.3; XXI, 4.4. For this second kind of renunciation, cf. ibid., III.8–9.

[68] Cf. ibid., VIII.3; X.3–6; XIV.1–2, 9–10; XV.2; XXIII.3–5, etc.

> The starting point of our salvation and wisdom is, according to Scripture, the "fear of the Lord." From fear comes healing compunction. From compunction of heart comes renunciation, that is, the disappropriation from and the despising of wealth. From disappropriation comes humility. From humility comes the mortification of the will. Mortification uproots vices and kills them. The rejection of vices allows the virtues to bear fruit and to grow. The fruit of the virtues is purity of heart. One who possesses purity of heart will also possess apostolic charity.[69]

From this passage we can see that while the goal and the end of the monastic life are distinct, related to each other as proximate end to final end, so that by means of the first the second can be attained, they are nonetheless linked by charity or love of God, beginning here on earth and final and complete in heaven.

Adalbert de Vogüé provides helpful insight into this connecting role of charity in Cassian. He writes:

> When he distinguished the final end and the intermediate goal, the *telos* of life eternal and the earthly *skopos* of purity of heart,[70] Cassian shows that these two ends are intermingled. Their relationship one to the other is neither extrinsic or arbitrary. . . . The kingdom of God is already in us, since it is justice, peace and the joy of the Holy Spirit.[71] Every soul in which these virtues are to be found are like angels, seen as heaven here on earth. Thus, the monastic soul, striving toward perfect charity and unceasing prayer is, for the Church, the prefiguration of eternal joy.[72]

If Vogüé is correct about the connecting role of charity, there is, for Cassian, only one end *(finis)* to purity of heart, namely, life eternal. But the one who has arrived at purity of heart already exhibits, even in this life, the qualities of life eternal: justice, peace, and the joy of the Holy Spirit. These qualities are so many signs of the perfection of charity. In Cassian one finds, then, a proleptic eschatology where the fulfillment of the eschaton is still awaited even though it is being anticipated, in part, in the present.

The Master and Benedict

Do the Master and Benedict regard the end of purity of heart in the same way as Cassian? In order to answer this question, I will first compare their ascetical traditions with that of Cassian.

---

[69] Cassian, *Institutes* IV.43.
[70] Cf. Cassian, *Conlationes* I.2.
[71] Cf. ibid., I.13. Cf. Luke 17:20-21; Rom 14:17.
[72] Adalbert de Vogüé, "Monachisme et Eglise dans la pensée de Cassien," *Théologie de la vie monastique: Etudes sur la tradition patristique* (Paris: Aubier, 1961) 212–40, esp. 234–5.

One would be hard-pressed to find in either the Master or Benedict the "active-contemplative" vocabulary of Cassian. But the absence of this kind of vocabulary should not be surprising. Cassian uses it only in his *Conferences* when writing about eremetical life; it is not mentioned in the *Institutes*.[73] But, as Vogüé observes:

> Cassian's silence in the first part of his work is sufficient enough to show that one must not interpret the silence of the old Latin rules as a rejection of his theories of the two kinds of life. Our legislators do not reject it. One can not even conclude that they are not interested in it. The only thing that their silence affirms is that an exposition of these two ways of life are not part of the rudimentary beginnings which these rules lay down.[74]

What are the "rudimentary beginnings" that *RM* and *RB* lay down? According to Cassian's terminology, the Master and Benedict are legislating for the cenobitic and, therefore, "active" life by which the monk strives to eliminate vices and acquires virtues. Even so, both the Master and Benedict characterize the life of the hermit, too, as a "fight against the devil," a solitary combat against the vices of body and mind.[75] Neither the Master nor Benedict seems to take up Cassian's definition of contemplation which is concerned with the knowledge of Scripture.[76] But while neither employs the terminology of "contemplation" in the Cassianic sense, both have a developed sense of *opus Dei* and holy reading as a means to unceasing prayer.[77] Benedict, however, as we will see shortly, shows more concern for the quality of the monk's prayer than the Master does.

In spite of the absence of Cassian's explicit "action-contemplation" vocabulary, one must be careful, then, not to build an impregnable wall between the active and the contemplative lives in *RM* and *RB*. As we have seen, *praktikè* is a necessary prelude to *theorètikè*. In some senses, cenobitism is a preparation for anachoretism. Thus the Master, followed by Benedict, writes that it is not in the first fervor of religious life that hermits embrace the solitary life, but only after a prolonged training in the cenobium.[78] While neither the Master nor Benedict develop this line of thought any further, remaining content with the bare outline

---

[73] Cf. Adalbert de Vogüé, "La Règle de saint Benoît et la vie contemplative," *Collectanea Cisterciensia* 27 (1965) 93. For a discussion on the relationship between the *Conferences* and the *Institutes* see Stewart, *Cassian*, 30–2.

[74] Ibid., 93.

[75] Cf. *RM* 1.3–5 = *RB* 1.3–5.

[76] Cf. Cassian, *Institutes* V.33; *Conlationes* I.15.1.

[77] Cf. *RM* 3.62 = *RB* 4.56.

[78] Cf. *RM* 1.3 = *RB* 1.3.

that they found in Cassian, nevertheless, both the Master and Benedict see the eremitical life in some sense as a "flower" of cenobitism.

This being said, one is left with the impression that the active life is subordinate to the contemplative life. But concerning the different modes of living *praktikè*, Cassian writes, "for there are many ways that lead to God, and therefore each person should finish the one that he has taken up, intent upon his course, so that he may be perfect in his profession, whatever it may be."[79] Cassian also places life in the desert alongside the governance of cenobia and charitable works. This is but one form of the active life. Cassian does not say that a monk should abandon one way of life to go to another. Each way of life, pursued faithfully to the end, has in itself that which is necessary to perfect the one who has chosen it. It should not be surprising, then, to find in the Master and Benedict the injunction to persevere in the monastery *usque ad mortem*.[80]

Cassian is a tributary for the Master and Benedict, both of whom cannot but have been influenced by his descriptions of Egyptian monastic life. What is clear is that both the Master and Benedict legislate for cenobites and not for hermits. The principal tasks of this so-called "active" life are the elimination of vices and the acquisition of virtue in view of attaining to purity of heart. But within this shared tradition, there are two important differences between the Master and Benedict.

First, Benedict, as I alluded to earlier, is interested in the quality of the monk's prayer in a way that the Master is not. Prayer can be prolonged under the inspiration of the Holy Spirit (*RB* 20.4). For Lent Benedict prescribes private prayer in place of the common prayer of the Master (*RB* 49.5). These private prayers are always associated with tears and compunction (*RB* 20.3; 49.4; 52.4). But prayer is also accompanied by *intentione cordis* (*RB* 52.4), of which the two most important elements (indeed, the key to understanding *intentio cordis*) are purity of heart and compunction.[81] Compunction and tears are but manifestations of the heartfelt personal response of the monk to the presence of God and the progressive elimination of everything in the monk which is opposed to the acquisition of purity of heart.[82]

Second, if the elimination of vices and the acquisition of virtue remains the first task of the monk, Benedict nevertheless subordinates this to the demands of charity, evident especially in the "horizontal" relationships of the monastery. Thus, charity is to be the norm of the

---

[79] Cassian, *Conlationes* XIV.6.
[80] *RM* Ths 46 = *RB* Prol 50.
[81] Cf. Michael Casey, "Intentio Cordis (RB 52.4)," *Regulae Benedicti Studia* 6 (1980) 105–20, esp. 119.
[82] Cf. ibid., 120.

monastic life and not only when the monk has climbed the ladder of humility (*RB* 7.67).[83] It should already be present in the monk's relationship with the abbot (*RB* 72), the brothers (*RB* 72), the sick, (*RB* 36), the old and young (*RB* 37), and the guests (*RB* 53). But charity is subordinate to the monk's final end: the kingdom (*RB* Prol 50).

These differences between the Master and Benedict are critical for our understanding of how each one views the end of purity of heart. According to Vogüé, Cassian sees the proximate and final ends of purity of heart as intermingled in a way that is neither extrinsic nor arbitrary, such that the kingdom of God is already in the monk who practices charity.

Can the same thing be said of the Master and Benedict? Benedict's redaction of the Master's conclusions to his chapters on the holy art (*RM* 3.78–94) and humility (*RM* 10.94–120) indicate that one cannot. Let us compare these conclusions.

The Master ends his chapter on the holy art with a long, almost florid description of the delights of heaven which he has borrowed from both *Visio Pauli* 21–3[84] and *Passio Sebastiani* 13.[85] He borrows again from *Passio Sebastiani* 13 in order to complete his chapter on humility.

In adopting these chapters for his own rule, Benedict omits the Master's long eschatological texts, retaining Cassian's basic pattern that humility leads from fear to love. Like Cassian, Benedict is interested in the earthly goal of the monk's spiritual development.[86]

The omission of the Master's eschatological passages does not imply, however, that Benedict has completely lost sight of the heavenly goal of the monk's life. He concludes his prologue with the hope that those who patiently share Christ's sufferings may deserve also to share in his kingdom (Prol 50). In chapter 72, also, Benedict establishes a link between everlasting life and the practice of charity which finds concrete expression in good zeal (cf. *RB* 72.2, 12).

By the same token, the Master's interest in the future joys of heaven should not be construed as a disavowal of the life of charity here and now. Words like *amor, caritas,* and *diligere* appear frequently in his rule. This being admitted, it remains a fact nevertheless that the Master ends two significant chapters with lengthy descriptions of the

---

[83] In fact, Benedict alters both Cassian and the Master by inserting the notion of "the love of God" as early as his third step of humility. Cf. *RB* 7.34.

[84] Cf. Thomas Silverstein, *Visio St. Pauli: The History of the Apocalypse in Latin Together with Nine Texts* (London: n.p., 1935) 136–8.

[85] Cf. *PL* 17.1118.

[86] Cf. Michael Casey, "Saint Benedict's Approach to Prayer," *Cistercian Studies* 15 (1980) 329, n. 4.

delights of heaven, descriptions that do not appear in Cassian and that are clearly rejected by Benedict.

Notwithstanding the Master's frequent use of the language of charity, or Benedict's references to life eternal, the latter, unlike the former, shares Cassian's confidence that the process of exaltation is not completely deferred until the future life. In this regard, Michael Casey writes, "[a] life lived in fidelity to Gospel teaching begins to be suffused by the outshining of eternal life; the final realities are already in the process of being realised."[87]

CONCLUSION

At the end of this study, it is clear that while the Master and Benedict are indebted to Cassian and share with him a common ascetical tradition regarding both the beginning and end of purity of heart, Benedict remains closer to the Cassianic tradition than does the Master. While Benedict does not give us a neatly-packaged definition of purity of heart as such, he does provide us not only with its initial and final stages, but also with its contours: a life cleansed of vices and sins with the help of the grace of the Holy Spirit (cf. *RB* 7.70); a life characterized by a love- motivated practice of the virtues (cf. *RB* 7.68); a life that, even now, exhibits that love of God and neighbor which will come to full fruition in the kingdom of heaven (cf. *RB* Prol 50; 4; 72).

---

[87] Columba Stewart notes that Cassian is ambiguous about the present possibility of achieving the beatitude of heavenly existence. He is more confident of it in *Inst.* V (cf. *Inst.* V.14.4), which prepares for his remarks in *Conf.* I (cf. Conf I.10.51), less so by the time he writes *Conf.* XXIII Cf. Stewart, *Cassian,* 56–7. See also Casey, "Saint Benedict's Approach," 329.

"The Deepest Conviction of the Heart": A Probe into an Expression of St. Benedict (*RB* 7.51)

TERRENCE G. KARDONG, O.S.B.

In the seventh rung of his Ladder of Humility (*RB* 7.51–54), St. Benedict insists that the monk not only confess that he is of no account, but really believe that is the case: "The seventh step of humility is surmounted if the monk not only confesses with his tongue, but also believes with the deepest conviction of his heart that he is lower and less honorable than all the rest." To make this point, Benedict uses the expression "the deepest conviction of his heart," a colorful term contrasted with "tongue" in the concrete fashion often employed by the Bible. In fact, the principle is not absolute, since in the twelfth step of humility Benedict teaches that the body *(corpora)* is to express the humility that exists in the heart *(cor)*. For those who hold that the Ladder of Humility is a true progression, the external expression of rung twelve is a higher state of spiritual progress than the internalization of step seven.[1]

The expression is more remarkable in the original Latin: *intimo cordis credat affectu.* A literal translation of those four words would be: "let him believe with the inmost feeling of his heart." Yet I myself did not render it that way in my recent translation, nor do any of the English translations that I have seen.[2] None of us speak of "feeling," probably because we suspect that Benedict is not speaking about emotions,

---

[1] In my commentary on *RB, Benedict's Rule: A Translation and Commentary* (Collegeville: The Liturgical Press, 1996) 162–9, I argue against the progression in the Ladder of Humility.

[2] My original translation did not use the words "deepest conviction," but simply "with all his heart." After making the present study, though, I believe a stronger translation is warranted. A random sampling of other translations: *RB 1980:* "convinced in his heart"; J. McCann (1951): "in his inmost heart believe it"; St. Meinrad (1937): "with inmost conviction"; Fort Augustus (1948): "in his inmost heart." It would be too diverting

215

but of something more fundamental. Furthermore, there does seem to be a redundancy, for "heart" and "feeling" are generally thought of as one and the same. But this assumes that we know what *"affectus"* and *"cor"* (heart) mean for Benedict. It is the purpose of this essay to clarify these two words, especially the second.

BENEDICT'S USE OF "HEART" (*COR*)

Although I have no intention of conducting a complete word study of *cor* in the *Rule of St. Benedict*, it would be helpful to have some basic statistics to provide a framework in which to situate *RB* 7.51. First of all, Benedict makes rather frequent use of *cor,* which appears no less than thirty times in his Rule. By way of comparison, the *Rule of the Master* uses the term sixty-six times. Since the *RM* is three times longer than the *RB*, this suggests that Benedict has something of a predilection for "heart" compared to his literary prototype, for *cor* appears at a 1:2 ratio for *RB/RM.*

But this point should probably not be pressed, since fully two-thirds of Benedict's usages are copied from the Master. These borrowings occur mainly in the first seven chapters of *RB*, which are heavily dependent on the Master. Moreover, no less than ten of Benedict's usages of *cor* are found in the chapter on humility.

This clustering also applies to the Prologue, where there are six usages, and four other usages occur in *RB* 4. Thus twenty of the thirty usages of *cor* are limited to three chapters. This is no surprise, since the same phenomenon is true of the Master: *cor* appears ten times in Prologue/Thema; five times in *RM* 33 *(Ars Spiritualis)*; thirteen times in *RM* 10 (Ladder of Humility).

More relevant for this study is the fact that a great number of these instances of "heart" in *RM/RB* come directly from Scripture. About one-third of the cases are simply quotations of the Bible, for which "heart" is very common terminology. *RB* 7.51 as a whole is not a direct quote from the Bible, but the words *affectus . . . cordis* have a biblical resonance. Therefore, to understand Benedict's use of "heart," we need to look at the biblical theme in general and *affectus cordis* in particular.

THE BIBLICAL THEME OF THE HEART

The Hebrew language is extremely concrete, so much so that it does not even have words for the various human faculties such as

---

to go into the various foreign translations, but Adalbert de Vogüé has "l'intime sentiment de son coeur" (*La Règle de Saint Benoît* [Paris: Cerf, 1972] 487). He translates *affectus* by "sentiment," a French word that can mean either "feeling" or "opinion."

memory, will, and intelligence.[3] Rather, their operations are attributed to various bodily organs taken metaphorically. Thus the eyes judge: "That appeared good to his eyes [judgment]." What job, then, does the heart (Hebrew: *leb*) perform? We might assume that it would be the organ of passion and feeling, since that is the way we normally use "heart" in English.

But that is not the way the Bible normally uses the word. In no more than 20 percent of hundreds of cases does the Bible use heart to refer to feelings.[4] For Hebrew writers, the appetites and feelings were located in the soul *(nefesh)*, not in the heart. For them, *leb* is the moral faculty with which one comes to understanding and makes moral decisions. A phrase such as "speaks the truth in his heart" (Ps 15:2, quoted in *RB* Prol 26) may jar us a bit, but it is a typical biblical use of "heart."

When the Bible speaks of the heart as a human faculty, it tends to understand it as an active power. Compared to the soul *(nefesh)*, the heart is more vigorous in its activity, not so much being acted upon as acting; the soul is passive and subject to the suasions of outside powers. From this point of view, the heart is the deepest, most fundamental part of the person; it is closer to what we would call the conscience.

Scripture also speaks of the heart as a metaphorical place. Although the biblical writers know well enough that the heart is literally a muscle for pumping blood, they use it to mean the inmost part of the person.[5] This is the moral center, true interior, where only God can see. Indeed, we often do not even understand our own hearts—they are hidden from our own eyes. The heart is the inmost part of a person or thing.

Usually the Septuagint renders biblical *leb* with the Greek terms *nous* or *dianoia* (mind). Such a translation is by and large accurate, but it also locates thought or decision in a different place than the Jews did. Of course, the Greek language has a word for heart, which the writers of the New Testament use in their own fashion. For them, *kardia* is connected to thoughts and intentions, just as *leb* was for the Jewish writers.[6] Along the same line as the Hebrew Bible, the New Testament used *psyche* (soul) as the place of feeling or appetite.

---

[3] This section and the next are based on A. Lefevre's article "Cor/Cor Affectus," *Dictionare de Spiritualité* (Paris: n.p., 1952) 2.2278–2308. Although this article is over forty years old and does not attempt to cover the whole subject, it is far more useful than its counterpart in *Theological Dictionary of the New Testament*, ed. Gerhard Kittel (Grand Rapids, Mich.: Eerdmans, 1964–).

[4] Lefevre, "Cor," *Dictionare de Spiritualité*, 2.2278–2281.

[5] A. Guillaumont, "Cor," *Dictionare de Spiritualité*, 2.2281.

[6] According to Lefevre (n. 4), Paul sometimes "relieves the term [heart] of some of its [semantic] overload" by using words like *nous* or *suneidesis* for thought or intention.

THE HEART IN EARLY CHRISTIAN SPIRITUALITY

When the Church Fathers used "heart," they often followed the biblical usage.[7] But since they were also affected by various Greek philosophical currents, they sometimes gave the term new nuances and twists. For example, the Stoics used *kardia* to indicate the guiding intellect *(hegemonikon)*, which Gregory of Nyssa also used to explain the heart in the Canticle of Canticles.[8] But this is not at odds with the biblical usage, which also emphasized the active, controlling role of the heart in the human moral and spiritual life.

We have seen that one of the typical biblical usages of "heart" is to indicate the inmost part of the person.[9] The Greek Fathers sometimes deepened that theme by claiming that there is also an inmost part of the heart. Sometimes they said that the spirit *(nous)* dwells within the heart, which then leaves the heart somewhat externalized. The spirit is the divine part, but the heart is human. As such, the interior of the heart is the place of encounter with the divine.

Yet not all the Greek Fathers were comfortable with language that localizes the heart and its operations. The Origenist school preferred to use the heart in a broader sense than a term such as *psyche*. The latter was often used to refer to the "sensible life" or the natural spirit.[10] For the Fathers, however, "heart" is broader, corresponding to the biblical term, which refers to the whole interior or spiritual part of the person rather than a specific faculty.

Although the Greek theologians generally spoke of the heart in the way that the Bible does, there is one significant exception. Pseudo-Dionysius restricts the term to the affections.[11] In doing this, Pseudo-Dionysius is being true to his intellectual heritage, which lies more in Platonic philosophy than the Bible.[12] Like the Greek philosophers, Pseudo-Dionysius probably finds *kardia* (heart) too vague, and so

---

[7] This part of the *Dictionare de Spiritualité* article (by A. Guillaumont) is limited to the Greek Fathers of the fourth to the seventh centuries. The research is based chiefly on Pseudo-Macarius, Diodochus, and Hesychius.

[8] *In cantica* 7; PG 44.937d. Origen has the same usage: *In cantica, Origenes Werke* 8, ed. W. A. Baehrens (Leipzig: n.p., 1925) 93.

[9] Guillaumont, "Cor," *Dictionare de Spiritualité*.

[10] Ibid., 2.2283.

[11] This is the analysis of A. Guillaumont. See *Dictionare de Spiritualité*, 2.2287, "Oraison du coeur et mystique du coeur." Regrettably, Guillaumont does not give any citations of Pseudo-Dionysius in his article. Presumably, these would be found in his full study of the subject: "Les sens des noms du coeur dans l'Antiquité," *Études carmélitaines* 29 (1950) 41–81.

[12] The thesis of A. von Harnack that the thinking of the Bible differs fundamentally with that Hellenistic philosophy is no longer accepted by a consensus of scholars. For a

tends to use it pejoratively and also rather rarely. We will soon see how this kind of thinking has affected the Bible itself and, in a less direct way, Benedict's Rule. But neither Benedict nor most of the other Church Fathers can be placed in the Platonic, intellectualist camp of Pseudo-Dionysius.[13]

Affectus Cordis

Besides the general biblical use of "heart," it is also relevant to our topic to notice that *affectus cordis* is itself a veritable theme in patristic and medieval spirituality.[14] Almost all of these usages occur in commentaries on Vulgate Ps 72:7, which Jerome translates as *Prodiit quasi ex adipe iniquitas eorum, transierunt in adfectum cordis* ("Their eyes stand out with fatness, they have more than the heart could wish," King James Version).

It is interesting to compare this with a modern version such The New American Bible: "Out of their crassness comes iniquity, their fancies overflow their hearts." This is reasonably close to Jerome's version, but we should note that "fancies" are different from his *adfectum* (passion, desire). Since Jerome, like almost all of the Church Fathers, normally associates feeling with "mind" or "soul" and not "heart," we may wonder why he chose the latter here. Apparently because he misunderstood the Hebrew term that he rendered *adfectum*.[15] This may

---

major work based on the opposite point of view, see Hans Dieter Betz, *The Sermon on the Mount*, Hermeneia Series (Minneapolis: Fortress Press, 1995).

[13] Commenting on use of "heart" in *RB* Prol 1, Aquinata Böckmann remarks that Benedict belongs to the "experiential stream" that includes Origen, John Climacus, Antony, and Diodochus of Photike, rather than the intellectualist stream. See Aquinata Böckmann, *Perspektiven der Regula Benedicti* (Münsterschwarzach: Vier-Turme-Verlag, 1986) 24. Here again, though, not all contemporary patristic scholars believe in the split between these two "streams" in the Church Fathers.

[14] So much so that the *Dictionare de Spiritualité* article on "Cor" includes a special subsection "Affectus Cordis in the Middle Ages" by J. Chatillon (2.2288–2300). Fortunately for our purposes, Chatillon covers the sixth to the eleventh centuries in his study, so *RB* 7.51 becomes in effect his first witness.

[15] At least this is the contention of Chatillon (see previous note). The Greek translators of the Septuagint give us *diathesis* (judgments, thoughts), but apparently Jerome thought it was a question of feeling, so he used *adfectum*, a term he usually associates with the Greek *pathos*. Most medieval commentators on Ps 72:7 also thought of "feelings" in a negative way. J. Chatillon lists the following commentators for this pejorative use of *affectus cordis*: Ps. Jerome *Brevarium in Ps.*, PL 26.1031c; St. Bruno, *Expositio in Ps. 72*, PL 52.1101cd; Ps. Rufinus (Letbert of St. Ruf) PL 21.943a; Ps. Bede (Mangold of Lautenbach) PL 93.870b; Ps. Aymo of Halberstadt (Anselm of Laon) PL 115.439b; Ps. Remi of Auxerre, PL 131.519b; Peter Lombard, PL 191.671c.

have happened because the Hebrew word is virtually unintelligible.[16] The Greek translators of the Septuagint give us *diathesis* (judgments, thoughts), but apparently Jerome thought it was a question of feeling, so he used *adfectum*, a term he usually associates with Greek *pathos*.

AFTER ALL OF THIS, RB 7.51

How is it that Benedict parted company with the standard patristic treatment of *affectus cordis*? First of all, Benedict probably did *not* use *affectus cordis*! The words are not placed together in *RB* 7.51 *(intimo cordis credat affectu)*, nor is there any indication that Benedict is commenting on Ps 72:7.[17] None of the modern commentaries list that psalm as a background for *RB* 7.51. Furthermore, we should point out that Benedict is not "on his own" in this passage, but is copying the *Rule of the Master* (10.68) verbatim. So it is not so easy to sort out Benedict's attitude from the Master's in this case. Indeed, Benedict may have no particular opinion about this verse, but may merely pass it along somewhat mechanically.

As for the Master, we can at least say that he liked this turn of phrase, for he used it twice. In both his seventh step of the Ladder of Humility (10.68) and also at the end of his long Rule (93.72), he has employed the terms *affectus* and *cor*. *RM* 93.72 concerns the abbot's designated successor. The main virtue that the Master requires of that monk is humility, and he repeats many of the points he made in the Ladder of Humility. As with *RM* 10.68, 93.72 requires the abbot-designate to consider himself lower than all the other monks.

But when we attempt to find out what the Master meant by *affectus . . . cordis*, we run into the same problem that we encountered with *RB* 7.51. That is, the Master did not himself craft the verse, for it appears in identical form in the prototype of the Ladder of Humility, namely, the ten indices of humility found in Cassian's *Institute* 4.39.2. Cassian was writing in the early fifth century, so it is quite possible that he did not pick up the phrase from the Vulgate Bible, which was written

---

But there were a few medieval writers who used the term *affectus cordis* in a positive way. One of them was Gregory the Great, or whoever wrote the Commentary on First Kings that has come down under his name. Far from criticizing the "feelings of the heart," this writer says that when they are turned toward heaven, they can ward off the temptations of the flesh. In his *Moralia* (XXV.5, 7), Gregory also says that "steps of the heart" *(gressus cordis)* motivate the heart toward God.

[16] S. Bullock, *New Catholic Commentary on Scripture* (London: Nelson, 1969) 467.

[17] According to Chatillon (*Dictionare de Spiritualité*, 2.2291), Benedict is not alluding to Ps 72:7 in his seventh step of humility.

about the same time. At least we can say that Cassian did not attach any stigma to *affectus* or *cor.*

Since the Master and Benedict lived about a century later, they both were probably aware of Jerome's negative use of *affectus cordis* but they did not see fit to modify the Cassianic text. Perhaps they understand that by *affectus* Cassian means something different from Jerome. He was not talking about emotion, but about conviction.

Although Benedict was speaking about the heart, he did not mean it in the modern sense as the locus of passion or emotion but rather as the moral core. And even though he says that the monk must know with all the *affectus* of his heart that he is the lowest of all persons, this does not refer to "affections" but to moral conviction. That is not the usual patristic use of the term, but it seems to be what Cassian, the Master, and Benedict mean.

For example, A. Blaise[18] gives many meanings and examples for *affectus:* (1) state of human nature, (2) disposition, (3) desire, (4) depths of the soul, (5) feelings of affection. Granted that some of these are not quite the same "passions," and granted also that some of the examples he cites may not refer only to passion, the regular meaning of *affectus* is emotional.

In conclusion, modern translators would be wise to avoid the word "feelings" or "passion" in their rendition of *RB* 7.51, but one should keep the word "heart" and represent the term *affectus* by some term such as "conviction." This should be done out of faithfulness to ancient usage and not out of prejudice for thought and against feeling.

---

[18] *Dictionare latin-Français des Auteurs chrétiens* (Turnhout: n.p., 1954) 49.

EPILOGUE
The Life of Sister Juana Raasch, O.S.B., 1927–1974

LINDA KULZER, O.S.B.

INTRODUCTION

"You are not free until you have been made captive by supreme belief." The significance of this statement by poet Marianne Moore is wonderfully expressed in the life of Sr. Juana Raasch. This gentle monastic woman whose earthly life ended in 1974 at age forty-seven was eminently free. During her undergraduate years the Christianity of her childhood began to take on a profound meaning. It marked the beginning of that deep interior life which would gradually become obvious to all who were privileged to know her. She was by nature a free spirit, and this quality, coupled with a deeply spiritual outlook, seemed to liberate her from concerns for human respect, appropriate outward appearance, and correct external practices. She chose the freedom of the monastic life and as a "scholar monk" used her brilliant mind in monastic and scriptural studies. Sister Juana pursued in a particular way the study of the concept of purity of heart.

Now twenty-four years after her death we pause to remember her in a special way. The significance of Sister Juana's life and work lives on after her. Our community continues to receive requests about, as well as messages of admiration for, her seminal work on the topic of purity of heart. As members of her monastic community we wish to pause in order to examine anew with appreciation, love, and reverence her life among us. This chapter is devoted to the story of her life. We are fortunate to be able to begin with a selection written by Avis Raasch Worthington, Juana's only sibling. Avis, herself a published writer, gives us an animated description of Sister Juana's early life. What follows this account is an exploration of the events of Juana's life as a member of St. Benedict's Convent (now referred to as monastery) in St. Joseph, Minnesota. The author thanks all those sisters who willingly and graciously shared their memories of Juana. In particular she acknowledges the invaluable help of the archivist of St. Benedict's Monastery, Sr. Ruth Boedigheimer, O.S.B., as well as Sr. Etienne Flaherty, O.S.B., who did the oral interviews with sisters who knew Juana well.

EARLY LIFE OF SR. JUANA RAASCH BY AVIS RAASCH WORTHINGTON

Elaine Raasch was born on September 7, 1927, and weighed seven pounds, seven ounces. My mother always considered seven to be her lucky number. The future Sister Juana was born in Milwaukee, Wisconsin. My father had finished his undergraduate work in geology at the University of Wisconsin and returned to work at the Milwaukee Public Museum as he had on and off since his teen years. Later he went back to graduate school at Madison. He was curator of the geological museum there at the time. In 1931 I joined the family.

Elaine was always shy, but she could be a harum-scarum little girl. My parents were horrified when she led me across the ice of one of the Madison lakes when I could barely walk. Later on when we lived for a while in Oklahoma, she would dive off quarry cliffs from heights that frightened my father. Once when we were out on a family field trip she climbed down into a crevasse in the ground and got stuck with only her head showing. The crevasse went down a long way, and my father never forgot digging her out. One of the dearest memories of both Raasch girls was the time we spent with our extended family from the Polish side on a lake in northern Wisconsin playing Tarzan and Robin Hood with homemade bows and arrows.

But Elaine was always a book person. My father had named her after Elaine the Lily Maid of Astolot and would read to us such poems as "Winken, Blinken and Nod." An important occasion in our family was the day each girl was old enough to be granted a public library card. Throughout her life Elaine was frequently found lost in the library.

The Depression and World War II reduced the family's fortunes. We returned from a few years in Oklahoma and Kansas to live in Milwaukee, where my father again worked at the Museum under WPA. After war was declared my father enlisted as an officer in the United States Air Force. Elaine began high school in what would today be considered a ghetto school. At this time her interest in languages appeared, and she became proficient in Spanish. Upon graduation she began college at what was then the extension of the University of Wisconsin in downtown Milwaukee. Then the war ended and my father began working at the Illinois State Geological Survey on the campus of the University of Illinois in Urbana. Elaine entered the University of Illinois and began an association with Latin American intellectuals that she found very rewarding. I think it likely that the Catholicism of the Spanish culture added to her religious interest. At this time she returned to the Church that had baptized her and in which she had made her first communion. Our family was split religiously with my mother's side Catholic and my father's Catholic, Lutheran, and agnostic. During our family travels during the Depression we had stopped attending church.

Elaine graduated Phi Beta Kappa from the University of Illinois in 1949. She began graduate work at the University of Kansas, but her shyness and vocational confusion led her to drop out. Returning to the University of Illinois in Urbana, she completed an MA in Spanish in 1952. After this she went to New York, working for a time as a translator. It was around this period that she found her religious vocation.

I have not written much about my mother, but her warmth and love bathed us all in a feeling that we were deeply cared for. Mother was a vivacious woman who, as she said, talked to us constantly as toddlers so that we became "word" people. Both Elaine and I eventually became writers.

Mother worried about Elaine's absentmindedness. She was often preoccupied with her thoughts, and the sisters at St. Benedict's told me they would see her cross a street reading a book. There may be some family heritage in this. When I began studying family history I came upon a Father Theobald Spetz who was my grandmother's first cousin. Fr. Theobald was a teacher at St. Jerome's College in Ontario and was often so lost in thought that he would pass his colleagues without noticing them enough to greet them. So perhaps genetics does play a part in these things.

ENTRY INTO RELIGIOUS LIFE

What was it that brought this bright, promising young woman to consider entering Benedictine life at the Convent of St. Benedict in St. Joseph, Minnesota? It is likely that Avis Worthington's observation about the significance of Elaine's association with the Catholicism of the Spanish culture is also a key factor in her considering the possibility of the religious life. In addition, Avis tells us that Elaine read about life at St. Benedict's and that the lakes and woods of Minnesota reminded her of happy family times in northern Wisconsin.

In September of 1954 Elaine arrived at St. Benedict's and began her postulancy. During that year she taught Spanish at the College of St.

Benedict. In June of 1955 she was part of a group of twenty-five young women who received the Benedictine habit. At that time she was given the name Juana. Her choice of name reflected her interest in Sor Juana, a saintly Spanish Carmelite whose deep interest in the intellectual life caused her a life-long struggle.

Interviews with some of the sisters who were a part of her novitiate period provide us with a glimpse of a gentle, unassuming young woman. Her classmates soon recognized her as someone who was well-educated, intensely interested in ideas, unceasingly kind, and hopelessly absentminded. They all agreed that Juana quickly endeared herself to each member of the group. She was not adept at many of the manual duties that fell to novices. However, when it came to discussions, research, and creativity, she stood out. Her classmates recall her ability to pose searching questions to the convent chaplain who came to provide regular classes in theology to the novices. They indicated that at times her questions may have challenged and/or frustrated the chaplain. On one occasion Fr. Harold Fuchs, O.S.B., stated that everything in the world that God created was important. Juana asked him about the mosquito. What purpose did it have? Those recalling the story said that she was perfectly serious and hoped for a serious answer.

Juana's musical ability soon became obvious to those around her. She had a strong, beautiful soprano voice, and singing Gregorian chant in the convent choir was a special joy for her. She played the guitar well and became known in the community for her ability to organize and lead sing-alongs. In the years to come she would be noted for a hymn text she wrote and sang. Mary Joy Probst listened to her sing it and wrote down the musical setting for "Creator, Savior, Rich in Grace." Her hymn is still in the collection of Evening Prayer hymns sung by the monastic community.

On July 11, 1956, Juana professed her first vows. At this point she and the other members of her class moved to the Juniorate. Juana again taught Spanish to college students. After three years in temporary vows, she was accepted for final vows which she professed on July 11, 1959.

TEACHING AND RESEARCH

Juana taught Spanish at the College of St. Benedict for seven years. Gradually it became clear that, although she herself was proficient in six languages (and would add two more in her lifetime), teaching a foreign language to undergraduates was not her forte. Her strong bent for research was recognized, and in 1964 she was given the opportunity to study at Rosary College in River Forest, Illinois, to do an MA in Research Librarianship. The years that followed were particularly happy for her because she was able to devote herself to the research work she loved. Sr. Mariella Gable, writing in the *ABA Language and Literature Newsletter* (June 1966), expressed a certain envy at Juana's good fortune: "Sister Juana Raasch is that rarest and most fortunate of persons who has as her monastic assignment simply to engage in research. *Mirabile Dictu!* Had you known that there could be such an assignment?"

The period from 1965 to 1970 was spent in research. Her accomplishments in those five years were phenomenal. During the summer of 1963 she began her association with the Benedictine Institute of Sacred Theology (BIST) at St. Benedict's Convent. This program begun by Sr. Mary Anthony Wagner, O.S.B., and Fr. Paschal Botz, O.S.B., provided the opportunity for Benedictine women to do summer graduate work in both theology and monasticism. This was the beginning of an ongoing friendship and work relationship between Sister Mary Anthony and Juana. One of the prominent faculty members in the BIST program was Fr. García Colombás, O.S.B., a monk from the Abbey of Montserrat in Spain, who was editor of the journal *Studia Monastica* and a recognized monastic scholar. During the summers of 1963 and 1964, Juana was asked to help Father García translate his lectures into English so he could deliver them to his American audience. She took two of Father García's courses: Commentary on the Rule of St. Benedict, and Early Monastic History and Spirituality. This association was the beginning of some important scholarly developments for her. Father Garcia encouraged her to help him in editing, translating, and writing on pre-Benedictine monasticism. Since Cistercian Press had agreed to publish the English version of their joint work, Juana began working on this project. She referred to these two pending works as *Monastic Origins I, History* and *Monastic Origins II, Spirituality.* She had the first volume ready for publication in 1970 and had sent it to Fr. Basil Pennington, O.C.S.O., who was heading Cistercian Publications at the time. The work was never published because she was not able to prepare the second volume.

Another important work resulted from the encouragement given her by Father García. She started work on a series of articles on purity of heart in the early Church for publication in *Studia Monastica.* Here was the initiative behind what was to become Juana's most original and outstanding contribution to the field of monastic history. This book-length work, "The Monastic Concept of Purity of Heart and Its Sources," was made up of five articles written between 1966 and 1970. As a result of the excellence of this series she was asked to provide an article on purity of heart, "Katharsis," for *Dictionnaire de Spiritualité,* the French encyclopedia of spiritual theology.

During this time she also contributed articles for publication. These reflect her own particular interests at the time: her book review of *A Love of Learning and a Desire for God* by Jean Leclercq, O.S.B., in *Studia Monastica,* vol. 3, 1961; "Monasticism in the United States: Efforts towards Definition and Renewal," *Yermo* 1965; "Survey of New Monastic Trends," *American Benedictine Review,* June 1967; "Benedictine Renewal and Its Bibliographic Requirements," accompanied by "A Bibliography for Benedictine Renewal with Excerpts," presented to the American Benedictine Academy, 1967.

As can be noted from her writings, this was the period when Juana's interest in "simple monastic living" took on a special urgency. In a statement she prepared on her educational and professional background she states, "I might add that I am very interested in forming a simple monastic foundation." Around this time (1968—1970) the community at St. Benedict's Convent had been studying the possibility of setting up a separate house for a group interested in simple monastic living. Sister Juana was a member of the committee conducting the study and took a keen interest in the possibilities being considered. In 1969 the community established such a house, which came to be known as the House of Prayer (also known as Millstream House). Once it was set up, Juana was happy to be invited occasionally to share her background in monasticism with the sisters in this group. In April 1970 she became a member of the House of Prayer. There was not, however, much possibility of a long stay with this group because she had for some time been requesting permission to pursue a Ph.D. and had already applied to three universities for scholarships for Ph.D. studies.

Toward the end of this five year period (1969—1970), she had completed an MA in theology from the Graduate School of St. John's University in Collegeville and studied Hebrew there with Rabbi Shulman. It was at this time that her interests began to shift from continuing her study of early monastic spirituality to Judaic studies. In a description of her educational and professional background she spoke of her interest in the roots of Christian spirituality:

> I should like to single out the field of Judaic studies for special emphasis. I have long been interested in the primitive Judaic strand in early Christianity, as it is closer to the sources of revelation and in many ways represents a purer tradition than those spiritual tendencies influenced by Hellenistic philosophy. . . . More recently I have extended this interest to include other aspects of Judaism as a foundation for ecumenical dialogue.

GRADUATE WORK IN NEW YORK

In May 1970, in a letter to the prioress, Mother Henrita Osendorf, Juana indicated that she had accepted an NDEA (National Defense Education Act) Scholarship in Hebrew Studies at New York University. The fall of 1970 was to be the period for launching a new scholarly venture for Juana. In a letter to the community dated October 2, 1970, she spoke of driving to New York with Sr. Donald Corcoran, O.S.B., and that the two of them attended a Cistercian Studies meeting at St. Joseph's Abbey in Spencer, Massachusetts. She indicated that she gave a report on the progress of the books she was writing with Fr. García Colombás. She thoroughly enjoyed her courses at New York University and was pleased to receive word in the spring of 1971 that her NDEA scholarship had been renewed for another school year.

While Juana lived in New York, she found a delightful haven with sisters of her own monastic community who were missioned at St. Anselm's College in Manchester, New Hampshire. These sisters welcomed her when she was on vacation during the school year. St. Anselm's College had been founded and was sponsored by the Benedictine monks of St. Anselm's Abbey at Manchester. She found the monastic atmosphere at St. Anselm's and the welcoming hospitality of the sisters a great boon.

Her second year in New York proved even more exciting than her first. She had planned on her return from Minnesota to live in the same apartment in the Bronx but found it necessary to look for new lodgings. In a letter from New York on September 26, 1971, she recounts the serendipitous way in which she found new housing.

> One evening I was invited to dinner by the priests of the local parish church, St. Joseph's on 6th avenue in Greenwich Village, as the pastor, [Fr. Wilde,] a Greek scholar, was very interested to hear that I had a scholarship to study Hebrew and that I was a Benedictine. I told the priests my plight and the pastor suggested that I might possibly stay in the vacant rooms on the fourth floor of the "Parish Building" next to the Church—actually the Rectory. After I had exhausted every other possibility and we had discussed the matter with the two other priests, this turned out to be what happened. I moved in here yesterday. They want me to take my meals with them. . . . I demurred at that at first, but they insisted. They thought I would add to the conversation a scholarly tone at the dinner-table! . . . Two of the priests—the pastor and another priest and I are going to start praying Lauds in the mornings at twenty to eight.

Interestingly these three were soon joined by lay people who also wanted to join in this prayer. This practice went on in St. Joseph's parish for many years following Juana's departure. It is clear that the year and a half she spent at the rectory was mutually enjoyable and that her presence was valued by the priests in the rectory. Father Wilde wrote a touching letter of recommendation in January 1973:

> I have known her as a serious, full-time, respected student who is an adornment in any academic community. I have known her as a Religious, with a deep and life-giving commitment to Gospel faith and the Benedictine tradition. I have known her as a woman who lived in this house with us, and whose presence at the table and at our discussions we always looked forward to, and whose absence we always missed. She entered fully into the life of this house and was included in all our programs and projects.

In one of her letters to the community (Saturday before Palm Sunday in 1972), Juana mentions that she had been teaching an adult education course in Spanish in the parish and that she found the class enjoyable and the members appreciative. She also indicates that she had been chairing the Evaluation Committee for the church decorating program.

When Juana requested a dissertation scholarship for her third year at New York University, she also asked for additional money to go to Israel during the second semester of her third year. She wanted to go because she believed that Dr. David Flusser of the Hebrew University and others there could be very helpful with her dissertation topic, a comparison of the Qumram Manual of Discipline with the First Letter of Peter. Before she left for Israel she was pleased to announce in a letter to Mother Henrita Osendorf (January 1, 1973) that Father Simon, the prior and head of the department of religious studies at St. Anselm's College in Manchester, New Hampshire, had offered her a part-time job there for the next year, teaching Hebrew to the clerics and a seminar on Judaism to the college students. She was happy with this arrangement because it meant that she would also have time to work on her dissertation and go once a month to New York to meet with her advisers.

The only information available about Juana's experiences in Israel come from two references in letters she wrote to the prioress (Mother Henrita Osendorf). The first was written in the early part of her stay there, February 5, 1973: "Don't know how I deserved to have this time here, but I'm certainly trying to make the most of it, and to be grateful. . . . Galilee is even more beautiful than I had thought it would be, and it certainly gave me a new feeling for the Gospel stories." It was two months later when she wrote the second letter (April 8, 1973), and it was evident that the Holy Land had made a profound impression on her psyche:

> I would like to recommend the Holy Land as a place for you to visit. I never had any great desire to come here, but now that I'm here, I find it very hard to tear myself away. In fact, I know I'm going to be homesick for the rest of my life.

It was during Juana's stay in Israel that she received her first intimations of the cancer that would take her life within the next sixteen months. According to her sister, Avis (e-mail, November 19, 1997), "Once she had discovered the lump [in her breast] in Israel she acted upon it as soon as possible, abandoning her research until she got better." She came home to St. Benedict's and had a mastectomy early in the summer of 1973. All indications are that she recovered quite rapidly from the surgery and was unaware of the possibility of further complications. Following her surgery she and a friend, Joan Binzen, traveled with Avis and her children to Canada for a visit with her parents.

LIFE AT ST. ANSELM'S

That fall Juana was pleased to begin her new teaching assignment at St. Anselm's College. She had enjoyed the welcoming hospitality of the sisters at St. Anselm's many times during her vacation periods while attending New York University. The sisters always looked forward to her visits and particularly loved her anecdotes about living in the rectory at St. Joseph's in Greenwich Village. The sisters who welcomed her on August 23, 1973, were Srs. Carmen Mulcahy, Christopher Weber, Gonzaga Plantenberg, Patrick Joseph Flynn, and Nivelle Berning.

The first semester of that year at St. Anselm's was a halcyon period. She liked teaching Hebrew to the clerics and, according to Brother Andrew, O.S.B., her students enjoyed her (letter received April 21, 1997). He speaks of a "general impression of her kindness and gentleness" and then becomes more specific: "As I recall, S. Juana would let you bluster along about something you thought you knew and then completely derail you with a correction that always began 'That's funny, I thought. . . .' More often than not, the dialogue ended with a giggle that was infectious."

Sister Nivelle reported that Juana was loved by her colleagues in the faculty for her scholarship, warmth, and genuineness. It seems apparent that her deepest joy during the time at St. Anselm's resulted from the community she found among her own sisters there. Again Sister Nivelle's comments help us understand:

> She liked being at St. Anselm's and often remarked that her months here were some of the happiest in her community life. She felt accepted and could be herself . . . [she] was especially exuberant when during the

course of the year, she learned she could look forward to another year's assignment to teach and complete work on her dissertation.

In Sr. Gonzaga Plantenberg's oral history (tape four, side 2, archives, St. Benedict's Monastery) there is also a reference to Juana's life with them that year. After saying how happy the sisters were to have her with them, she goes on to specify the qualities she appreciated in her: beautifully simple, unsophisticated, thoughtful, and very prayerful. She indicated that Juana did not pay much attention to details that were not important. Sister Nivelle also noted that "she liked to prepare meals for the sisters, but her forte was not in domestic tasks. There are many stories to support the fact that the practical and/or pragmatic were not her primary concern."

CANCER PREVAILS

During the second semester of that year at St. Anselm's, those around Juana noted her increasing health problems, particularly her unrelenting cough. After some urging she went in for a check-up. She learned that cancer had returned and had spread to her lungs and possibly her bones. This was frightening news in the midst of what had seemed to Sister Juana an ideal situation. Her friends at St. Anselm's grieved as they saw her finish up her main obligations at the college and, in late April 1974, return to St. Benedict's in Minnesota to seek further treatment.

Early in May of that year she went to the St. Cloud Hospital for surgery. The exact nature of that surgery is not clear, but she wrote a rather hopeful letter from the hospital to the sisters at St. Anselm's (May 11, 1974). She noted that while the last X-ray of her chest showed no change, the doctor did indicate that at her age she had a good chance of a remission of from three months to three years. She indicated her own ambivalence: "My ideas about what will happen to me change drastically from day to day, but I am always willing to accept God's will, whatever it may be." A characteristic interest that sustained her through all the days of her illness was her love of reading. She remarked that during her stay in the hospital she read Abigail McCarthy's autobiography.

She left the hospital on May 12 but returned for another chest X-ray on May 20. She wrote to the sisters in Manchester on May 21 and again sounded hopeful: "The results [of the X-ray] show a decrease in pleural effusion, and I forget the other technical phrase. Anyway it looks like a remission, although it's too early to be sure." She was pleased to tell the sisters that she had received a call from the two priests at St. Joseph's in Greenwich Village, stating that they would be flying out to see her on May 28. She also stated that she would leave for Calgary on May 29 to spend three weeks with her parents.

While at her parents' home in Calgary she wrote, "I seem to have gotten a little stronger, but have been plagued with vomiting, coughing, etc." Her condition worsened after this, and on July 5 she was anointed in the infirmary at St. Benedict's. Sr. Giovanni Bieniek, O.S.B., the nurse who was Juana's major caregiver, continued the correspondence with the sisters at Manchester. On July 11, she thanked Sister Nivelle for the phone calls and the letters and related that twenty-five sisters were present when Fr. Vitus Bucher, O.S.B., chaplain, anointed Juana. In that same note Sister Giovanni told how Juana wanted to know just where she stood:

> She asked me about her true condition. I explained it fully to her, and yet giving her hope in prayer for healing if God so wills. I advised her to pray, "Thy will be done" and not place any obstacles in His way. She said, "yes." . . . She is really beautiful and is a source of edification to those who see her and visit her.

Early in July, Juana had phoned her sister, Avis, in Berkeley and asked her to come. She knew it was time. Their visit extended over a four-day period in mid-July. Avis later captured the high points of that memorable time in an essay entitled, "Death at St. Benedict's." In it she spoke of weeping over a letter that Juana had received "from our father remembering her [Juana's] babyhood" and of how Juana, noting this, begged her not to be sad. There was a close bond between the two sisters, and the final farewell was painful. Avis noted the following about their last exchange: "Weeping in the face of her calm I said just before I left, 'reach down [from heaven].' She nodded as if this were not too surprising a request, and then I left her. It was not something I had expected to say."

From this time on it was evident that Juana had accepted the imminence of her own death. She requested that all the research and dissertation writing she had done thus far be handed over to Fr. Paul Dinter, a priest who had lived in the Greenwich rectory at the same time as Sister Juana. He was a doctoral student at NYU and was doing his graduate work in the same area. She wanted her work to be of benefit to his research. She also wrote a farewell letter to her friend, Fr. García Colombás, the monk from Spain who had been so instrumental in her early writing career. In 1997, when Fr. García was contacted about his memories of Sister Juana, he referred to the message he received: "Some weeks before she died, she wrote me a farewell letter which I do indeed have, preserved between the pages of my Bible. It is a very short letter, but full of her sincere spirit."

During the final weeks she was visited frequently by close friends, particularly Srs. Johanna Becker, Emmet Corcoran, Annette Brophy, and Sheila Rausch. Sisters took turns reading out loud to her. Sister Sheila remembered reading from the Dorothy Sayer's *Gaudy Night* mystery trilogy. Sister Linnea Welter read to her from C. S. Lewis's Narnia series (Letter to Sisters in Manchester, September 2, 1974). By August 19, when Sister Giovanni again wrote to Sister Nivelle, she reported, "For the past four days she has been suffering much with severe pain in her neck. . . . But through this all she is very patient, at peace and beautiful."

Sr. Cathan Culhane, O.S.B., wrote of spending some time with Juana on Sunday, August 25 (letter to sisters at Manchester, September 1, 1973). She indicated that she found her restless and, it seemed, somewhat frightened. She remarked that it was Sister Johanna who seemed to be able to comfort her. On Tuesday, August 27, around 6 p.m. Sister Giovanni noticed a definite change in Juana's condition. She called Sisters Johanna, Emmet, Sheila, and the sisters at Caedmon to her bedside. Sister Annette was absent because her own father was dying. Sister Cathan reports that Sister Kenneth Pahl (herself a patient in the infirmary) spoke of how she was present when Sister Giovanni told Juana she was dying. She recounted that Juana answered "yes," that she was ready to meet Jesus, and "yes" that she wanted to renew her vows.

Sister Cathan shared her memories of the final hour: "I think she was conscious most of the hour that I was there, but she did not speak as we prayed and sang and waited and longed with her . . . she continued her shallow breathing with much effort to the end." Sister Giovanni in recalling these last moments with Juana says: "At one point I asked her if she could say 'Jesus, I love you!' This she did with some difficulty. Moments later she died." All those present at her bedside (including the author of this article) noted that after she took her last breath the struggle in her features disappeared and her face took on a beautiful serenity.

Juana died at 8:15 p.m. on the evening of August 27, 1974. Her parents were called immediately. They knew the end was near and were dreading the news. Juana's sister Avis could not come for the funeral, but she recounted her reaction to the news of Juana's death:

> Though I was grieved, my spirits rose. I felt a kind of exultation. The period of waiting and worrying was over. She had been afraid of pain, but God was a reality to her. . . . I wrote in my diary that night: "She died with absolute, simple, and admirable faith greater than my pen can write. . . . She did not teach me the secret of her faith, only its beauty. If

only I could graft onto my character some of her strengths. When I left her at the convent this summer I told her 'reach down' and she nodded. About 9 p.m. this night I felt her touch and her love" (from "Death at St. Benedict's").

SERVICES FOR SISTER JUANA

Juana's wake took place the next day, August 28. Sr. Dunstan Plantenberg in a letter to the sisters at Manchester speaks of the wake: "When I viewed sister's body today there was evidence that she had suffered, but the serenity and quiet dignity that were Sister Juana were also evident. She is wearing her blue dress and has her glasses on." Sister Cathan recalled that when Juana's parents arrived, her father indicated that he did not wish to view the body but wanted to remember her the way she was. Of Juana's mother's reaction she said, "Her mother was sad, and kept saying those first minutes, 'My daughter, My daughter.'"

Juana's funeral took place at 4 p.m. on Thursday, August 29. Sister Cathan commented on the celebrants:

> Four priests concelebrated, all introduced properly, of course, by Father Vitus, who mentioned briefly each one's connection with sister: Father Tom Wahl, who was at the Biblical Institute in Jerusalem this year, and returned recently; Father Patrick Riley, who visited S. Juana when she was in the hospital in St. Cloud in May, Father Jonathan Fischer, chaplain, and himself. Father Gunther Rolfson was also present but did not concelebrate.

Sister Emmet did the first reading and made a few remarks before it, mentioning that Juana loved to play and sing the Shaker hymn, "Tis a Gift to be Simple." She invited the community to sing it together in response to the reading. Sister Johanna gave a touching homily in which she described Juana as a "scholar monk, who quietly succeeded in achieving the delicate balance Dom Leclercq described in his book, *The Love of Learning and the Desire for God.*" She went on to say of her, "Although she was perceptive and sensitive by nature, I have never heard her speak in judgment of another person, in defense of herself, or without charity."

Sr. Linnea Welter, in a letter to the sisters at Manchester (September 2, 1974) described the next part of the service: "For me the most moving time at the funeral came at the Offertory when [Juana's] parents and Sister Mary Reuter [subprioress] carried the gifts to the altar." For the meditation at Communion time Sister Mary Helene Juettner sang the hymn composed by Juana. The first verse reads:

> Creator, Savior, rich in grace,
> God merciful and good;
> Your will is love, not punishment,
> Not death, but life renewed.

The sisters and monks at St. Anselm's had also been watching and waiting as the end drew near. On the day after her death, the feast of St. Augustine, a Mass was offered for her at St. Anselm's Abbey. Abbot Joseph Gerry, O.S.B., closed his homily with the following thought:

> In the words of St. Augustine whose feast we celebrate this day, Sr. Juana can now cry out: "You have called . . . and have pierced my deafness. You have lightened, you have shone forth, and have dispelled my blindness. You have sent forth your fragrance and I have drawn my breath and yearn after you. I have tasted you . . . and I am all inflamed with your peace."

CONCLUSION

What is the message of Juana's life? Sister Johanna's homily at her funeral gives at least one dimension of that message. She states that when Fr. Vitus celebrated a Mass in Sister Juana's room close to the time of her death, he asked her for a message. She responded, "Only to trust to God's love for you, and believe that whatever happens is for your good." Her obituary card contained a passage claiming that purity of heart characterized her. It would seem that it was her very life among us that was her most eloquent message. Psalm 73[1] seems to capture in a few short phrases a description of that life and its meaning:

> Those who are pure in heart find that God is good!
> O God, You are heaven to me!
> I desire nothing on earth as much as I desire You!
> Though my body wastes away and my heart faints and fails,
> You are the rock of my soul!
> You are the treasure of my heart!
> I will cherish you forever.

---

[1] (Ps 73:1, 25-26, from *Swallow's Nest: A Feminine Reading of the Psalms* by Marchiene Vroon Rienstra).

Contributors

Douglas Burton-Christie is associate professor of spirituality in the department of theological studies at Loyola Marymount University. He is author of *The Word in the Desert* (New York: Oxford University Press, 1993). His book on spirituality and the literature of nature is forthcoming from the University of California Press.

Deirdre Ann Dempsey is assistant professor of theology at Marquette University. She received her doctorate in Northwest Semitic languages, with a specialty in biblical Hebrew, from The Catholic University of America. She is author of articles in *Vetus Testamentum, Biblische Notizen,* and *The Bulletin of the American Schools of Oriental Research.* She is currently working on the revised translation of the Old Testament for the New American Bible.

Jeremy Driscoll, O.S.B., has been a monk of Mount Angel Abbey since 1973. Father Driscoll teaches in Mount Angel's seminary one semester each year; the other semester he teaches at the international Benedictine Collegio di Sant' Anselmo in Rome. He has published several books and articles on Evagrius Ponticus, including *The Mind's Long Journey to the Holy Trinity: The* Ad Monachos *of Evagrius Ponticus* (Collegeville: The Liturgical Press, 1993).

Mary Forman, O.S.B., member of the Monastery of St. Gertrude, Cottonwood, Idaho, has a doctorate in medieval studies from the University of Toronto. She serves as spiritual director at the Spirituality Center, Sacred Heart Monastery, Richardton, North Dakota, and teaches theology at the University of Mary in Bismark. She is a visiting lecturer in monastic spirituality and history at the School of Theology, St. John's University, Collegeville, Minnesota.

Gertrude Gillette, O.S.B., is originally from South Bend, Indiana. She took her solemn vows as a Benedictine in September 1984 at St. Scholastica's Priory in Petersham, Massachusetts. She received her doctorate in patristics from The Catholic University of America in 1996 and is presently in Rome assisting the Abbot Primate in setting up a new program in the area of monastic formation at the international Benedictine Collegio di Sant' Anselmo.

Alexander Golitzin is a monk of Simonopetras, Mount Athos, Greece, and associate professor of theology at Marquette University. He received his doctorate from Oxford University. Father Alexander is the author of *Et Introibo ad altare Dei: The Mystagogy of Dionysius Areopagita* (Thessalonike: Patriarchikon Hidryma Paterikon Meleton, 1994), and translator of St. Symeon the New Theologian's *On the*

Mystical Life: The Ethical Discourses (Crestwood, N.Y.: St. Vladimir's Seminary Press, 1995–), 3 volumes, and articles on Pseudo-Dionysius.

Benedict Guevin, O.S.B., is a monk of St. Anselm's Abbey and an associate professor of theology at St. Anselm College, Manchester, New Hampshire. Father Benedict holds a Ph.D. in history of religions and religious anthropology from the University of Paris-Sorbonne, and an S.T.D. in moral theology from the Institut Catholique de Paris.

Terrence Kardong, O.S.B., is a monk of Assumption Abbey, Richardon, North Dakota. He is the editor of the *American Benedictine Review* and the author of articles on the Rule of Benedict. His publications include *The Benedictines* (Wilmington, Del.: Michael Glazier, 1988) and *Benedict's Rule: A Translation and Commentary* (Collegeville: The Liturgical Press, 1995).

Linda Kulzer, O.S.B., a member of St. Benedict's Monastery in St. Joseph, Minnesota, holds a Ph.D. in education with a minor in religion and culture from Syracuse University. She is co-editor and contributor to *Medieval Women Monastics: Wisdom's Wellsprings* (Collegeville: The Liturgical Press, 1996) and has had a long-term interest in monastic history.

Harriet A. Luckman holds a master's degree in systematic theology from St. Thomas Theological Seminary, Denver, Colorado, and is a doctoral candidate in historical theology at Marquette University. She has contributed articles to *Medieval Women Monastics: Wisdom's Wellsprings* (Collegeville: The Liturgical Press, 1996), *Word and Spirit*, the *American Benedictine Review.*

Irene Nowell, O.S.B., director of community formation at Mt. St. Scholastica in Atchison, Kansas, is adjunct summer faculty member of St. John's University, Collegeville, Minnesota. Her publications include three books with The Liturgical Press: *Jonah, Tobit, Judith* (1986), *Sing a New Song: The Responsorial Psalm in the Sunday Liturgy* (1993), and *Women in the Old Testament* (1997). She is also working on the revised translation of the Old Testament for the New American Bible.

Placid Solari, O.S.B., a native of Richmond, Virginia, entered the Benedictine community at Belmont Abbey, Belmont, North Carolina, in 1974 and was ordained in 1980. Father Placid holds a doctorate in theology from the Pontifical Patristic Institute "Augustinianium" and teaches at Belmont Abbey College.

Columba Stewart, O.S.B., is a monk of St. John's Abbey, Collegeville, Minnesota. A native of Texas and graduate of Harvard, Yale, and Oxford Universities, he teaches monastic studies at St. John's University. Father Columba is the translator of *The World of the Desert Fathers* (Fairacres, Oxford: SLG, 1986), and author of *Working the Earth of the Heart: The Messalian Controversy in History, Texts, and Language to A.D. 431* (New York: Oxford University Press, 1991), *Cassian the Monk* (New York: Oxford University Press, 1998), and *Prayer and Community: The Benedictine Tradition* (Maryknoll, N.Y.: Orbis Books, 1998).

Mary Anthony Wagner, O.S.B., member of St. Benedict's Monastery, St. Joseph, Minnesota, holds a Ph.D. in theology from St. Mary's, Notre Dame, Indiana. She has taught theology at the College of St. Benedict, St. Joseph, and has been dean of the Graduate School at St. John's University, Collegeville,

Minnesota. Her publications include *The Sacred World of the Christian: Sensed in Faith* (1993) and the editorship of *Sisters Today*, both of which are published by The Liturgical Press. Sister Mary Anthony, together with Fr. Paschal Botz, O.S.B., of St. John's Abbey, Collegeville, began the Benedictine Institute of Sacred Theology at St. Benedict's Monastery in 1958—later to become the School of Theology at St. John's University, Collegeville. It was during sessions at this Institute that Sister Juana first made her acquaintance with Fr. García Colombás, O.S.B.

Greek Terms

aisthesis, 116
anachoresis, 51, 58–9
anapagseta, 149
apatheia, vi, 8–9, 11, 113, 141–3, 146–7, 150, 153–7, 163, 165–6, 173
aphrones, 149
arete, 82
askesis, 6, 11, 49, 170, 173
axioma, 127

chora, 97

dialogismoi, 124
dianoia, 169
diatheses, 220
diatyposis, 126

eidosin, 148
ennoia, 148
epekteinomenos, 51
epithymetikon, 77

gnosis, 141, 149

hegemonikon, 78, 218
hesychia, 98
hodos, 50–1, 56
homoisis, 71

kardia, 9, 19, 22, 26, 33, 78, 152, 163, 165–6, 168–9, 174, 218–9
katharos, 9–10, 17, 19, 26, 33, 143, 163–4

leitourgoi, 127

logismoi, 124, 126, 128–9, 161–2, 164, 168–74
logistikon, 77, 143
logos, 6, 73–4, 86, 102, 174

metaballo (metabole), 126
monachos, 115
monos, 53

nous, 9

paredroi, 127
peira, 116
plattein, 74
plerophoria, 116
pneuma, 76, 168
poiein, 74
praktiké, 11, 144, 147, 149–52, 154–7, 172, 174, 211–2
pronesis, 149, 167
prosueche, 169
psyche, 76, 78, 143, 170–1, 217

sarx, 79
scopos, 198, 208–9
soma, 76
spermatikos, 102
synaxis, 126

telos, 198, 208
theoria, 12, 153
thumikon, 77, 143
topos, 47, 49–50

xenon, 128

Hebrew Terms

bāḥan, 27
bār, 17, 19, 23–4, 33

derek, 20

hekhal, 119
hesed, 20

kibbes, 17

lēb, lēbāb, 18, 21–2, 24–6, 27–8, 32–4, 217

mišpāṭ, 20

nāqî, 33
nĕqî kappayim, 23

nepeš, 23, 217

ṣārap, 27
sĕdāqâ, 23, 25

tāhôr, 17, 19, 24–5
tepillātî, 33
tôb, 25
tōm, 19, 20–1
tummô, 19

yāṣar hārá, 17, 19
yāšār, 17, 19, 24
yōšer, 21

zāk, 19, 25, 33
zikkîtî, 33

Latin Terms

adfectum, 219
affectus, 216, 219–21
amor, 213
anima, 208

caritas, 213
conversatio morum, 11
cor, 215–6, 221
cordis, 212, 219, 220–1
corpora, 215

discernere, 200–4, 208
discretio, 199, 200, 202, 206, 208

emundationem, 199

finis, 208
fuga mundi, 14

habitus, 207

intentio, 208, 212

mens, 9

probationem, 199
puritas cordis, 2, 8, 142, 163, 209

sagaci, 199
scopos, 198, 208–9
senpectae, 205

visio dei, 110, 111

Syriac Terms

brîray, 33
bûyānâ, 36

dakyâ (dky), 32–4, 37–44
dke blebbeh, 32, 38

gby, 33

haymānûtâ, 35
hî rûtâ, 36

îhîdāyê, 43, 115, 137

lebbâ, 32–44
lebba dakya, 32

melkâ, 36
myattĕrātâ, 43

rehmĕtâ, 36

taybûteh dmāran, 43

General Index

abbot, role and virtues of, 202–8, 220
Abel, 37
Abimilech, king of Gerar, 21
Abraham, patriarch, 21, 137
Adam, 86, 99
    and Eve, 75, 84, 85
Akiba, Rabbi, 119
Alexandria, school of, 5, 9, 68–77, 80, 109, 112, 124, 152
almsgiving, 165–6, 178, 187–91, 195
altar, 5, 39, 136–7
Ammonas, 103, 129
Amstutz, J., 115
anchorites, 14, 42, 43, 174, 205–6, 211–2
angels, 40, 70, 74, 111, 118–9, 120, 125, 195
anger, 9, 13–14, 36, 43, 100
Anthony of Egypt, 1–15, 45–64, 70, 94, 96–7, 109, 198, 200
apatheia, vi, 8, 9, 113, 141–3, 146–7, 150, 153–7, 163, 165–6, 173
Aphrahat, the Persian sage, 32–4, 36–8, 101, 109, 111, 114, 116–7, 129, 137, 139
apocalyptic, 95, 98, 111, 114, 117–20, 125, 129
Apophthegmata Pateron, 109, 162, 200
asceticism, Christian, vi, 12, 50–3, 57–8, 64, 89, 94, 145, 172–3
ascetics, vi, 49, 105–6, 114
    Syrian, 115–6, 145, 163
askesis, 6, 11, 49, 164, 170, 173
Athanasius, 6, 13, 45–65, 70, 96–7

Augustine of Hippo, vi, 4, 142, 175–95

Balás, D. L., 97n.
baptism, 5, 39, 72, 99, 108, 123, 125–6, 132, 137–8, 185
Barnabas, epistle of, 90
Basil of Caesarea, vi, 89–106, 109, 135
Beck, Edmund, 35n., 36n., 115
Becker, Johanna, 234–6
Benedict of Nursia, vii
    Rule of, 197–221
Bernard of Clairvaux, 113
Berning, Nivelle, 231–4
Betz, Hans Dieter, 219n.
Bienert, Wolfgang, 68n.
Bieniek, Giovanni, 233–4
body, 7, 14–15, 19, 39–40, 43, 54, 64–5, 69, 72–9, 80, 87, 93, 95, 98, 105, 123–4, 136–7, 151–3, 176, 179, 180, 188, 198, 211, 215, 217
Bongie, Elizabeth Bryson, 162n., 163n., 164n., 165n., 166n., 167n., 168n., 169n., 170n.
Bonian, Stephen J., 136n.
Botz, Paschal, 227
Boulleuc, A. Le, 76n.
Brakke, David, 47n., 56, 63n., 97n.
Brock, Sebastian, 34n., 36, 38–9, 39n., 41n., 42, 43n., 101n., 115, 136n., 137n., 138n., 139n.
Bröckmann, Aquinata, 219n.

245

Brown, Peter, 7n.
Brueggemann, Walter, 22n.
Bucher, Vitus, 233
Bullock, S., 220n.
Bundy, David, 31n.
Bunge, Gabriel, 7n., 143n.
Burton-Christie, Douglas, 167

Caiaphas, high priest, 183
Camelot, P. Th., 72n.
Casey, Michael, 212n., 213n., 214n.
Cassian, John, 2, 6, 8–14, 109, 142–3, 163, 197–200, 205–14, 220–1
Castelli, Elizabeth, 162n.
celibacy, 5, 90
  see also chastity
chastity, 14–15, 167–8, 174, 185
Chatillon, J., 219n., 220n.
Christ, 166–7, 173, 175, 180, 183, 190, 193, 202, 206, 213
  body of, 93
  as bridegroom, 137, 168, 194
  clothed in, 86
  commandments of, 101–3
  eucharist and, 134–8
  glory of, 110, 121–2, 125
  image of, 35, 39–40
  image of God, 73
  imitation of, 72
  as mediator, 85–7
  participating in, 69
  power of, 54, 64
  saving work of, 65, 69
  as virtue, 73–85
church, 5, 35–6, 38–9, 48, 53, 60, 68, 73, 92–7, 105–6, 111–2, 177, 187–8, 210
  inner, 136
  as sacred space, 49
  soul as, 126–7
  types of, 38–9, 127
circumcision of the heart, 34, 133–4, 138, 165–6
Clark, Elizabeth, 71n.
Clark, Mary, 176n.

Clement of Alexandria, 9, 71, 72n., 80, 83, 109, 110, 157
Climacus, John, 6
Collins, John, 117–8
Columbás, García, 227, 229, 233
community, 28, 52ff., 103–4
compunction, 11–12
contemplation, 12, 13, 63, 78, 91, 99, 112, 148, 150–3, 156–7, 165, 172–4, 209, 211, 212
Courcelle, Pierre, 6n.
Covenant, Sons and Daughters of the, 36
creation, 4, 7, 10, 12, 27, 37n., 71, 74–8, 87, 99, 104, 106
Crouzel, Henri, 71n., 72n., 75n., 76n., 79, 85
Culhane, Cathan, 234–5
Curtis, Monica, 164n.
Cyprian of Carthage, 36, 135

Dadisho, 32, 41–2, 93
Daly, Robert J., 87n.
Daniel, prophet, 118
David, king of Israel, 20–2, 24
Davidson, Arnold, 6n.
death, 4, 40, 48, 60, 63, 65–6, 71, 99, 145, 195
Defarrar, Roy J., 91n.
demons, 52–8, 62, 74, 96, 99, 113, 144–5, 148, 150, 162, 164, 183
devil (Satan), 52, 56–7, 111, 118, 124, 152–3, 164, 168, 199, 211
Didache, 134
Didymus the Blind, vi, 67–88
DiLella, A. A., 22n., 23n., 26n.
Dillon, John, 7n., 87n.
Dinter, Paul, 223
Dionysius Areopagita, (Pseudo), 112, 127, 218–9
discernment, 6, 36, 124, 164, 202–3, 206
discretion, 197–214
Donatists, 185, 189
Donna, Rose Barnard, 135n.
Dörries, Herman, 93n., 108n.,

109n., 111n., 117, 126n.
Doutreleau, Louis, 67n.
Draguet, René, 43n.
dreams, 15, 145, 155
Driscoll, Jeremy, 8n., 11n., 70n., 148n., 150n., 151n., 152n., 154n., 155n.
dualism, 4, 7
    dual creation, 74–5
    ethical, 118

Eberle, Luke, 200n.
Eckhart, Meister, 113
Elihu, 24
1 Enoch, 117–8, 120
2 Enoch, 119, 120
Ephesus, Ecumenical Council of, 111
Ephrem the Syrian, 35–6, 115–6, 137–8
Eucharist, 126, 134–6, 138
Eustathius of Sebaste, 91–3, 105
Evagrius Ponticus, 6–9, 12–15, 68, 70–1, 109–10, 112, 129, 141–59, 163–6, 171, 173
Ezechiel, 119–21, 128–9, 132–3, 137

faith, 24, 35–7, 42–3, 54–5, 82–3, 88, 97–8, 124, 133, 135, 154, 158, 168, 181–3, 185, 193, 195
Fall, the (original sin), 15, 72, 75–6, 78, 80, 84, 86, 99, 124, 199
fasting, 40, 90, 96, 131, 136, 155, 169, 171, 187–90, 195, 198, 201, 209
Fedwick, Paul, 93, 96n., 97, 98n.
fire, spiritual, 37, 56–7, 110, 121
    divine, 125, 131–2, 135, 137, 139
Fitzmyer, Joseph, 31n.
Fleteren, Frederick van, 176n.
Flusser, David, 230
forgiveness, 37, 39, 183–5, 187
    of God, 194
Forman, Mary, 163n.
Fossum, Jarl, 117
Frazee, Charles, 92
Freud, Sigmund, 3

Friel, Philip, 187n.
friendship, 14, 98, 104
Fuchs, Harold, 226

Gable, Marietta, 227
Gabriel, archangel, 37
Gangra, Council of, 92, 105
Gemser, B., 18n.
Germanus, 198–9, 208
Gerry, Joseph, 236n.
Gesché, A., 68n., 82n.
Gibeon, 20
Gihin, P., 143n.
Gillette, Gertrude, 194n.
Glory, throne of the, 118, 120, 122
    of God, 118, 122ff.
gnosis, 141, 144–9, 154–7, 172, 181
    see also knowledge
gnosticism, 117
Goehring, James, 47n.
Golitzin, Alexander, 127n.
grace, 8, 10–12, 43, 63, 93, 112–3, 125–7, 139, 166, 173, 185, 192, 207
Greer, Rowan, 7n.
Gregg, Robert, 46n., 48n.
Gregory Naziansus, 92, 104
Gregory of Nyssa, 218
Gregory of Sinai, 127
Gribomont, Jean, 92n.
Griffith, Sidney, 35n.
Gruenwald, Ithmar, 95n., 119n.
Gryson, Roger, 5n.
Guillaumont, Antoine and Claire, 8n., 13n., 14n., 70n., 115, 129n., 143n., 145, 147n., 217n., 218n.

Hadot, Pierre, 6n., 7n., 11n.
hands, as symbol of heart, 18, 20, 23, 26
Harl, Marguerite, 115
Harnack, Adolf von, 218n.
Hausherr, Irenée, 11n., 112–7, 123
heart, vi, vii, 3, 9
    as altar, 39, 136–7
    as center of emotion, 161, 217
    as center of the person, 37,

148, 217
circumcision of the, 34, 133–4, 138, 165–6
divided, 35, 177–9
double, 22, 90, 178, 180
enlarged, 151–2
empty and open, 23–4
eyes of the, 123, 176
place of faith, 35
freedom of, 23, 26–7, 137
gentleness of, 150, 155
Hebrew concept of, 18ff.
human actions and responsibility in, 28, 125–6
as inner self, 20, 101–2, 123–4
integrity of, 21
purity of, *see* Purity of Heart
simplicity of, 22, 90, 178
singleness of, 22, 102, 137
source of life, 34
uncircumcised, 132
uprightness of, 24
wholeness of, 21–2, 132
heaven, 5, 9, 11, 13, 24, 37, 39, 42, 47, 91, 99, 110, 118–20, 124, 127, 129, 132, 158, 199, 208–10, 213–4
Hemera, Robert A., 193n.
Hesychast spirituality, 112, 113, 117
Himmelfard, Martha, 120
Holmes, Michael W., 90n.
Holy Spirit, 72, 77–80, 88–91, 93–4, 96–9, 103, 106, 109–11, 121–9, 132, 136–7, 162, 167, 183, 185–6, 194, 201, 206–7, 210, 212, 214
Horn, J. H., 83n., 87n.
humility, 6, 94, 124, 133, 137, 165–8, 174, 202–4, 206, 210, 213, 215–6, 220

Ignatius of Antioch, 135
ignorance, 152–3
Irenaeus of Lyon, 109–10
Isaac, 137
Isaac of Nineveh (the Syrian), 32, 41, 137–8

Isaiah, Abba (Isaiah of Gaza), 42
Isaiah, prophet, 5, 19, 118
Ishmael, 119

Jacob, God of, 23
Jeremiah, prophet, 27
Jerome, 8, 67, 69, 141–2, 219–21
Jesus, and purifying rituals, 5
example of, 48, 161
see also Christ
Jewish holiness codes, 5
Job, sufferings of, 182
John of Apamea, 136, 139
John the Baptist, 132
Johnson, Maxwell E., 138n.
Joseph, abbot, 131, 139
Joseph the Visionary, 138
Jung, Carl, 3
justice, 91, 99
identified with Christ, 86
moderator of virtues, 82–3
title for virtue, 86

Kardong, Terrence, 9n., 202n., 203n., 207n., 215n.
Kehl, A., 68n.
kingdom of God, 91, 99, 109, 180, 208–10
kingdom of heaven, 208, 213–4
Kitchen, Robert, 94n.
Kmosko, M., 111, 127n.
knowledge (*gnosis*), 4, 51, 53, 56, 72, 121, 141, 144–58, 172, 181
self-knowledge, 51, 53, 65, 72
Kramer, B., 68n.
Kretschmar, G., 115

language, 2–3, 42, 55–6
Leclerq, Jean, 228n., 235n.
Lentini, Anselmo, 203n.
Letter to Cyriacus, 32, 40
Levison, John R., 96n.
Levites, 24
holiness codes of, 5
Liber Graduum (Book of Steps), 32, 38–9, 94, 97, 111, 116, 127, 136–7
light, 35, 39, 44, 54–5, 74–5, 85, 112

114, 117–8, 122–4, 128, 137, 145, 158, 177, 179, 182, 190, 193, 198
liturgy, 5, 112, 117
    of heaven 120, 126–7, 131, 134–8
logos, 6, 74, 86
Lot, Abba, 131
love *(agape)*, 5, 9, 10, 13, 20, 36–7, 39, 40, 42–4, 46, 61–3, 94, 99, 101–6, 112, 124, 128, 133, 154, 165, 168, 174, 183–6, 188, 189, 194, 198–9, 201, 203, 206, 209–14
    purity of heart as, 90, 94
    of God, 101, 183
    of neighbor, 103, 112, 172, 185–6
    as prescence of the Holy Spirit, 110, 133, 154, 165, 172, 183–4, 188, 189, 194–5, 198–9, 201, 206, 210, 212–4
Louth, Andrew, 112n.
Luislampe, Pia, 95n.
lust, 13
Lydia, seller of purple, 133

Macarius (Pseudo), 93, 107–29
Macedonianism, 95
Manichaeism, 111, 113
Marsili, Salvatore, 142n., 143
Martyrius (Sahdona), 32, 41–2, 138
Mary of Bethany, 13
Mary of Egypt, 10
Mary, Mother of Jesus, 133
Master, Rule of the, vii, 197–214, 216–21
Maximus the Confessor, 127
McCarthy, Abigail, 232
McCreesh, T., 18n.
Meier, C. A., 164n.
Melania, 70
Mendieta, Emmanuel Amand de, 90–1, 95n.
Merkabah, 119, 129
Merki, H., 71n.
Merton, Thomas, 12, 131n.
Messalianism, 111–3, 116
Methodius of Olympus, 109
Meyendorff, John, 111n.
Middle Platonism, 71

Miles, Margaret, 177n., 186n.
mind *(nous)*, vii, 9, 22, 27, 41, 73–4, 78, 80, 129, 136–8, 145, 148, 182, 187, 211
    identified with heart, 80, 87, 101, 129, 148, 153–7, 168–70, 174, 179–80, 186, 192, 199, 202, 208, 217–9
    humble, 133, 137
Mitchel, Nathan, 134n.
monasticism, 2, 7, 46–7
    in Egypt, 50ff., 68, 70, 92, 97, 103
    goal of, 141, 154–5, 173, 205, 209, 212
money, 56–7, 78, 191
Moore, Marianne, 223
Moses, 2, 110, 122, 124, 131
Moses, Abba, 198–9, 208–9
Moses, the bandit, 10
Mühlenberg, E., 68n., 73n.
Mulcahy, Carmen, 231
Murray, Robert, 115, 116n.
mysticism, Jewish, 119

Nagel, P., 115
Nautin, Pierre, 68n.
Neoplatonism, 71, 98, 105
Nussbaum, Martha, 102n.

obedience, 21, 28, 52, 90, 95, 112–3, 133, 164, 202–3
O'Connor, Flannery, 10
Olphe-Galliard, M., 197n., 199n.
Origen, 5, 7, 9, 36, 67–71, 74–79, 80, 83, 85, 86, 88, 92, 99, 108–10, 112, 148
Origenist crisis, 69, 71
Origenist monks, 70
Origenist school, 86, 218
Osendorf, Henrita, 229–30
Owen, G.E.L., 87n.

Pachomian Koinonia, 93–4
Pachomius, 94, 109
Palamas, Gregory, 112
Palladius, 69n., 70
Paripatetic school, 82

Parisot, J., 34n.
passions, 5, 9, 40, 43, 94, 98,100, 111, 113, 124–5, 144–7, 150–1, 155–7, 165, 169, 217, 221
Paul of Tarsis, apostle, 2, 51, 73
  ascent to heaven, 121
  conversion, 121
  teachings, 124, 133, 134–5, 168, 180
Pelagianism (Pelagius), 113, 194
Pennington, Basil, 227
Peter, apostle, 132–3, 181, 183
Philo of Alexandria, 5, 9, 71, 73n., 74n., 80, 109
Plantenberg, Gonzaga, 231–2
Plato, 3, 4, 129
Platonic, 3, 4, 7, 9, 13, 98, 218–9
  divisions of soul, 77, 80, 82, 143–6
Platonism, 3, 7, 9, 13–14, 108, 110–2, 117, 129
Plotinus, 3, 7, 87
Pneumatomachianism, 95
Poemen, 6
Polycarp, Bishop of Smyrna, 135
poverty, 165–6, 168, 173
prayer, 5, 9, 11–12, 28, 33-43, 60, 63, 70, 90, 92, 96, 100–1, 105, 111, 113, 131, 136–9, 145, 158, 163–4, 168–73, 183, 187, 190–2, 195, 211–2
pride, 24, 43, 155, 165, 170–1, 178, 189, 193
priesthood, 120
Proba, 191–2
Probst, Mary Joy, 226
prudence, 149, 150–1, 156, 203
Psalms, as use for prayer, 5, 40, 43, 137, 201
psychology, 3, 49, 118
purity, 4, 6, 9
  of heart, vi, vii, 1–2, 8–10, 13–17
  as *apatheia*, 142, 147
  biblical understandings of, 8, 19, 20–7
  and the body, 4, 14–15
  and chastity, 14–15
  as clarity of vision, 13
  and conversion, 10
  and discipline, 11
  and fear of the Lord, 28
  as gift, 141–7
  as goal, 97, 131
  goal of, 23, 28
  and health of soul, 13
  innocence and, 10
  as *katharos*, 10
  and love, 9
  monastic purity, 2, 46
  moral purity, 4–5, 17, 19, 25–6
  and prayer, 11–12, 136
  and repentance, 10, 11
  ritual, 4–5
  as sincerity of speech, 28
  as spirit-bearers, 89
  and vision of God, 17
  as wisdom, 20
Pythagorean, 6

Quispel, G., 115
Qumran, 90, 114, 230

Raasch, Juana, v, vi, vii, 1, 6, 8n., 15, 17, 31, 36–8, 89, 90, 101n., 102, 103n., 104, 106–14, 116–7, 124, 129, 141n., 142n., 143, 146n., 161, 162, 163n., 165n., 169n.
  early life, 223–5
  early monastic years, 225, 226
  illness and death, 232–6
  life of, 223–36
  at St. Anselm's College, 231–2
  teaching and research, 226–31
Ramsey, Boniface, 9n., 198n.
resurrection, 7, 71, 74–6, 80, 123, 134–5
Reynolds, S. C., 79n.
Richardson, Cyril, 134n., 135n.
Rist, John, 98n.
ritual cleanness, 17
Rousseau, Phillip, 90n., 99, 104n.
Rowland, Christopher, 118

Rubenson, Samuel, 70, 97n.
Rufinus, 69–70, 100

Salandini, A. J., 119n.
Sarah, wife of Abraham, 21
Sarapion of Thmuis, 137
Saul, 183
Scholem, Gershom, 119, 128, 129n.
Segal, Alan, 117
self-awareness, 6
    as knowledge, 53, 72
Severus of Antioch, 115
sex, 5, 56, 111
sexuality, 14
Shepherd of Hermas, 90, 96
Sheridan, Mark, 142, 151n.
Shulman, Rabbi, 228n.
Silverstein, Thomas, 213n.
Simonetti, M., 75n.
sin, 13, 17, 21–3, 26–7, 32, 39, 40, 43,
    84, 99, 102–5, 125, 134, 136,
    153, 161, 170–1, 176–7, 181–2,
    185, 189, 191
    memory of, 194, 206–7
Sirach, Ben, 5, 22, 26
Skehan, P. W., 22n., 23n., 26n.
Socrates, 4
Solomon, King, 20–1, 24
Song of Songs, 67, 151, 218
soul, 7, 13–15, 23, 40–1, 54–5, 59,
    60, 62, 69, 72–87, 94–5, 98,
    100–3, 110, 123, 125–8, 132,
    139, 144–7, 150–3, 155–7, 167,
    169–73, 175, 182, 187–8, 192,
    208, 217, 219
    God's image in, 73
    microcosm of Church, 126, 217
    Platonic divisions of, 77, 82,
        144–8, 157
Spetz, Theobald, 225
Spidlík, Thomas, 169n., 171n., 172
Spirit, fruits of, 44,
    and flesh, 77,
    as distinct from soul, struggle
        with the body, 79
    see also nous, Holy Spirit, and
        soul

Stephen, Saint, 121
Stewart, Columba, 2n., 6n., 7n., 8n.,
    9n., 11n., 13n., 14n., 97n., 116–7,
    198n., 208n., 210n., 214n.
Stoicism, 3, 5–8, 71–2, 76, 80–3, 87,
    102, 105, 109
    apatheia in, 141–2, 218
    virtues, 81ff.
    spermatikos logos in, 102, 105, 110
suffering, as purification, 182, 191–2
Sutera, Judith, 47n.
Suzuki, Daisetz T., 12
Symeon the New Theologian, 127
Syncletica, Amma, vi, 161–74

tears, gift of, 39, 43, 136, 212
temple, 5, 20–1, 24, 100, 107–09, 110,
    122–4, 126, 129, 134–6
    Christian as, 121, 136–7
Tertullian, 36
Theodore, Abba, 199
Theodore of Mopsuestia, 115
thoughts *(logismoi)*, 6, 15, 23–4, 26,
    39–43, 48, 54–5, 98–9, 101, 106,
    124, 126, 128, 131, 136, 139,
    144–5, 148, 155, 161–5, 168–73,
    191, 199, 202, 217, 220
    control of, 43, 54, 99–100, 128,
        131, 139
    evil, 144–5, 148
Timothy, 133
Tolstoy, Leo, 13
Transfiguration, 121
Trinity, 72, 75, 84, 134
    contemplation of, 146, 151, 154,
        156–7

veil of Moses, 124
virtue, vi, 6, 13–14, 41, 43, 50, 69,
    124, 144, 153, 165, 169, 176, 186,
    198, 209, 212, 214
    Christ as, 80ff.
    as divine clothing, 86, 100
    goal of, 84–6
    God as source of, 83
    as habit, 83
    as image of God, 84

as right faith, 82
vision of God *(visio dei)*, 110–1,
  175–6, 179, 184, 186, 193, 195
Vogüé, Adalbert de, 200n., 203,
  210–1, 213, 216n.
Vööbus, Arthur, 94n., 115

Wagner, Mary Anthony, 227
Wagner, Monica, 90n.
Ward, Benedicta, 162n.
Ware, Kallistos, 125n.
wholeness, 20–2, 29
  as integrity 5–6, 8, 10, 19–21,
  29, 53–4
wisdom, 5, 18, 20, 22–4, 26–9, 50, 86
  of God, 149
  and knowledge, 148–51, 155–6,
    158, 186–7, 198, 210
  literature, 5
  search of, 50
  sign of, 29
  value of, 148
worship, 5, 6, 8, 19, 26–7, 29, 40, 97
  angelic, 40
  place of, 97, 136
Worthington, Avis Raasch, 223–4,
  231, 237